The London Correspondence of Anthony William Boehm

The London Correspondence of Anthony William Boehm

A Hub of the Global Network of Pietism

ANTHONY WILLIAM BOEHM

Edited, German translation, and Introduction by
DANIEL L. BRUNNER

Latin translation by PAUL J. GRIFFITHS
Foreword by JONATHAN STROM

◆PICKWICK *Publications* • Eugene, Oregon

THE LONDON CORRESPONDENCE OF ANTHONY WILLIAM BOEHM
A Hub of the Global Network of Pietism

Copyright © 2025 Daniel L. Brunner. All rights reserved. Except for brief quotations in critical publications or reviews, no part of this book may be reproduced in any manner without prior written permission from the publisher. Write: Permissions, Wipf and Stock Publishers, 199 W. 8th Ave., Suite 3, Eugene, OR 97401.

Pickwick Publications
An Imprint of Wipf and Stock Publishers
199 W. 8th Ave., Suite 3
Eugene, OR 97401

www.wipfandstock.com

PAPERBACK ISBN: 979-8-3852-1898-1
HARDCOVER ISBN: 979-8-3852-1899-8
EBOOK ISBN: 979-8-3852-1900-1

Cataloguing-in-Publication data:

Names: Böhm, Anthon Wilhelm (1673–1722) [author]. | Brunner, Daniel L. [editor and translator] | Griffiths, Paul J. [translator] | Strom, Jonathan [foreword writer]

Title: The London correspondence of Anthony William Boehm : a hub of the global network of pietism / Anthony William Boehm.

Description: Eugene, OR: Pickwick Publications, 2025 | Includes bibliographical references and index.

Identifiers: ISBN 979-8-3852-1898-1 (paperback) | ISBN 979-8-3852-1899-8 (hardcover) | ISBN 979-8-3852-1900-1 (ebook)

Subjects: LCSH: Böhm, Anthon Wilhelm (1673–1722) | Pietism—Germany—History. | Great Britain—Church history—18th century.| Germany—Church history—18th century.

Classification: BR1652.G3 B64 2025 (print) | BR1652.G3 (ebook)

In memory of my *Doktorvater*,
John D. Walsh (1927–2022)

Contents

List of Pictures | viii
Foreword by Jonathan Strom | xi
Acknowledgments | xiii
Abbreviations | xv

Introduction | xvii
    Characterizing Pietism | xviii
    Pietism and Evangelicalism | xx
    Piety vis-à-vis Spirituality | xxii
    Subjects and Themes in the Letters | xxiii
    On "Indians" and Slavery | xxvi
    The Original Editor | xxviii
    Translation and Structure | xxviii
List of Letters | xxx

Erbauliche Briefe [Edifying Correspondence]
    Preface by original editor | 5
    Early Years (1700–1708) | 12
       Letters 1–14
    Pastoralia (1709–1710) | 30
       Letters 15–44
    Outreach Through the SPCK and Beyond (1710–1714) | 101
       Letters 45–103
    From Queen Anne to George I (1714–1716) | 206
       Letters 104–130
    Later Years (1717–1721) | 267
       Letters 131–152

Bibliography (Pre-1800) | 303
Bibliography | 312
Index | 317

List of Pictures

Photograph of John D. Walsh
Etching of Anton Wilhelm Böhme
Title Page from *Erbauliche Briefe*

Anton Wilhelm Böhme[1]

1. From Frontispiece in *Der Königl. Dänischen Missionarien*, vol. viii.

Foreword

FROM HIS PRIVILEGED POSITION as a court preacher in London, Anton Wilhelm Böhme enjoyed an extraordinary perspective on some of the most remarkable religious movements of the early eighteenth century. As this correspondence reveals, he stood at the center of several overlapping networks that were reshaping Protestantism in the early eighteenth century. Part of what makes these letters so helpful for historians is the way that they show how Böhme brokered connections across continents and promoted his own understanding of a non-sectarian Protestantism. He mediated between Cotton Mather in New England and August Hermann Francke in Halle. A powerful advocate for the Danish mission in Tranquebar, he secured funding, corresponded directly with the missionaries, and endeavored to send a printing press halfway around the world to aid their work. Exiled from his own territory for suspected spiritualist inclinations and at the same time beneficiary of powerful patrons at court in Britain, Böhme remained particularly attuned to the predicament of religious migrants and refugees, especially the French Prophets and the Palatines from Germany, even as he could be critical of their views and motivations. Böhme embodies many of the aims of the Halle Pietists, and he employed a publishing strategy that would disseminate their ideas not only to the English-speaking world but well beyond that through translations and editions of devotional works.

For students and scholars interested in how new evangelical movements such as Pietism began to challenge traditional Protestantism to transcend national and narrow confessional confines, this translation affords a close look at the religious motivations and strategies of an ardent German Pietist abroad who aimed to implement his views in a wider cosmopolitan context. In these letters we glimpse how Böhme engaged the Protestant world around him with ingenuity and zeal to achieve his increasing global vision of Christianity. Böhme's curiosity and non-sectarian approach—still at root Lutheran as numerous letters suggest—allowed him to converse with radicals about their experiences and explore diverse religious phenomena. At the same time his privileged, outsider status afforded him insights into the divisions within the Church of England and dissenters in Britain. Yet, here, we can also glimpse limitations in Böhme's perspectives. His irenic instincts in no way extended to Catholicism, and anti-Catholicism imbues many of the letters. Nor does his tacit acceptance of slavery distinguish him from most other European Protestants at this time; his all too easy acceptance of enslavement reveals starkly the limits of his moral vision.

The transformations of Protestantism in the eighteenth century marked by the rise of Pietism and related movements are critical to grasping modern manifestations of Christianity in a global context. The excellent translations and superb annotations here ensure that this collection will lead readers into greater engagement with Böhme and the networks he employed to further his distinctive vision of Christianity.

Jonathan Strom
Emory University

Acknowledgments

IN A 1717 LETTER, Böhme made this suggestion for translating a sermon: "Should circumstances otherwise permit, if you were to devote only half an hour to it every day, it would soon be possible to translate it."[1] In the summer of 2014, sitting in the Upper Reading Room of the Bodleian Library in Oxford, I committed myself to spending thirty minutes a day translating Böhme's London correspondence. My only expectation was that the regular discipline would keep me academically connected to the person who had been the central figure of my doctoral work. I started that translation process armed with an online DeepL translator and a 1909 Flügel, Schmidt, and Tanger German-to-English dictionary. Ten years later that journey is finally coming to an end.

Many people have supported me along the way. In 2022, after finishing two passes at the translation, I enlisted a friend, Stephanie Gehring Ladd, to proofread my work. Her corrections and suggestions were invaluable, and I and this translation are indebted to her work. She also introduced me to Paul Griffiths, who translated so excellently the nine Latin letters in *Erbauliche Briefe*. Jonathan Strom, a foremost scholar of Pietism, graciously agreed to write the foreword.

In the fall of 2023, I received a two-month grant from the Dr. Liselotte Kirchner Scholarship Programme of the Franckesche Stiftungen. That grant allowed me to make use of the unparalleled resources of the library and archive of the Franckesche Stiftungen in order to prepare footnotes and annotations for this critical edition. I offer my thanks to Holger Zaunstöck, director of the scholarship programme, and his colleagues for their kindnesses during my stay in Halle. Particular thanks go to Dirk Glettner and his staff in the Lesesaal der Stiftungen.

---

1. Böhme to de Ners, London, 7 May 1717 (Letter 133).

ACKNOWLEDGMENTS

George Fox University provided research grants that allowed me to do some initial explorations in the libraries of both Oxford and Halle. The staff at George Fox's library, especially Kate Wimer, has been exceptionally responsive to my requests. Over the years my colleagues at Portland Seminary have encouraged me in my academic endeavors; it was a joy to serve with them until my retirement in 2023.

The editorial team at Wipf and Stock and its subsidiary Pickwick Publications have been most understanding and accommodating. It is particularly gratifying to be able to work with an Oregon publisher.

My family and friends, too numerous to mention individually, have always expressed interest in this work, even when my explanations have only quickly left them glassy-eyed.

My parents, Louis and Glenna Brunner, raised my sisters and me in a home rife with a healthy Lutheran Pietism. I was not able to identify that background as pietistic, however, until I went to seminary, where I was introduced to historic Lutheran Pietism by Gary Sattler. This work is dedicated to the memory of my late *Doktorvater*, John D. Walsh, whose unique intermingling of warm-hearted Methodist piety, attentiveness to his students, and academic excellence remains, for me, the exemplar, personally and vocationally, of a life well lived.

Abbreviations

AFSt/H   Archive of the Franckesche Stiftungen in Halle
SPCK   Society for Promoting Christian Knowledge
SPG   Society for the Propagation of the Gospel
         in Foreign Parts

Introduction

THE ATLANTIC WORLD SAW wave after wave of religious revivals and spiritual renewal from the seventeenth century through the nineteenth century, including Puritanism, Pietism, Methodism, and the Great Awakenings.[1] In the eighteenth century Pietism provided a "crucial nexus" for diverse swells of reformation, and August Hermann Francke's institutions at Halle served as "an international clearinghouse" for a religious correspondence that eclipsed all previous endeavors.[2] One of the centers of that communications network was London, where Anton Wilhelm Böhme (or, when anglicized, Anthony William Boehm) operated in the first quarter of the eighteenth century.[3] Böhme, a student at the newly formed university in Halle and chaplain at the German Lutheran Royal Chapel at St. James's, was a well-placed representative of the increasingly global outreach of Francke's endeavors.[4]

Böhme, however, was more than an ambassador for Halle: he was a preacher and pastor (though not ordained), translator, and author in his own right. He was one of the few foreign Protestants invited to become a subscribing member of the Anglican Society for Promoting Christian Knowledge; not only was he an active member, but he influenced and introduced a number of the Society's most important early endeavors.[5]

---

1. See Lehmann, "Pietism in the World," 13–22; Ward, *Protestant Evangelical Awakening*; Noll, *Rise of Evangelicalism*, 45–68.

2. Butler, "Spiritual Importance," 103.

3. On Böhme, see Brunner, *Halle Pietists in England*; Sames, *Anton Wilhelm Böhme*.

4. On the connection between London and Halle, see Brunner, *Halle Pietists in England*; Zaunstöck et al., *London und Hallesche Waisenhaus*; Schunka, "Zwischen Kontingenz und Providenz," 82–114. For the religious context of the Halle-London relationship, see Schunka, *Ein neuer Blick*.

5. See chapters 3–6 in Brunner, *Halle Pietists in England*.

INTRODUCTION

But the purpose of this volume is to draw attention to and document Böhme's role as a worldwide correspondent.

In 1737, fifteen years after his death, over one hundred and fifty of Böhme's letters were published as *Erbauliche Briefe* [*Edifying Correspondence*]. The letters are representative of his correspondence, but not exhaustive.[6] Very little of the correspondence of early German Lutheran Pietism has been translated into English. These letters offer an English-speaking readership an enlightening glimpse into the theology, pastoral heart, spirituality, and life of a Halle Pietist whose reach extended from London to the Continent, Russia, the Malabar coast of India, and the fledgling American colonies.

CHARACTERIZING PIETISM

F. Ernest Stoeffler, who in 1965 wrote the first major scholarly work on Pietism in English, said that Pietism is "one of the least understood movements in the history of Christianity."[7] Defining Pietism continues to prove elusive to scholars over half a century later. Among the various approaches to the study of Pietism that have emerged,[8] two are significant for our purposes. The first denotes moderate forms of Pietism that sought the religious renewal of—not separation from—Protestantism on the Continent.[9] German scholarship historically has tended to focus on the more ecclesial forms of Pietism, such as Philip Jakob Spener in Frankfurt, Theodor Undereyck in Mülheim, Francke in Halle, or Johann Albrecht Bengel in Württemberg. These leaders, and others, sought to reform their respective German church communities by reviving the practice of Christianity through personal spiritual renewal. Certainly, there have been scholars who have brought to light the importance of this distinct understanding of German Pietism to specific denominational traditions in North America.[10] Nonetheless, Stephen J. Stein claims,

---

6. Much of Böhme's correspondence with Halle in the archive of the Franckeschen Stiftungen is not yet translated, though some of it has been published in German. See Sames, *Böhme*, 156–95.

7. Stoeffler, *Rise of Evangelical Pietism*, 1.

8. See the summary in Strom, "Problems and Promises," 536–54.

9. Wallmann, *Pietismus*, 7; Roeber, "Problem of the Eighteenth Century," 125.

10. Among numerous other specific denominational works, see esp. Stoeffler, *Continental Pietism*.

INTRODUCTION

"Historians in the United States have failed to give sufficient attention to Pietism as a religious movement of significance in North America."[11]

The second approach to Pietism significant for this volume is represented by Hartmut Lehmann.[12] Lehmann's perspective builds on and expands the work of W. R. Ward;[13] broadly speaking, one can also include in this camp Martin Brecht's understanding of Pietism as a "crisis of piety," Ted Campbell's "religion of the heart," and Stoeffler's "experiential Protestantism."[14] Lehmann describes Pietism "as part of a series of religious revivals in the Atlantic World." What we call Puritanism or Pietism or Methodism or the Great Awakenings are labels for aspects of "the sequence of waves of revivals and awakenings since the seventeenth century in various European countries and in North America." What characterizes and unites these reform movements is "the belief in renewal and rebirth on the individual and the community or congregational levels, and the belief that earnest and committed Christians should devote their lives to labor for the growth of the Kingdom of God." And often these transatlantic revivals became aware of parallel awakenings and networked with them through stories, correspondence, and the sharing of devotional literature and other resources.

Anton W. Böhme can undoubtedly be placed in both of these approaches. The earliest history of Pietism to appear in English was penned by Böhme himself in 1705, as a preface to his translation of Francke's history of the Halle orphanage, *Pietas Hallensis*.[15] Böhme narrowed his understanding of Pietism to three key figures within the German Lutheran Church: Johann Arndt, Spener, and Francke. Böhme described three aspects of Pietism.[16] The early Pietists modeled an oppositive element; there were "abuses" in the Lutheran Church, including dead orthodoxy and pulpit logomachy. Secondly, they pursued personal holiness and practical piety as a fruit of justification. Lastly, Pietists sought spiritual renewal and a vital relationship with God through new birth and a living

---

11. Stein, "Some Thoughts," 23.

12. On what follows, see Lehmann, "Pietism in the World," 13–22.

13. Ward, *Protestant Evangelical Awakening*; *Early Evangelicalism*.

14. Brecht, "Einleitung"; Campbell, *Religion of the Heart*; Stoeffler, *Rise of Evangelical Pietism*.

15. Francke, *Pietas Hallensis*. For an analysis of Böhme's "short history," see Yoder, "Rendered 'Odious' as Pietists," 17–26.

16. Böhme's preface in Francke, *Pietas Hallensis*, xxxv.

faith. These characteristics are a representative summary of ecclesial German Lutheran Pietism.

At the same time, Böhme was in a unique position to become aware of other Protestant awakenings or revivals, whether among children in Silesia, or within French Huguenot and Swiss Reformed traditions, or in the American colonial Puritanism of someone like Cotton Mather, or among the religious societies, societies for the reformation of manners, and voluntary societies in Anglicanism that garnered the backing of both Whig and Tory leadership. In cosmopolitan London, Böhme was effectively situated to network with a notable diversity of people, opinions, and interests. Stoeffler has written, "If Pietism is to be seen truly it, like other historical movements, must be seen with reference to its center, not its circumference."[17] Böhme was the unique kind of person who could hold onto the center of his convictions as a German Lutheran Pietist and exhibit openness and understanding to many of the diverse ways revival and renewal were emerging.

PIETISM AND EVANGELICALISM

Already in 1976, Stoeffler could affirm: "There can no longer be any doubt that the evangelicalism which became the dominant pattern for the individual and corporate religious self-understanding of American Protestants is heavily indebted to the Pietist tradition."[18] Nevertheless, the relationship between Pietism and American evangelicalism remains debated within evangelical scholarship. Theologian Roger Olson observes that a number evangelical scholars, especially those aligned historically with the Princeton school of Reformed orthodoxy, continue to "malign" Pietism for experientialism, individualism, and perfectionism.[19] However, a cadre of evangelical scholars have observed that "most of the communities that have come to identify themselves as evangelicals are rooted more in the revivalism of the nineteenth century—a movement and phenomenon which has far more in common with Pietism than with Protestant orthodoxy, both historically and theologically."[20]

---

17. Stoeffler, *Rise of Evangelical Pietism*, 12.
18. Epilogue in Stoeffler, *Continental Pietism*, 267.
19. Olson, "Pietism," 4.
20. Introduction in Collins Winn et al., *Pietist Impulse*, xxii.

INTRODUCTION

Part of the difficulty is coming to a consensus on what is meant by evangelicalism. David Bebbington suggests four marks of evangelicalism: *conversionism*, the conviction that lives can be changed; *activism*, expressing the gospel in lived experience and action; *biblicism*, a particular regard for the Scriptures; and *crucicentrism*, a stress on the centrality of Jesus Christ and his life, death on the cross, and resurrection.[21] Although the "Bebbington quadrilateral" has its critics,[22] it remains, in the eyes of one historian, "among the most well-known definitions in the study of religion."[23] Although one can point to nuanced, though important, differences between these four marks and the theology and praxis of Pietism, the parallels are significant. Mark Noll observes that the "convictions, practices, habits and oppositions" of evangelicalism "resemble what Europeans describe as 'pietism.'"[24] Böhme is a key figure in this regard. His uniquely anglicized Pietism during the "tunnel period" in Britain between the fall of Puritanism at the Restoration in 1660 and the Evangelical Revival under George Whitefield and John Wesley in the 1730s earns him the moniker of those who were, in the words of Geoffrey Nuttall, "Evangelicals before the Revival."[25]

One last note: not only has the connection between Pietism and the rise of evangelicalism drawn the interest of academics on both sides of the Atlantic,[26] but, at the same time, there are an increasing number of works accessible to lay audiences, texts that highlight the significance of Pietism for understanding evangelicalism and contemporary church renewal.[27]

---

21. Bebbington, *Evangelicalism in Modern Britain*, 1–17.

22. For useful colloquia on Bebbington's definition, see Phillips, "Roundtable"; Bebbington and Jones, *Evangelicalism and Fundamentalism*; Haykin and Stewart, *Emergence of Evangelicalism*.

23. Porterfield, "Bebbington's Approach," 58.

24. Noll, *Rise of Evangelicalism*, 15.

25. Nuttall, "Methodism and the Older Dissent," 261. See also Ward, *Christianity under Ancien Régime*, 142–45. On Böhme's "evangelicalism," see Brunner, "'Evangelical' Heart of Boehm."

26. Ward, *Early Evangelicalism*; *Protestant Evangelical Awakening*; Collins Winn et al., *Pietist Impulse*.

27. Olson and Collins Winn, *Reclaiming Pietism*; Gehrz and Pattie, *Pietist Option*; Clifton-Soderstrom, *Angels, Worms, and Bogeys*.

INTRODUCTION

PIETY VIS-À-VIS SPIRITUALITY

When I submitted some of my earliest writing to my doctoral advisor, John D. Walsh, a leading Wesleyan scholar, he commented that I was using the idea of "spirituality" too frequently; in Europe, he noted, the preferred term was "piety." What was true then remains true now: the nomenclature of "spirituality" is considerably more common in North America than "piety." For decades, many American seminary professors resisted quite vehemently the language of piety and Pietism, citing well-known scholars like Karl Barth and Wolfhart Pannenberg—"Whatever I am, there is one thing I am *not*—a Pietist!"[28] However, this critique was more than the well-worn theological clash between Pietism and Orthodoxy. For many leaders within American mainline denominations, including my own, it was personal: they had been raised in pietistic (read: restrictive) homes and wanted little to do with any kind of subjective, heart-over-head religion. As a counterpoint, for more than twenty-five years I taught numerous courses at an evangelical seminary on the history, theology, or practice of Christian spirituality. Part of my qualifications to teach spirituality in an academic institution was my doctoral work on Böhme and German Lutheran Pietism.

The "tone" in Böhme's correspondence represents not only the *praxis pietatis* of Pietism, but also a genuine, vital spirituality. Olson aligns with Stoeffler and argues "that real Pietism is no longer a movement but an ethos or spirit that has filtered into especially American religious life."[29] The leading historian of evangelicalism in America, Mark Noll, has written that the era from the late seventeenth century through the eighteenth was "when pietism on the Continent and evangelicalism in Great Britain emerged as powerful movements that (depending on one's perspective) opened a way to inward spiritual renewal or threatened to subvert society."[30] His reference to "inward spiritual renewal" would have warmed Böhme's heart.

As a life-long Lutheran, raised in a pietistic home, I have found it natural to talk about what Eric Lund has called a "Lutheran spiritual tradition" that began with Luther and was revived first by Johann Arndt.[31] Berndt Hamm states that scholarship is increasingly open to seeing

---

28. Quoted by Roger E. Olson in Olson and Collins Winn, *Reclaiming Pietism*, 4.
29. Olson, "Pietism," 6; Stoeffler, *Rise of Evangelical Pietism*, 13.
30. Noll, *America's God*, 7–8.
31. Lund, "Johann Arndt."

INTRODUCTION

Luther as "the founder of an evangelical mysticism and as someone at home in a Protestant mystical spirituality."[32] Carter Lindberg referred to Pietism as the second Reformation, not unlike Böhme who referred to Pietism as a "New Reformation," a "Practical Reformation," and even a "more Universal Reformation."[33] I am a proponent of a "spiritual" thread that runs from Luther's "faith mysticism" through Johann Arndt and historic Pietism to a spirituality that embodies both contemplative prayer and *praxis pietatis*.[34]

SUBJECTS AND THEMES IN THE LETTERS

This book brings to light primary source material on a wide range of subjects in religious and cultural history. The following descriptions sketch primary themes in Böhme's correspondence.

Starting in 1708, over ten thousand German Protestants from the Palatinate in Germany passed through London on their way to the American colonies and elsewhere in Europe.[35] Böhme spared no effort to make sure the "poor Palatines" were cared for, physically and spiritually. Nonetheless, he was not persuaded of their motivations for leaving Germany. He wrote a tract in 1711 to discourage further migrations of Germans to London,[36] and offered his reasoning in a letter to a correspondent: "The worst thing is that the poor people are not willing to recognize that this is a time of divine judgment which must be removed not with outward flight but with the eradication of inner sinfulness."[37] Böhme maintained an ongoing correspondence with many of these and other German leaders in New York, Pennsylvania, and Carolina. The last letter of the collection, from 1721, is to a German tailor, Johann Bernhard van Dieren, who had passed through London laden with Bibles and devotional literature from Halle, and was preaching to small Lutheran congregations in New York.

---

32. Hamm, *Early Luther*, 191.

33. Lindberg, *Third Reformation*; Böhme's preface in Francke, *Pietas Hallensis*, xxxvii.

34. Brunner, "Luther's Mysticism," 20–28; Hoffman, *Theology of the Heart*, 202, traces the origin of the descriptor "faith mysticism" to Söderblom, *Tre livsformer*.

35. See Otterness, *Becoming German*; Olson, "Huguenots and Palatines," 269–85.

36. Böhme, *Das verlangte, nicht erlangte Canaan*.

37. Böhme to Mr. D. H. C., London, 14 Oct 1709 (Letter 17).

INTRODUCTION

The translation, publishing, and distribution of devotional literature, especially Johann Arndt's *True Christianity*, occupied a goodly portion of Böhme's correspondence. Böhme mentioned *True Christianity* in nineteen different letters. He regarded Arndt's work as "an Instrument of the Divine Blessing in the Conversion of many Souls into the true and Interior Christianity."[38] He took an active role in the translation, printing, and distribution of the Bible and New Testament in numerous languages, including Turkish, Estonian, Portuguese, and Arabic. He was tireless in his efforts to secure devotional literature and Scripture for German emigrants in the American colonies.

Böhme was a central figure in maintaining the complicated relationships between Halle Pietism, the Danish royal court, and the SPCK in their "ecumenical" collaboration around the first Protestant missionary outreach to the southeastern coast of India.[39] A sizable portion of Böhme's correspondence aims specifically at attending to details, monitoring relationships, and easing tensions that arose between an Anglican voluntary society, German Lutheran Pietists, and Orthodox Danish Lutherans. Böhme's mediating skills were put to the test when the Anglicans in the SPCK learned that there were conflicts among the missionaries themselves and that the catechism used at Tranquebar was overtly Lutheran; the Archbishop of Canterbury feared the spread of "sectarian Lutheranism" when he saw the name "Luther" on the title page of the catechism printed by the missionaries in India.[40]

Böhme's relationship to Puritanism, mysticism, and the more radical expressions of Pietism or mysticism is fascinating and provides evidence of his own spirituality and the limits beyond which his theology and sensibilities would not allow him to trespass. He was grounded in some of the classics of Puritan literature; in his letters he mentions works by Joseph Alleine, John Bunyan, Thomas Goodwin, Ezekiel Hopkins, John Eliot, Richard Baxter, Lewis Bayly, Cotton Mather, and Jeremiah White.[41] In the last letter of the collection, Böhme says of Bunyan's *Pilgrim's Progress*: "It was one of the first books through which God worked

38. PBöhme's preface in Francke, *Pietas Hallensis*, xvii.

39. The literature on the East India Mission and Halle-SPCK cooperation is extensive. A good place to start is Lehmann, *It Began at Tranquebar*. Probably the most thorough is Gross et al., *Halle and the Beginning*. Vol. 1 is *The Danish-Halle and the English-Halle Mission*.

40. Note esp. Letters 72, 73, and 91. See Brunner, "Collaboration and Conflict"; O'Connor, "Lutherans and Anglicans."

41. See McKenzie, *Catalog of British Devotional*.

on my heart and persuaded me of the nature of a living Christianity."[42] Additionally, he exhibits clear proclivities toward the mystical side of Christian faith and practice; he favorably alludes to and/or engages in correspondence with Thomas Bromley, Jakob Böhme, Johann Kelpius, Johann Gottfried Seelig, John Pordage, Johann Wilhelm Petersen, Johann Tauler, Catherine of Genoa, Thomas à Kempis, Christian Knorr von Rosenroth, and others. At the same time, he had to address the complicated connections between Pietism and radical mystics and movements like Richard Roach, Francis Lee, Jane Leade, and the Philadelphia Society; for example, he maintained a close collegial friendship with Francis Lee. Böhme sharply condemned the extreme inspirations and gesticulations of the French Prophets, while also praising the generosity of one of the prophets, Richard Bulkeley, and supporting the publication of a book on miracles in England.

The sharp divide between High Church and Low Church wings of the Church of England rankled Böhme; on many occasions he addressed the chasm between the two parties and advocated for understanding and moderation. In a lengthy letter to a Pietist colleague in Pennsylvania, Böhme wrote: "It will be unnecessary to add anything about the High and Low Church parties into which the Church of England is now divided, and which are constantly at war with each other. . . . The saddest thing is that neither party is concerned for the glory of God, but only for its own interest, with the exception, perhaps, that the leaders of the moderate party have a little more natural honesty, and are better patriots than their opponents."[43] For the sake of reform and mission, Böhme sought to remain aloof from party differences and walk a *via media* between the parties.[44] In a letter to Samuel Urlsperger he made his opinion plain: "For the essence of Christianity is not exclusive to any sect—I call every outward form a sect, if the spirit of Christ, which alone can enliven and inspire the form, is lacking—but flows through every party, and here and there saves a few from the widespread corruption that sours all parties."[45] To another correspondent he wrote that "no party is so corrupt that God has not retained a holy seed within it. Such good souls, who are, as it were, salt in the midst of decay, are undoubtedly found most often among the simple

---

42. Böhme to Johann Bernhard van Dieren in New York, n.d. (Letter 152).
43. Böhme to Johann Gottfried Seelig, London, 18 Aug 1714 (Letter 104).
44. On "confessional impartiality," see Malena, "Confessional impartiality," 43.
45. Böhme to Samuel Urlsperger, London, 22 Dec 1709 (Letter 21).

INTRODUCTION

and lowly crowd."[46] Tensions between Anglicanism and Lutheranism were that much pricklier with the accession of a "Lutheran" to the throne in 1714.[47] The writer of the original preface elevated Böhme as someone who respected differences and could engage conflicting opinions with generosity and understanding, even if he disagreed with them.[48]

The diversity of people with whom Böhme communicated stands out. Not only did he correspond regularly with key Pietist leaders, but twenty-eight of his letters were to a French Huguenot émigré, Seigneur de Ners, and a second-generation émigré from the Palatinate, Jane Slare, whose brother was a member of the Royal Society and a laboratory assistant to Robert Boyle. He communicated with royalty and government officials, and remained in touch with former members of the *collegium pietatis* he held on Monday evenings.[49] Hartmut Lehmann has written that even within diverse Pietist groups, one of the matters they held as most important was "the solidarity with all of those with whom they felt close as brothers and sisters."[50] Böhme is an exemplar of such a comprehensive solidarity, as noted at the end of the original preface: "True friends of the Bridegroom will have no doubt that he [Böhme] too belonged to their number, and that he will certainly shine along with them like the radiance of the sun and like the stars forever and ever."[51]

ON "INDIANS" AND SLAVERY

Two particular subjects in Böhme's letters deserve attention. The first is related to the evangelization of and missionary outreach among the Indigenous peoples of the American colonies and East India.[52] In a 1711 letter to Francke, Böhme introduced him to John Eliot, Puritan missionary among the Massachusett and Narragansett peoples of New England. Eliot had translated the Bible into Massachusett, the first Bible printed in America, as well as Lewis Bayly's *The Practice of Piety* and Richard Baxter's *A Call to the Unconverted*. Böhme recounted an anecdote of the

46. Böhme to Mr. K., London, 12 Jan 1714 (Letter 92).
47. Brunner, "Anglican Perceptions."
48. See esp. [Jacobi], Preface §11.
49. See Böhme to Mr. V. B. at H., London, 8 Sept 1713 (Letter 87); Böhme to Mr. H. in P., London, 31 Dec 1713 (Letter 90).
50. Lehmann, "Communities of Pietists," 351.
51. [Jacobi], Preface §12.
52. See, for example, Cox, *British Missionary Enterprise*, 22–51; Jeyaraj, *Inkulturation*.

INTRODUCTION

mutual love shared by Eliot and his Indigenous friends.[53] In another letter, Böhme relates a graphic, gory account of Yamasee raids on English settlers in South Carolina. Böhme interpreted the raids as divine judgment on the Christian settlers, adding: "This much is certain, these Indian raids should be regarded as something unparalleled, since they are not in accord with their nature, which is kind-hearted, gentle, and tolerant."[54] One challenge for translation is Böhme's frequent use of *Heiden* or *Heidentum*—traditionally translated as "heathen" or "heathenism"—when referring to Indigenous peoples and enslaved Africans in the colonies and West Indies, to Malabarians in East India, or to the unconverted in general. Worth mentioning is a footnote in Johannes Ferdinand Fengar's history of the East India mission: "The Malabarians do not like to be called Heathens (*Anyani*, i.e., Unwise)."[55] Out of respect for Malabarian preferences, as well as Böhme's unambiguous emphasis on evangelization and conversion, our translation uses "Malabarian," "pagan," "unconverted," or "Gentile," depending on the context.

Even more problematic for modern readers is Böhme's citation from a 1711 sermon by the Anglican preacher and economist William Fleetwood, Bishop of St. Asaph. Christopher Wendt, secretary of the Mission College in Copenhagen responsible for the mission in Tranquebar, had asked Böhme "how native peoples and slaves were treated with regard to baptism and similar matters in the English plantations in the East and West Indies." In response, Böhme quoted at length Fleetwood's sermon delivered to the SPG, a sister society of the SPCK.[56] A British general named Christopher Codrington had bequeathed to the SPG two plantations on Barbados, along with three hundred enslaved African men, women, and children. Codrington directed that the enslaved be treated humanely, catechized, and baptized, and that their children be catechized. Fleetwood sought in the sermon to counter three objections frequently raised as to why the enslaved should *not* be catechized and baptized; Böhme's purpose in citing the sermon was to support efforts to convert the enslaved in the West Indies. Nonetheless, the sermon is further evidence of Jeffrey Cox's claim that "the Church of England was deeply implicated in the system of slavery that was the foundation of the

---

53. Böhme to Francke, London, 16 Feb 1711 (Letter 62).
54. Böhme to N. N., London, 28 July 1715 (Letter 121).
55. Fengar, *History of Tranquebar Mission*, 58n.
56. Böhme to Christopher Wendt, London, 30 June 1715 (Letter 119).

British Empire of the eighteenth century."⁵⁷ In this respect, it is important to note that the USPG (formerly, SPG) has established the Codrington Reparations Project "to seek to engage critically with and take reparative action in response to USPG's shameful links to slavery through its ownership of The Codrington Estates in Barbados."⁵⁸

THE ORIGINAL EDITOR

The original editor and author of the preface is unknown. *Erbauliche Briefe* was published in 1737. Johann Jakob Rambach, who translated, edited, and penned the preface to Böhme's *Sämtliche Erbauliche Schriften* and drew up Böhme's *Memoirs*, died in 1735.⁵⁹ Johann Albert Fabricius wrote the preface to Böhme's *Acht Bücher von der Reformation der Kirche in England*, but he died in 1736.⁶⁰

The most likely editor of *Erbauliche Briefe* is Johann Christian Jacobi. Jacobi was a student at Halle, Böhme's colleague at and keeper of the German Lutheran Royal Chapel, and a translator of religious tracts and of Rambach's biography of Böhme. In the preface to Böhme's *Memoirs*, Rambach said that he lacked materials to write about Böhme's life, "had I not been furnished since with several of Mr. *Boehm*'s own private Letters, to give some Insight into the outward and inward Dispensations of Providence he met with in his Life-time."⁶¹ Since so many of the private letters in *Erbauliche Briefe* were to correspondents in England, it is likely they were collected by Jacobi.⁶²

TRANSLATION AND STRUCTURE

The title page of *Erbauliche Briefe* states that the original letters were written in German, Latin, and English; however, they were published only in German and Latin. Since the original English letters are lost, we are only able to recover them by translating them back from the German.

---

57. Cox, *British Missionary Enterprise*, 40. The SPG owned and ran the estates as a business with slave labor until 1838.
58. USPG, "Renewal and Reconciliation."
59. Böhme, *Sämtliche erbauliche Schriften*; Rambach, *Memoirs of . . . Boehm*.
60. Böhme, *Acht Bücher*.
61. Preface in Rambach, *Memoirs of . . . Boehm*, vii.
62. See Sames, *Böhme*, 37.

INTRODUCTION

Paul Griffiths translated the nine Latin letters (Nos. 12, 19, 56, 82, 83, 108, 112, 115, and 117). In a 1717 letter, Böhme asked the Frenchman Seigneur de Ners if he would be willing to translate one of Böhme's sermons into French: "It is not necessary to be bound by the literal words; a translation must be free to express in the best way the sense and emphases of the author."[63] Our goal as translators has indeed been to express the sense and emphases of the author. Where we were able, we expanded names of people and places beyond initials. Brief biographical details of many of the people Böhme mentions are put into footnotes, when that information is available.

The letters follow the same ordering and numbering as the original publication. Italicized text is in the original. At times, lengthy paragraphs have been divided to make reading easier; in order to save paper, eighteenth-century letter writing usually made minimal use of new paragraphs. These organizational categories were added:

Preface by initial editor
Early Years (1700–1708)
Pastoralia (1709–1710)
Outreach Through the SPCK and Beyond (1710–1714)
From Queen Anne to George I (1714–1716)
Later Years (1717–1721)

There are two bibliographies: the first is for works published before 1800, usually ones to which Böhme makes reference; the second bibliography is for secondary scholarship in footnotes and the introduction. A thorough index provides references to names, authors, and subjects.

It is my sincere hope the translation and publication of these letters will provide academic and lay readers, especially those with limited access to primary source material in English, with insights into and appreciation for both the central role of this particular Halle Pietist in London but also his unique Pietist theology, inclusive churchmanship, pastoral presence, and deeply rooted spirituality.

---

63. Böhme to de Ners, London, 7 May 1717 (Letter 133).

List of Letters

Preface by Johann Christian Jacobi[?]

Early Years (1700–1708)

No. 1	A. W. Böhme to the Countess of Waldeck
No. 2	A. W. Böhme to the Countess of Waldeck
No. 3	A. W. Böhme to the Countess of Waldeck
No. 4	A. W. Böhme to Anna Elisabeth Böhme[?]
No. 5	A. W. Böhme to Dr. Frederick Slare
No. 6	A. W. Böhme to Anna Elisabeth Böhme
No. 7	A. W. Böhme to Dr. Frederick Slare
No. 8	A. W. Böhme to Anna Elisabeth Böhme
No. 9	A. W. Böhme to N. N.
No. 10	A. W. Böhme to Miss Jane Slare
No. 11	A. W. Böhme to Miss Jane Slare
No. 12	A. W. Böhme to I. A. Lubomirsky
No. 13	A. W. Böhme to Miss Jane Slare
No. 14	A. W. Böhme to Christian Friends in Germany

Pastoralia (1709–1710)

No. 15	A. W. Böhme to Henry Newman
No. 16	A. W. Böhme to Miss Jane Slare
No. 17	A. W. Böhme to Mr. D. H. C.
No. 18	A. W. Böhme to Carl Hildebrand von Canstein
No. 19	A. W. Böhme to M. Z. G., Rector of the School of O.
No. 20	A. W. Böhme to Mrs. Dr. O., née of S. in C.
No. 21	A. W. Böhme to Samuel Urlsperger
No. 22	A. W. Böhme to Professor August Hermann Francke
No. 23	A. W. Böhme to Loth Fischer

LIST OF LETTERS

No. 24	A. W. Böhme to Samuel Urlsperger
No. 25	A. W. Böhme to Justus Falckner[?]
No. 26	A. W. Böhme to C. R. at M. in the Earldom of W.
No. 27	A. W. Böhme to Justus Falckner, farmers, and residents in New York
No. 28	A. W. Böhme to Johann Gottfried Seelig[?]
No. 29	A. W. Böhme to Professor Johann Heinrich Michaelis
No. 30	A. W. Böhme to J. P. H., Pastor at Lower R. in Thuringia
No. 31	A. W. Böhme to G. H. at F. in Holstein
No. 32	A. W. Böhme to Samuel Urlsperger
No. 33	A. W. Böhme to Loth Fischer
No. 34	A. W. Böhme to Mrs. S. in C.
No. 35	A. W. Böhme to Dr. Johann Wilhelm Petersen
No. 36	A. W. Böhme to Professor August Hermann Francke
No. 37	Mr. B. in the Earldom of J. to A. W. Böhme
No. 38	A. W. Böhme to Mr. J. U. and Mr. B.
No. 39	A. W. Böhme to Professor August Hermann Francke
No. 40	A. W. Böhme to Mr. B. C. S. from P.
No. 41	A. W. Böhme to George Keith
No. 42	A. W. Böhme to Professor August Hermann Francke
No. 43	A. W. Böhme to Seigneur de Ners
No. 44	A. W. Böhme to Carl Hildebrand von Canstein

Outreach Through the SPCK and Beyond (1710–1714)

No. 45	A. W. Böhme to John Chamberlayne
No. 46	A. W. Böhme to Seigneur de Ners
No. 47	A. W. Böhme to Professor August Hermann Francke
No. 48	A. W. Böhme to Seigneur de Ners
No. 49	A. W. Böhme to Professor August Hermann Francke
No. 50	A. W. Böhme to Seigneur de Ners
No. 51	A. W. Böhme to Mr. N. C. in the Earldom of W.
No. 52	A. W. Böhme to Mr. C. R. in M.
No. 53	A. W. Böhme to Joshua Kocherthal[?]
No. 54	A. W. Böhme to Loth Fischer
No. 55	A. W. Böhme to Professor August Hermann Francke
No. 56	A. W. Böhme to Bartholomäus Ziegenbalg and Heinrich Plütschau

LIST OF LETTERS

No. 57	A. W. Böhme to Bartholomäus Ziegenbalg and the rest of the German missionaries in Tranquebar
No. 58	A. W. Böhme to Seigneur de Ners
No. 59	A. W. Böhme to Seigneur de Ners
No. 60	A. W. Böhme to Mr. R., Merchant in Frankfurt am Main
No. 61	Mr. R. to A. W. Böhme
No. 62	A. W. Böhme to Professor August Hermann Francke
No. 63	A. W. Böhme to Seigneur de Ners
No. 64	A. W. Böhme to Mr. E. in the city of M. in Moscow
No. 65	A. W. Böhme to Miss Jane Slare
No. 66	A. W. Böhme to Miss Jane Slare
No. 67	A. W. Böhme to Georg Melchior Ludolf
No. 68	A. W. Böhme to Dr. Heinrich Lysius
No. 69	A. W. Böhme to Professor August Hermann Francke
No. 70	A. W. Böhme to Mr. S. S., a Preacher in E.
No. 71	A. W. Böhme to Anna Elisabeth Böhme
No. 72	A. W. Böhme to Bartholomäus Ziegenbalg
No. 73	A. W. Böhme to Johann Ernst Gründler
No. 74	A. W. Böhme to Zacharias Dezius
No. 75	A. W. Böhme to Professor August Hermann Francke
No. 76	A. W. Böhme to Miss Jane Slare
No. 77	A. W. Böhme to Miss Jane Slare
No. 78	A. W. Böhme to Miss Jane Slare
No. 79	A. W. Böhme to N. N.
No. 80	A. W. Böhme to Miss Jane Slare
No. 81	A. W. Böhme to Heinrich Plütschau
No. 82	A. W. Böhme to Mr. H. F.
No. 83	A. W. Böhme to Mr. R.
No. 84	A. W. Böhme to Miss Jane Slare
No. 85	A. W. Böhme to Monsieur V. B. in H.
No. 86	A. W. Böhme to Mr. O. H. at R. near L. in H.
No. 87	A. W. Böhme to Monsieur V. B. in H.
No. 88	A. W. Böhme to Mr. T. in B.
No. 89	A. W. Böhme to Samuel Urlsperger
No. 90	A. W. Böhme to Monsieur H. in P.
No. 91	A. W. Böhme to Bartholomäus Ziegenbalg and Johann Ernst Gründler
No. 92	A. W. Böhme to Mr. K.
No. 93	A. W. Böhme to Georg Heinrich Neubauer

LIST OF LETTERS

No. 94   A. W. Böhme to Mr. H.
No. 95   A. W. Böhme to Samuel Urlsperger
No. 96   A. W. Böhme to Henry Newman
No. 97   A. W. Böhme to Professor August Hermann Francke
No. 98   A. W. Böhme to Henry Newman
No. 99   A. W. Böhme to Christopher Wendt
No. 100   A. W. Böhme to Mr. K.
No. 101   A. W. Böhme to Professor Joachim Lange
No. 102   A. W. Böhme to Heinrich Plütschau
No. 103   A. W. Böhme to Loth Fischer

From Queen Anne to George I (1714–1716)

No. 104   A. W. Böhme to Johann Gottfried Seelig[?]
No. 105   A. W. Böhme to N. N.
No. 106   A. W. Böhme to Georg Heinrich Neubauer
No. 107   A. W. Böhme to Samuel Urlsperger
No. 108   A. W. Böhme to Dr. Johann Georg Pritius
No. 109   A. W. Böhme to Bartholomäus Ziegenbalg and Johann Ernst Gründler
No. 110   A. W. Böhme to Mr. F. at Edinburgh
No. 111   A. W. Böhme to Christopher Wendt
No. 112   A. W. Böhme to Dr. Cotton Mather
No. 113   A. W. Böhme to Seigneur de Ners
No. 114   A. W. Böhme to Professor C. S. in L.
No. 115   A. W. Böhme to Dr. Johann Georg Pritius[?]
No. 116   A. W. Böhme to Carl Hildebrand von Canstein
No. 117   A. W. Böhme to Mr. P. F.
No. 118   A. W. Böhme to Professor August Hermann Francke
No. 119   A. W. Böhme to Christopher Wendt
No. 120   A. W. Böhme to Miss Jane Slare
No. 121   A. W. Böhme to N. N.
No. 122   A. W. Böhme to Monsieur V. B. in H.
No. 123   A. W. Böhme to Carl Hildebrand von Canstein
No. 124   A. W. Böhme to Miss Jane Slare
No. 125   A. W. Böhme to Bartholomäus Ziegenbalg
No. 126   A. W. Böhme to Mr. C. V. in W.
No. 127   A. W. Böhme to Mr. U. in W.
No. 128   A. W. Böhme to Mr. K. in S.

LIST OF LETTERS

No. 129   A. W. Böhme to Georg Heinrich Neubauer
No. 130   A. W. Böhme to Mr. B. on the C.

Later Years (1717–1721)

No. 131   A. W. Böhme to Seigneur de Ners
No. 132   A. W. Böhme to Seigneur de Ners
No. 133   A. W. Böhme to Seigneur de Ners
No. 134   A. W. Böhme to Seigneur de Ners
No. 135   A. W. Böhme to Seigneur de Ners
No. 136   A. W. Böhme to Anna Elisabeth Böhme
No. 137   A. W. Böhme to Henry Newman
No. 138   A. W. Böhme to Miss Jane Slare
No. 139   A. W. Böhme to Miss Jane Slare
No. 140   A. W. Böhme to Miss Jane Slare
No. 141   A. W. Böhme to a preacher in the country
No. 142   A. W. Böhme to Monsieur Williams
No. 143   A. W. Böhme to Henry Newman
No. 144   A. W. Böhme's reflections on the love of God (not included in the previous letters)
No. 145   A. W. Böhme to Monsieur Williams
No. 146   A. W. Böhme to Monsieur Williams
No. 147   A. W. Böhme to Monsieur Williams
No. 148   A. W. Böhme to Monsieur Williams
No. 149   A. W. Böhme to Monsieur Williams
No. 150   A. W. Böhme to Dr. Isaac Watts
No. 151   A. W. Böhme to Mr. B.
No. 152   A. W. Böhme to Johann Bernhard van Dieren

Anton Wilhelm Böhmens
weiland
Sr. Königl. Hoheit, Prinz Georgens von
Dännemark, Hof-Prediger zu London,

Erbauliche Briefe,

welche
in teutscher, lateinischer und englischer
Sprache von ihm geschrieben worden;
mit einer

Vorrede,

in welcher von dem Herausgeber nach dem
Exempel des sel. Verfassers
gezeiget wird:
Daß man einen jeden müsse
sein Recht geniessen lassen,
wenn man von ihm urtheilet.

Altona und Flensburg,
Verlegt von den Gebrüdern Korte. 1737.

The Edifying Correspondence

of Anthony William Boehm,

formerly,
court preacher at London to His Royal Highness,
Prince George of Denmark,
Which he wrote in German, Latin and English;
with a Preface
in which the editor shows, following the example
of the blessed author:
That one must do right by everyone
when passing judgment on them.
Altona and Flensburg:
The Korte brothers, 1737

Preface

by Johann Christian Jacobi[?]

§1

One should undoubtedly let every person be right in those matters in which they are right, and we clearly consider it unfair when anyone acts contrary to this rule in what concerns us. Nevertheless, it is quite common to do just the opposite of this rule. We poor people are all too inclined to pass judgment on things before we are fully informed about them. It often takes quite a bit of effort to get to the bottom of a matter. We want to spare ourselves that trouble, and are therefore satisfied if we only have an idea of what it is. Now we should not assert anything other than that for which there is sufficient reason. This presupposes clear ideas of the nature of things, as well as of the connection between them. But how can one assume that this is even probable, if the heart either shuns the effort altogether, or does not willingly see their true nature and true context, and would rather have it otherwise; and if one does not admit to having seen things wrongly, nor to have made an unfair decision? Opinion and passion infinitely deceive people. And, what is most deplorable, they generally do not want it to be better. But who is untainted by it, and who is able to remain untainted by it?

§2

I like to say that there is a very big difference to be noticed: People are not the same; nor are the times the same.

Of course, the improvement of the mind and will clearly stands one in good stead. Indeed, it would be speaking too narrowly of grace if I wanted to claim that in this respect it does not create a very important change in people. The Sun of Righteousness will steadily dispel darkness in those who are counted worthy of the discipline of the Spirit, and will soon put an end to falsehood. The times, also, are very different. When souls are serene, and when the graced watch and pray, it is certainly different from when they let themselves be taken out of that state, and when they are negligent in these two things. However, living an ordinary way of life, it is almost impossible not to come to all kinds of opinions. And is it odd, then, that people are called students when they seek out such things diligently and take special pleasure in the abundance and variety of them? By this a mind is obviously corrupted, so that afterward it becomes quite problematic to realize what a great difference it is when one only has an opinion on a proposed issue and when, on the other hand, one thinks something about it with good reason.

§3

Much of it probably stems from a weakness of the intellect; but if only this weakness did not often result from the fact that a fine intellect has been dulled, so to speak! Most of the blame for all of this can be attributed to passion. Unfortunately, people do not come to this or that conclusion because it is most likely, but because we find it the most respectable and secretly wish that it would be so. And precisely this mother of all passions, the corrupted will, is the main source of mistaken judgments and conclusions. How ought the will drive the intellect to investigate the true nature and context of a matter, both of which the person does not want to know? And how many countless times must the intellect be clouded, and directed and applied in a completely different way than is entailed by the nature of the soul's powers and the order of its actions?

§4

I readily admit that this often happens so subtly that people are quite unaware of it, unless they are accustomed to becoming wary of the darkening of their hearts, and of their inner restlessness, and of the unsettledness in the hidden powers of the soul, and to suspecting that there is something wrong. But it is much more common that people knows very well that passion is involved; even though it is denied inwardly, they just cannot break free from its slavery. At least those hearts which are not yet completely depraved, in the beginning cling to their passion with considerable reluctance, though it diminishes with time, and perhaps even stops over time with some people. This reluctance and restlessness are sufficient evidence that a higher hand governs human actions; but they also make passion all the more culpable. Not only to want something, but also to want it constantly, and, as far as possible, to put it into practice, the falsehood and unreasonableness of which a person can see and feel, is obvious proof of turning away from God and of a stubborn persistence in it.

§5

In the meantime, it happens that people generally act according to their opinions and passions when they decide on what they want to do, especially when it concerns certain people and especially when it concerns religious matters. After we have considered something true or false, right or wrong, useful or harmful, and whether it is pleasant or unpleasant, advantageous or disadvantageous, only then do we finalize our judgment. If the Scriptures did not actually speak clearly of the deep corruption of human nature, it would be difficult to understand to any degree why people hold their chosen opinions so rigidly, and why passions then tend to be aroused with such a sense of rightness. What unspeakable misfortune has always resulted from the fact that people have been zealous for God out of ignorance! With many people it is as though all obligations, which nature and grace prescribe, had ceased as soon as another person does not speak or act in accordance with our current opinion in matters of religion. If, therefore, one has occasion to pass judgment on someone in regard to religion, it is certainly rare to hear neither opinion nor passion, and to hear the matter judged with the genuine reason and fairness, which the characteristics of human nature and human life, and especially the teachings of Christ, indicate. Meanwhile, no reasonable person, much less an enlightened Christian, doubts that it should be so.

§6

One should do right by everyone. The question is: whether a person should, can, and will believe or do something? Very often it is necessary first to find out whether a person should do this or that, and whether or not these actions are, in fact, errors and unlawful, or at least foolish, things which he is supposed to accustom himself to do because someone else thinks he should. Consequently, it is a very great inequity to reproach in a person that which should rightly be praised, and to be moved to regard with disdain and disapproval that which should rather inspire us with esteem and heartfelt love toward the person. The fact that something has been believed and done from ancient times, and even by many respected people, is poor evidence that the thing is right. The three ways of arriving at conclusions—of the senses, of reason, and of faith—are not always found in the places where one most expects them, but have not infrequently, especially the conviction of faith, been given to those in whom one would have least expected to find it. It is quite common for the most delicious goods to be packed in coarse cloth and shoddy barrels. What a wonder that the wisdom of God has often bestowed its most important gifts on those who are regarded as very unworthy people. Someone else can utilize very good reason in certain things, even if I might still lack it. A closer examination and a faithful appeal for wisdom have revealed to many a detail that otherwise would not have been discerned, or even that one would have assumed to be the opposite. What is clearly discerned by reflecting on the source of all knowledge and derived from correct conclusions cannot and should not be taken away from a person. Because we are right in these things, we should also let others be right in them.

§7

If we do not want to do injustice to anyone in our judgments, we must first examine carefully whether people are able to know and practice what they should otherwise understand, believe, and do. It is indisputable that an indescribable amount depends on the circumstances in which people have been situated at different times of their lives and in which they find themselves now. Everything that can be understood is to be derived partly from the things themselves, partly from divine revelation, and partly from the revelation and accounts of others. Then we should consider: What opportunities have been given to people by birth, upbringing, and events in order to perceive and use these three sources of understanding? It is important not to forget the furnishings of human nature, and to remember the differences in disposition and temperament that exist in humankind. One must also ponder: Is the person's intellect capable of it? One must not lose sight of the wise distribution of the gifts of grace. After innumerable considerations, and after careful reflection on every circumstance, one will only be in a position, when judging, not to do another person an injustice, if one should decide to make an explicit remark that is disadvantageous to him. Is it not in fact difficult to discern with sound reason, and consequently also to determine, whether something is after all right or wrong, done well or done poorly? However, when we apply this thinking to certain situations common to people whom we like or dislike, and since we can easily be influenced by a word or a suggestion, the safest path is to let love prevail, at least to speak conditionally: if such and such is the case with people, then we can come to this and that conclusion about it. If this is the case with humans, then this and that is to be judged by it. Perhaps a person cannot think and do otherwise; and if we were in the same situation, perhaps we would not even do it as well. O! what a depth of God's wisdom and understanding is to be observed in the order of nature and the affairs of humankind! How dare we, then, master this wisdom worthy of adoration, and not accept and look upon people as they are able to be, and not at least be willing to speak positively where we find so much to be concerned about!

§8

If we do not want to do injustice to others in our judgments, we must first of all determine whether they actually want something, and whether they also *want* to know and do what they *should* and *could* have known and done. To begin with, nothing is crueler than to take from people's words and statements, provided nothing else, anything more or less than they want to say and imply. Therefore, whoever wants to do right by others must not be content by just taking bits and pieces from their words, but must make every effort to find out what they really meant. In doing so, it is imperative that one inquires exactly how they view the matter; from which perspective are they imagining it and what things are they comparing? Otherwise, it is impossible not to misunderstand each other and to end up at odds with one another, especially when people do not have the gift of explaining themselves clearly, and may even use and adopt words in a completely different sense than one is accustomed to. Only then can we hold the opinion that they do indeed believe what we think and say that they do.

§9

From this it likewise follows that it often happens that some things are well meant by others but miss the mark, and that it is important to take such things into proper consideration when judging them.

After all, if God Himself judges humankind only according to the intentions of their hearts, how can we avoid gross wrongdoing when we do otherwise? We must therefore make a great distinction between the counsel, intention, purpose, and designs of people and their outward actions and what results from them.

Their intentions are governed by their free will, but the actual carrying out of their intentions is not necessarily governed by their free will. Therefore, one can only say that they desired what they had intended in their hearts and what was in fact their goal.

§10

At the very least, however, the *main thing* must not be confused with *peripheral things*, so that we do not do gross injustice to others when making our judgments. Now, we must be very careful to make the important distinction between one part involving *desires, wishes, appetites*, and *affects*, and the other part involving *intentions*. The main question is and remains: What is the people's business? What is and remains their main purpose, and what, on the other hand, only happens occasionally without having any particular influence on their inner self or on all their doings or leavings? Are they concerned about *God* and the *Savior*, or about *themselves* and the *world*? Does the *Spirit* or the *flesh* win with them? Are they faithful to the limited light and little strength they have, and is it evident that they have not received them in vain? Do they truly intend, according to the power that is at work in them, *to live for the one who died and rose again for them*, setting aside and putting to the test that which is considered inferior, partly by reason, but especially by Scripture? We would have to exalt ourselves improperly; otherwise, we probably cannot help but confess willingly that there are many things going on in humankind that are impossible to approve of. There are all kinds of thoughts, desires, cravings, and emotions that are highly objectionable. If it were to happen to us, if our actions were not to be regarded according to our intentions, we would decry the violation and injustice of it all. How could we not let others have the same rights as we do? In truth, then, we must take the greatest care to differentiate the intentions of others from the notions and impulses that otherwise appear in them. If we do not do so, they have every reason to be given to understand that we, with great unfairness, are not letting them enjoy their rights.

§11

Grace has taught the blessed *author* of these letters to take into account all of these important factors, so that I can present him as an uncommon example of a person who, in passing judgment, has *allowed others to enjoy their rights*. It is a particular pleasure to note how he always viewed everything according to the main purposes of those he spoke with, and whether he approved or disapproved, he was guided strictly by these intentions. And therefore, no one will be surprised if he should find one and another thing in these letters that does not seem to him to apply, if it is measured according to the usual yardstick of those who ignore the revealed principles. It is not enough for the hungry that something is very beautiful to look at, if it doesn't provide them with food. If this is the only benefit one gets from practicing Christianity, that one's head is occupied with images, and that one feels content, even though one's heart remains unfulfilled, then the effort will have been poorly spent. Wherever souls treasure the Savior, a little hay and stubble can be overlooked; and there is reason to find them preferable to those in whom one cannot sense such treasuring, even though they may appear to be pure of the hay and stubble.

§12

I cannot deny that if I had written the letters, I might not have voiced one or another sentiment, and some expressions would have come out differently than they did by the blessed author. Righteous indignation against the enemies of the cross of Christ has sometimes moved him to express himself quite vividly. However, I thought it more appropriate to leave his words unchanged, especially since I found throughout that love for the crucified Savior and for souls was his primary motive. Nevertheless, true friends of the Bridegroom will have no doubt that he too belonged to their number, and that he will certainly shine along with them like the radiance of the sun and like the stars forever and ever.

Early Years (1700–1708)
Letters 1–14

No. 1

A. W. Böhme to the Countess of Waldeck[1]
Arolsen, January 1700

I was quite disconcerted that the writing against me was dealt with in such a way. After their admonition, I will gladly accept the truths it contains and use them to clarify my teaching, especially since I seek nothing but the truth in daily denial of my reason. Even if it should be wrapped in a bitter shell and thereby cause my old nature to suffer in its stubborn selfishness, I will willingly use all of this for a more complete mortification and shattering of such natural tendencies. Through this process, I hope to reach a higher echelon in the life of Christ, especially since the nakedness of false Christianity has been so vividly revealed to me!

---

1. Sophia Henriette of Waldeck (1662–1702), by birth a Princess of Waldeck and the Countess of Saxe-Hildburghausen by marriage to Ernest Heinrich George. On Böhme's contentious encounter with the orthodox Consistory in Waldeck over his spiritualist proclivities, see Sames, *Böhme*, 58–106.

No. 2

A. W. Böhme to the Countess of Waldeck
Arolsen, 15 February 1700

    Those who want to whitewash the old with the new disgust my soul, since we know from long experience that the old will soon shine through again, and the new whitewash will become old through familiarity. Indeed, it is no different than an upset stomach with undigested food in it, which deprives the body of the nourishing power of the new food, and thus causes more trouble. I do wish that during the reading and hearing of my writing, people would lay aside their reason and wrestle after the truth hungrily! Which is why, Your Excellency, on the day of retribution the King of Truth will honor you in return, if you have honored His truth and what is bound up with it here, and if you have not resisted the same power that wounds our old human nature.

No. 3

A. W. Böhme to the Countess of Waldeck
Arolsen[?], 19 March 1700

    You may still remember how that same week I was given some documents in which they expressed their opinion of my previous teaching which, by God's providence, has now been put in writing. This was much more valuable to me because it showed me that we should examine ourselves by the measure of grace and not allow everything to depend on the words of the scholars, which so often miss the mark. And I assure you before the Lord that the more you free yourself from human interference in such things, the more He will transfigure your inner eye, and you yourself will see where Christ is born. I recognize that your gaze at times focuses on the center and mid-point of divine truths; but should it lose focus, it often lets itself be triggered by reason and prejudice, because the resolutions are unable to reach the goal. Therefore, it will do you good if, when considering the mysteries of the kingdom of Christ, you close off the eye of reason, so that all the power of vision may be concentrated solely on the interior life. Reason belongs in the outer room, where it can regulate external things; but if we were to take it into the inner room, it would only produce false ideas, and, instead of a living, true existence, it would only yield lifeless playthings that are meant for children. Moses had to take off his shoes and drive back the livestock, if he wanted to know the secrets of God clearly. The merchant had to forsake his entire house when he wanted to find the pearl of great price.

No agreement can be reached here, nor haggling over this and that. All that is in us must be presented to the Lord through a constant surrender, renouncing all coarse and subtle nonsense; thus, the cold and hard winter of our hearts will soon be transformed into a lovely spring. We have already experienced enough of what results from such dangerous mixtures of the spirit of God and the spirit of the world. Where are the fruits of a blessed government? Where are the fruits of all our previous prayers and prayer meetings? The Lord has to return empty-handed when he comes looking for fruit. The curse is surely felt, but who will be the first to break loose from it and to provide the model for a blessed rebirth in others? Oh, what glorious reward awaits the firstborn in a homeland, house, and family in the kingdom of Christ!

Doesn't such a pending ruin necessarily convince us that the root has not yet been sufficiently permeated with the sap of life, and that the interior must be well watered if the branches are to blossom? Everyone should begin with themselves and carry out their work from a pure foundation: what is more, the Lord would like to spread the leaven of his grace from us to others; otherwise, the Lord will continue to sweep with one broom after another, until the lost coin of his faded image is restored to its proper character. Oh, that we could be cleansed by lesser trials! With what will we finally remove the corruption? By serving the pious? But even if they were angels, it would not be removed until we bring our will completely under God's control. Yes, they would only bring curses, if we do not accept their testimony. The rulers and princes must first flee from their corruption, and then the land, the people, the children, and all that they possess will follow in a wonderful suite. If this does not happen, patch it up as you like, but the gap will never be filled before it becomes even larger.

Therefore, let everyone be warned, and flee from corruption; but remember Lot's wife, lest they stop halfway and become a stone! After the visitation of love is ended, the bowls of wrath will begin to drip, and the cedars will be broken by the voice of the Lord. These words have flowed out of love. If it is received in this way anew, it will be a balm for your head and will inspire me to strive even more before the Lord for your soul, which has been redeemed from the earth by the Lamb. But if it should be rejected, though I do not believe it will be, the blessing that I am daily assisting you, to the best of my ability, in petitioning the Lord for your salvation and that of your children—over whose sorrow my heart is so often plunged into deep grief—will return to me.

No. 4

A. W. Böhme to Anna Elisabeth Böhme[?][2]
London, 30 March 1702

I have heard that our L. will now be with you again, which I am glad to hear. I have written to her once, and urged her, where I thought it appropriate, to refrain from her travels and to experience the blessedness of peace and quiet. Who would want to venture out in this difficult time, when circumstances require that one first reflect on oneself? Who would want to go out in such wind and weather with so faint a light, since we often cannot tell if it is blowing from morning or evening? The more the kingdom of Christ arises, the more the kingdom of the anti-Christ will move in and out among us. When Christ is born in us, Herod comes and wants to kill Him in us, which one does not experience until Christ reveals himself as a king and wants to reign in the soul alone. So, when you are together, use your time to bless and encourage one another, and all the more because the day is drawing near. Be faithful in your original grace, lest it be taken from you and given to others: to the one who has, it shall be given.

God is certainly at work in this country, but the strong influence of the spirit of the world makes it nearly impossible to notice from outside. The Word shines in a very dark place, but humankind does not want to recognize it. In Germany, the external movement of the gospel is quite different from what it is here. What the Lord will use here is in his hands. Do not forget to read the Scriptures diligently with one another and seek nourishment for your souls in them. A few days ago, August Hermann Francke sent me a booklet on how to seek Christ as the core of Scripture

---

2. The letter was addressed to "the author's sister"; Böhme had other correspondence with Anna Elisabeth, so she is the most likely recipient.

and thus nourish a person's inner self;[3] if you have the booklet, it can give you good guidance for this essential practice.

No. 5

A. W. Böhme to Dr. Frederick Slare[4]
London, 8 April 1702

Those who want to live here, as Lot did in Sodom, and keep their conscience, will benefit greatly if an angel comes to them from time to time, I mean, if they are encouraged by a friend of the Lord to attend to their souls, so that the inner fire and strength of the spirit will not be extinguished under so many dead coals. The Enochian way[5] is described here in a small tract with ink and pen, but those who lead it are not readily visible to others; as has been the nature and manner of God's friends in virtually every age, they have hidden themselves from others and carried out the great work of salvation. A few days ago, I visited an old man who lives alone about an hour from here. As a way of removing himself, he left the noise of this city several years ago. He had been a wealthy and well-liked solicitor here, he told me; but when out of love he became keenly aware of his eternal salvation, he left everything and chose a way of life not like his old ways. The projects he had for the Church and its improvement did not seem central, but I found that his quiet, austere, and world-defying undertakings were evidence of a higher principle that had awakened in him.

To mention something from the kingdom of this world, the newspaper will no doubt have long since reported the unexpected death of the King, who is mourned by so many. It is said that the body (which is supposed to be buried in pewter and two wooden coffins) is now to be laid in state and, just before the coronation of the new queen, is to be placed in seclusion in an appropriate place. Queen Anne is now honored

---

3. Francke, *Christus der Kern Heiliger Schrifft*.

4. Dr. Frederick Slare (or, Friedrich Schlör) (1648–1727), FRS, was a second-generation émigré from the Palatinate, an active member of the SPCK and SPG, a supporter of charity schools and the Palatine emigrants, and a laboratory assistant to Robert Boyle. Both Theodore Haak (1605–1690), his cousin and early founder of the Royal Society, and A. W. Böhme died in his home. Hall, "Frederick Slare, F. R. S."

5. The "Enochian" language was regarded by some as the lost language of the angels.

by everyone as a newly rising sun, and there is great hope that she will vigorously promote the public interest. The day before yesterday, I was with some friends at Westminster, where all kinds of arrangements were being made for the future coronation ceremony in a church dedicated to such solemnities. Some ships have departed from Holland to bring over velvet and other valuable things, because what is in London will not suffice. On April 23rd, St. George's Day, on which kings in England are usually crowned, the solemnities will proceed, according to the Royal Proclamation. Whitehall Castle, where former kings had their court, but which is now overgrown with grass after it was burned down in a fire, is also to be rebuilt.

No. 6

A. W. Böhme to Anna Elisabeth Böhme
London, 2 February 1704

Dear sister, I use this opportunity to greet all of you and hope that you are healthy in the faith. I would like to hear from you more often and write to you from here, but the remoteness of the place, especially during these wars, does not allow it. Let us be faithful to the One who has called us and run together toward one goal, so that, if we do not meet on the way, we will certainly meet at the end of it and rejoice in every mercy that the Lord has bestowed on our souls. It is a great burden to live in such a far-flung world, in which, by the will of God, I find myself planted, and do not know for how long! If you in the villages do not want to save your souls, city people can easily excuse themselves, because here the soul is subject to the senses, and the senses are so much more subject to the world's vanity. There are sins going on in London that are not known in Ösdorf! Therefore, be aware of the time of our visitation. Those who fear the Lord have great peace. Pray for me, that the Lord may preserve me like Lot in Sodom. There is nothing holding me here (as far as I know) but the hand of God, and if God releases me, I will gladly fly away, even though there is little evidence of it.

No. 7

A. W. Böhme to Dr. Frederick Slare
London, 3 February 1704

I thank God that the winter is now hastening to an end. I have endured many headaches this winter, especially during the night, and if it should continue, I will probably have to create a diversion for my mind and body by traveling, because I am almost never healthier than when I travel. But these are human undertakings, and it seems as if they want to entangle me more and more here. To date I have turned down numerous favorable opportunities, and have learned to be content with what is at hand, so that my mind may be all the more unfettered. What people are seeking in the world is not to be found in it. The sorrow and misery are so much greater, the less they are recognized by people. Thus, instead of working their way out of their misery, everyone runs deeper and deeper into it, making the path to hell even harder.

About a fortnight ago, a solemn day of fasting and repentance was proclaimed and observed throughout the entire empire to pray to God, in order to avert the judgments hovering over this land, of which the violent windstorm was a harbinger. In front of the most prominent churches, small tracts were distributed. Some of the local religious societies had excerpted many of the blasphemous, offensive, and disgraceful discourses from the printed comedies of the godless comedians. They thrust into the consciences of all honor-loving people the question of whether they can thus deliver themselves and their children—who are dragged in almost as soon as they can walk, and are thus sacrificed to the spirit of the world from their youth—to the devil's slaughter bench! These and similar approaches by well-meaning persons have had some, but unfortunately limited, effect.

Queen Anne published a proclamation that from now on comedies should be performed more decently and without such disorderly outbreaks, and that a large number of whores, who gather in swarms around such houses at night (since comedies are performed in the light), should be apprehended and imprisoned, and that all women should be ordered to enter without masks. But whether this will suffice, or whether such schools for sinners can be corrected and improved without a complete ban, others may judge. Thus, some among the clergy are beginning to see how the wrath of God is being provoked by these things. One of them has written a whole book against the English comedies, and, when a comedy lover answered him in another writing, he defended his book with new reasons.[6] Everything is so corrupt that sin itself finds its defenders and patrons who write great apologies for it and portray it so virtuously that the silly love it and the foolish are driven into misery as oxen to the slaughter. I hereby commend Mr. D. to the eternal love of Jesus. May the Lamb be his lamp and light until the day he enters into the rest of the saints.

No. 8

A. W. Böhme to Anna Elisabeth Böhme
N.p., n.d.

He who is called the beginning and end, Alpha and Omega;
may his goodness prevail over you!

Perhaps it has not pleased the Lord, from whom our journey originates, to let me enjoy your company now; for I have not asked for anything other than that the Lord, if it was his will that I should travel, should remove the obstacles from the way, of which there are not a few, and if it is not his will, that he should put even more obstacles in the way. For although I love you and your gracious lady dearly, I would rather, by the will of God, be denied your outward presence and not see you in the flesh, than come to you in a spirit of selfishness, by which we would both be more likely to suffer harm than gain. Meanwhile, I am often with you in spirit and see your equanimity in the will of the Lord and your patient waiting for the full day of Christ's grace, which is sure to follow the dawn. Blessed are you if you keep awake and have your loins girded! At the wedding banquet of the Lamb the guests come together; there we will proclaim how great—oh, how great!—the goodness of the Lord has been to our souls. But here we must labor faithfully in our vineyards, and not look back until the Redeemer comes, bringing with him the olive leaf of peace in the evening, as a sign that the waters of unrest and the

---

6. Jeremy Collier (1650–1726), *Short View of the Immorality*; William Congreve (1670–1729), *Amendments of Mr. Collier*; Collier, *Defence of the Short View*.

judgments of wrath have passed, and that the feast of peace is at hand; then our mouths will be full of praise, and our tongues full of laughter.

These, dear sister, are certain and trustworthy words! Be still and hide yourself under the wings of your Savior, so that you may be kept safe for the hour of temptation that will come upon the earth. Oh, those who would be wise and vigilant, when they see the clouds gathering, know there will be a storm, and it is time to run or to stay! These are the nail-prints of Christ's wounds, for there one finds a safe anchor and harbor in the storm, shade in the heat, and a sweet consolation amid fears. Oh, indeed, love Christ, for he has redeemed you from the world, that in him you may have peace; and he also petitions the Father for your faith, that it may not fail you in sifting. Many will yet be sifted, and it will be revealed whether they were a noble grain of wheat or worthless chaff scattered by the wind. The Lord has swept his threshing floor and has the winnowing fork in his hand: Oh Lord, let us be wrapped in your sheaf forever! This will happen if we allow ourselves to be purified; the dross must be separated by fire and our nature must die, whether or not it hurts the old person: Christ's death must be revealed in us with its power, whether or not it alienates the world. Let the world treat you with contempt, since Christ will once again taste so sweet under the cross.

But to get to the last point of your letter concerning the person we know, who asks for your advice in a matter of conscience on a certain matter, I have brought it before God, but I have no certainty which direction to take; my human counsel, however, is to go slowly, and see if you can discern some of God's footsteps as time goes by. One must not run ahead of the Lord in any matter; if He does not guide us with His eyes, we will fall as easily on the level as on the slippery paths, but if the Lord leads us by the hand, every mountain and hill shall be made low, for in this way He shows that He is the Lord who can keep creatures from becoming a snare to us.

No. 9

A. W. Böhme to N. N.
N.p., n.d.

I wish with all my heart that my heavy responsibilities would allow me to reply adequately to Your Grace's esteemed letter, but I regret that I am so overwhelmed that I can hardly manage. I often groan under the burden of Egypt and patiently await the promised deliverance. Meanwhile I do not want to set out on my own, lest the Lord, who himself must provide the help, let me sink. The trumpet is blown, and its sound becomes stronger the longer it lasts. Meanwhile, in certain places, many voices resound like great waters, but their roaring does not produce anything that can be understood. Other voices are like thunder that awakens and terrifies humankind, while others do nothing but produce a harmonious and proportionate sound that is quite low (see Rev 14:2–3). We note the different voices; some are pitched too high, others too low, yet each has a good intention; but because they will not learn from each other, the harp will not yet be in tune until, by the Lord's grace, each will gradually revive and learn to think, speak, and do nothing but the Lord's will. We are certainly living at such a time, when the children of God are not harmonizing, and the new song cannot yet be sung. But the Lord will bring into harmony all those who allow themselves to be governed and tuned by His Spirit.

I am sorry about dear N., although I have not received an actual report of what the accusations are. In the meantime, I am convinced and have come to realize that the clergy in your region are not capable of understanding or judging him, especially since they are filled with many prejudices and lack a spirit of discernment, as long as N. does not push things too far or neglect to extend a little compassion to those who do not know what they are doing. On the surface, I hear that he speaks highly of Mr. N. Now it goes without saying that this man has excellent insight in many matters; but I think that he still has a lot of willfulness and pushes things too far. His harsh spirit still needs to be humbled, so that he may tune his strings more softly. I have written this in confidence, because the children of the world, when they hear such things, reject also the good. May the Lord cleanse and purify all of us, so that we may look to Him always, test everything, and keep what is good.

No. 10

A. W. Böhme to Miss Jane Slare[7]
Windsor[?], 26 July 1705

I hope my letter will be so fortunate as to reach you before you start your journey, so that I can assure you of my heartfelt wish that you will

---

7. Jane Slare (ca. 1653–1734) was Dr. Frederick Slare's sister, a regular correspondent of Böhme, and a supporter of the Halle orphanage.

receive a true and lasting benefit from your journey, and that it will contribute to the welfare of soul and body, which indeed unfailingly happens when you have learned that all things work for the best for those who love God. On my return I was persuaded by some good friends to go to Oxford, where we stayed a day and visited the colleges. I wish you had been with us, and am sure the pleasant walks would have afforded you some delight, though among the throng of students, there is probably little to satisfy a soul that has tasted something of the other world and has grown past the paltry, pitiful notions in which reasonable worldly people set such stock. Oh, how little Christ is known among them, and what a great mystery is the Christ who was crucified.

So, I am more and more persuaded that neither carnal wit, nor human reason, nor scholarly learning is in itself capable of communicating the tiniest drop of a saving knowledge to a soul. There is no other means than that we humbly offer ourselves to the Father's persistent pull, that He may bring us to his Son, after He has made us realize our wretched and lost condition; to the end that through Him, as the ultimate restorer of our lost condition, we may be established in life, light, and power. The Father's discipline teaches us the fear of the Lord, and when our hearts have been established in a holy fear and awe, being somewhat reluctant to take hold of the pearls of the kingdom, He then reveals His mystery to us, but not all at once; rather, He leads the soul in a gentle way, step by step, according to how much or how little we have grown in humility. This is the long and hard lesson we have to learn; I mean the one that a poor layperson fortuitously taught the eminent Johann Tauler, who was filled with human erudition but empty of real experience. He was told that his vessel was not pure, so he first had to learn the ABCs of true religion, namely humility and poverty of spirit, if he wanted to expect a richer inflow of divine grace. Therefore, let us seek only to have a will that is constantly directed by God's will. This will give us serenity and contentment in every circumstance in which the Lord places us for us according to His wisdom; indeed, it will give us a foretaste of the peace and cheerfulness of mind here that we shall enjoy in eternity.

No. 11

A. W. Böhme to Miss Jane Slare
Windsor[?], 4 October 1705

When I consider every aspect of the gracious providence of God, and the many traces of His undeserved grace which I have experienced in England, I have every reason to take this gracious providence to heart, for the growth of the inner life, of which the Lord has so graciously given me a taste. If all of God's overflowing grace were to flow back into the original fountain from which it flowed, after having had the right effect in the soul, then I would have reason enough to cringe when I ponder my performance against all the excellent proofs of divine providence that I have previously experienced. This observation overwhelmed me as I thought of my departure and considered how I might have made use of the blessing of the solitude that divine providence had afforded me for a time. But I find that all external means of help are of little use to us whenever we forget the vigilance that we should have over ourselves. The restless desire of our own fantasies is all too inclined to lead us into another world, even if we are confined to a small room, and to distract us to the point of losing ourselves in the great sea of our heart's restlessness, instead of sinking deeper and deeper into the inexhaustible fountain of God's love, whose movements are sweet, still, and accompanied with a peace of mind and serenity that is found in God Himself. May the Lord bestow on us the enjoyment of the same.

No. 12[8]

A. W. Böhme to I. A. Lubomirsky[9]
London, 28 April 1707

[Böhme footnote to the letter:] At the end of 1706, I. A. Lubomirsky, a Pole by birth, arrived in England. He was a Franciscan and missionary for twelve years in China. At the request of his mother, he had received permission from the pope to return. But when he was traveling from Italy

---

8. Original letter written in Latin.
9. SPG, "No. 85"; "Nos. 195–96"; "20 December 1706."

to Poland, he converted to Protestantism in Switzerland. When the pope found out about this, he excommunicated him; he then went to Holland to ensure his safety and finally arrived in England. He was referred to me by Mr. Charles Bridges,[10] and at first things went badly for him; but subsequently he received about £20 from the Society for the Propagation of the Gospel. He provided many witnesses, from which it was clear that his claim about his Chinese mission was true. He had converted 6,607 people to Catholicism in China. Some time later, we became aware of his carnal heart: he had secretly promised himself to a woman, without having said a word about it to his friends. The Society, which was about to bequeath him a pension of £50 per year, withdrew it. There were several proselytes in London at that time—among them Pertack a Bohemian[11] and Casotti an Italian—and I had the opportunity to have a weekly conversation with them, to which Lubomirsky also wanted to come after his troubles were over. He wrote to Pertack to make that request of me, and I replied as follows.

Dear Mr. Lubomirsky,

I am quite surprised that in your letter to Pertack there is mention of desire for spiritual colloquy—something which I have now and then provided to proselytes.

I cannot see that such a thing would be of any interest because you already know more about the business of religion than you have yet put into practice—which is that to which everything should be directed. Please bear in mind the weight of the warning the Savior gives in Luke 12:47: "The servant who knew his lord's will, and who neither prepared himself nor acted in accord with it, is severely punished; while the one who did not know it, and acted in way that warrants punishment, is punished lightly." In no colloquy I have given have I intended to teach others with a scholar's erudition, or to burden anyone's brain with a lot of superficial ideas about the business of religion. Instead, I have always intended to convince you, together with the other proselytes who have separated themselves from papism in an external and physical way, that

---

10. Charles Bridges (ca. 1672–1747) was an agent of the charity schools in Britain, an active early member of the SPCK, and a correspondent of Francke. He would later go on to be a respected painter in Virginia. Brunner, *Halle Pietists*, 72–79.

11. Pertack was a priest from Prague who was recommended to the Society by Robert Hales, the itinerant English layman who worked for Anglican interests and Protestant church union on the Continent. Bultmann, "Layman Proposes Protestant Union."

a merely external exit from that disordered throng of errors is of no use unless accompanied by both a sincere separation from that internal chaos of confusion, greed, error, and desire under which mortal hearts labor, and an internal denial of the flesh and the world which the Savior commended to all his followers as the way to lay the true foundation of conversion. When this is done seriously, and when the intemperate impetuosity of one's own will is bridled to some degree by self-denial, then the great restorer of fallen nature can more easily and felicitously shape and reshape the human soul by means of His spirit, and perfect the work of regeneration, or new creation, in the same.

And if you, Mr. Lubomirsky, had thought a little more deeply, while no longer resisting the Spirit of Christ when coming upon a little divine ray of conviction in yourself, you would have found no reason to glory in your departure from Babylon when, alas, your heart lies buried by sin's defilements, the world's filth, and the confusions of both the world and your own will, so that you have until now unhappily suppressed, with a very obstinate opposition, the Spirit's invitations which call mortals to a better life. You would, as a result, see clearly how much your sins have grown. I do not doubt that the grace of God, which shines on everyone (Titus 2:11) and calls to true repentance those who wander from salvation's path, will fill even your heart with deeper convictions; but what good can conviction do so long as you hide behind the veil of hypocrisy and find your own miserable soul sunk in misery, unless it leads to true conversion, rescuing the soul from the power and kingdom of darkness and leading it to the kingdom of light? For those whose corrupt hearts put on hypocrisy's mask are savage to themselves, and therefore accumulate, by piling sin upon sin, the wrath of God for themselves like a treasure-house, for the day when the just judgment is rendered (Rom 2:5).

Consider with what disposition of the soul you would be able to talk with others about spiritual things such as true and inner conversion if at that same time your heart should be filled with the defilements of the flesh and the spirit of lies, and should despise all warnings! Alas! Approach true repentance humbly. Entreat the God of mercies with untiring prayers that He might create a new heart in you and place a new spirit in your belly. Do not any longer be deaf to the Redeemer's voice within your heart inviting you to celestial love. Alone in your private room with that very one who is alone (Matt 6:6), present the intimacies of your heart for reformation, so that after the expulsion of the spirit of lies and hypocrisy the fruits of His most pure spirit may grow there. Do not defer the offering of your heart to the Lord, and as that moment of grace dawns upon you, grasp it before it slips away. Let your eyes be opened here and now in order that they not open too late.

Believe that as I write these things to you no personal dislike moves me; rather, I pray eagerly for your eternal salvation.

No. 13

A. W. Böhme to Miss Jane Slare
Windsor, 11 July 1707

I hear that the movements and disputes in matters of religion are still continuing in Germany as heatedly as ever. So, some Reformed leaders are also awakening and beginning to see the dead nature of their party, and to concern themselves with a more spiritual theology. But what is most remarkable is that the best of the Lutherans joins with the best of the Reformed and become aware of a much truer foundation in each other than either sect can provide alone. On the other hand, the wicked Lutherans join with the wicked Calvinists, and stand by each other in denouncing and persecuting the pious in both parties. This, to my mind, is a part of the mystery of both godliness and wickedness. The first shows that the best approach to union is true conversion from darkness to light, by which souls, whatever sect or party they may be, unite with Christ and consequently with all His living members; the other shows that Christ, the living ground of religion, is persecuted in His members, and that the walls of sectarianism, by which they are ordinarily distinguished from one another, should fall down, rather than that Christ should remain unpersecuted in His members. These are evil days, and as there are depths in God (1 Cor 2:10), so there are depths in Satan (Rev 2:24.). If the one moves in his own ways to promote light and love, so the other is not idle in his efforts to send forth hatred and darkness. So it is in the whole world outside of us, and so it is in the small world within us. The spirit of darkness will never rest where the spirit of light is active. This is the daily cross that Christians have to take up, and they need to count these daily temptations as joy (Jas 1:2), because they teach him that the Lord is working on their souls while Satan is at work. So, a Christian must not only struggle but also suffer; and this latter is much more arduous because it requires stillness and forbearance. May the Lord make us faithful in both, and teach us not only to do His will alone, but also to suffer, and then we shall be crowned.

No. 14

A. W. Böhme to Christian Friends in Germany
London, 22 July 1707

> *To all those who seek the righteousness that is in Jesus*
> *and its increase in themselves and others:*
> *Blessings and peace!*

Just as the eternal love of God has now and then kindled in some souls a desire for the true good that is found in Him alone, and has also nourished that desire in a true, though often hidden, way, so it has also been evident among some friends in Pennsylvania, who, being quite distant from European Christians and therefore slow to hear what the Lord is doing among them, are all the more eager to receive accounts of their growth and other breakthroughs, including written testimonies, and to rejoice in the gifts of mutual love and fellowship.

They have repeatedly testified to their heartfelt delight in the spiritual books, which are so essential in this time of weakness, that we have sent them. There are several testimonies to this from their letters, but here is just one from April 19, 1707:

> We have received the books sent to us, and have been using them with considerable blessing; we thank God with heartfelt humility, as far as we are capable of it, that He still inspires devout hearts not only to remember us but also to demonstrate His love in action as an encouragement to our hope. In our prayers for you we are asking that the Lord Himself may be your reward! etc.

Some friends here are able to help them with English or Latin books, if the purpose of the book is to edify, but they have not been able to do so with German books, because there is a great shortage of them here, and it is therefore impossible to provide them for others.

Now, however, some God-loving friends in Pennsylvania are not only diligently teaching young Germans, Swedes, and other settlers who are ignorant of the German language, but are also working with the elderly and adults for their edification, and are trying to do as much as they can to strengthen true Christianity in the midst of so many sectarian divisions. To this end, they need some books that promote a living Christianity according to the Holy Scriptures. So, through these letters we want to communicate with those who want to promote edification, and leave it to their own discretion, or rather to the Lord's, how far they might be moved to offer a hand. If anyone would like to help purchase and provide such books, I make the following simple suggestions:

I) As far as the *type* or genre of the books themselves is concerned: (1) Bibles will be required above all, usually in a small format, so that all the more people can be served with them. (2) New Testaments bound separately from the Old Testament, to be placed as a beginning into the hands of children and young people. (3) Some of the writings of Johann Tauler and any others that stress an authentic Christianity. (4) In particular, Johann Arndt's *True Christianity* and in the smaller edition, in order to disperse it to more people. (5) It would be desirable to include a good number of small practical and edifying books—such as the small tracts on Christianity by Johann Schade[12] and others—from which people have often received more blessings than from large books. These can be given away more easily, and because they are not too long, they will be read by more people. To these could also be added some hymnals, especially the new spirit-filled hymnals printed in Halle and Darmstadt.

II) As to the *acquisition* of such books, every one is free to decide voluntarily what they want to contribute to such Christian works. But there would soon be a good number of books if everyone would donate just one of their own, especially since people often have several copies of a book and can therefore let go of the extra ones. For there is nothing wrong with the fact that a book has already been used for a while. One may also say something like this: "Cast your bread upon the water."

III) It would be necessary to have the books donated to this cause bound. Namely, (1) because our friends in Pennsylvania are not of such means that they are able to invest very much in the binding of books; for

---

12. Johann Kaspar Schade (1666–1698) was a Pietist preacher, author, and poet, acquainted with both Philipp Spener and A. H. Francke.

this reason, then, many a book is likely to remain unused. (2) I do not know if it will be possible to do this easily. If it were assumed that they would be bound in England, then we must report (3) that German books, which are usually printed on poor-quality paper and therefore have to be flattened, cannot be bound in England, or at least not without great expense, since no one here knows anything about flattening, since books are usually printed on writing paper. If the books were to be bound unflattened, which would be the case here, we know that this often ruins the book or makes it unpleasant for the reader. It may be that there are some who, out of the principle of supporting the edification of their neighbor, give the books unbound, and others who, out of the same principle of love, have them bound.

IV) When these books have been collected, they must be properly stored in a chest of strong boards, then either locked or nailed shut, and sent on their way.

V) This chest, then, should be sent to a friend in Holland who is willing to take care of it—because in times of war it is not often possible to go to England from Hamburg—and the freight should be paid in full. The chest should be addressed to me with the initials A. W. B. And then what is required to send it from here to Pennsylvania should faithfully be provided. May the Lord guide our work to His praise and the edification of our neighbor!

Pastoralia (1709–1710)

Letters 15–44

No. 15

A. W. Böhme to Henry Newman[1]
Heringen[?], 23 July 1709

After divine providence brought me here safe and sound, I have culpably neglected to send you these few lines. The work of reformation in this country thankfully carries on under divine blessing. Professor Francke, who sends his cordial greetings and kind remembrance to the Society, was very pleased with the package of books that I brought to him. He immediately had all of the titles translated in order to share them with his friends and supporters of the Lord's work. The Land and Agrarian Manual is actually already translated and will be printed shortly. However, it has been improved and expanded with some notes from another English author, John Flavel, who wrote a book several years ago called *Husbandry spiritualiz'd*.[2] The theological writings of Robert Boyle have recently been reprinted here in German.[3]

---

1. Henry Newman (1670–1743) was the American-born secretary of the SPCK from 1708 to 1743. He was vital to the inner workings of the SPCK and became one of Böhme's most important connections to the Society. Cowie, *Henry Newman*.

2. John Flavel (ca. 1630–1691), *Husbandry Spiritualized*.

3. Robert Boyle (1627–1691) was a distinguished Anglo-Irish natural philosopher who made contributions in numerous scientific fields and helped found the Royal Society. He also wrote Christian devotional and theological tracts and supported mission activity.

We are told that the King of Prussia[4] has ordered his soldiers, who are garrisoned here and there, to be catechized, and to this end has distributed many New Testaments among them. The New Testament, in both old and new Greek, is also being printed at the orphanage's bookstore, paid for by a gentleman for distribution among the Greeks. The vulgar text was taken from the copy printed in London some years ago at the expense of some English gentlemen; as soon as the printing is finished, two thousand copies are to be bound and sent. May the Lord extend His kingdom more and more. Truly, the harvest is plentiful, but there are still few laborers.

No. 16

A. W. Böhme to Miss Jane Slare
Heringen[?], 24 September 1709

Under the protection of the Most High, I will soon reach the coast to depart once again for England. I have been delayed in my return journey a little longer than expected, but now I hasten to enjoy once again what I can of the good company you have given me in Great Britain. I have encountered many fragrant flowers on my journey so far, and the garden of Christ seems to be blossoming here and there in Europe. The harvest is plentiful but the laborers are few. It is almost impossible to describe the inner hunger and thirst that is beginning to reappear in some souls. And though some fall from the stem like rotten fruit, others, in spite of the enemy, continue to spring up and spread in the power of Christ. Many who were first may be the last. However, when God begins to work, Satan does not rest. Some people convey a false and counterfeit conversion, and Satan, mimicking God, tries to make the Lord's work seem suspicious through his intrigues and tricks. The same sun that produces good and healthy creatures also discloses evil and cursed ones, and all this through the same light. And how is it among my friends in London? I hope they will have grown as living branches of Christ, drawing strength and life from Him, for He alone can make us persevere to the end. May the Lord strengthen you by His Spirit, and fulfill all His promises to you for His glory and the welfare of your souls, etc.

4. Frederick III, Elector of Brandenberg, and Frederick I of Prussia (1657–1713).

No. 17

A. W. Böhme to Mr. D. H. C.
London, 14 October 1709

After I arrived in Hellevoetsluis under the good hand of God, we set sail on September 29th at eleven o'clock. The wind was very favorable to us when we departed, but it did not last more than three hours and began to blow from the west, turning us back toward Holland. The captain and skipper, unwilling to lose what they had gained in the three hours, sailed against the wind, intending to accomplish by maneuvering what they could not by means of a good wind. So, we sailed steadily through the day, the following night, and the following Monday, and would have reached England on Tuesday, if a violent storm had not arisen that destroyed all previous efforts. It arose about three o'clock Tuesday morning and lasted until eight o'clock, during which time our ship was tossed to and fro like a ball on the immense sea. The waves came crashing down on the ship ferociously, so that I got almost completely wet, along with the others who had rented the same cabin. After this, they quickly took measures, as best they could, to counter the storm, which was now raging. The sails were hauled in, the water was pumped out, and everything was put in place to save our lives. As the day dawned, which everyone was longing for, the sky shone like a red glowing iron, and as the fog from the weather rose, the view of a normally lovely sky became quite frightening; it was as if the fiery sky was covered with a veil. The waves stood like mountains on both sides of the ship, and the skippers, working on deck, testified after the storm had ended, that two enormous waves had completely gone over the front of the ship, and if a third had hit there, the power of the waves would have broken and sunk the ship. At last God gave a merciful rain that broke both the power of the wind and the fury of the waves, and enabled us to sail back to Holland, having almost reached the coast of England; if it had been daylight, we would have seen land. At five o'clock in the evening, our ship sailed into the harbor at Hellevoetsluis, and everyone was glad that, even if we had been driven back, we still had carried our lives away like spoils. We waited 13 days for the wind to change. At last, an east wind began to blow, which in about 16 hours drove us the 34 German miles (according to the skippers) happily ashore in England. Let us praise the Lord's great grace to us!

I noticed several things in these circumstances that left a lively impression on me. In my cabin there were several officers from the army in Flanders who intended to go to England. When the weather was fair, they spent their time in idle gossip, carousing, joking, and other foolishness, and continued to do so until the storm grew so fierce that they were forced to refrain and wait in anxious silence for it to pass. I took the opportunity to speak to them, and to submit that this storm was a trumpet call to repentance, never to be forgotten; some pondered my admonition sincerely, but others turned a cold shoulder to it. Then, about eight o'clock in the morning, when the wind died down, one of the skippers threw open our door and called out: "How are you gentlemen, are you still alive?" To which an officer answered: "Yes, what good news do you bring us?" He replied: "The storm seems to be coming to an end and the sea is calming down." To which the officer immediately replied, "That's good, young man; bring in bottles of wine." All fear disappeared straightaway, and he started up again where he had left off. I called to mind *that it is not judgment but grace that converts people, and how easily fear disappears if it is not accompanied by grace and love.* A certain German student, who was waiting for me at Wesel and wanted to go to England with me, was terrified by this storm and turned back as soon as we had reached dry ground. He testified in no uncertain terms *that in all the years he had spent at universities, he had not learned as much real theology as he had during the three days confined in a small uncomfortable ship's cabin.* He called it *the university chair in which God himself was teaching him,* while he himself had to struggle constantly with his own conscience. And when his heart warned him that his intention to travel in England was not sufficiently pure, he turned back in order first to make himself even more fit for such a journey.

Other than this, the Lord has brought me here without any resistance, as if on eagle's wings. In the midst of the storm, I called to mind the many heartfelt requests that had been passed on to me by upright people during my journey through Germany and Holland. I hoped that some of them could still be realized in England. So, I was indeed filled with divine joy on my return, because I was not drawn here by any natural curiosity or forwardness, but in part by a common love to work for my neighbor's salvation to the best of my ability, and in part by other circumstances.

Moreover, I discovered five thousand poor Palatines when I arrived here, some of whom are to be sent to the West Indies and others elsewhere. The Catholics among them, who cannot settle here according to the fundamental statutes of this empire, have been sent back to Holland. However, the Queen issued a travel allowance of five Reichsthalers to each soul, thus bearing witness that the Protestants are not entirely without love. Eleven to twelve thousand Palatines have arrived here, and the royal commissioners have had their hands full providing for them, although many have perished in misery before adequate provision could be made for them. The worst thing is that the poor people are not willing to recognize that this is a time of divine judgment which must be removed not with outward flight but with the eradication of inner sinfulness.

No. 18

A. W. Böhme to Carl Hildebrand von Canstein in Berlin[5]
London, 18 November 1709

The weekly newspapers in Germany will undoubtedly have reported that since May 1709 a multitude of poor Palatines have fled to England, hoping to be sent to Pennsylvania, Carolina, or some of the other plantations that the English own in the West Indies. One could say a lot about what actually drove these people to do this, if space in this letter allowed. From a spiritual perspective, it is easy to see that by this outward flight they are trying to escape God's judgments, which are gathering here and there like clouds, but they do not want to recognize the signs of grace, which are universally revealed in the midst of the outward plagues of the land, and which drive people in the inner depths of their conscience not so much to try to escape suffering as to sanctify suffering in the flesh for the salvation of their souls. But as almost everywhere, there is a lack of sound guidance toward a living Christianity and right discernment of the signs of these times, a lack that can be clearly seen in the majority of the Palatines; for they mainly lack a true knowledge of the most necessary aspects of Christianity, and thus do not know how to submit to suffering, or how rightly to recognize God's grace which comes to them in the suffering.

As for the original impulse that caused so many people to come to England, it is likely that those Palatines who first arrived here earlier

---

5. Baron Carl Hildebrand von Canstein (1667–1719), close friend of the Pietists and founder of the Canstein Bible Institute.

this year have given the strongest impetus to this exceptional migration, the like of which will not easily be found in the history of their country. Those 53 men, women, and children, as soon as their cause became known, were welcomed by the English, so much so that Her Majesty herself, after having the matter presented to her, graciously ordered that each soul be given one English shilling (about six German groschen) every day. Not to mention other contributions, which were collected for their wellbeing by friends here and there. After they were provided with basic necessities, new clothing, and all kinds of building and farming equipment at the Queen's expense, they were then transported free of charge to New York in America in September 1708. They landed happily with the new governor Lord Lovelace, who however died there soon after his arrival.[6] Four souls died during the passage, reducing their number to about fifty. The success of these few—about which they sent messages to their compatriots before they left England—gave the others the hope of receiving similar rations, which led to such large numbers undertaking such an unpleasant journey. To which, of course, other causes, too far-reaching to be discussed here, could be added.

The first of this last group landed at the end of last April; there were about eight hundred souls. And because I had given the above-mentioned fifty some guidance as to how and where they should make their concerns known, I was also immediately approached by some of this most recent group, in such difficult circumstances and in a country whose language they did not speak, to offer them a hand: but since I was about to set off for Germany, it was not possible for me to do so. But on my return, I found out that the number of those who had come over from Germany had grown, unbeknownst to me, from eight hundred souls to between eleven and twelve thousand, at last count. From these, in what was then summer weather, various camps were formed, which probably looked like large annual festivals or folk fairs. Some were located on the so-called Blackheath near Greenwich, others near Camberwell, and others elsewhere. Her Majesty the Queen was demonstrably pleased when the fifteen hundredth tent was handed out from the Tower for refugees. The influx of people from London, both gentry and commoners, to see these new encamped guests is said to have been immense, although most of them probably came more out of curiosity than any more noble purpose. And at that time, when the numbers were still moderate and

---

6. John Lovelace (1672–1709), 4th Baron Lovelace, was appointed governor of New York and New Jersey in 1708.

the whole thing was regarded as a novelty, these poor people were well provided for. From the Queen's treasury, large sums were distributed to support them, and a public collection was gathered under royal authority throughout the country. Not to mention the various gifts and alms given to the people by private individuals who came to see them in their camps. In these efforts, Her Majesty has given the whole country a shining example of overflowing love and charity, and has inspired others to follow.

While I am thinking about the public collection, it is worth knowing that a special letter, in which the hardships of these people were described, was sent under royal authority to every preacher throughout England, to be read from the pulpit to the congregations under their care, exhorting them, given the poverty of these people, to make a charitable contribution toward their relief. While the amount collected out in the rural areas by this means may not have been very high, in the city of *London*, with the refugees in closer view, £10,000 was collected and used for their welfare. More than a few people were surprised at the amount of money that was raised, especially in such difficult times, when almost all commercial activities, such as the silver mines from which this country derives its wealth, are depressed due to the war. It is noteworthy, with regard to this substantial collection, that both Episcopal and Presbyterian congregations have acted laudably and donated generously. Would to God that these two important parties, which up to now have not wanted to come to a common religious concord, would be united more closely from a foundation of genuine love, of which they have given an example here; then the remaining disputes, which up to now have not been resolved by any debate, would in time fade away of their own accord.

But I have lost sight of the most important thing, to which all material benefits must be directed, and which should therefore be mentioned first: namely, the care that was taken for *the edification of the people* when distributing the material charity. This care was undertaken in good part by two High German Lutheran pastors, who were joined by two Swiss Reformed pastors who had just arrived here.[7] These pastors, who were

---

7. The Lutheran pastors were John Tribbeko (1677–1712), Böhme's colleague at the German Lutheran Royal Chapel at St. James's, and George Andreas Ruperti (d. 1731), pastor of St. Mary-Le-Savoy German Lutheran Church. It is unclear who the Swiss Reformed were—possibly Conradus Wornley and Ulrich Scherer—but from other sources it is clear that pastor Johann Jakob Caesar of the German Reformed Church of St. Paul in the Savoy was also involved. One anonymous 1711 document says: "It would be hard to say how much the court preacher, now an inspector at Magdeburg, John Tribbeko, spent in behalf of the Germans." See "Being a Short Account of those

also appointed members of the Royal Commission, preached here and there among the people, exhorting them to use the alms they had received in a godly manner, and to conduct themselves in such a way that they would leave behind a pleasant aroma of irreproachable behavior to a foreign nation. In the beginning, before the numbers became so great, no one heard of any particular disorder breaking out. However, with the immense influx of new arrivals almost every week, there has at times been some damage, that has deterred many otherwise good-hearted people of this nation from further outpourings of love. *For it is generally the case that people attribute any missteps to the entire group*, irrespective of the fact that only a few are to blame for it. This should certainly awaken everyone to the need for prudence, so that they do not hurt themselves and others through disorderly behavior, and so that those who are still so weak that they cannot do good to the wicked are not hindered even more in the practice of love. In addition to the sermons and exhortations that were preached to the people in the various camps, a Church of England priest readily offered his own church to the Lutheran pastors for the same purpose. The people have now heard sermons once a week in this church, and it should continue until the people are sent off to the West Indies or other places are assigned to them for their accommodation.

The pastors working with them cannot adequately describe the ignorance of these people. Very few seem to have a sufficient knowledge of the most necessary aspects of Christianity. I myself saw proof of this soon after my return from Germany. Because some friends in Germany had sent me a number of Bibles, New Testaments, and other spiritual books to be distributed among the American Germans who have settled in Pennsylvania, New York, and other provinces, the poor Palatines, when they heard of the books, often asked if I would provide them with a Bible, hymnal, or prayer book before their departure. Which shows how few of them had a desire for the Scriptures or other spiritual books, because they had taken so little interest in them when they left, and were only convinced of their importance when they were in a foreign country. But it is apparent that very few people could be supplied with this travel necessity, and therefore even those who felt a love for the word of God had to depart without a book that could strengthen their good desire.

Germans who, as it were through some Species of Enchantment, in 1709, sailed over the Sea into England. How it fared with them, when they arrived and where they afterwards took up their Abode," in Diffenderffer, "German Exodus," 395.

Three thousand Palatines alone have been sent to Ireland. In Dublin, the nobility and other wealthy residents divided the refugees among themselves by lot, so that very few remained together in one area, but were scattered here and there throughout the country. And since under such circumstances some of them will not have a pastor, while others are unfamiliar with the English language, and therefore cannot attend an English church, and since they have few, if any, spiritual books, it is easy to assume that in time this people will become feral. Therefore, without any spiritual guidance and teaching, they will become like a field that has not been planted, fertilized, or cultivated. To say nothing about those who will go to the Isles of Scilly, to Carolina and perhaps to other distant countries. I had to turn most of the multitude of refugees away with the promise that, if the Lord would inspire good friends to whom I would bring their request, to provide edifying books out of mutual love and to promote the salvation of their neighbor, then I would remember them and send the books after them.

And from these circumstances, my lord, I think it is easy to see what a wonderful work of love it would be if God-loving people were so deeply moved by the eternal salvation of the Christians in the West Indies, whose number is growing daily, that they sought to help out with a small donation of not just physical but spiritual works of love. Such alms, because they are meant primarily for the salvation of souls, would be consecrated immediately and established in the true foundation from which all physical gifts must flow, and consequently be that much more exalted and ennobled. A friend from Pennsylvania wrote the other day, after German friends had sent him some spiritual books:

> We thank you very much for the books you sent us. The names of the benefactors will always be held in blessed remembrance among us. . . . Among all the books that were sent, the most beloved and valuable are Johann Arndt's *True Christianity*, the Bibles, and the New Testaments. But we still need more (1) Bibles, average print; (2) the books of *True Christianity*; (3) a couple dozen copies both of Johann Arndt's *Paradise Garden*, not of fine but good, average print; (4) and of the best and most complete newly printed German hymnals. In particular, please also ask for several copies of Joachim Neander's songs, and some of Angelus Silesius's spiritual shepherd songs.[8] The good people

---

8. Joachim Neander (1650–1680), *Glaub und Liebes*; Angelus Silesius (ca. 1624–1677), born Johann Scheffler, also known as Johann Angelus Silesius, and author of "Wilt Thou Not, My Shepherd True—Hymn to the Good Shepherd."

around me are very desirous of these books and have asked me to write on their behalf. I hope that the love for my neighbor that moves me will easily excuse me, and give the boldness that I am using in this matter a different shape.

From this presentation, your lordship can see that even in the plantations of the West Indies, and especially among the Germans who have settled there, a hunger for the Word of God is beginning to unfold. If the Lord should awaken some souls in Germany to contribute to this cause, the blessing would spread throughout the West Indies as a sweet fragrance emanating from the European Scriptures, and in time make these dark corners of the earth bright and sweet-smelling by its power. I will gladly see to it that these books are properly sent on from here and distributed among the Germans in the various plantations. If the books were put on a ship in Hamburg or Bremen—after they have been bound and flattened, because they won't know to flatten them here—then rest assured that they will be delivered under God's guidance and bear much fruit in due time. May the Lord teach us to do good, because we have time to sow seeds for a rich harvest.

Since I started writing this letter, I am told that the Royal Commission has determined that three thousand souls are to be dispatched to New York on the 15th of December. Whether or not it will happen, time will tell. The misery that these poor people are enduring, with these cold winter days and the deficient care they receive, is almost impossible to describe. Therefore, many of them die, and many have an unadvisable wish to migrate, since they have not received full assurance of all the circumstances surrounding time and place. And now that they have been here so long and have become a burden to the country (especially during the ongoing war), love is growing cold among many citizens, but especially ordinary people are growing angry, and are complaining to the mass of guests that the price of bread has soared for some time, and has not yet fallen. For in spite of the fact that the commissioners spare no effort to find ways and means to further care for the people, it seems as if there is not enough to go around.

To that end they have just now published a seventeen-page document titled: *Piety and bounty of the Queen of Great Britain: With the charitable benevolence of her loving subjects, toward the support and settlement of the distressed Protestant palatines.*[9] That document first of all reports

---

9. *Piety and Bounty of the Queen.*

the actual situation of these poor people, in their own words, which they presented to the government in June 1709 as soon as they arrived. It also includes the aforementioned advertisement, which was published on June 28th under the Great Seal of Great Britain. In it the wretched state of the Palatinate and especially of the Protestants there, so affected by the ongoing wars with the French, was presented movingly, and therefore everyone, men and women, servants and maidservants, foreigners and natives, were earnestly exhorted to take in these refugees as brothers and sisters, and to let them benefit from their love in such troubling circumstances. This was followed by the Archbishop of Canterbury's letter appealing to the clergy in his jurisdiction with moving reasons to ardently promote this labor of love in the parishes entrusted to their care. Many bishops have followed this laudable example and have written to the priests under their care, exhorting them to do likewise. The intention of this whole document is that by publishing a Royal Proclamation in this matter, as well as the letters of exhortation issued by the archbishop and bishops, people would be more fully informed of the whole context of this work and would be inspired to contribute further. It concludes with a detailed account of similar works of love that in years past, under King Edward VI and Queen Elizabeth, were shown to foreign Protestants by the English.

No. 19[10]

A. W. Böhme to M. Z. G., Rector of the School of O.
London, 26 November 1709

Most illustrious one, supporter, much-admired friend,

After divine providence drew me to England it deprived me for a while of intercourse with local patrons and friends. And so, in the meantime, since the occasion grants it, I send you these lines on a small piece of paper to show my gratitude to you. I recall clearly, most illustrious one, when I was beginning the study of literature in Lemgo under your direction, that you helped me along the path upon which I had set out, even though it seemed to be blocked by the uncertain circumstances I found myself in. Ever since then, I often recall the kindness I received.

---

10. Original letter written in Latin.

The clarity which came to me then, which never fails to be of use, and which makes itself available to all who attend to it, has, I hope, continued to strike deeper roots in my mind. It was by divine mercy that an illustrious man such as you directed my studies.

So much of what is done in these matters is worthless: it is clear that there is a lack of good people for the work of clarifying divine judgments. If the modern Christian schools are examined a little more closely, one finds scarcely one or two among the teachers (to say nothing of students motivated by anything more than appearing in a good light to their teachers) who strive with all their hearts to instill above everything else in the minds of students a living knowledge of Jesus Christ derived from the very guts of the Scriptures by which filth worse even than that of the pagans encountered in the schools may be cleansed. Would that all this would resound from the thrones of the doctors, and that fear of the Lord drawn from the wisdom of Scripture would once again be the starting-point! But when the study of the sacred texts is either entirely set aside, or treated as incidental, and time is spent on giving instruction in the terms and concepts of vulgar philosophy, it is no wonder that the more exalted affections of the young, left undisciplined, should eventually enslave the mind, with the result that an infinitude of errors is engendered in the intellect, and those same faculties of the mind are made incapable of absorbing more solid teaching. The result is that the ears eventually become deaf to the inner promptings of the Spirit of God (who constantly pricks us in an effort to return our minds to a healthier state of conviction); the superficial memory of concepts is then chaotic, and the activity and vigor of reason when deprived of proper development lead the young precipitately into great error.

I wish, most illustrious one, that it should be agreed that the uneducated young should follow the divine order. Not that preparatory studies should be completely eliminated, but that they should be restored to their proper place of service to the Christian light as primary, and if they are able to serve a more sublime and warmer erudition, they should be studies only for that purpose. Then everything mundane will be made pure; when, on the other hand, the heart is empty of the knowledge and fear of the living God, then all good things, though licit in themselves, become impure. I hope, most illustrious one, that you are in agreement with me. And since divine grace has moved people here and there to work energetically for the improvement of the schools, with special attention to the introduction of sounder teaching methods, I trust that you will help them in their difficult business, and promote work of such great importance. Usually, joint effort is stronger. And since the light shines more strongly in these days, more and greater things are expected of us. I doubt that anyone will be reported to bear a greater weight of glory than those who did not hesitate to be among the first who, with great courage, led the churches and schools which were afflicted and approaching perdition toward healing.

Farewell, most illustrious one—kindly accept my *Enchiridion Precum* [*Handbook of Prayer*] for the use of students,[11] as well as Dr. Francke's *Manuductio Ad Lectionem Scripturae* [*A Guide to Reading Scripture*], published here together with my preface,[12] for whatever use they may be.

No. 20

A. W. Böhme to Mrs. Dr. O., née of S. in C.
London, 2 December 1709

Although I remembered you often before the Lord, I did not want to write until I had seen how our things would fare at Court. The poor Palatines, who have been arriving here steadily since May, number around twelve thousand; in the beginning, almost all of them received funds from the Queen's treasury, but as a result, the treasury has been greatly depleted. It is said that the Queen has spent £20,000 from her own resources for this cause; thus, she has lacked neither opportunity nor willingness to be rich in good works, according to the apostle's admonition, and to sow good seed for a future harvest. In all these unprecedented developments, anyone with an eye to see can clearly read the harbingers of divine judgment. The people run from one country to another hoping to escape their vague sense of impending judgment, and do not realize that they are plunging into new ones, which might be that much more difficult for them, since they are less prepared for them, especially in a foreign country. There are still five thousand souls here, all suffering considerably during the cold winter days and bad conditions. Three thousand, by Royal Commission decree, will be going to New York in the West Indies around the middle of this month. Several hundred

11. Böhme, *Enchiridion precum.*
12. Francke, *Manuductio Ad Lectionem.*

young Palatines have agreed to become marines to sail to the East Indies with the next fleet; in this way, the poor people are being scattered in different parts of the world.

O! that they, or even a few of them, might take with them a living foundation of truth in their souls, that they might be salt and light in the dark corners of the earth, and thereby prevent everything from falling into stench and blindness! But now it is *so commonly the rule that, wherever the so-called Christians come, it seems to be true*: in both the East and West Indies, most of the sins originate with the Christians, who not only themselves boldly commit all kinds of atrocities, but also draw pagans into the fellowship of their vices. Thereby, Christ's name becomes a mockery, because they conclude from the evil works of the Christians that the whole foundation of their worship must be wrong and perverted. It also seems that this people is daily falling into thicker darkness. The three thousand who were dispersed in Ireland and distributed by lot among the residents of Dublin are going without pastors and shepherds. And since they do not yet know the English language, and therefore receive no edification from their conversations or sermons, the people may in time become like a tree that is neither pruned nor tilled. The Lord, however, may awaken a deeper hunger in souls and fill them, when external means are exhausted. He alone can do this, for He has more inroads than we do into human minds, and can open hearts through His Spirit. It was a sad foreshadowing that so few of them were provided with a Bible or any other spiritual book. Only here in England were they convinced that it was important.

May the Lord teach us to discern the signs of the times and the unprecedented movements in the world, both great and small! Certainly, He has set out to move heaven and earth, heavenly and earthly powers. For because the kingdom of God, which has until now been, out of righteous judgments, like a silent grain, is beginning to become a mustard seed again, and to reveal its small power (Rev 3:8) and potency in some people, we must not think that the devil will rest when God is at work. Innumerable deceptions wear the masks of truly spiritual actions. There are *spiritual malevolences among the celestial powers*, and over time they will penetrate deeper and deeper, as the healing powers in the kingdom of light are unlocked. A *simple eye* probably remains the safest guide in the midst of so many detours and deviations.

The so-called *French Prophets*, who previously caused a great stir among some people here, are now rarely spoken of, now that their affairs have failed. But they are said to have a few followers in Scotland. Finally, I send my heartfelt love to dear Miss R. Following the apostle's admonition, she has every reason to look beyond everything and only to Christ, so that her journey may be secure on the gentle path of peace. May the Lord keep her steadfastly on this path and, under the guidance of heavenly wisdom, carry her through to the goal! Thank you for all the love you showered on me during my journey, and I remain gratefully yours ...

No. 21

A. W. Böhme to Samuel Urlsperger, Theology Student in Utrecht[13]
London, 22 December 1709

It has been difficult so far to obtain naturalization for young Mr. B., in spite of the fact that the process, which in previous years cost £12–£20, now costs almost nothing. For the Lord's Supper has become a necessary and indispensable qualification for all those who want to acquire the right and privilege of naturalization, which is why Mr. B. has not been able to obtain it, since he lacked this prerequisite. Neither did anyone in the Baptist communion—they greatly dislike being called Anabaptists or rebaptizers here because they do not consider infant baptism to be a valid baptism, and so do not feel they can rightfully be called rebaptizers—want to admit him to the sacrament of the Lord's Supper without prior baptism. Since it now appears that he will remain in the Baptist denomination, I advised him to get acquainted with a Baptist pastor, who was recommended to me by a friend as one of the best, in order to receive instruction in this matter. For because he must take the Holy Sacrament locally and bring proof of it from the party in which he received it, a Mennonite baptism in Holland—which I understand is done by simple sprinkling, as is customary among Protestants—would not serve him here. The Baptists here are so rigid that they do not recognize any

---

13. Samuel Urlsperger (1685–1772) was a German Lutheran Pietist theologian. After completing his studies at Halle, he traveled to London where he became a close associate of Böhme and served with George Ruperti at St. Mary-Le-Savoy German Lutheran Church. Some of Böhme's most transparent letters were sent to Urlsperger. His early connections with the SPCK would ultimately serve the Salzburger emigrants to Georgia in the 1730s.

baptism as valid except one that is done by complete immersion of the whole person; consequently, they do not administer the Lord's Supper to anyone who has not been baptized by immersion. Thus, everything has fallen into external appearances; the essence and inner power have been lost, for the different parties are at war with each other over form.

Moreover, I was reluctant to advise young B. toward either form, but have left it to his conscience to decide for himself which denomination he would be most comfortable with. For the essence of Christianity is not exclusive to any sect—I call every outward form a sect, if the spirit of Christ, which alone can enliven and inspire the form, is lacking—but flows through every party, and here and there saves a few from the widespread corruption that sours all parties. However, if Mr. B. is to receive the more apostolic form of baptism—as immersion undoubtedly is, in that sprinkling was introduced into the Church as part of the corruption that so gradually penetrated it—I will take the liberty beforehand of urging him to manifest those fruits of the Spirit that bear witness to the power of Christ's and the apostles' teaching. For this reason, I also spoke with the Baptist pastor yesterday and cautioned him not to present his act of baptism as apostolic, which they tend to do in such circumstances, but to emphasize more explicitly that baptism means putting to death and burying the body of sin; for the empty form cannot save those who rely on the form, but do not want to step into its essence.

In terms of our dear friend's letter, I wish that I could make suitable suggestions for his support here. I admit that I would like to have a Christian student who would be available to be placed among the English, should an occasion arise. This happens now and again, if one can take the time to learn the language, without which one is useless in this country. I would imagine that our friend would be able to live here as cheaply as he could in Holland, if he had another friend who would give him guidance on how to do so, which he should not lack. I have often eaten for six shillings, and one can probably make do with that. He could have a small room for 12 or 18 shillings a week. And then we could see on the ground whether there would be any information or other opportunity that would arise to help support him in comfort. He should ponder these things in his conscience before God, and wait for God's guidance in it. I am not in the habit of lightly advising travels to England, especially for young people, because of the many temptations that they will encounter here in more ways than one. However, I am also not in the habit of advising against it, because I know that there are still many things to be learned here, which students can apply beneficially. In particular, many a person has been liberated from deep-seated prejudices by such a journey, and has been delivered from the bitter theological zealousness that rules and enchants minds almost everywhere in Germany. Those who fix their hearts solely on the fear of God can use everything for good: For the fear of the Lord is the beginning of wisdom, etc.

No. 22

A. W. Böhme to Professor August Hermann Francke in Halle[14]
London, 30 December 1709

I am at last able to transfer the enclosed 80 Reichsthaler to feed the twelve students mentioned in my previous letter and to begin providing for them in the name of God. I would have liked to have provided it sooner, but I was unable to find a merchant who knew how to transfer it directly. As soon as the funds are collected in Leipzig, twelve worthy students can be accepted and selected to receive this benefit. Of course, it is not possible to obligate the students directly to let themselves be sent to foreign countries, but it can be said in general terms, without obligation, that such would not displease those who made this contribution. Perhaps in time—if God blesses these small beginnings—a means can be devised to provide small scholarships for certain students, and thereby put the work on a better footing; but this cannot be done when the work is just beginning. It also would not hurt, if the opportunity presents itself, that they practice themselves in English and French, and thereby become proficient in something that would further the whole undertaking.

In addition, I wish that these twelve students would come together once every two weeks, if not weekly, and unite in prayer and thanksgiving to God for these benefits. Likewise, that they would take that occasion to pray for their benefactors in England, and to remember particularly the Lord's work that is going on here and the whole country. For it is not the least certain that this benefit will continue, but we must leave it to the Lord's gracious provision how and for how long the students will receive this gift; therefore, the participants have all the more reason to pray to God for its continuation, or for the awakening of more benefactors. In

14. AFSt/H C 829:56.

addition, I would be grateful if someone would take the trouble to keep a proper invoice of these contributions, which could be presented to those benefactors who require it every three or six months, if it were deemed necessary. The postage for letters and other small expenses which may be incurred when bills of exchange are cashed could also be included in this invoice.

I have translated and prepared an abstract of the illustrious examples of divine providence that took place at the orphanage in 1707 and 1708, about which there have been inquiries here and there. It takes up a third half-sheet in print, and will be finished today. When the examples from 1709, which I saw in the manuscript when I was there, are ready to print, send me several copies as soon as possible, so that I can print the complete continuation in English by the end of the year.

P.S.

When the letters from Malabar arrive, have them transcribed and sent in letter form.

No. 23

A. W. Böhme to Loth Fischer in Utrecht[15]
London, 14 January 1710

I am grateful for the love I received from you and your children during my journey. If I can obtain some information about Robert Gell's life, I will write it down on paper and, God willing, send it to you in the spring.[16] I hear that some of Gell's relatives are still living. I plan to ask them what they know about him. Dr. Francis Lee told me that a catechism written anonymously, has been published, which some attribute to Gell because of similarity of style. I have not seen the book myself, since it appears to be quite rare, but I have heard that it is written in

---

15. Loth Fischer (1640-1723) was a translator and editor. He translated Jane Lead's *Heavenly Cloud* into German. He was then commissioned by Baron Ernst von Knyphausen (1678-1731), an administrator at the court of Frederick III, Elector of Brandenburg, to translate her other works into German.

16. Robert Gell (1595-1665), DD, one-time chaplain to the Archbishop of Canterbury and rector of St. Mary, Aldermanbury, London. At the Restoration, he urged peace between religious parties. In his biblical writings, he sought to make the Scriptures accessible and approachable (see Letter 91).

the style of the mystics. I am grateful to you, dear brother, for the interest you have taken in Thomas Bromley's small tract, *The Journeys of the Children of Israel*, which I translated from English several years ago.[17] I have heard from a friend in Halle that Mr. M. in Leipzig is willing to coordinate the printing and have it ready by Easter. He also requested that I send Bromley's theosophical letters to him, in order to add them to the small tract; however, I have declined this request, because I would first have to gather them from friends here and there, and then put them in order. Some friends have another writing by Bromley, although only in manuscript, in which he, by making certain observations about some of the local writers, describes the character of true and false visions and other spiritual powers; this work might be of use in these difficult times. *But it appears that our young and newly recruited soldiers are reluctant to learn from the old warriors who have been trained in true knighthood.* So, books and other such testimonials are unlikely to find much use.

Some extracts from Jacob Böhme's *Seraphinisch Blumen-Gärtlein* [*Seraphine Flower Garden*] were taken by lovers of such writings to New York in America, where the over three thousand poor Palatines are now being transported.[18] However, there is still a lot of work to be done before the American wilderness can become a Seraphine flower garden, especially since our so-called Christians are in the habit of promulgating all sorts of atrocities among the pagans, of which they know nothing, and thus transforming paganism into a full desert. I commend you, beloved brother, to the eternal love of the Lamb, and remain . . .

P.S.

I forgot to mention that there is also another small tract by Bromley, *The Law of Circumcision*, in which he discussed the subject of marriage as he saw it.[19] But at this time, I would not advise starting with a writing like that one. Enclosed is a statement about *universal love* and the harm that arises from sectarianism, which I wrote in English to a friend last year, who had it printed here without my knowledge during my trip to

---

17. Thomas Bromley (1629–1691) was a companion to John Pordage (see Letter 33) and a member of the community that eventually evolved into the Philadelphian Society. He was greatly influenced by Jacob Böhme, as evidenced in his primary work, *Way to the Sabbath of Rest*, which appeared in German as *Weg zum Sabbat der Ruhe*. Böhme's connection to this edition is unclear.

18. Jacob Böhme (1575–1624), *Seraphinisch Blumen-Gärtlein*.

19. Bromley, "Necessity of Mortification."

Germany.[20] Consequently, it is missing certain details, although it otherwise expresses my thoughts on this matter fairly accurately. Along these same lines, an old Englishman, who loves such writings, tells me that a sermon by Dr. Gell on Matthew 2:2 is still available; in it he deals with the right and wrong use of astronomy.[21] He had it printed at the request of astronomers in London. Such small tracts tend to be very rare, otherwise this sermon could easily be added to the other translated works of this author that you already have.

No. 24

A. W. Böhme to Samuel Urlsperger, Theology Student in Utrecht
London, 14 January 1710

Dear friend, now that young B. is returning, after finally received naturalization, I will answer the important details in your letters, all of which I have duly received. As for the reflections you mentioned, there are several different examples; I hope the one enclosed, which is only half a sheet and written in French, is the right one. It has been drafted by Heinrich Ludolf, a cousin of the famous Hiob Ludolf and former secretary to my own Prince;[22] in it, he has portrayed today's corrupted religion quite clearly, to the best of his knowledge. The disreputable Dr. Henry Sacheverell's two sermons, for which he was summoned before Parliament and is still held in custody, are also enclosed here.[23] We will soon hear the verdict in his case. Often here in England ignorant zealots who preach nothing but quarreling and hatred will get little protection from the authorities, but also minimal punishment. Here, moderate and gentle people are identified and placed in the most important offices; but unruly

---

20. Böhme, *Universal Love*.

21. Gell, *Aggelokratia Theon*.

22. Heinrich Wilhelm Ludolf (1655–1712) was a German Pietist, renowned linguist, and world traveler. He met Böhme in 1701 on board ship from Rotterdam to England, befriended him, and introduced him to Prince George of Denmark. On Böhme's friendship with Ludolf, see Letter 67. Böhme preached Ludolf's funeral sermon (see Letter 69) and edited Ludolf, *Reliquiæ Ludolfianæ* (see Letter 83).

23. Henry Sacheverell (1674–1724), *Communication of Sin; Perils of False Brethren*. Sacheverell was a High-Church Anglican, Tory, and controversialist whose sermons led to his impeachment from the House of Commons.

theologians, who under the pretense of religious zeal vent their passions, are restrained, so that they cannot do much harm with their hatred of priests (which is on the whole very bitter).

And would that it were in our Germany, too, that the eyes of many authorities would be opened wide, so that they would not so blindly submit to their Consistory and its accusations against different parties, nor would they so quickly scrap from office and service those who, according to their clergy's mood and opinion, do not completely agree and comply. Indeed, I cannot believe that those who preach strife, envy, and discord reflect the spirit of Christ, nor that a particular church or religious group is the bride of Christ (as this doctor in his sermon wants to argue); but I can certainly believe that the bride of Christ is hidden in every denomination and party that embraces Christ as the beginning of restoration.

Because Monsieur B. stayed here for a long time, waiting for naturalization, he did not have any money to purchase the books he wanted. Therefore, I used the money that my former traveling companion owed him, twelve English shillings, for that purpose. Books are very expensive in England, and are sold bound. As a token of my love and remembrance, he was willing to accept from me *Enchiridion Precum*, which I put together several years ago at the request of some friends, together with the funeral sermon I preached for Prince George of Denmark.[24] The remaining tracts, which I consider very edifying, I purchased for the twelve shillings mentioned. It will be gratifying to publish the new edition of Francke's *Manuductio ad Lectionem Scripturae cum, qualicunque mea Praefatione de Impedimentis Studii Theologici*. At least it can be seen from the prefixed recommendation of the well-known Frenchman Pierre Allix, what kind of esteem some people here have for the theology professors at Halle.[25] *Vita Bonelli*, which is enclosed, is very edifyingly written, and full of good meditations. Joseph Alleine was a fiery preacher in his time.[26] His life is included in extract in *The Lives of the Faithful*, published

---

24. Böhme, *Enchiridion precum*; *Life of a Christian*. Prince George of Denmark and Norway (1653–1708) was the husband of Queen Anne of Great Britain. In 1705, the prince, at the recommendation of Heinrich Ludolf, invited Böhme to be his chaplain and court preacher at the German Lutheran Royal Chapel.

25. Pierre Allix (1641–1717), celebrated French Huguenot pastor and refugee, who came to England initially at the invitation of Gilbert Burnet. Allix was a copious author and well-connected, personally and ecclesially. Böhme mentions a number of conversations with him and refers to him as a friend.

26. Joseph Alleine (1634–1668) was an English Noncomformist pastor and author, whose primary work, *Alarm to the Unconverted*, was published posthumously and

in Halle in 1701 under Gottfried Arnold's name.[27] But the beautiful letters and encouraging writings are missing, which were printed here in the original. I have also included a whole volume of sermons by Gilbert Burnet, printed in quarto, which are hard to find individually.[28] If I knew the subject of the sermons he wanted, I would gladly request them.

With regard to any histories of England published in Latin and French, the reality is that the English write almost all their books in their mother tongue, since they can express a thing in their own language most emphatically. So, I cannot recall any history written by a native Englishman, nor a history of England in Latin from Cromwell's time on, of the sort you want. But when it comes to foreign authors, who have either written about English affairs or translated books into Latin or French, those books are more likely to be found in Holland and France than in England. I do remember that I have seen various histories of the English state in French, but almost all of them were printed in other countries. Also, it is not clear whether you want ecclesiastical or political histories. But it is very helpful, in every occasion but especially in letters, to speak precisely and distinctly so that the other person can answer the thing in question. I can, if desired, name quite a number of English authors who write about the many changes in state of English ecclesiastical or political affairs.

No. 25

A. W. Böhme to Justus Falckner[?], Pastor in New York and Albany in America[29]
London, 16 January 1710

Your esteemed letter of June 1709 has come to my attention after my return from Germany, where I was traveling this past summer. German

---

reprinted frequently. See Baxter et al., *Life and Death of . . . Joseph Alleine*. Böhme's reference to *Vita Bonelli* could refer to an earlier publication of Alleine's biography.

27. Arnold, "Leben des . . . Joseph Allein."

28. Gilbert Burnet (1643–1715), *Collection of Sermons*. Burnet, bishop of Salisbury, was a Scottish historian and prolific author, actively involved in many of the political and ecclesiastical controversies of his lengthy career. A number of Böhme's correspondents took an interest in Burnet.

29. Even though Letter 25 is addressed, "Hrn. J. T. Predigern zu Neu-Yorck und

Bibles and copies of Arndt's *True Christianity*, like those sent in 1708 with the Palatines sailing from here to New York—but which did not come into the hands of your Dutch congregation—are now being distributed for the benefit of the three thousand Palatines who have now arrived here. I will be sure to acquire, as well, a supply of Dutch Bibles and spiritual tracts privately and send them to your congregation for their comfort and edification; but I have not been able to get to that as yet.

Thank you very much for the booklet you sent me, which you wrote in Dutch for your congregation, and which Joshua Kocherthal handed on to me.[30] As I looked through it, I concluded from some of the questions that there must be disputes with other religious parties in the West Indies, and that it was therefore necessary to include such questions and answers in the tract. *What a blessed time it will be when all these unfortunate conflicts will be relegated to the abyss they came from, and nothing but a universal confluence of love will be left!* I have often wished that such religious quarreling would bleed to death in Europe, and would by no means become known among the poor people of the East and West Indies. I have also thought that if the providence of God should send me to such a remote land, I would proclaim from my own limited experience nothing but repentance and faith, rebirth and renewal, or, in a word, the living knowledge of Christ, and leave all other quarrels aside. If I were to be encroached upon by quarrelsome people, I would pretend not to notice, so that I would not, by a mistaken attempt to save the truth, be deprived of a greater blessing nor confine myself so narrowly that few would enjoy my gifts. But it is certain that my knowledge and experience will become more virtuous the more I reach out with it, and offer myself for the use and benefit of others who are not strictly of the party I belong to. This can be practiced much more easily in the West Indies, where there is complete freedom, and one is not constrained by the yoke of an unyielding Consistory as in other countries. As an example, I know of a Lutheran pastor who for a while proclaimed Christianity, straightforwardly and devoid of controversy, in a large city where there was no Reformed preacher at the time. His edifying sermons were attended not

---

Albanten in America," the strong likelihood is that the recipient is Justus Falckner (1672–1723), a student of A. H. Francke in Halle at the same time as Böhme and the first Lutheran to be ordained in the American colonies. Pardoe, "Confessional Spaces," 249–53; Williams, *Journey of Justus Falckner*.

30. Justus Falckner wrote *Grondlycke onderricht* in a catechetical, question-and-answer format. It was the first Lutheran catechism published in America. Falckner, *Fundamental Instruction*.

only by Lutherans, but also by the Reformed. However, on one occasion he confronted and refuted the Reformed—I don't know the specifics in this case—and they stayed away from his church from that point on, and so were deprived of the edification they had otherwise enjoyed. This example occurred to me as I was going through some writings my friend left behind, and found in them a sound grasp of repentance, regeneration, and other practical matters; but I quickly realized that the Dutch Reformed, of whom I hear there are many in New York, would derive little benefit from them because of the controversial points they touched upon. During my travels in Germany, to my great satisfaction, I encountered here and there, among Lutherans and Reformed alike, souls who are united in a mutual bond of love and disregard every controversy and distinctive name. In time, these will fall away, so that nothing remains but the one Spirit of Christ, and all believers are bound together as *one* through the divine nature.

Last year, shortly before my departure for Germany, I explained in more detail my ideas about this matter in a letter to an Englishman. Once, on a chance occasion, I was talking to him about the excellency of universal love and the great harm that results from an overly zealous approach to religious controversies; afterward, he asked me to explain it to him in writing. I have enclosed a few copies of the abstract of the examples of divine providence that took place at the Halle orphanage in 1707 and 1708.[31] Because I published the first part in English in 1705, some have asked to see the Continuation; I trust this abstract fulfills that request. At the end I have added a small appendix of the most important aspects of the work of Reformation in Germany, which I trust proves useful to read.[32] If something edifying in English should otherwise come to light here, I will be glad to help you with it, if it is something you desire. May the Lord graciously prosper all planting and watering, and may there soon be light everywhere.

---

31. Francke, *Pietas Hallensis; or, an Abstract of the Marvellous Footsteps.*
32. Francke, *Pietas Hallensis . . . Together with a Short History of Pietism.*

No. 26

A. W. Böhme to C. R. at M. in the Earldom of W.
London, 20 January 1710

The love I bear for you and your house cannot be expressed in paper and ink. Your name sprouts in my heart before God, since I often remember you when the Lord moves me to love and compassion for my neighbor. Up to now, we have seen many lamentable pictures of human misery here, which are able to portray with vivid colors the dawn of God's judgments on Europe to those who do not have a stony heart.

The extraordinary migration from the Palatinate and several other places in Germany to England has been sufficiently reported in the public newspapers. It seems that most of them cannot themselves give a good reason for the desires that brought them here. Of the twelve thousand who have come here, three thousand are now being loaded onto ships to take them to New York in America. A large number (some reckon four thousand) have died, partly for lack of adequate care, although the Lord has also awakened souls throughout this nation who have sought to alleviate misery and poverty through generous contributions. However, with such a multitude of people and the increasing price of bread, it is not enough.

While I am thinking of the poor Palatines, I should also mention the so-called Prophets, who arose here some years ago and spoke of a new dispensation that was to be established with them; a number of them have done works of mercy for these people. A noble and learned gentleman associated with the Prophets, Sir Richard Bulkeley, distributed about £300 among these poor people, having been awakened to it by means of an inspiration, as it is called, which one of the Prophets had.[33] He himself walked among the people. He brought wine and other refreshment to the sick among them. He clothed others from head to foot and distributed many other gifts among the people. At the beginning of December, the following happened: A certain German physician, who was entrusted with the oversight of the sick by the Royal Commission, seeing Sir Richard's generosity, asked that he, the physician, be allowed to refer the most

---

33. Sir Richard Bulkeley (1644–1710), 2nd baronet of Old Bawn, Dublin, Ireland, and Ewell, Surrey. Bulkeley was a scientist, horticulturist, benefactor, and author; he suffered from innumerable ailments and afflictions, which drew him ultimately to the millennialist French Prophets. See Letter 97.

miserable and feeble patients to Sir Richard, in order to let them share in such outflowing love before others did. But he refused, saying that the same spirit that had first awakened him to this compassionate love would, on invocation, also indicate to him the persons who were to receive the benefit. However, this resulted in some of the poor receiving garments twice, while others received none at all, since the patron did not recognize many of those who came twice. Thus, some conclude that the Spirit, who instructed him to do this, had not made a real distinction in this matter. At almost the same time, a half-sheet notice was printed and sent to the homes of the richest residents in London. It depicts the hardship and distress of the poor Palatines in a very sensitive way, and is thought to have been written by Bulkeley himself. Among other things he wrote:

> I appeal to you who have a warm fire and a full table and live in abundance every day, and to you who ride in exquisite carriages and waste your money at wine and comedy houses. I appeal to you who have two coats: because you call yourselves Christians and profess Christianity, make haste and bring one of them to these poor members of Christ, lest they perish and their blood become a burden to you. You who are so attached to your bellies and to your animals and to your walls.... You prelates and teachers who have silken beds, convert all of this into an offering to help these poor members of Christ. It is a time of judgment, of weeping and wailing, in which you should exchange your expensive garments for sackcloth.... You great Nimrods of the land, who allow yourselves to be worshiped as gods, and say, who is master over us? You care little for the suffering of Joseph; but know that in the end you will receive a severe punishment. Remember how easy it would be for the Lord to upend the wheel, and for you who now soar above to fall down and be crushed under it.

This letter has indeed had good effects with some people here and there. A friend of mine told me about a prominent lady who visited the poor people and was so moved by the sight of their misery that she immediately sold all her jewels and distributed the money among the Palatines. Does the Lord not teach us to discern the signs of the times, and give us eyes to see into the silence of Christianity and bring in love? At the end of December, the royal commissioners had a small broadsheet printed here in High German, warning people not to come over to England, unless they themselves had the funds required for their upkeep and passage.

This short notice is to be distributed in Germany in order to stop people from fleeing.

But there are other things I almost forgot to write about. The other day I received a letter from Pennsylvania, requesting that a few copies of the illustrious Christian Knorr von Rosenroth's spiritual songs, called *Helicon*, be sent over to encourage the Christians there.[34] Now I wouldn't have known how to proceed, unless dear Mr. C. had offered a hand and procured about a dozen copies from Nuremberg. I don't have a copy of it myself, but I remember that the songs in question were printed by Felsecker in Nuremberg. Since, if I remember correctly, Mr. C. is his relative, it occurred to me that this might be a way to acquire the books they requested. They are very grateful for the books that were collected in Germany some years ago for the edification of the German Christians in America, to which Christians in W. also contributed; and it is to be hoped that in time the way will be paved for the kingdom of God in the West Indies. Such visible testimonies are useful in these days of weakness, when we have only a small star to guide the searching soul to Christ. When it is day and the sun reaches its height, the tiny lights are snuffed out, and the stars are swallowed up by the expansive power of the sun.

No. 27

A. W. Böhme to Justus Falckner, farmers and residents in the province
   of New York in America[35]
London, 21 January 1710

In the love of Jesus

Dear friend,

I have just received the letter that you wrote to me from New York. I hope you will faithfully guard the good desires God has placed in your heart, and strive to fortify them by daily prayer, watchfulness, and supplications against the attacks and temptations of evil. Every position and lifestyle have their own special temptations, and you cannot get rid of them simply by fleeing from them. For the evil kindling that catches

---

34. Christian Knorr von Rosenroth (1631–1689), *Neuer Helicon*. Rosenroth was a Christian Hebraist and hymn writer.

35. See footnote on Letter 25.

the fire of temptation and ignites the soul in worldly lust lies within us. In this case, evil must be overcome and all the doorways of the heart must be constantly guarded, if one wants to keep the inner life of grace, so precious a gift, untarnished. As you may recall, I often warned them when they were here that it would be of little help to them to run from one country to another, dragging their evil and selfish hearts with them wherever they went. Oh, that but a few of them might be true salt, so that by its pervasive power and sharpness it might prevent everything from falling into stench and foulness! And oh, that a few of them would shine like lights, so that the pagans and brutes around them might see something godly, if not by their words, then in their deeds! Christ's name has unfortunately until now been blasphemed among the pagans by the un-Christian life of the Christians. Yes, the Christians have manifested all kinds of sins and abominations that the pagans knew nothing about. From now on, the Christians should shine, in the midst of the pagans, with a godly power that bears witness to the glory, love, humility, gentleness, purity, and joy that is in Christ and His members.

It is written of the first Christians that they were like blazing coals. When unbelievers, like so many dying coals, approached them, they were awakened and set on fire by the power of the Christians. Perhaps many unbelievers might still be warmed by the fire of Christians, namely, they might be convinced that the living God is truly with us, when they find in Christians what they are still lacking. The time will come when even those poor hearts that are still in darkness and death will see their light and life and be led to Christ, the living spring that restores all unrighteousness Therefore, dear friends, see to it that you shine in the land like lights that are lit from above. Warm and awaken one another, so that the small strength that began to stir among you may not be extinguished, but may rather burst forth from that flame into a veritable bonfire, illuminating the dark corners of the earth and remote wastelands. You now have complete liberty where you are to seek the Lord with one mind, and to unite in prayer and song to the praise of the Most High, if only you are not lacking the will and joy. *It is often the case that the more freedom people have to serve God, the less they make use of it; indeed, they tend to make it their own and become confident in the flesh. They are more likely to be driven to God by plagues, burdens, and grievances arising from the authorities.* O what a dangerous snare is confidence in the flesh! How soon people cease from the works of the Spirit, when the flesh is again given some air and freedom. In many a soul nothing remains but a lifeless glaze and shadow, even though it may have once tasted the love of Christ. The firstborn have a great promise in the Scriptures, and a special blessing is bestowed on them.

See to it then, beloved friend, that you are one of the first in America to bear witness to the grace, power, and love of Christ. May you join with the few who have tasted the righteousness that is in Jesus. *For in the loving unity of hearts there is great blessing.* As long as the burning coals lie close together, they sustain each other; but if they are thrown apart and scattered, they soon die out. As long as upright hearts dwell together in harmony, and refresh one another through prayer, encouragement, and sweet conversation, there is still hope that something will remain of the truth once tasted. But if one wants to go this way and the other another way, and they get into quarrels and disputes over opinions, everything will be disrupted and thrown into chaos. To be sure, where *love* is lacking, the first and foremost quality of a disciple of Christ is lacking. But where love is rooted in the soul, there can be no great disruption, even if one has one opinion and the other another in ancillary matters. *For the kingdom of God does not depend on this or that opinion, but on power, love, friendship, joy, righteousness, humility, and following Christ.* Whoever abides in Christ's love and humility has a secure and insurmountable fortress. And this is precisely the fortress the evil one tries to lure us out of through the weighing of diverse opinions.

I am taking this opportunity to send you some booklets, both in German and English. You can distribute the German books, along with my heartfelt greetings, to our fellow Germans as you wish, especially to those in whom you observe a longing for the grace of God. Perhaps such a booklet can become a seedling from which, in time, yet more fruit can grow in their deserts. Germany lies under heavy judgment of God. Three thousand souls have arrived here from there, weary of the driver and hoping to find some peace in the West Indies. But I am afraid that most of them are bringing with them that which is the origin of all evil and misery. Whoever drags this restless impulse—that is, *selfishness* and *stubbornness*—with them will have little chance of escape. You can spread the enclosed English pamphlets among some of our British friends and make use of them as best you can. Say to our friends on my behalf: "Take care that you do not cultivate the field more than your souls. Do not let your spiritual life become a desert, while you are cultivating the earthly desert and making it fruitful." I commend all of you to the sweet and gentle love of Jesus and remain . . .

No. 28

A. W. Böhme to Johann Gottfried Seelig[?] in Pennsylvania[36]
London, 10 February 1710

After I sent my last letter, something occurred to me, which I would like to hear your opinion about, beloved brother. In Germany, there is a striking movement among both the wealthy and the poor to leave their homeland and migrate to the English plantations in America. I cannot speak here to the intentions that each of them may harbor. This much is certain: they are weary of being oppressed by their rulers and are seeking peace. But they are unlikely to find it as long as they do not thoroughly remove the inner root and main cause of all unrest and strive to enter the Center of peace.

Since Christians are obliged to observe the interests of their Lord in all kinds of revolutions that take place in the outside world, I have been wondering whether it would not be expedient to set up a bookstore in America with actual books, and thereby help to promote the salvation of this poor people as best we can, as long as the days of degradation are still with us. As I reflected on this idea, I mentioned it to a friend who was just with me, and he thought it would be quite feasible, and that I should prepare a small proposal, which could be sent to you, beloved brother, to get your opinion on it, since you are quite familiar with the American state. I have therefore, for the sake of better clarity, summarized the whole project in the following questions for you to answer:

(1) Would one, presuming naturalization, have entire freedom to set up a bookstore in America, and particularly in Pennsylvania?

(2) Which city would be considered the most appropriate for such an enterprise?

(3) Would the Quakers, who are the dominant group in Pennsylvania, be able to prevent it from happening? I ask this question because the Quaker bookseller in London carries almost nothing but Quaker books, disregarding all other books, so that his own sect

---

36. Probably Johann Gottfried Seelig (1668–1745), mystic and hymnist. He was a native of Lemgo, Germany, where A. W. Böhme was a student, and a member of Johann Kelpius's mystical community on Wissahickon Creek (see Letter 35). He was a bookbinder who brought his tools with him to Pennsylvania. Sachse, *German Pietists*, 335–40.

restricts itself so strictly that others cannot benefit from his business. Whereas the bookstore in America should carry the best and most valuable books of those in all parties and sects whom God has raised up as witnesses of the hidden life of grace, so that anyone, whatever their party, may find a powerful witness to the truth and be edified by it.

(4) Is there any hope that someone could make even a meagre living from this kind of enterprise? For that person should be selected who is free from self-interest and is only concerned about the general welfare of the kingdom of God, yet he would need to earn his keep from the work of his hands.

(5) Would it therefore be possible, through a comfortable correspondence, to spread throughout all the American provinces where there are Christians, edifying writings aimed at the salvation of one's neighbor?

(6) Are the houses in Pennsylvania expensive, and how much rent would be required annually to establish such a business?

(7) From which European nation do most of the people in America come, in order acquire the most books in that language?

Please answer these questions as soon as possible. If anything else should occur to you, you are welcome to add it, since not everything comes to mind at once. The main purpose of the whole project is upbuilding the kingdom of God through the salvation of souls. Therefore, the whole enterprise should be made as *universal* as possible, so that all nations and parties in their respective languages and religious convictions can benefit from it. I have a particular hope that through this means the Word of God in Bibles and New Testaments could be scattered throughout the land, and that in this way a holy furor would be brought among the people that in time would imbue many a soul. Should conscientious missionaries be chosen and sent there, such an undertaking could support them in many good ways. I am well aware that the English have also established libraries here and there in the American plantations. However, their aim was not so much general edification as the strengthening and expansion of their Church; whereas, this work should be placed on a completely different footing and be led from basic principles, that is, its purpose would not be the propagation of denominations but of true Christianity. Care should also be taken that the so-called polemical writings, by which Europeans have until now been so violently provoked against each other and separated from each other, are not propagated in the West Indies, but that, along with the Scripture, those books are sent which reinforce the essentials of Christianity and pave the way for universal love. May the Lord make us faithful in this dispensation in which we stand, and may the door once opened be opened wider and wider, so that Gentiles and Jews may enter and find the way to the hidden treasures of the gospel.

No. 29

A. W. Böhme to Johann Heinrich Michaelis, Professor of Theology and Oriental Languages at Halle[37]
London, 18 February 1710

In the love of Jesus

Dear brother, as promised I am sending John Bunyan's works, or rather the first volume of them.[38] The rest of his writings can only be obtained individually here and there; however, in time they should also be collected into a single volume, if, as the publisher told me, enough subscribers could be found who would help promote the work by making advance payments, which is customary here. As for Bunyan himself, whose books have brought great blessing in England, Holland, and Germany, and also partly in France—since some of his writings have been translated into French—it may have been a special providence that his position and vocation have not become widely known; for many who judge by reputation might have been precluded from the edification which they could have otherwise derived from his books. He was a Baptist, a very oppressed party at the time he lived. He was a tinker by trade, but he was much less industrious in his trade when, after an arduous penitential struggle (*Bußkampf*), he was called to be a teacher among his fellow Baptists. Should his other works eventually be printed

---

37. Johann Heinrich Michaelis (1668–1738), German theologian, studied under Hiob Ludolf at Frankfurt and was named professor of Oriental languages at Halle in 1699 and professor of theology in 1709.

38. John Bunyan (1628–1688), *Works of . . . John Bunyan*. Bunyan was a renowned Puritan author and preacher.

in a single volume, I can also get it into your hands. I would like you to accept this, beloved brother, as a small testimony of my gratitude for the love enjoyed from your dear relatives during my last journey to N. and F. Please send Mrs. M. the enclosed prayer booklet, which we use in our chapel and is taken mostly from the English liturgy. And because Mr. D. asked me for a copy, I have also enclosed an unbound one for him, which could be handed over to him at an opportune time. I would like to know whether the man continues to disrupt others with his opinions, and likewise, whether Halle's answer, which was made last August when I was traveling through, has had some effect either on him or on others? I would have liked to have talked with him in more detail at that time about his opinions, but my hurried situation did not allow it. It is regretful that some opinions become so entrenched that essence and substance are often forgotten over them. But may the Lord lead us ever closer to the goal!

No. 30

A. W. Böhme to J. P. H., Pastor at Lower R. in Thuringia
London, 27 February 1710

The copies of the Eisleben Testaments have been duly sent to me by Mr. E. as a fruit of his love. May the Lord, who moved him to this outpouring of love, be his reward on the day of retribution. He has indeed cast his bread on the waters, especially since there are still hungry souls both here and in the West Indies; and even much more so, since there is much less of the outer witness of the Word in the West Indies, in particular in Pennsylvania, where the local Christians express their great gratitude to those in Germany who come to their aid with such gifts. I wish that others would follow in your footsteps, beloved brother, and provide us with enough copies of Arndt's *True Christianity* to support the dispersed Germans in the East and West Indies.

PASTORALIA (1709–1710)

No. 31

A. W. Böhme to G. H. at F. in Holstein
London, 6 March 1710

I found your letter from May 1709 when I returned from Germany in October. I have not found opportunity to answer it sooner, although I have been diligently searching for it. I also received Otto Lorentzen Strandiger's tract, which was enclosed with those letters, and I am grateful for it.[39] It reaffirms in me the realization that religious matters are increasingly fermenting everywhere, and that our ordinary systems are no longer sufficient to decide all the disputes that might arise. Much less will our successors be able to wear our robes or measure themselves according to our standards. However, I must admit that I now wish that those who see and walk in God's light would turn the power they have been given against the root evil and avoid small side disputes, for which this time does not yet provide sufficient light. Here in London we have quite a few Anabaptist congregations that in all seriousness campaign against the baptism of children and, in their own words, will baptize only those who have received the beginning of grace. But the decay is as visible with them as with other denominations. If the best of outward forms is approached with a defiled hand and heart, it is immediately corrupted, and there is scarcely any fruit of substance to be found in it. Therefore, I have often wished that those who recognize the corruption would begin the work of reformation from a spiritual, inward foundation, and leave the outer form alone until the inner is right; then the outer would be borne out of the inner, and the form out of the spirit, even as the fruit and the leaves come out of the root. The inner foundation must form and shape the outer. But everyone has their own understanding. And because corruption is so manifold, the Lord also requires manifold instruments to detect and attend to it. Those who remain faithful to the position assigned to them will receive a reward. For God's kingdom is wide and expansive, and requires many laborers to build and establish it.

Here and there I have heard talk of R.'s decline, but nothing certain. Often a soul falls, so that it will stand all the firmer once it is raised up again. This may be particularly true of those who, by the Lord's wise allowance, are led through formidable trials and breakthroughs, and are

---

39. Otto Lorentzen Strandiger (1650–1724), *Bekänntnüs von dem Kirchlichen.* Strandiger was a German theologian and separatist.

conceived and born, as it were, in a single day. These people, having reached the top rapidly, need a singular humiliation that transcends reason, so that they may persevere in the pure foundation of grace, which gives everything to the Creator and takes everything from the creature. So, when the opportunity arises, please give me some information about R.'s current circumstances. At the same time, let me know if E. is still in A. and is still opening the abyss of darkness to others. Because goodness is moving, evil is also moving to hinder it. May the Spirit of Christ search our hearts and make us faithful and teach us to persevere—since so many are falling away—through him in every adversity! I remain . . .

No. 32

A. W. Böhme to Samuel Urlsperger at Utrecht
London, 14 March 1710 (OS)[40]

The last letter I have seen from you was from the 13th of this month, along with an enclosure from the esteemed Mr. F[rancke?]. I will answer him next, after I will have received some remarks on the life of Dr. Robert Gell from Dr. Francis Lee. An old English preacher has also told me about some collections, which I expect will be delivered in due time. On the first of March there was an enormous uproar of rioters here because of the infamous Henry Sacheverell. I have never seen such a convergence of people in London. But I could see and hear everything clearly, because Sacheverell was right outside the door where I currently have my room, before he had to leave when the time came for him to appear in court at Westminster Hall. The mob ran in unbelievable numbers to the carriage, and surrounded it until it entered the house where he was to be interrogated. By the time he returned between seven and eight that evening, the mob had grown even more, and the alleys through which he was passing were becoming quite unsafe due to the insurrection of the scoundrels and insolent who were perpetrating it. But the uprising reached its height during the night. As they accompanied him home with loud acclamation, the agitated spirit of the people would not settle down. At nightfall

---

40. In England before 1752, the Julian Calendar was used in which the new year began on 25 March; it is called Old Style (OS) dating. Since 1752, the Gregorian Calendar has been in use.

they began to tear down the Presbyterian churches, or meeting houses as they are called here, with a savage fury. Together they dragged chairs, benches, books, pulpits, etc. to a certain place and made gleeful bonfires. Seven such meeting houses were either completely torn down or made temporarily unusable. Some Presbyterian preachers have left their homes and moved to other more secure places. And indeed, due to the furor that swept over the people, many of them were dealt with terribly. During the riots, some are said to have been killed, others crushed, and others miserably hacked to pieces by the Royal Guard, which had been dispatched from the Court between ten and eleven o'clock to disperse the mob. However, the people had broken off into various groups so that they were spread out even further; therefore, the soldiers could not immediately control the rampage that had erupted. So can a human tongue pour out fire and flames when it has been lit by hell! We witness here a vivid commentary on James 3, especially vs. 6, about the *cycle of nature*, which is set on fire by the tongue and once set in motion is so difficult to restrain. The bitter spirit of discord and sectarianism is propagated from one generation to the next, and people learn from others shameful language that should be buried in eternal oblivion. Much good could be done in Utrecht if teachers of a universal love were available. I am sure that in time such teachers will be sought after here and there, and the falsely famous orthodoxy will lose its credibility.

Dr. Johann Jäger's *Church History* is known here, although I have never seen the book myself.[41] Several scholars publish monthly critical reviews of new books here, in which I found the book reviewed. One of them told me that the Philadelphian Society, in case he attributed unorthodox things to them, would publish a response in Latin and have it printed here.

---

41. Johann Wolfgang Jäger (1647–1720), *Historia Ecclesiastica*. Jäger was a German Protestant theologian who became chancellor of the University of Tübingen.

No. 33

A. W. Böhme to Loth Fischer in Utrecht
London, 24 April 1710

Let me respond briefly to your last letter. I have written to Halle about the tracts of Thomas Bromley that I translated into German, but have not yet heard whether anything further has been done about it. Currently, some of his small works are being printed together in English: (1) *The Way to the Sabbath of Rest*; (2) *The Journeys of the Children of Israel*; and (3) *A Treatise of Extraordinary Divine Dispensations*.[42] The first one has been published several times, but the last two have only been kept among friends as manuscripts. The daughter of the well-known Dr. John Pordage inherited these writings and has willingly handed them over for printing.[43] Because she has limited financial resources, a few enthusiasts of such books have advanced money for the printing; thereby, the heiress can keep any profits, and the friends can purchase copies of the book for themselves at the current price. As soon as it is finished, dear brother, I will give you a copy. An elderly pastor who knew Dr. Robert Gell has shared with me a few circumstances of his life, which I have enclosed. However, Dr. Francis Lee, whom I likewise approached to find out whether some memorabilia of Dr. Gell's life might be preserved, has not come up with anything. I searched diligently among old books for the sermon he is said to have given on astronomy, but could find nothing. Such small tracts, which may consist of just a few sheets of paper, are usually soon lost unless they are incorporated into larger works and thus preserved for future reading. Should I yet be able to discover some of Gell's writings or life circumstances, I will send them to you promptly. In the meantime, you can proceed with the printing and, if something should appear, it can be added at the beginning or the end of the work. . . .

The delegated preacher, who is about to travel to Pennsylvania, has delivered your booklet to me, dear brother. What you write is certainly true, that the poor people are being *misled by the deceitful* (I add, lying) *spirit of earthly reason*. Not long ago, I received a lengthy letter from people I had never heard from before in the J. region of the Palatinate. In

---

42. Bromley, *Way to the Sabbath of Rest . . . To Which Are Now Added.*

43. John Pordage (1607–1681), physician, Anglican churchman, and mystic, was the founder of the Behmenist group at Bradfield, Berkshire, that later became the Philadelphian Society under the leadership of his disciple and successor, Jane Lead.

it, they posed many questions about the status of the English plantations in America, which I intend to answer in the near future, in order to put a stop to the actions of this people. They promise themselves nothing but golden mountains in the new world. They say they are looking for rest, but they do not realize that it must be born in one's inner being and cannot be attained in the external world. I think of Johann Tauler's familiar saying about those who limit God to time and place: "The sun that shines in Cologne also shines in Paris."

No. 34

A. W. Böhme to Mrs. S. in C.
London, 4 May 1710

Beloved friend,

I have often remembered before the Lord my dear friends from C., after having enjoyed myself with them last August. It is always a great joy for me to be able to be edified and rejoice with the children of peace in the presence of the Lord. It is high time that believers unite in heartfelt love, for the provocations that divide us are increasing everywhere. In my heart I became quite convinced that God has a rich seed in C. I am looking forward to a future harvest, which is already starting to turn a bit white. There is no doubt that the evil one will strive to sow tares wherever the Lord sows the fine wheat. Only those who are awake will recognize what the evil one has in mind. Some souls have received the seed of new birth, but it is very slow to break through. The weight of human fear and people-pleasing oppresses and presses them down, so that they can neither draw nourishment from below, nor can they grow and bear fruit upward.

Not only have other souls received the seed of rebirth, but it has also begun to germinate and emerge. But this happens only in good weather and lovely sunshine. When the heat of testing from within and all kinds of opposition from without arise, it loses all its power and in some cases is even lost. Oh, so much is required for the seed of God to flourish to a truly healthy maturity in the soul. When the grain of wheat is sown, the sweet vision of summer is still present; in other words, the soul is sweetly drawn to receive the word of life. But this is followed by the cold winter, which covers everything with cold, frost, and snow. Here everything seems forlorn and dead, and there is almost no grass that grows from the seed that has been scattered. This, dear friend, is the spiritual season in which the soul must undergo the hour of testing and prove its faithfulness. Many fall away at this point. Since they are immersed in spiritual poverty and must delve deeply into their own nothingness, and must also truly understand their own inward sinfulness, they do not want to hear of anything but spiritual comforts. This often gives rise to widespread immaturity. Many find themselves again clinging to the decaying creature, seeking external comfort from it, since they are lacking inward comfort. Some puff themselves up in the enjoyment of spiritual gifts, because they have not sufficiently laid a foundation in true grace, by which they should reject those gifts. Every gift should lead back to this grace, so that God would be more exalted by the gift, while the person would be more humbled. For this is the right use of spiritual gifts.

Other souls seek deep mysteries, and talk more about knowledge than love. They are like trees, which spread out into many extensive branches, but do not bear much fruit. Love, on the other hand, is a tree that bears healthy fruit, from which one's neighbor can eat and be satisfied. The way of love is noble, assured, and graceful. It is noble, because it leads everything into the noblest foundation, namely into God Himself. In this way, the lowliest works are made great and, as it were, ennobled. It is assured because one cannot easily stray from it. Love simply takes and gives, and does not let the left hand of reason know what it is doing. The way of love is also *graceful*. It does not let any roots of bitterness grow in it. Those who follow this path receive all souls in an extended spirit of love. They do not receive them in opinion, but in love. With them love prevails and conquers everything. They want everyone to have the same love, even if they have differing opinions and understandings in this or that matter. Now, beloved friend, may the Lord teach you the straight and narrow way of salvation, together with all your friends in Christ, some of whom I met when I was there. *I hope they will abide with the one who called them. If they are united in love, their strength will grow; when they are divided, their strength is weakened and finally lost.* I am enclosing the discourse on Luke 9,[44] which was given in the residence of Mr. O, and which you, in hope of some edification, then requested in writing. God is able to bless even a small testimony.

---

44. Original editor's note: "This discourse can be found in the second part, p."

No. 35

A. W. Böhme to Dr. Johann Wilhelm Petersen at Magdeburg[45]
London, 3 May 1710

Most reverend ...

Your Honor's letter was duly delivered to me by Mr. G.[46] After reading it, I realized that you must not be aware of local government regulations, and so I thought it advisable to pass on that information. The Foreign Protestants Naturalisation Act, which was finally passed in 1709 after a long period of opposition—because it hindered the self-interest of a few merchants and private persons—was established and published under Royal and Parliamentary authority only for the benefit of foreigners.[47] Briefly, the content is: All foreign Protestants who want to settle in England and be regarded as naturalized citizens shall: (1) receive Holy Communion in the denomination in which they were raised (it is not required to receive Holy Communion in the Church of England); (2) swear allegiance to the government; and (3) bring a certificate signed by several witnesses of having received Holy Communion in a Protestant assembly. Whereupon the person's name is recorded and added to the public registers. But all this must be done according to the laws of the land here in England; the Queen herself, because it is a parliamentary matter, can do nothing further about it, and therefore all written or oral requests to her would be useless. After the publication of the Naturalisation Act, the costs have even been reduced, and a small gratuity is given to the one who records the name of the one being naturalized. Beforehand, it could it cost 70, 80, 90 to 100 German dollars. Now you can have it recorded for three or four dollars, plus incidental costs. Only time will tell whether this privilege will be permanently granted to foreigners, or whether the Naturalisation Act will be revoked (as many suppose).

---

45. Almost certainly Johann Wilhelm Petersen (1649–1727), a German theologian and friend of Philipp Spener and the Pietists. He and his wife, Johanna Eleonora (1644–1724), a remarkable theologian and writer in her own right, developed their own unique mystical, millennial, pietistic spirituality.

46. Possibly Johann Georg Gichtel (see Letter 122). On the connection between Petersen, Gichtel, and Jane Lead, see Martin, "'God's Strange Providence.'"

47. The Foreign Protestants Naturalisation Act was passed on 23 March 1709 (1708 OS), primarily for the naturalization of French Huguenots who had fled to Britain since the revocation of the Edict of Nantes in 1685.

Otherwise, things seem to be going rather confusingly with the 25,000 acres that the Frankfurt Company has in Pennsylvania.[48] From time to time, I receive letters from my friends there, in which they express their concern about the danger facing those Germans who have not been naturalized. In 1707, the now blessed Johannes Kelpius wrote:

> William Penn, when he came to Germany about 25 years ago, convinced the Germans that he himself could naturalize foreigners.[49] He even wrote a specific law towards that end. However, for reasons unknown, he did not have it confirmed in King James II or King William III's time, which he could have done quite easily. Therefore, William Penn's law concerning naturalization, together with various others, was rejected, for the Parliament in England wanted to reserve that particular prerogative for itself. Now our German people indeed expect, as long as William Penn is alive and reigns over the land, they are in no danger. But if he should die soon, or otherwise be deprived of his governorship, they fear, and perhaps not without reason, that the hungry lawyers would force the Germans into all kinds of processes—although they were often the first inhabitants in the land, helping to break the ice, setting up a linen factory, and otherwise doing a lot of good to the country, thus proving to be faithful and quiet subjects—and would put them, together with their families, into extreme misery.[50]

Kelpius then made an impassioned appeal that I asked Prince George to take to the Queen the matter of whether suitable measures could be taken for their protection. I then presented the whole matter to a few knowledgeable persons, as best I could, but have heard nothing more; nor can I, in my present circumstances, provide any further assistance. Finally, the Germans who have purchased land in Pennsylvania should consider how they might weather such a storm and protect their property by means of a general naturalization. I am mentioning this here for your mature consideration, your honor, out of the principle of love, since

---

48. The Frankfurt Land Company was composed of German Lutheran Pietists who hoped to locate in Pennsylvania, under the agency of Francis Daniel Pastorius (1651–1720), the founder of Germantown, Pennsylvania.

49. William Penn (1644–1718) toured Germany in 1677, promising a new kind of religious freedom in the American colonies.

50. Johannes Kelpius (1667–1708), musician and mystic, was the leader of the German mystical community, "Society of the Woman in the Wilderness," on Wissahickon Creek near Philadelphia in Pennsylvania. The source for Böhme's quote is unknown, although he was in correspondence with Kelpius.

I have not set foot in Pennsylvania; and since, besides, I rather believe that mere human institutions, no matter how strongly they are guarded by the authorities, will finally fall to ruin and will not provide adequate protection against the judgments of God.

P.S.

The well-known Frenchman Dr. Pierre Allix is writing about the French Prophets; he told me the other day that he wants to prove among other things that both the old and the new chiliasts—with whom he himself agrees—had incorporated many Jewish interpretations into their account of the Prophets, and thus had considerably weakened their version. Dr. Francis Lee, the late Jane Lead's son-in-law, just visited me as I am writing this and sends his warmest greetings to you and your dear wife.[51] Things are still very muddled with our so-called Prophets, and time will tell how much of God has been in this matter. The physical agitations, which some still exhibit, are quite violent, and even enter others around them who are not firmly fixed against them.

No. 36

A. W. Böhme to Professor August Hermann Francke in Halle
London, 19 May 1710

I am delighted that the final £25 which Dr. Frederick Slare managed has now been properly received. The name of the nobleman who honored the orphanage with the gift is Sir Hugh Fortescue, a parliamentary lord, whose name could be printed at the end of your next narrative.[52] A certain preacher of the Church of England, named Henry Shute,[53]

---

51. Francis Lee (1661–1719) was a physician, nonjuror, and High-Church Anglican. He knew both Pietists and followers of the mystic Jacob Böhme. He became associated with the Philadelphia Society and married the widowed daughter of Jane Lead, although he broke with the Society after Lead's death. Jane Lead (1624–1704) was a mystic after the theology of Jacob Böhme and a prolific early modern English female writer. She was a member of John Pordage's Behmenist community and later became the head of the Philadelphian Society. Hessayon, *Jane Lead and Her Transnational Legacy*.

52. Sir Hugh Fortescue (1665–1719), a Whig in the House of Lords from Penwarne, Mevagissey, Cornwall.

53. Henry Shute (d. 1722), lecturer at St. Mary's, Whitechapel, and treasurer of the SPCK from 1700 to 1722.

had presented the translated accounts of the orphanage to Sir Fortescue, together with another treatise; upon reading them, he was inspired straightaway to contribute the above sum. After the last continuation of the Footsteps, containing Noteworthy Examples of Providence, published from 1707–1708, some Presbyterians also found themselves emboldened to contribute. Indeed, an elderly Presbyterian preacher named Richard Stratton[54] sent the *Biblia Polyglotta* to be included in the orphanage library.[55] Others have promised various other books, which will be delivered to you in due course. The previous gifts were all given into my keeping by members of the Episcopal Church; therefore, this turn of events seems all the more noteworthy to me.

I have not been able to give my attention to the project of the English Table for the orphanage. The matter of the Palatines has kept our best people so occupied that we have almost no access to the benefactors, much less can we propose anything new. However, now that almost all of the Palatines have been shipped off, the Commission will soon be disbanded. Then there will be time to attend to the matter. So far, I have heard that they are more likely to send a number of relatively grown-up boys or young men than children, which is perhaps better because they will be available for public service sooner than children would. . . . I am now working on collecting a small English library from among friends to use at the English Table and with others who want to learn the language. In this way, many original books would be made known in Germany and, in time, translated. By the end of the year, I intend to provide the names of the contributors to the English Table that you requested. As soon as the 44 copies of Arndt's *True Christianity* arrive, I will distribute them among the Christians in America as usefully as possible, and perhaps I will also be able to distribute them in areas outside of New York where Germans are to be found. Good-bye and love . . .

---

54. The name in the German is "Strutton," but it is probably Richard Stratton. According to Lothrop, *History of the Church*, 48–49, on August 4, 1699, Benjamin Colman (1673–1747) was ordained by the London Presbytery "by prayer, with the imposition of the hands of the Rev. Richard Stratton, John Spademan, Robert Fleming, and Christopher Taylor." Three months later, Colman began his ministry at the Brattle Street Church in Boston, which he served until his death.

55. Brian Walton (1600–1661), *Biblia Sacra Polyglotta*. A copy is in the library of the Franckesche Stiftungen (Signature: S/THOL:XX 021:1).

PASTORALIA (1709–1710)

No. 37

Mr. B. in the Earldom of J. to A. W. Böhme
15 March 1710

A letter from Mr. J. U. providing news on the conditions in the English settlements in America.

... The great revolution to emigrate to America, which arose last year on the Rhine and Main Rivers to the utter displeasure of the authorities in every region and religion, is now beginning to emerge anew. Many are already preparing to make such a move; others are still struggling and arguing over such ideas, unwilling to venture into the unknown. Therefore, the enclosed letter has been drawn up by good-hearted people with the worthwhile intention of seeking the advice of godly people on this matter. Since I was assured of your kindness toward the friends of God, I am also sending this to you, among others, because a friend is about to embark on this journey, in the hope that you will be kind enough to respond lovingly and impartially to the following points after carefully examining the matter. There are already up to ten families of well meaning people resolved to emigrate, and several more are still considering it. If you could find out something favorable and certain from the appointed landlords of these regions, it would be a great service and benefit to these friends. It is reported here that Queen Anne would have the people transported at her expense. However, because, as word is spread, this would entail something binding and because these friends love their own people, they would rather delay than be trapped in a bad situation for so long. Please, if you would, give us some information as to whether the Queen will extend this mercy, and how it will actually happen. The attached supplement will provide several matters to be answered, etc.

Here are the questions which they would like answered.

Since the recent times and events of certain families—who, for the sake of conscience, can no longer remain in their previous homes and positions and are partly in exile and partly on pilgrimage awaiting God's further command and providence in the region of M. where they are staying—have particularly led them to consider and deliberate over what the Lord God intends to do with such a great movement, in that it not only opens a door for the Europeans to America and the British islands, but also gives many Germans the courage in their hearts to go there. They are not afraid of the great danger and burdens that they will have to take on. And because the signs of these times certainly point to the fact that the Lord God is chastising Germany in particular, which has brought about the migration, and that the Trabitii, Cotteri, and other prophecies seem to be coming true, it has been reported that some families have come to think that the Lord God has opened a door for them, so that they can flee with their loved ones from the destruction and judgments of God. Some of them are gifted with children, which can be cheaply kept to do external work, so as not to give way to secret wickedness through idleness; however, there is little or nothing to do here, especially in the way of honest work, aside from cultivating fields and tending livestock. Because, for the sake of conscience, they have no permanent place to go, they are on the verge of being overcome, even apart from the apparent plagues and judgments of God. Therefore, they have been advised first of all to offer up their affairs to God's holy rule and direction, and then, making use of their reason and God-given insight in these external matters, to seek counsel from good friends. To which end the following points are put forward.

I. Whether it is advisable that people who, for the sake of conscience, can no longer submit to a specific denomination, and are therefore tolerated almost nowhere, and who, for these reasons, are inclined to make this journey, but have no real certainty of God's will, should do so. Are they free to act?

II. Is it more advisable to go to Pennsylvania or Carolina?

III. Whether there is a significant difference between the two destinations, and, if so, what is it?

IV. Whether there is full freedom of conscience in Carolina as well as in Pennsylvania to worship God in a non-sectarian way?

V. Whether the food in both destinations is expensive?

VI. Whether one can acquire a piece of land suitable for cultivation, along with other amenities, at a reasonable price from the proprietors in Carolina, since the foremost of them is supposed to be Lord Granville in England?[56]

VII. Likewise, whether one can still acquire land in Pennsylvania from the owner, William Penn, which is not too remote, and at a reasonable price, or at no cost?

---

56. John Carteret, 2nd Earl Granville, 7th Seigneur of Sark (1690–1763).

VIII. Since most of them are inclined to pay their own transportation costs, to preserve their freedoms and other rights completely, what more would be required?

IX. Because not only several families in this resolution but also other exiles are included in this consideration, but several of whom do not have the means to pay for transportation, could not a means be found that such be brought across by the property owners?

X. What is the cost now for transportation and board from England to America, and what is the price difference between men, women, and children? Also, how is the baggage transported?

XI. Whether there are iron factories already established in America, or are we required to bring our own weapons and the like?

XII. Whether it would contribute to a lowering of the costs if some of the money left over were put to carrying over some goods, and which would be best?

XIII. Whether stocking weavers would be allowed to bring their iron chairs with them? Or, whether on this or previous points the West Indies Company in England would make things difficult?

XIV. Whether, while waiting in England for the ships to depart, one can find employment in stocking knitting factories, carpentry, or some other work?

XV. At what time of the year does the fleet usually leave? And what time would you suggest to be the safest and most suitable?

XVI. Whether some, if they were to remain living quietly in England, would be tolerated in freedom of conscience?

XVII. Whether it is expensive to eat in England, or if having the necessary means of living comes at an affordable price?

No. 38

A. W. Böhme to Mr. J. U. and Mr. B.
London, 26 May 1710

Here follows answers to Mr. J. U.'s questions

Dear friend,

Around the middle of last month, I received your letter, together with the questions that you asked me to answer. However, I have not been able to answer until now, because I have had to inquire with friends here and there, and consult several books, in order to be able to answer with greater certainty the questions, most of which concern the present state of affairs in America. I will now, however, take the liberty of saving the first question for the end, and proceed directly to answering the other questions in order as follows:

(2) Is it more advisable to go to Pennsylvania or Carolina?

Answer: Because I see from our dear friend's letters that he and his friends are mainly concerned with the place where they are assured that they can serve the Lord in full freedom of conscience, the question could be asked, for the sake of clarity: *Whether it would be more advisable, in terms of religion or freedom of conscience, to go to Pennsylvania or Carolina?* And then the answer would be: that now in both Carolina and Pennsylvania every sect or religious party has full liberty to settle and worship according to their beliefs. See the answer to the fourth question. But if the question is aimed at the external conditions of the region, namely, whether one could live most cheaply in Pennsylvania or Carolina, then the following should be noted:

Carolina is divided into South and North Carolina. South Carolina is very hot, although the heat is tempered by cool winds blowing through it, and therefore it is not as easy to grow European grain as in North Carolina. But it is all the better situated for wine growing. Therefore, both white and red wine, according to an informed report, would grow there, if there were enough people to tend to the wine growing and to distill it at the right time and in the proper manner. In North Carolina, wheat, rye, oats, rice, buckwheat, and other similar grains grow. Rye is not widely planted; instead, the inhabitants sow Indian corn, which is what they call maize. It is said to be very nutritious and can be prepared in various ways for eating. Some Indians and negro slaves eat nothing but this crop, dressed with a little salt. In some places, where the soil is exceptionally good and fertile, it bears seven- to eight-hundred-fold; however, it does not like any sandy ground. The residents brew beer or other beverages from its stalks or stems, which are said to have a sweet and pleasant taste.

Apart from that, animal breeding is quite common, and almost every species of European cattle can be found there. The pork is supposed be particularly tasty, because the pigs are fattened with nuts and acorns. Although quite a few people have found that life's necessities are available in Pennsylvania quite cheaply as well, Carolina surpasses Pennsylvania in having more goods available, some of which can be shipped to America and others transported to Europe. These goods include silk, all kinds of fur, animal skins, rice, wheat, corn, turpentine, and various kinds of rubber and the like. For those, then, who would like to engage in trade either with foreigners or with other American regions, Carolina would be the first choice. On the other hand, it is noteworthy that more German colonists have settled in Pennsylvania than in other English domains in America, which might be important to those people who would like to hope for help and assistance from fellow compatriots when they first arrive. Several people offer this suggestion: Pennsylvania is most suitable for people from Lower Saxony, who understand agriculture, while Carolina is better for those from the Palatinate and elsewhere who know wine making, because the wine is better in Carolina than in Pennsylvania. Other than that, Pennsylvania lies in the 39th to 40th latitude, while Carolina lies in the 29th to 36th, which naturally results in different produce from each region. And this would also basically answer the third question about *the differences between the two regions.*

The Fourth Question

Whether there is full freedom of conscience in Carolina as well as in Pennsylvania...

Answer: Yes. In the Royal Privilege granted by Charles II to the property owners, the following is stated: All persons who wish to settle here may at all times freely and undisturbedly follow their own religious beliefs and conscience throughout the land; however, they must live peacefully and not abuse this freedom insolently or in any way that may cause offense or disruption.

The Fifth Question

Whether the food in both destinations...

Answer: In Carolina, a bushel of English wheat costs about 3 shillings, which is about 18 German groschen, but sometimes it costs as much 3 shillings 6 pence. In Pennsylvania, however, a bushel of English wheat comes to nearly 4 shillings. In Carolina, a bushel of corn is sold for 2 shillings. Fish, fowl, beef, and pork can be bought very cheaply in both regions.

The Sixth Question

Whether one of the property owners in Carolina...

Answer: In Carolina, you will pay £20 (about 100 Reichsthaler) for a thousand acres of land. But if parties should join together, and become one, to bargain for a large tract of land, or a certain tract, they can commonly obtain it from the proprietors for an even more reasonable price, and for £10 or £12 they can obtain as much as they could for £20. In addition to this, they annually pay an English shilling in rent for a large piece of land; in the county of Albemarle, however, only half a shilling is required. The most distinguished of the present proprietors are His Excellency William Lord Craven Palatine,[57] His Grace the Duke of Beaufort,[58] His Excellency John Carteret,[59] among others. Note: the rent is not paid until the land has been actually taken into possession and made fit for use.

In Pennsylvania, a hundred acres are generally sold for £6, £7, or £10, for land that is still relatively nearby and good and fertile. However, if the land is more remote, a hundred acres can be bought for £5–£6. Those who are naturalized in England before their departure (which can now be obtained for very nominal fees) enjoy all the rights and privileges that English citizens have. This also answers the seventh and eighth questions. As for Pennsylvania, one can deal here in London with Governor William Penn himself, or his deputy, and obtain from him thorough instruction on all the details of that province.

The Ninth Question

Because not only several families but also other exiles . . .

Answer: Nobody should have the slightest hope of a free passage. The proprietors say that they have enough people from England and their own countries to occupy their land if they were to bear the cost of transportation. Many foreigners who have come to England in the hope of going straight to America have fallen into great poverty and misery and had their hopes dashed. Indeed, the fact is that in the past year about fourteen thousand souls, some from the Palatinate and others from elsewhere, have come to England, hoping to be transported directly to Carolina. Since this throng of people cost the nation a great deal to maintain (some say seventy to eighty thousand pounds), many of the English have become very bristly, particularly among the common people and especially in these difficult and prolonged times of war. But most of those who arrived in England, in spite of the benefits received, have not only made themselves odious by grumbling, impatience, unpleasantness, laziness,

---

57. William Craven, 2nd Baron Craven (1668–1711).

58. Henry Somerset, 2nd Duke of Beaufort (1684–1714).

59. Second Earl Granville.

lust, and other outbursts of bad will, but also barred the way for others, who intend to make the journey for better reasons and to seek out special assistance, especially since the matter is still fresh in everyone's mind. This in no way casts blame on the few who were like salt among this rabble and bore witness to their righteous character, nor does it excuse those among the English who were too harsh on the miserable people and showed little Christian kindness.

Many of these people, wanting to escape judgment in their homeland, have now fallen into even more difficult ones, and have thus received the reward of their impatience. Many have perished miserably for lack of adequate care; some have gone with the East India fleet to the East Indies and have been scattered there; many young people were dragged into the war as soldiers; others were sent to Ireland, where they still find no rest. They complain about the mercilessness of the local citizens, who in turn complain about the laziness and inertia of the refugees. Some have run back to England, and survive by begging, but as a result fall into all those sins found with those who beg. Three thousand were sent to New York in the West Indies because the Royal Commissioners were able to hire ship captains at a lower rate; however, with such crowded conditions, the people had to lie in several ships so compactly that many, before they even left the English coast, were miserably plagued by stench and vermin. To say nothing of the fact that those quartered in the lowest floors of the ship could neither breathe fresh air nor enjoy any daylight for their respite. The small, tender children often died in these circumstances, or were swept away during major storms. Neither parents nor children are left remaining from many families; old and young have been wiped out. The last letters from Portsmouth, written in April, report that about eighty souls in one ship died, and that about a hundred are still sick, many of whom, if past experience holds true, will likely follow. The cause can be ascribed partly to the tight and compact quarters and partly to the mercilessness of the ship's masters, who do not provide them with good and healthy food, but rather profit from the death and demise of the people. From all of this it is important to see that the original fourteen thousand refugees have been torn apart and four thousand have succumbed to death. Of late, out of the principle of Universal Love, which warns one's neighbor of misfortune, I have earnestly been trying to make the point that no one who does not have the financial means should dare to embark on such a fretful journey, much less let it come down to a little luck and good fortune.

The Royal Commissioners have found themselves convinced of this very thing; therefore, already this past December they have had the following short declaration and warning printed and dispersed here in the German language, which I am enclosing as confirmation of what I have been saying. It reads:

> Last summer a large number of poor people from various parts of Germany arrived here in England; they were accommodated by Her Royal Majesty and then over time sent to the West Indies and to Ireland. But because more of these poor people have come here since then, we have sent news to Holland and elsewhere that such are longer being admitted, much less being maintained. Those, too, who have arrived here since the first of October are to be sent back to Germany via Holland at the first opportunity. As a result, we are informing all those who still intend to come here to abandon their journey, which will certainly be fruitless, unless they are able to support themselves. London, 31 December 1709.

But now I move on to . . .

The Tenth Question

What is the cost now for transportation and board from England to America . . .

Answer: Adult males and females going to these (not islands, but contiguous) regions pay the same price for board and transport. So, an adult traveling from England to Pennsylvania or Carolina (which is actually southern Virginia, a three-day journey over land from Carolina) pays £7. Sometimes you can find it for a few shillings cheaper, depending on what you agree to with the skipper. For children under six years of age, two are considered as one adult. There is no charge for infants. Baggage is free. But if you bring goods from Germany that you intend to sell, they must be shipped to the customs house in London, and the customs officers must inspect them to see if they are in good condition and to ensure that the owner pays the customs duty on them, which in England is usually very high.

The Eleventh Question

Whether there are iron factories already established in America . . .

Answer: There are iron factories here and there in America, but, due to a lack of able workers, they are not yet sufficiently developed to provide the land with enough iron equipment. Therefore, it is necessary that those traveling there from Europe bring those things with them. However, it is not advisable for any German to lug heavy equipment from Germany to England, partly because it is not worth the effort and expense to carry such heavy things so far, and partly because they can be bought in England at a reasonable price. But you can probably take some ploughshares and other agricultural equipment that are not too heavy or easily obtained in London.

The Twelfth Question

Whether it would contribute to a lowering of the costs . . .

Answer: The proprietors of these regions who reside in England usually advise travelers on which goods to take from England, and how most advantageously to use their money. But if people want to put money into German goods, they can bring along Osnabrück and other kinds of coarse linen, which is lacking there. But for these goods, as mentioned above, the usual customs in London must be paid.

The Thirteenth Question

Whether stocking weavers would be allowed to bring . . .

Answer: It is not worth the effort to engage in the stocking weaving trade in these regions, because stockings can be purchased very cheaply. Newcomers can spend their time much more advantageously growing rice and grain and other similar pursuits. Nevertheless, if someone in the stocking business wants to establish a factory or drag over weavers' chairs, it will not be forbidden by the West India Company.

The Fourteenth Question

Whether, while waiting in England for the ships to depart, one can find employment . . .

Answer: There is little or nothing to be earned by stocking knitting in England. Ever since the Huguenots fled from France, so many such factories have been set up in England that it would be better if their number were reduced rather than increased. There is a constant hatred and resentment between the English and French weavers, and it often breaks out into uncivil insolence and acts. Such things originate in the evil of self-interest, since everyone is only concerned with what belongs to them and not with what belongs to the other person. With regard to carpentry or other such work, nothing is certain: however, I know instances of German craftsmen, after becoming acquainted with the English and proving themselves trustworthy, being employed for such work.

The Fifteenth Question

At what time of the year does the fleet usually leave? . . .

Answer: It is generally thought that it is best for ships to depart in autumn, or, if that is not possible, to leave early in the year. This is because the months of July and August are considered to be the sickliest months in these regions, and when newcomers arrive, they generally come down with a fever. But this is prevented if one comes into the area some time before or after those months.

The Sixteenth Question

Whether some, if they were to remain living quietly in England . . .

Answer: Yes, they would. The current government tolerates all parties and denominations, including those that want to escape their denominations.

The Seventeenth Question

Whether it is expensive to live in England . . .

Answer: A distinction must be made between London and England. In some counties food is very affordable, especially in those that lie to the north and west. In London, everything is more expensive because of the number of people, and bread in particular has not in human memory been more expensive than in the previous year. This increase in the price of food continues even now, despite the efforts of the parliament to find a means of stopping it. A pound of mutton or beef now costs 4 half-shillings or 1 German groschen, 9 pfennigs; a bushel of the finest wheat flour is 16 shillings, and the cheap kind is 14 shillings.

And I trust this is sufficient to answer the questions about the condition of the region and travel there. As for the first question: "Whether it is advisable that people who, for the sake of conscience, can no longer submit to a specific denomination, and are therefore tolerated almost nowhere, and who, for these reasons, are inclined to make this journey, but have no real certainty of God's will, should do so. Are they free to act?" I hereby advise that they seek the answers to these questions in their own conscience. However, out of love, which wishes no ill toward any creature, I must remind them to ponder the costs, internal and external, that are required for such a long journey. The external costs I have noted are more difficult to estimate than is stated here, since many unexpected events occur on journeys, which require costs that cannot be foreseen, much less quantified. Above all, may they pay attention to the internal motive or inspiration of such an important journey, and may their eyes be resolute in the Spirit of Christ, that they may be preserved from the twisted ways of the snake.

Many have told me that they *seek tranquility* and want to go to the new world for that reason. I have reminded them of Johann Tauler's saying: "The sun that shines in Cologne also shines in Paris." Tranquillity must be born within. One's own housemates, self-will and obstinacy, are the greatest disturbers of peace. If these are not resisted and conquered in the power of Christ, there will be no more tranquility in America than in Europe. I have also had people who have a good opinion of Tauler read his conversation between the learned man and the poor beggar who was lying in front of the church door, in order to help them reflect internally and prevent them from running away prematurely. It is in the 66th chapter of *Medulla Animae*, the title of which is: "An exemplary form of a mature person, that we stand true, and learn to let ourselves be in all things as it pleases God."[60]

I can also report that many of those who were seeking tranquility in America got into such physical and mental turmoil that some, after much winnowing, were finally convinced that it was not the right way to achieve an earnest and God-pleasing tranquility. Others, however, have let themselves be entangled in the crude, wretched love of the world in the very place where they intended to escape the temptations of the world completely and find the pearl of the kingdom of God. I regard such vivid examples as warnings that no one should allow himself to limit the Lord, whose Spirit fills the world's travails, to place and time. *Every new way of life has its new temptations.* And this is something that people do not always see in advance. They tend to awaken inwardly only after the person has achieved that outwardly, in which lust and desire were invested. Some people, after acquiring their own fields in America, have laid aside the staff of their inward spiritual pilgrimage and have planted themselves in their fields as property lords. Eventually, they lapse to such an extent that they are more concerned with cultivating their fields than their souls, since the honest work of cultivating fields and tending livestock has become a snare to them. They stand before our eyes as so many sad memorials, *so that we may not let ourselves lust.*

---

60. Johann Tauler (1300–1361), "Cap. LXVI. Ein Exemplarische Form eines vollkommenen Menschen, daß wir gleich stehen, und uns in allen Dingen, als es Gott beliebt, lassen lernen," in *Medulla Animae*, 584–88.

Others have said to me that *they see the judgments of God beginning to befall Germany, and that they would therefore deem it advisable to seek an ark, a Zoar, or a Pellam for their protection when the time comes.* But I have asked them to consider whether or not they have contributed to the kindling of these judgments through unbelief, love of the world, contempt for God, abuse of His creatures, and other sins. If this is the case, then it is reasonable that they also bear their share of the judgments, or at least wait until the Lord *bids them enter the ark and closes the door behind them.* Those who allow themselves to be swept along by the spirit of doubt and deceit can easily fall into all kinds of unfamiliar temptations and succumb to them. But if through the judgments they endure all kinds of opposition and persecution from the authorities, who have been agitated by their zealots and orthodox church leaders, it is clear that the Lord will bestow glorious blessings on those who suffer for the sake of the truth. But people lose this blessing when they walk in darkness and flee from persecution before it is time, before their witness against the overall corruption is perfected, and they themselves are purified and made useful for further service to the master of the house.

The blind zeal of the clergy has until now been deficient, yet the authorities have allowed themselves to be taken in by it to such an extent that the corruption of the upper classes has become so visible that no whitewash will any longer be able to cover over what is everywhere apparent. The so-called spiritual orders see that souls who have tasted something of the power and freedom of the gospel no longer want to be pacified with systematic formulas and circulars, but are eager for something nobler and more substantial; and where they do not find such things, they eventually go to extremes and separate and isolate themselves from the entire external structure of the Church. Many reckless zealots have now come to the point of thinking that their office, authority, and teaching are being insulted and disregarded; and in order to keep their reputation and respect, they incite the authorities and get them to use their power to expel and banish those whom the clergy have declared to be unruly leaders and disturbers of the peace.

But if the rulers here would just open their eyes and investigate objectively the cause of the disruptions that have so far occurred in Germany, they would soon realize that they themselves and their clergy had caused most of the disorder. If the authorities, who now take care of filling offices and posts, were to set apart trustworthy teachers for this purpose, or, in the absence of such, were to make them capable of carrying out the office by means of appropriate preparations, others would have less cause to distance themselves from them. But as long as it is apparent that the authorities are not really concerned that their subjects are shepherded with sound doctrine and divine discipline, but only that this and that self-made hireling, who has been put forward as a court favorite, receives plenty of food for the belly, then it is no wonder that others, who seek to save their immortal souls, but find no pasture for it, look around for something else, and often, before they have adequately received the spirit of moderation, allow themselves to be seduced into all sorts of extremes, and finally separate and isolate themselves completely from all church fellowship.

And this careless and immature conduct by the two responsible classes must now also be regarded as one of the reasons why there has been such an enormous migration of so many Germans in these years, and it isn't over yet. Many people in authority, regardless of the fact that they stand under the judgment of God as much as others, live in such splendor and extravagance that their subjects are forced to give everything they can scrape together to support the state, and therefore often have no bread in their homes. Now, if the authorities rob people of their bread and the preachers appointed by them rob their souls, one should not be surprised that such disruptions occur; for if the head is so dangerously ill, the whole body, together with its members, is carried away into severe convulsions. For while everything is supposed to be maintained by the upper classes and held together in proper order through every joint and marrow, the members ultimately tear themselves away from their head, and would rather withdraw to the farthest corners of the earth, risking life and limb, and consume their bit (as they like to say) in silence and peace, than to let the yoke of the authorities and the hatred of their priests, who restrict their consciences, bear down on them any longer.

Mind you, even if these people (or most of them) run away from the school of the Lord God, and try to escape judgment before its appointed time, their arguments, which they have certainly learned from painful experience, are so powerful to them that very few can be convinced of a better solution by other ideas. Thus, this ignorance of most people around the most necessary aspects of Christianity is so large that almost no foundation can be found on which to build a good admonition. Very few of the people mentioned above, after arriving in England, had with them with a prayer book, or any edifying book, by which they could have lifted their spirits in the face of the grief and misery that was to follow;

even less often was the New Testament or the Bible to be found among them. They would also probably have remained without such valuable provisions, if Her Majesty of Great Britain had not been persuaded, out of the goodness of her heart, to donate money graciously for the acquisition of good German books, and thereby to help promote not just the physical but also the spiritual salvation of this people.

These disturbances have multiplied in Christianity to such an extent that those who preside over Church and police affairs have to admit that the means of assistance that were applied before in order to alleviate the disorders that had arisen are now completely inadequate. Indeed, many theologians see that their systematic distinctions, decisions, and responses are no longer sufficient to tip the scales dictatorially in one fell swoop on the controversies that have previously been put on the table. In the same way, many of the brightest statesmen and politicians must admit that they are now bogged down with their previous political maxims, no matter how polished and artificial they may be, and that they often, when it comes to applying them, only make more obstacles for themselves and the whole business worse.

It is just here that leaders in both offices should give glory to the Lord, and say, "This is what God has done, the one who slays the wisdom of the wise, and shames the mighty, that no flesh may boast before Him." Then the princes would begin to dig for the root of corruption and all evil, and the sins of injustice, tyranny, and oppression of the destitute, and thereby to lay aside their stinginess, wrath, finery, and pride. And the teachers in churches and schools would have to deny their untheological quarrelsomeness, hatred, envy, greed for honor and money, compulsion of conscience, lust for power, heresy, and other Pharisaic vices, so that these disruptions would be prevented over time.

But to return to the original question, I confess that I cannot yet see how Christians, because of the past oppressions or the bondage of the rod, as our beloved friend addresses in his letter, should leave their homeland and flee to another world without a sufficient knowledge of God's will. So . . .

(1) It does not behoove Christians to flee from judgment—especially since it is only beginning to gather and has therefore not yet broken through to its full severity—which they have provoked as much as others. Rather, they should submit to them, and let themselves be cleansed from the root cause of the judgments, namely, sin and unbelief.

(2) If God grants them grace in the midst of these corrupt times, they should bear witness to the grace they have received by their words and deeds in that very place. The apostle commands us not to run away from the perverse and wicked, but *to be blameless and innocent, children of God without blemish in the midst of a crooked and perverse generation, in which you shine like stars in the world* (Phil 2:15), which, according to the apostle, must be possible even in the midst of such corrupt company. Those who withdraw from the base and unconverted crowd also deprive that crowd of the needed edification that it could receive from the converted. A Christian should be a salt, who through his righteous walk prevents everything from falling into stench and decay; through which otherwise the judgments of God would be kindled to break through completely. But they can better accomplish this aim in their own country than in a country so far away, where they are inexperienced in the language and the whole lifestyle of the people, and so encounter numerous obstacles to this purpose.

It is indeed proper that Christians, in the same place where they have borne rotten fruit or thorns and thistles, should now also bear the good and ripe fruits of the Spirit. Where before they had been a thorn bush, they must now blossom like a rose or a lily, and give off a pleasing aroma for the edification of others, testifying to the power and sweetness of the gospel. Where they had left behind traces of vanity, they must now leave traces of virtue and truth, and take upon themselves, with humility and patience, any ridicule the world may inflict on them. In this way, they would glorify the power of God and attest to the possibility of true Christianity.

(3) I cannot understand what is being reported on any action toward freedom. *Christians have surrendered themselves and their entire will and deeds to their Lord and master. He has bound the human will to His yoke, from which all those who want to remain faithful to the Lord must not break loose again. And from this surrender of the will to God, a sweet and lasting rest is born; for the human will is then in the hand of God—the instrument in the hand of the master—who guides it, so that it never moves on its own, but only by a power outside it.* Herein lies the true rest of souls; but it is lost when one seeks to find rest out of one's own self-chosen freedom. This true rest can be sustained even in the most severe persecutions, as the examples of the first Christians often demonstrate. For the Lord indeed knows how to care for His children and protect them in the midst of the outpouring of judgment. For while those who do not

belong to God are slain in Jerusalem, those who lament and wail over every abomination will be marked with a sign and saved from the slayer. Let everyone see that they live among the wicked like Lot did in Sodom, conducting themselves as ambassadors of the Lord in their appointed place; they must not flee from judgment, for the Lord will lead His children, and they must be led only into suffering obedience.

Finally, quite a few people have told me that *the spirit of sectarianism is so dominant in Germany that people are almost never tolerated if they do not accept all the forms and ceremonies of the denomination in which they were raised.* Now, a few words on this report...

Certainly, the love of denominations, like other lowly, earthly attachments, must die, so that Christ alone may become all and solely in all. It does not follow, however, that those who discard this or that form or ceremony, or even leave the external forms of Lutheranism and Calvinism, are not sectarians. Just as it does not follow that, in the present dispensation, all those who remain in their denomination or in this or that form are sectarians. It has been sufficiently demonstrated in these last years that many leave *Babel* and rebuild *Babylon*. Many leave their former mother church, but build a daughter church not far from it, which, since it is a mere fabrication, full of many fresh religious inventions, opinions, and statutes, is all the more pleasing and appealing to one's corrupt reason, which is always lusting after something new. Consider, however, whether the religious practices that touch the inner spheres or powers of the heart are not to a certain extent more dangerous than the common traditions handed down to us by our ancestors? For since these have been derived from deeper and more spiritual speculations, and have been tossed from one model into another by the imagination, *spiritual counterfeits* arise, in which self-love, the root of all sectarianism, is so mirrored and established that the soul captured by it cannot be convinced of its illusory and deceptive nature by any other means than submitting greatly to the cross and to discipline. Indeed, experience shows that spiritual idolatry, in which people engage with their own selves and offerings, is often more dangerous than that to which they are tempted by the ingrained habits of their creaturely nature.

Now, getting back to Pennsylvania: those who are seeking a non-sectarian Christianity would do well to consider whether it would be easier to find non-sectarian Christianity in a place where there are many sects than in a place where there are few. For this much is certain: there are more sects in Pennsylvania than in Germany. All sects have a free pass there; all those who have previously been wounded and chased away by national religions in France, Switzerland, Germany, etc. have gone there. Therefore, it is easy to imagine the plethora and hodgepodge of sects, parties, opinions, and other religious movements that are to be found there, the number of which, by all accounts, is more likely to increase than to decrease. At this point, people must be assured that they are prepared for all such sectarian provocations and that they will not be lured out of their strongholds by one or the other. For although papist coercion of conscience is not tolerated there in the least, there are still many other more secret and subtle ways of contaminating the soul with a sectarian spirit, and eventually even taking it captive, if it does not keep its guard up. I know several examples of people who have traveled the sect circuit from beginning to end, because they were trying to flee from heavy-handed sectarianism. And these were not unsophisticated people driven by self-interest or other worldly motives, but people with good desires, yet who did not yet realize that *Christianity was not a sect*.

But should they intend to settle down in the quiet of a particular place and not have much contact with other parties, thereby avoiding the danger of sectarianism, they would do well to ponder how easily they could fragment and spin out infinite forms of religion from among them, unless they have a leader who is gifted with such a measure of the Spirit, that he knows how to keep souls united in Christian discipline and order, not by papist or sectarian domination, but through the power of gentle love and divine moderation, and how to respond with humility to all sectarian divisiveness (such as that which flows from a corrupted self-love). What is written about Samuel (1 Sam 19:20) is critical: *Samuel was the overseer of the prophets*, that is, he was appointed over them to keep them in proper order and discipline, and to prevent the influences of our fleshly nature, which like to interfere with God's work. This is a useful reminder at a time when so many people are quickly rising up, and hardly interested in hearing the advice of the old guard, although there may still be few righteous and skilled *overseers* to be found.

In general, in my opinion, non-sectarian Christianity stands in the *love of God and neighbor*. The former is the foundation of the latter. The more universal the latter becomes, the more non-sectarian it will become. A sect narrows the heart, but a non-sectarian love expands and broadens it, and offers itself for the enjoyment of all without partiality. And such enlarged souls are still to be found here and there, even in Germany. And who would doubt that there are not also, as already mentioned, several among them who are still outwardly in a denomination; they look beyond the denomination, but remain in it, in order, by the grace of God, to do their part for the good of the denomination and to urge those souls whom the Lord has preserved in it as His own to build Zion.

And these, beloved friend, are my thoughts about his questions. If he finds in them the slightest guidance to satisfy his mind, let him thank the Lord for it. Moreover, I well know how difficult it is in these times to give an adequate answer to the kind of scruples that spiritual pilgrims can sometimes encounter both inwardly and outwardly on their pilgrimage. May the Lord make us faithful from the heart in what He has given us and teach us to do the will that we know, so that the will that is still unknown will also be revealed to us when it will be useful to us. I remain . . .

No. 39[61]

A. W. Böhme to Professor August Hermann Francke in Halle
London, 20 June 1710

Now divine providence has once again generously provided me the opportunity to deliver a third contribution for the English Table. It comes to 51 Reichsthaler, 16 German groschen, which Andreas Kock will pay out as soon as the circumstances of the Table require it.

Just this week an anonymous pamphlet in French has come out here with the title: *Sentimens désintéressez de divers théologiens Protestans; sur les agitations, et sur les autres particularitez de l'état des Prophetes* [*Impartial Sentiments of various Protestant Theologians on the Agitations and other Particularities of the State of the Prophets*].[62] The pamphlet seems to have been edited to protect the so-called *Prophets* and their extraordinary movements, if we can call them that. In it the author wants to prove, among other things, that God has always awakened extraordinary prophets, if the ordinary ones fail in their duty or allow all kinds of errors to creep in. To the latter he attributes the main cause of all errors in teaching and life, and quotes with great respect your name and the sermon in which you said that *most pulpits in every denomination are*

---

61. AFSt/H C 229:62.
62. *Sentimens désintéressez.*

filled with false prophets. He had taken this quote from the short account of Pietism, which was appended to the first abstract of *Pietas Hallensis*.

Some time ago, a number of well-meaning persons established projects for lending money to the poor in return for a pledge, which would both help the poor and control the usurers who ruthlessly exploit the poor when they are in need. These projects were presented to the Queen, who approved them. It can favorably be compared to the so-called *Monte di Pietà* [*Mount of Piety*] in Italy; the author is said to be Bishop Pietro Barozzi of Padua, who in 1490, in order to put a stop to the profiteering of usurers, organized such a work.[63] The aim here was to imitate such a good provision for the poor. Such works of love are called *Lombardica Officia* [The Lombardy Services], because the Italian institution for the poor subsequently spread further into Lombardy, and has there especially been brought to fruition. So far, however, it has not been able to come up with a proper constitution here. There are two parties. One calls its institution The Charitable Fund; the other, The Charitable Corporation. Those who belong to the former project make suggestions on how, for a given pledge, money can be advanced to the poor without interest. The latter, however, do not consider this feasible, and therefore want to take a moderate profit. Both parties have recently clashed in writings, with one accusing the other of self-interest and other unseemly things. One party refers to the institutions at Halle; the other responds that *Pietas Hallensis* reveals an extraordinary providence of God, which one can admire but not so easily imitate—"as to the Instance of *Pietas Hallensis*, it looks so like an extraordinary Providence of God, as seems rather to be admired, than like to be imitated"—as if God was not as powerful in England as in Germany. Although the people were intent on serving others in love, their unity crumbled and they spent their time on projects that could have been used to provide real help to their poor neighbor.[64]

---

63. The actual role of Pietro Barozzi (1441–1507) in the *Monte di Pietà* is unclear. The Franciscans were the primary initiators of these charitable institutions.

64. See *Rules and Orders for a Charitable Society*.

No. 40

A. W. Böhme to Mr. B. C. S. from P.
London, 23 June 1710

The circumstances of our chapel have already been made known to your Excellency. So far God has not withheld blessing from our work in it; for, especially among young people who have happened to come, a revival has taken place, and here and there some have been saved from the widespread ruin. It is worth noting the evening prayer meeting, which we began while the Prince was still alive, and in which we speak more freely and simply about the ways of God; although few of our own people attend, they are frequently visited by outsiders who benefit from them. It has served to convince many, and has even brought a few of them to a genuine improvement of their lives.

I wanted to mention this briefly, your Excellency, in order to assure you that your visit to the Queen on behalf of the chapel was not without every blessing. And now, because divine providence is apparently directing the heart of our Queen to continue this benefit, I am so glad to hear that your Excellency, out of Christian concern, has recommended a capable subject for the position created by Mr. Tribbeko's departure.

I have then taken the liberty, on such occasions, to ask Your Excellency most respectfully to examine the matter in such a way that, through the right choice, the little good that has been fostered here so far may be furthered.

It is not my intention to go into particulars, or even to propose anyone; rather, with your approval, I am leaving that to Your Excellency's provision. But I have no qualms over suggesting that generally speaking a person is needed, who is suited to this place and these circumstances. Someone whose head is only filled with a sterile, academic knowledge of the articles of faith, as they are ordinarily meted out at universities, and who has learned to drum their orthodoxy, will not get far here. We ourselves would get into quarrels and make life difficult for each other; even more so, such irritations would hinder and crush any edification in others, to whom we should shine in love and humility.

I am well aware that contemporary theology, as it is taught at most universities, has become a skeleton of what it was; therefore, I willingly admit that it would be difficult, if not impossible, for me to be harnessed to that present system. My way is to awaken people's consciences through the Word, so that they find and feel inwardly what they hear outwardly, and thus become convinced of the truth of the matter. If people have other ideas, I willingly leave them to them, only that they grant me the same freedom. I have wanted to present the above to Your Excellency impartially, because I have seen so many distressing examples of contentious preachers and the offenses they give to others. If Your Excellency shies away from proposing someone who has the hated name of a Pietist, I can appreciate your caution; however, if he simply preaches a living Christianity with earnestness, he will not last three months without being branded with that name. There are examples of people who would never associate with those to whom this name was initially attached and who have studied at an Orthodox academy for six years. But in this matter, too, one can discern certain strategies of Satan, through which he seeks to make not only people but the truth itself suspect, even though it finally breaks through, and by its light puts to shame all unfounded objections.

May the Lord give Your Excellency the necessary wisdom also for the matter at hand! . . . As I, by the grace of God, will furthermore strive in this matter to promote not my own self-interest but the edification of souls for the kingdom of God, so I hope that Your Excellency, after the faithfulness that you have previously shown in promoting the good, will also continue to offer your hand in this matter.

No. 41

A. W. Böhme to George Keith[65]
London, 14 July 1710

Yours is a name that has been known to me for a long time, especially through translations of some English tracts, and it was brought back to mind when I received your letter. However, let me go straight to the content of the letter itself, if I trust myself well enough to give a report from an experience quite a while ago—toward the end of 1701, when I had just been driven from my homeland by the local clergy. Until now England has given food and sustenance to many people, including

---

65. Almost certainly George Keith (ca. 1638–1716). He was a Quaker from Scotland who converted to Anglicanism, a translator, friend of Henry More, and an admirer of particular mystics. In 1702 he was sent to America as an Anglican missionary by the SPG. Böhme would have known of him through the SPCK.

those whose ministries are despised in other places and who are expelled, because under current state policy, whether good or bad, everything here has complete freedom.

As for how to obtain a means of living, according to my experience and that of others, I can say that in the beginning it was somewhat difficult to get by; so, you should be satisfied to start with very little until you find yourself with broader opportunity. When I was sent here by the Lord's providence, my purpose was to establish a school among the Germans, which a few of them had requested. I started out with four or five children, and that number would probably have increased if some Lutheran pastors hadn't made my work suspect among the people, thereby hindering further progress. Meanwhile I had grasped enough of the language to be able to communicate with English people and to teach their children; so, I looked for a few children to teach in my home, but also kept the German school as long as I could. I also started translating into English Professor Franke's *account of the orphanage in Halle*, which I published in 1705. The publisher paid me £1 (five Taler) for each printed sheet—after an Englishman corrected the translation—which was a considerable relief for me at the time considering my very limited circumstances.

My purpose in telling you this, beloved friend, is so you can see that out of it, indeed out of all such things, that although the work might be quite trying, you can expect some assistance under the blessing of God. But this applies only to those books which, according to all accounts, will find admirers and be sold. With a position in the countryside, something might happen sooner. However, I would not advise anyone to do so, whom I hope, on the basis of universal love, has a nobler purpose in mind than the false *self* or superficial amusement. London is the heart of England, and both good and evil pour out from here through the whole country. So, I too am convinced that God has planted a rich seed in London; but there is still a lack of rain and sunshine to bring it to a true breakthrough and healthy maturity. If Christ's fire were lit only in London, it would soon begin to burn across the country as well. To say nothing of the fact that in the winter most of the prominent people from all walks of life congregate in London; as a result, those who have the gift of conversation find a very good opportunity to exercise it. So, now there are many Societies for the Reformation of Manners in and around London, which, by means of an ongoing correspondence, seek to spread the good that has arisen here throughout the country.

Whatever you, dear friend, are thinking of when you hear English provinces, I mean those regions in America that are subject to England. For a long time, we have sought to send a preacher among the Christians in America, one who would promote the pure and righteous character that is in Christ; but, though many have desired it, it still remains unfulfilled. We have not found anyone who would venture out; thus, it is also reasonable to have misgivings about persuading anyone to do so. Our poor Germans, since there are no teachers among them to keep them rooted in Christ with divine discipline and wisdom, run from one denomination to another, and at last find themselves on all sorts of desolate and wild paths. After the death of my Prince, I have several times had an inkling to go to the Germans in America and serve them with my few gifts. But since our Queen promised to grant us ongoing use of the chapel, and has just this week renewed her promise, it seems good to keep open the door which the Lord has granted us in England, indeed right in the middle of the court—which some regard as a particular providence—especially since the number of Germans here is more likely to increase than decrease.

And this is my response to your letter, dear friend. For things to change something will have to be risked. If we could expedite certain proposals for suitable conditions here, we would have a lot of German students; however, with those who want things to be certain, it generally goes worst.

No. 42[66]

A. W. Böhme to Professor August Hermann Francke in Halle
London, 18 July 1710

I duly received both the package of letters and the individual messages that brought news of the progress of the missionaries in Malabar. I have told Mr. Ludolf, who is in the country, about the complete copy of the New Testament in modern Greek. He takes great pleasure in this development, and as soon as he returns to London, he will send the names of some Greeks with whom he became acquainted on his travels in the East, so that, through their service, the books may be disseminated and

66. AFSt/H C 229:59.

bring blessing among the people. Some time ago he told me that the best way to spread the Word of God there would be to establish a seminary or college in Jerusalem, made up of young, clever people; but it would require a substantial investment.

John Chamberlayne[67] hoped that Mr. Plütschau[?] would consider giving him a copy of the modern Greek New Testament (it would have to be bound, though, because unbound books are rarely given away here). If one were to use the occasion to include a brief note about the Portuguese New Testament, for which there still seems to be some hope here, it would give the matter all the more emphasis. It is actually being printed in Amsterdam, and we expect only a sample of the print. We couldn't find anyone in London who had a sufficient mastery of the Portuguese language to be able to undertake such a work. However, if the printing can be organized in Amsterdam, then, as is customary here, the whole project will be publicized and presented to this world's rich and famous, since I have no doubt that the costs associated with it will not be raised easily. In time we will translate and distribute the parts of the reports from Malabar that people here will find useful.

With my next letter I want to write to Mr. Elers[68] about the 106 Reichsthalers collected for spiritual books for the American Christians, and specify those books I consider useful for that purpose. I want to purchase the sought-after English books. Thomas Goodwin's works are beginning to become quite rare and expensive.[69] They are printed together in different volumes, and the price will run up to 16 Reichsthalers.

---

67. John Chamberlayne (ca. 1668–1723), English author, translator, and courtier, was the first secretary of the SPG and an active member in the SPCK and other benevolent works.

68. Heinrich Julius Elers (1667–1728) was a close colleague of Francke who established the bookshop in Halle and worked with J. C. Jacobi to open a German bookshop in London.

69. Thomas Goodwin (1600–1680), English Puritan theologian, preacher, and chaplain to Oliver Cromwell. His sermons and works were collected and published together as *Works of Thomas Goodwin*. These volumes have been republished frequently.

No. 43

A. W. Böhme to Seigneur de Ners in New Windsor[70]
London, 14 August 1710

I beg your forgiveness for not answering your kind letter sooner. I am not able to guarantee reliable provisions for the young person in question. There are various French and German requests sent here, some of which are addressed to me, seeking such services and anticipating some assistance from me, but there are few whom I can serve as I would wish. The state of our affairs has changed a lot after our blessed Prince's death. Regarding this young person's change of religion, I can assure you, my lord, that I have conversed here with many proselytes from France, Italy, Germany, etc., but with almost no success in bringing them to a genuine fear of God. Many of them are satisfied with a professed formality, without the foundation of a true conversion that would bring them out of darkness into the light. I do not say this, my Lord, to withhold the practice of love, or to focus only on Protestantism, as I am fully convinced that the Christian religion is of a far greater reach and should not be confined within a single denomination. I only want to show you the difficulty of providing these people with satisfactory support. If he wants to come to London, I will do as much as I can, but I do not know whether I will succeed in my efforts. I commend you to the grace of God, and remain sincerely...

P.S.

If you know of some poor Palatines who need Bibles, I will provide you with as many as you want, as well as a few copies of *True Christianity*, which some friends have provided for their edification. Now I am busy translating the letters recently sent from the Danish missionaries in East India. As soon as I am finished, I will forward copies to you. Goodbye.

---

70. Peter Anthony Delon Seigneur de Ners of New Windsor, Berkshire, was a French Huguenot from Bas Languedoc. On 5 July 1713 he married Rachel Casamajor of Xavarreins in the Hungerford French Church, London. In his will, Seigneur de Ners left £5 each to the SPCK, the Tranquebar mission in East India, the Protestant mission at Fort St. George, the Protestant mission at Fort St. David, the charity schools, the Halle orphanage, and the orphanage of the Salzburgers in Georgia of the American colonies. See Ners, "Will of Seigneur de Ners."

No. 44[71]

A. W. Böhme to Carl Hildebrand von Canstein at B.
London, 29 August 1710

    I read with pleasure the recently submitted project concerning an inexpensive printing of the Bible, but it is not practicable in England. The University of Oxford, together with the royal printer, has certain privileges from the authorities; thus, the printing of Bibles and New Testaments have been conferred specifically on them. These then turn and lease out such benefits to other booksellers at a profit; and I doubt there are any in the whole realm who would dare to publish a Bible or New Testament, except these two parties, who run a monopoly on Bibles. That is why it is said that more effort is put into publishing almost every other book than the Bible, because publishers are afraid of reprinting them without being allowed to do so by the privileged parties. Now if I suggest to such people the idea of an inexpensive printing, they turn everything into self-interest, whereby little or nothing will come to the poor masses. I have long been willing to produce a New Testament with its parallels and other suitable additions, but because of these circumstances, I cannot dare to do so, especially since the University of Oxford, out of a misplaced love for everything old and other worldly intentions, is now trying to thwart everything new, no matter how good it may be. These fortresses must first fall, and the Lord must clear the way so that more freedom can be gained to do his work.

    The works of Thomas Goodwin, which you requested last year when I was leaving, were put on the Hamburg fleet eight days ago and sent to Halle along with other things. They are hard to come by, so they are getting expensive. There are 5 volumes which cost £3 or about 15 Reichsthaler, 12 Groschen. (The pound is calculated at 5 Reichsthaler, 4 Groschen). The money can be drawn from the discretionary account of the English Table at Halle. An abstract of the letters from the missionaries in East India is at the printer's here. It would be good, if over time a variety of capable subjects would be selected for the time when we could use a missionary. The opinion here is that those students, when it comes to their outside studies, should apply themselves not only to languages, but also to medicine and mathematics, together with the sciences that flow from them, since that is what the Catholic missionaries have often

---

71. AFSt/H C 229:58.

done on entering East India, although they have not used it for the right purpose. At the very least, it would be useful if a few young people, set aside for missionary work, then applied themselves to mathematics and medicine without stopping at the initial training.

An elderly nobleman here told me that, after his return from East India, he had spoken to the Frenchman François Bernier in Paris, who told him that he had been taken into the service of the Great Mogul to offer his knowledge of medicine and mathematics, and in this way learned many things that remained hidden from ordinary travelers. Just as his description of Hindustan [India], in which he himself mentions this matter—*The history of the late revolution of the empire of the Great Mogol*—is considered one of the most accurate.[72] The progress the Catholics have made with the help of these sciences, particularly in China, is apparent; although now most honest Catholics themselves complain that in these latter years the Jesuits, because of all sorts of national edicts, have introduced an errant religious ideology, consisting partly of pagan and partly of papal practices, and have mixed Confucian philosophy with Christianity.

If, in addition, a small library of geography books and various travel descriptions was collected at Halle, it would also be useful for understanding foreign lands.

Now that the modern Greek New Testament has been issued again, I hope that it can be proliferated broadly. Heinrich Ludolf thinks that the easiest way is to set up a college in Jerusalem with several bright people, in order to emulate the Catholics who established themselves there many years ago. Turkish protection could be easily obtained by the advocacy of the English or Dutch ambassador; but those who wanted to dedicate themselves to the project would at times have to use modern Greek, Arabic, and Turkish, so that with the help of these, they can aim to accomplish something worthwhile. Now that the Arab Solomon Negri is going back to Halle, there should be a suitable opportunity to learn these languages and pave the way for promoting many good things in the Middle East.[73]

While I am offering counsel about remote lands, I must turn from the East Indies to the West Indies and also report about the needs there.

---

72. François Bernier (1620–1688), *Histoire de la derniere revolution.*

73. Solomon Negri (d. 1729), a native of Damascus who spent time in Halle, London, and elsewhere, played a significant role in the SPCK's decision to print an Arabic Psalter and New Testament. For more on Negri, see Letter 116.

It is well-known that at the beginning of this year, three thousand emigrants, partly from the Palatinate and partly other Germans who had joined them, were transported to New York in the West Indies. The lamentable condition of these people often comes to mind. Their number is great, and yet there is not one among these poor people who can serve them with sound discipline and wisdom. The common result, therefore, is that, in a desolate land, they either run completely wild, or, if given the opportunity, run from one sect to another; and, since they find no peace, come in the end to consider all of Christianity a mere fantasy. It was up to the Royal Commission, which was in charge of the Palatine affair, to propose whether a German preacher should be appointed for these people; but, since no one was available right away, the matter has again been completely forgotten and is likely to remain so, now that the Commission will soon be dissolved. To be sure, when it comes to external subsistence, no aid can be expected from here, unless that preacher would be ordained in the Episcopal Church. Whoever is motivated to do such things out of love for the salvation of one's neighbor should experience no harm inwardly, but an advantage outwardly. Should your Highness come across a candidate—if you have a few in mind, it would undoubtedly have an even greater blessing—please remember this work of love. In this way one could investigate the situation in the West Indies more thoroughly, and see where the *land is open*, and how both pagans and Christians can best be helped. Here in England, it is those who have worn themselves out in service and now have no hope of being promoted who tend to sail there; one can easily imagine what one can expect from such hirelings.

Outreach Through the SPCK and Beyond (1710–1714)

Letters 45–103

No. 45

A. W. Böhme to John Chamberlayne
London, 31 August 1710

    I respectfully take the liberty of asking you to distribute some of the letters from Malabar among members of the Society, and at the same time to recommend to them the subject matter of the letters as a means of spreading Christianity in the East Indies. Good counsel is as necessary to these missionaries as external aid; and since the Society attests that the establishment of charity schools in various places in the country is now one of its highest goals, it is important to keep in mind that the more this work coincides with the main purpose with which our Society has been engaged for many years, the more the members of the Society must have acquired significant experience in such a vital work, and thus be all the more capable of supporting such an endeavor with good and beneficial counsel. My Lord, I leave it to your good judgment whether it would be wise to bring before the Society whether our missionaries, for the sake of this enterprise, could be accepted as corresponding members. So, I commend you and your efforts to the gracious assistance of God, and remain . . .

P.S.

I hope you will not forget the matter of the Portuguese New Testament; if it could be carried out before the departure of the English fleet to the East Indies, it would no doubt be a most delightful gift for the missionaries there.

No. 46

A. W. Böhme to Seigneur de Ners in New Windsor
London, 4 September 1710

I have received your letter of August 27th. Heinrich Ludolf, who intends to visit his friends in Windsor, will deliver it, together with two copies of the letters translated into English relating to the East India Mission. One is for you, and the other is for you to give those souls to read who have a passion for whatever concerns the spreading of the kingdom of God. Here we are occupied with collecting the costs of printing the Portuguese Testament for the benefit of the people in the East Indies, because Portuguese is known throughout the whole of the East Indies, and is therefore quite advantageous for furthering the Reformation among the pagans. I hope that over time it will fulfill that purpose. As for the young Catholic you mentioned, I advise him not to leave the small ministration he has with you, because at this time it is very difficult to find another one. A devout lifestyle is the surest way to make a lasting religious impact on someone who from youth has been opposed to the truth. The heart of religion consists in the love of God, which is also the eye that purifies the mind from all that is accursed and sinister, and gradually cleanses the will of everything that is worldly and contemptible. You do well, my lord, in assisting the poor Palatines with your good counsel for the sake of their souls. You share in the blessings that accompany works of love. I leave you to the love of God, and remain . . .

OUTREACH THROUGH THE SPCK AND BEYOND (1710–1714)

No. 47[1]

A. W. Böhme to Professor August Hermann Francke in Halle
London, 19 September 1710

A few days ago, abstracts of the letters from the missionaries in the East Indies were published in English. I promptly distributed a few copies among members of our Society, and in an enclosed letter I kindly asked them to give careful consideration to the fact that the whole work has *a close connection and kinship with the projects in which the Society has been engaged. Not only do the missionaries need outside financial assistance, but also good advice and encouragement, so that they are able to continue their work of reformation among the Malabarians with even greater joy. And since the establishment of suitable charity schools is one of its most recognized undertakings, the Society has now collected a wealth of experience and wisdom through many years of practice. Therefore, it would be extremely beneficial to the primary purpose of this mission if the Society was willing to assist them with good and sound advice.* Let me also mention the Portuguese New Testament, the publication of which would be a major contribution to the introduction of Christianity, in both the English and Danish plantations, and in the whole of the Orient. The matter was then presented twice to the Society, and finally a few days ago the secretary of the Society sent me the following resolution, which was reached and recorded in the minutes:

On 7 September 1710:

1. Decided to admit Mr. Ziegenbalg and Mr. Plütschau, the two Danish missionaries to Tranquebar, as corresponding members of this Society, and to order one of the Society's agents to prepare an appropriate letter to the missionaries and send it to them when the opportunity arises.

2. Decided that an appeal for the propagation of the gospel on the Coromandel coast, including necessary costs, should be drawn up and submitted to the Society for approval, and that Mr. Böhme should also be asked to appear at the next meeting of the Society.[2]

---

1. AFSt/H C 229:55.

2. 10 September 1710 marked the beginning of a century of cooperation between the Anglican SPCK and Halle.

This appeal is to be presented to wealthy people in order to encourage them to contribute. It is also to be presented to the East India Company, in order to get its opinion about it. There will be more to report in my next letter. A godly, humble heart will indeed be able to recognize the finger of God in this, and rejoice in it. For although the whole work is still a small, embryonic seed, from which it is not yet possible to harvest ripe fruit, it is already serving its purpose, since through the approval of such respectable people the project can be touted to others all the better and more emphatically and made known throughout the country. To say nothing of the fact that it already fosters good things internally and externally.

No. 48

A. W. Böhme to Seigneur de Ners
London, 20 September 1710

I received with joy your letter, along with the half guinea, for I highly value both the small nuggets of providence and the big ones. We have actually just begun to attend to the salvation of poor pagans by taking a collection to print the Portuguese New Testament; and you are one of the first to have contributed to it. The Society has willingly approved the project to print the New Testament and has named the first two missionaries as corresponding members. It is true that three more missionaries were sent and have arrived safely in Tranquebar. One is a Dane;[3] he is accompanied by two Germans who studied in Halle, one called Johann Ernst Gründler, the other Polycarpus Jordan.[4] I do not know the name of the Dane. With this letter I am enclosing a copy of Johann Arndt's *True Christianity* for the poor Palatines. I've enclosed various other small

---

3. The Dane was Johann Georg Bövingh (1676–1726), educated at Kiel and ordained for the mission by the Danish Lutheran Church. He did not hold to Pietist views. After leaving the mission in 1711, he wrote what Böhme called "uncharitable" things about the mission. See Letter 82.
4. Johann Ernst Gründler (1677–1720) studied at Halle and was ordained in Copenhagen before setting sail for Tranquebar. He would become Ziegenbalg's closest associate. Polycarpus Jordan was a student at Halle who came as an unordained assistant. He returned to Germany in 1714.

tracts for the same purpose. May the Lord bless their reading from above, for the true conversion of every reader.

No. 49[5]

A. W. Böhme to Professor August Hermann Francke in Halle
London, 13 October 1710

The cause of the missionaries in the East Indies has been, by the grace of God, well received by the people here; now, not only has the Society chosen Bartholomäus Ziegenbalg and Heinrich Plütschau as corresponding members, but it has also published a small pamphlet (a copy of which is enclosed) for the benefit of the mission and to promote its importance to the best of our ability. We are hoping for a considerable harvest, although the annoying strife that the clergy has aroused in this realm, if not completely defeating many existing projects, nevertheless makes many people, who could otherwise be useful, crazy, while making others cold-hearted toward works of love. We have already received about two hundred Reichsthaler for this work; for example, yesterday a godly woman whom I had never met before, the daughter of the famous English physician Sir Thomas Browne, who wrote the beautiful book, *Pseudodoxia epidemica*, brought fifty Reichsthaler to my home for this work.[6] The Society has decided that everything that is contributed will be used for printing the Portuguese New Testament, and then, if there is anything left over, further arrangements will be made. However, it will be impossible to have the New Testament ready by the time the next fleet leaves, no matter how diligently it is worked on. The fleet usually sets sail in January. I have requested that six thousand copies be printed, which, as long as the finances will bear it, has been granted.

We have received the following news regarding the transfer of money to the East Indies. There is no regular exchange rate; therefore, the money must either transferred as it is or it has to be secured here. By securing it here one forfeits 6 percent; thus, if 106 ducats or guineas

---

5. AFSt/H C 229:54.

6. Sir Thomas Browne (1605–1682), *Pseudodoxia epidemica*. The woman who brought the gift to Böhme was probably Frances (Fairfax) Erskine (1675–1719), the *granddaughter* of Thomas Browne. His daughter, Anne Browne, died in 1698.

are put forward here, one hundred are paid out in East India. But if you want to transfer the money as it is, it is safer and more convenient to give it to the Danish fleet, because it goes directly to Tranquebar, whereas the English fleet only goes to Madras, which is 36 German miles away, and to move the money between those two places would subject it to yet another danger.

Yesterday, the publisher of the letters from Malabar told me that the first edition, which appeared last year, has completely sold out, and that the Society for the Propagation of the Gospel in Foreign Parts, to which the volume was dedicated, had alone purchased five hundred copies at one time. Therefore, he requested that I revise the first edition, while he proceeded to the next edition.

No. 50

A. W. Böhme to Seigneur de Ners
London, 23 October 1710

You cannot believe what joy I have been given by the Littleton girls' present. It has inspired me anew to pursue a cause which, in time, may be a beneficial means of converting many Gentiles. Some of my friends doubt the realization of the project, because in the present circumstances there is so much stubbornness and coldness against the spread of the kingdom of God. We have now raised £60 for printing the Portuguese New Testament; we need £400 to complete the project. Enclosed is a copy of the proposal that our Society has published to inspire some devout souls to make a charitable contribution.

With regard to your request for an edifying booklet, I have found the tract, *A Discourse on the Great Duty of Mortification* by Bishop Ezekiel Hopkins, very thorough.[7] It costs about 30 pieces. This author notes the difference between a mortification under the law and one under the gospel, a difference that is very necessary to instill in someone a true taste of godliness and to show others what a difference there is between true Christianity and the web of a pagan morality. I also appreciate the tract *The Great Duty of Self-Resignation to the Divine Will* by Dr. John

---

7. Ezekiel Hopkins (1634–1690), *Discourse*. Originally a Puritan, he conformed to the Church of England in 1662 and was appointed Bishop of Derry in 1681.

Worthington, a devout theologian who translated *The Imitation of Christ* into English, which is the very best English translation available because of its sound, spiritually rich expressions.[8] This booklet is very useful to put into the hands of those who have a taste for sound piety; indeed, it is suitable for all kinds of people, and is also remarkable for the countless number of people it has converted.

P.S.

Kindly thank Mr. W. for the half guinea, which he wanted put to good use. Indeed, young people should practice works of love early on, before a spirit of love for the world and money gets the upper hand.

No. 51

A. W. Böhme to Mr. N. C. in the Earldom of W.
London, 3 November 1710

The people from S. you recommended to me arrived here last month. Up to this point simplicity has guided them safely, and I have no doubt that under its escort they will reach the end of their journey in blessing. They will set sail from here in a few days accompanied by a Christian friend who also intends to settle in Pennsylvania; and since he speaks English, he will be able to offer them a hand and speak for them if need be. Such people, whose eyes are fixed on the Lord without a lot of mental distractions, are generally led along the straight and sure path; while others, who live by reason alone, get stuck on many thorns and tend to pursue all kinds of diversions. I will give them letters to Mr. G. and Mr. B., who will hopefully have landed in Pennsylvania by this time. May the Lord give us rest under His wings!

---

8. John Worthington (1618–1671), *Great Duty of Self-Resignation*; Thomas à Kempis (1380–1471), *Christians Pattern* (trans. Worthington). Before the English Restoration, Worthington was master of Jesus College, Cambridge, and then vice-chancellor. He collected works on the German mystics Jacob Böhme and Hendrik Niclaes.

No. 52

A. W. Böhme to Mr. C. R. in M.
London, 6 November 1710

Because an acquaintance is traveling through Frankfurt, I wanted to give you these words, addressed to my brother, as a token of my love. Georg Andreas Ruperti has finally arrived, and last week preached his inaugural sermon in our chapel on the 21st Sunday of Trinity; we hope that he will be of further use to us for the edification of our German members. For although almost everywhere everything has fallen into such extremes and confusion that human conclusions and considerations are almost no longer sufficient in any matter, I have often been comforted by the fact that in the midst of such disturbances the Lord sometimes causes a star to rise, shining through the darkness from afar and bearing witness to a new grace. In particular, the work of the Danish missionaries in East India is a shining example: seeing that, after abstracts of their letters were published in English and sent out, we have already collected 800 Reichsthaler to support the needs of the newly converted Malabarians. One of the local Societies has especially taken up the matter and is willing to collect money for printing the New Testament in Portuguese. Since the missionaries both preach and catechize in Portuguese, it was deemed necessary to help promote their work with this book. We sent £20 to the missionaries on the last fleet in 1708, with which, according to their recent letters, they set up a Malabar school. They complain a great deal about the godless life of the Christians, by which almost all blessings would be beaten down. One might say here what the Lord said about the small world: "If the light in you is darkness, how great must the darkness itself be?" If Christians, who are to shine in the darkness of paganism, are themselves darkness, how great must the darkness be!

The Palatines and other Germans who sailed for the West Indies at the beginning of this year have finally landed there. There were three thousand when they left, but four hundred died at sea. A list of them was published here eight days ago. When this becomes known in Germany, many who are not following the clear finger of God will hesitate moving to such a remote country. Now that some of its people, who have been driven out of S. and have been staying in the region of W., are traveling there at their own expense, they have seen fit to write a warning letter to these scattered people and to have it printed here, so that it may reach all the more people and be distributed all the more easily in the various provinces.

No. 53

A. W. Böhme to Joshua Kocherthal[?][9] in New York, a Province in America
London, 14 November 1710

I am committing to your hands a number of copies of the New Testament, Arndt's *True Christianity*, and other edifying writings. These are graciously given by our Queen to the poor Palatines and other Germans dispersed in the American provinces for their encouragement, since they have long been dispatched from Germany for that purpose. The oversight of the books had been entrusted to my former colleague John Tribbeko, but because he was called back to Germany early last year, it has fallen to me to deliver the books.

So, I have sent the books bound for New York to you, dear Mr. Kocherthal, and have left their distribution to your fidelity and wisdom, since you are best acquainted with the circumstances there. Because I suppose that very few people can enjoy your encouragement and company in such scattered dwellings, it might be useful here and there to give the father of a home a Bible and a devotional book, with the request that he read from them to those who live around him on Sundays or at other times when they have a little leisure, so that the poor people are not left without all discipline and teaching in such a desolate place. I wish that in time another preacher could be sent to the West Indies to offer you a hand, and to assist the people with sound doctrine and instruction, but so far that person has not been found. When the occasion arises, give me a full account of the circumstances there, and, in particular, what would be required annually to support a preacher, in order to be able to advise me all the better by it.

---

9. Joshua Kocherthal, also known as Josua Harrsch (1669–1719), was a German Lutheran pastor from the Palatinate who led a group of fifty-three German Protestants to America. He met Böhme in London in 1708 en route to New York. He returned to Europe in 1709 and led a second larger group of emigrants to New York in 1710. At his death in 1719, he was succeeded by Justus Falckner.

Whatever else I considered worthwhile to lovingly remind our American friends of I decided to put in a printed letter, a few copies of which are enclosed in the case of books. If I can in any way be of some service to them in England or Germany, I promise to do so with full Christian goodwill. The judgments of God seem to be drawing near to the Europeans. In Poland and Courland, the plague has been so rampant that there were not enough people to harvest the bountiful crops that God had given. So also in Königsberg, Stargard, and other places, the plague has created a great rift; and since it still persists during winter days and is not broken by any cold, as is usually the case, many consider it to be a distinctive judgment.

No. 54

A. W. Böhme to Loth Fischer in Utrecht
London, 16 November 1710

Your last letter has safely arrived. I am glad to hear the report of J. T.'s ecstasy; it is a clear indication of the movements that are now taking place in the spiritual world. Is there a chance to get a few copies of the book, and thus be able to report whether and where the book is now being sold freely and unhindered? What is quoted on page 530 is a little harsh, where the author threatens a severe judgment on those who *hold even the slightest doubt* about the goodness of the work. From which one could almost infer that it should be embraced unexamined and recognized as divine, which I would not advise anyone to do at this time, when so many voices—*here is Christ!*—are jumbled, some too high, but others too low. Time will clarify everything, and the discerning Spirit of Christ in us will know how to put each one into its proper place, for it is he who testifies that the Spirit, in his manifold gifts and outpourings, is truth. Where the Spirit does not bear witness in the reader to the truth of such a writing and its dictates, nor confirm such truth by his seal, then it is fair, without acceptance or judgment, to leave the matter up to the Lord, who will separate everything in his time and bless the threshing floor. In the meantime, I will be glad if the manuscript can be sent to me at the first opportunity. I will hand it over to be printed together with all of Thomas Bromley's tracts.

No. 55

A. W. Böhme to Professor August Hermann Francke in Halle
London, 5 January 1711

Both packages with letters to East India have arrived in good order and on time. Jonas Fincke will have difficulty setting sail before the end of this month, even though the entire print shop, including the associated equipment, is now ready and is being taken to the ships straight away.[10] The Society has taken on the venture very earnestly, and several members have shown such zeal that they have met daily to confer about how to organize the whole project more conveniently. Mr. Fincke is to be given a salary in the first year of his service, which should be renewed if we see some blessing from this work. The draft, which I recently sent, has already been printed a second time in an expanded version, in order to ensure that this English nation also aims to prepare capable missionaries and send them among the pagans. The preachers serving the English factories in the East Indies have also been appointed as corresponding members of the Society; accordingly, they have been urged to cultivate a good rapport with the Danish missionaries and to initiate the establishment of good charity schools among the Malabarians. The sum collected to further this cause has grown to 2,200 Reichsthaler. Dr. Thomas Tenison, Archbishop of Canterbury, alone has sent in 30 guineas; and since he is the head of the moderate party, he has in so doing set a good example.[11]

---

10. Jonas Fincke (d. 1711) was a German recruited to serve as printer for the Tranquebar mission.

11. Thomas Tenison (1636–1715) was Archbishop of Canterbury from 1694 to his death in 1715.

No. 56[12]

A. W. Böhme to Bartholomäus Ziegenbalg and Heinrich Plütschau,
  Missionaries in the East Indies
London, 4 January 1711 (OS)

Reverends,
  You have found many in Europe among the godly who admire and judge important your work in the East for the propagation of the gospel; and you came to have special favor with the English as soon as the story of your progress was printed here. For just as the true church of our Savior is a body with many members whose structure is animated and strengthened in every part by the solid vigor produced by an influx of spiritual forces, so also each member of this body can do nothing other than rejoice inwardly when it perceives the whole body to increase Christ's stature. Neither will healthily godly worshipers rejoice less when they discover that the dry bones of the pagan peoples, destitute of heavenly life and spirit, are being stirred into life again by God's holier Spirit; and that, when the thick clouds of profane superstition are driven away, those pagans are disposed to receive the gospel's serene light.
  As a result, the Society for Promoting Christian Knowledge in England has not only approved your work of promoting the gospel in the East, but has also, because of your zeal in undertaking this work, elected you as corresponding members, as they are called, of the Society—this with the hope that by exchange of letters, Christian admonitions, and collaborative efforts, the Lord's work might be extended over time. It seems to be unnecessary that I should tell you in detail of the Society's origins, or of the happy growth it has undergone; you can learn about the nature and order of this and of the other societies which have recently come into being from the books sent herewith.
  The members of the Society mentioned have no doubt that the godly plans and purposes recounted there may, so far as the rationale of the institution permits, be further advanced where you are.
  In case I have not been clear: this is how far the work of reformation begun in Great Britain has reached—
  Some societies serve this end by working together with mind and hand to extinguish the flames of those evils with which we have lived in an ungodly way for centuries. They all have the same goal, but they use

12. Original letter written in Latin.

different methods. They want to remove obstacles which stand in the way of religion, so that others encounter fewer difficulties in renewing the foundation of solid godliness.

The first of these, called the Religious Society, came into being thirty years ago and continues.[13] It was begun by young people who met on certain days to read Scripture and to edify one another with hymns, prayers, and pious conversation. This Society was begun by a small number of young people, and with the passage of time was granted such success by divine power that soon there were forty of them in London and its environs. It is very true, as you say in your letters, that the young are more quickly brought to a good way of life than the old, for the old adhere largely to merely external and dead forms of religion, and so it is difficult to get them to taste the more life-giving truth.

I will not say more about this true Society now, since the Reverend Doctor Josiah Woodward has provided fuller information about its rationale, order, and form in a book written in English and also published in German.[14]

This Society was principally and closely concerned with the cultivation of godliness; from it came others with the same goal, distinguished by different names. Some were concerned to improve contemporary ways of life, others with promoting knowledge of Jesus Christ. Here is more detail about a few.

A first was set up to remedy the contagion of the vices of the present time, which are becoming more wicked by the day. The fact is that many of the great of the kingdom, together with some bishops conspicuous in their dignity, contributed to this situation by what they were doing. And we should say that in these things we find the unbridled enormity of sin opposed by the more severe discipline of the law; but the hope is that other kinds of work, having been so well begun, will gain the upper hand and will bring sinners, who previously had need of coercion by the restraining power of the law, to the paths of divine love by tempering the law's rigor with the gospel's gentleness. This is the order in which to do things so that not only are depraved ways of life corrected, but also so that the very heart itself, together with the soul's inner faculties, is imbued with the spontaneous principle of divine grace, and from the force working within acts in the various ways proper to a true Christian.

13. On the religious societies, see Kisker, *Foundation for Revival*.

14. Josiah Woodward (1657–1712) was an Anglican clergyman, moral reformer, and advocate of the religious societies. Woodward, *Account of . . . the Religious Societies*.

This Society is named for the living knowledge of Christ, and it has two principal purposes.

The first is that schools for the poor be established here and there by the kindness of others freely given for that end. Great progress has been made in this in just a few years, so that in London and its vicinity there are now one hundred schools in which the young of both sexes are educated in godliness and good habits. There are about 2,480 boys and 1,331 girls, and even the clothes for both are donated free of charge by patrons. But if we speak of the whole of Britain, there are five hundred schools established by the Society's assiduous work for the country's common use. In these schools, more than twelve thousand children are being educated free of charge; many are clothed by the kindness of patrons, and some are also provided with all the necessities of life.

In order to explain the Society's other end, I would like you next to know that catechetical pamphlets, which more than anything else urge the practice of godliness everywhere, and of which many have been produced at the Society's expense, are being distributed everywhere principally for the salvation of the poor—to the extent that they are permitted to consult them. In this way, many families whose small homes do not permit accumulation of books and other paraphernalia were supplied with Holy Bibles, books of prayer, and other ascetical works. And since the Society read in your letters that you do the same, and that you have translated various treatises into the Malabar language, it could do nothing other than unanimously support such a productive practice and pray for the Holy One's blessings upon your enterprises. It has for a long time been the usual state of things that support for the work of godliness has been mostly directed to Europe. But since there is reason to print books like this, and desiring, to the extent possible, to overcome difficulties in the way of doing so, the Society, by recommending the entire enterprise to good people, obtained enough money not only for a press capable of printing in roman type with all its necessary equipment, but in addition fifty English pounds for your support. The Society wishes only that those who have so freely contributed to this work might delight not only in that, but also in something greater, which is the freer sharing with others—principally with the pagan peoples—of goods already granted them.

Before I stop writing, I should add a word about a fourth society in England, that for spreading the gospel overseas. This does work very like yours in the East. I could tell you of people, both in the church and in politics, who apply themselves honorably to the illustrious work of propagating religion. It is reasonable to predict from this that great rewards will come in time to the churches, both eastern and western, if, as we hope, divine providence furthers these enterprises.

This, for the present, may suffice to inform you about the earnest application of the English to the work of reformation. Please, reverend ones, accept this brief narration tranquilly, along with an invitation to exchange letters in the future. May that stimulate whatever is needed from England. The greater the rapidity with which you advance toward your goal, the more people will go along with you in that effort. Do not lose heart if the enemy all souls have in common attacks you openly, or plots against you secretly; that one leaves nothing undone which might choke the Lord's work, which is like grass in its first growth. But truth always wins; even if pressed as hard as possible, it cannot be crushed. May your victory be in Christ's humility, and may catholic love, with patience as shield, fortify, surround, and protect you as that upon which all the weapons of adversaries break in the end.

Farewell in the Lord, revered and most studious ones—I commend you to the divine protection, which will endure . . .

P.S.

It has pleased the Society for Promoting Christian Knowledge to invite ministers of the Anglican Church, specifically George Lewis,[15] William Owen Anderson,[16] and George Watson,[17] to the same exchange of letters, or correspondence, if so it may be called. They are respectively in charge of the church which has been gathered to Christ from our nation in Madras, Bengal, and Bombay. The Society wishes that you, reverend ones, having established friendship with these pastors of the English nation, should diligently devote yourselves to the propagation of the gospel in the East, and should in that way support one another by mutual aid and counsel. This is what is meant by the Society's orders to the said ministers of the church.

---

15. Rev. George Lewis (ca. 1663–1729) was chaplain to the East India Company at Fort St. George in Madras from 1692 to 1714. He was a corresponding member of the SPCK and a keen supporter of the Tranquebar mission; he would play an important role in some of the conflicts surrounding the mission. Ansorge, "Revd George Lewis."

16. Rev. William Owen Anderson (ca. 1668–1710) served as chaplain to Fort William in Calcutta from 1708 to 1710. News of his death had apparently not yet reached Böhme.

17. Rev. George Watson served as chaplain in Bombay from 1709 to 1721.

Further, a particular noblewoman has, out of a singular interest in you, donated ten British pounds to support the work you are doing. The governor of Fort St. George, whose name is Edward Harrison,[18] to whose credit this money is pledged, will be pleased to hand it over to you upon presentation of this promissory note, signed by you, after he has safely landed in India.

P.P.S.

It is prohibited by the Kingdom's public statutes to export currency stamped with the character of Great Britain. The Society has therefore taken care to convert the above-mentioned gift of £50 into Spanish silver, and has added to it the amount of £40, which the Society granted to Fincke in the first year of his dealings with you, so that the work he was charged with doing could be carried on more successfully. From these £90, 345½ ounces of Spanish money will be given you. Of these, 180 are for Fincke. The Spanish thalers are to be paid as soon as they arrive in India. The remainder is at your disposal.

[Original editor's note:] The author drafted the above Latin letter to the Danish Missionaries at the request of the Society for Promoting Christian Knowledge, and, after it was signed by the secretary of the Society, was sent to East India through Jonas Fincke.

No. 57[19]

A. W. Böhme to Bartholomäus Ziegenbalg and the rest of the German missionaries in Tranquebar in East India
London, 23 January 1711

The work you were called by the Lord to lead has caused a stir here and there among many European Christians, some of whom have been inspired out of goodwill to actively promote the growth of this work. Among them, I count a few Englishmen who have not only expressed their pleasure with the letters that have been translated so far, but have also been eager to provide concrete assistance that might facilitate this work. To that end, you are going to receive a Latin printing press that can

---

18. Edward Harrison (1674–1732) served as president of Madras from 1711 to 1717.
19. AFSt/H Nachlässe und Deposita ALMW/DHM 6/9:15a.

serve you in spreading the Word of Truth. Then, at the first opportunity, you can thank the Society for Promoting Christian Knowledge in writing, and, since you have been named corresponding members, make a good start toward a worthwhile and lasting correspondence. May the Lord give you the necessary wisdom to do so, so that this small beginning may in time flourish into many blessings, and also inspire other nations to Christian imitation. I hope that the time is near when the Lord will have mercy on the poor Malabarians and pave the way for the fullness that is yet to come. The gifted Jonas Fincke will faithfully offer you his hand in the Lord's work, and fix his gaze with you on the same purpose. If your hearts become truly united in a gentle spirit of love, your victory will be all the more certain, and the whole of your progress all the more blessed. The unshakable unity that flourished among the early Christians was one of the most powerful means by which often wild and unrefined Gentiles were convinced of the truth of the gospel. "See how much they love one another!" they said. Love and humility are insurmountable vestments. Those who persevere in this have a double wall against the dangerous temptations of this time. Love will teach them to make themselves servants of all people, even of pagans, while humility will teach them how to return all blessings and progress to God, the original source. In this way, people persevere in spiritual poverty, where no enemy, no matter how great, can topple them. Oh, how many lose what they have received because they do not establish it wholly in God who gave it. *Nothing* must be the foundation, if *something* is to be built. May the Lord by His abundant power give you, dear brothers, whom He has chosen to send as firstfruits among the Gentiles, an enduring victory over all such temptations, and establish a fortified wall on your right and on your left, against which the temptations of the evil one and his devices will be destroyed! He has given you an open door and just a little power. What He opens, no one can shut. Only keep His word, and do not deny His name. Let it be said: *This is set for the fall and rising of many* (not only among the Gentiles, but also) *in Israel, and for a sign that will not be denied.*

As for an appropriate routine for corresponding, my unofficial recommendation is: (1) That some time before letters are to be sent off to Germany, England, etc., you confer with each other and deliberate on the subjects to be covered. (2) That you consider, in so doing, what is edifying and useful for each place and person. This prevents rash people from rushing to print those letters that contain particulars that are not appropriate to put before the eyes of everyone. (3) That you then set yourselves to elaborate in writing—which for England should be in Latin—on the main issue to be dealt with in the letter; but make sure that, after the letter has been drafted, it is read out again to all the members of the conference, their opinions on it heard, and thus, *mutatis mutandis* (once the necessary changes have been made), it can be sent on. (4) That you make copies of all the letters you send to Europe and put them in a special book, which can one day be useful for drawing up a complete history, or just be helpful for posterity to know. The same could also be done with your weekly conferences, namely, that everything that is discussed is incorporated into a special book and kept for others to read. This can have its benefits for many years: for in such a way one still speaks in death. May the Lord give us understanding in all things!

P.S.

The other questions you wanted to know about the East Indies and the circumstances there, I have included in some questions given to Mr. Jonas Fincke, which I have asked him to answer when the opportunity arises.

*** *** ***

Some questions, the answers to which should be sent on the return of the next fleet.

What is the situation regarding paper in the East Indies? Do they have the necessary ingredients to make paper there, namely, linen? In the absence of linen, could paper be made from cotton? The Jesuits in China make paper from silk; is this practical in other Eastern countries?

Are they able to make printer's ink there? The Dutch, who have a print shop in Batavia, could perhaps give instructions on this, in case some particular circumstances need to be considered.

Is the Portuguese language spoken in Malabar and other East Indian countries the same as that spoken in Europe? And if there is some discrepancy between them, is it so great that a European Portuguese could not understand the Portuguese spoken in the East Indies?

Could an accurate geographic map of Malabar and its borders be prepared? It would be so much better if it included a succinct description of the most prominent cities and what interesting things can be seen in them.

*** *** ***

Things for Jonas Fincke to observe on his East Indian Journey.

To keep an accurate diary of the events of the entire journey, and to record every evening what he has seen and heard. In particular, he should carefully note the difficulties he encounters, in order to enlighten or better advise those who come after him. On occasion, he should send out these and similar observations for the common good.

To visit the Dutch preacher at the Cape of Good Hope and give him a copy of Arndt's *True Christianity* in Latin. The first missionaries, who visited him in 1706 on their journey to East India, praised his love and joyfulness in the letters they sent out.

To visit the other Germans who have settled there, and to present them with some edifying German tracts. In their letters to Europe, the missionaries who visited Mr. B. and Mr. K. in 1709 remembered with gratitude the love and support they had witnessed there.

In addition to German books, to have an assortment of English tracts on hand, and to give some to the ship workers or other Englishmen, as occasion allows.

On such a long journey, the chest of books must be checked several times, and the books aired out in good weather, so that they are not water damaged or otherwise accidentally damaged.

To visit George Lewis, an English minister at Madras. When you hand him the books that the Society is giving him, you can commend the missionaries' cause as an opportunity for a fruitful correspondence. Also, to discuss with him whether or not such an initiative, which has the conversion of pagans as its purpose and which is highly praised in England, could be established in the English plantations.

To find out whether they have one or more Malabar schoolmasters at Tranquebar, who, if required, could be transferred from there to the English plantations and used as schoolmasters for establishing suitable charity schools.

If he gets to know one or another trustworthy person in the English plantations, to try to establish a suitable correspondence with him. At times he can reprint a one- or two-page English tract at Tranquebar, and try to sell and distribute it through such correspondents in every English operation.

Wherever he meets some true Christians and children of God, to carefully write down their names, addresses, particular leadership externally and internally, professions, etc., and, by means of an edifying correspondence, to share with them news of the good that the Lord has brought about in Europe over these last years. He can also acquaint them with good edifying books, thereby awakening and increasing that goodness.

To carefully note everything that belongs to the inner state of the Church since in all places and at all times God has still raised up some witnesses to the truth, who must testify against the corruption in all lands. A special message on the so-called Thomas Christians is desired; a more complete report ought to be made of their circumstances.

To visit the monasteries when arriving in Catholic areas, to see if some good souls, or rare and edifying books or manuscripts, might be found in them. Likewise, to see whether some footsteps of the lives of hermits, anchorites, etc. can be found here and there.

To carefully note where a particular case of providence, grace, or even judgment of the wicked occurs, and to make it known to the correspondents in Europe for their edification.

To inquire thoroughly about the progress the Dutch have made in planting Christianity among the pagans. What is the nature of the religious life among Christians and the converted, especially in Batavia, Ceylon, and other places under Dutch rule? To report back if he discovers something among them that might be imitated; but if with their works they rely on a merely outward conversion, without an inward change of heart, to report it as an admonition to be all the more cautious in choosing missionaries.

Because there are many German Lutherans at the Cape of Good Hope, and they are said to be without a preacher, could he find out from some well-disposed people whether there is any inclination to appoint a trustworthy preacher? With the help of such a person, correspondence with the East Indies could be established on better footing, and he could prove useful for many other good things.

To find out if there are any English people at the Cape of Good Hope, to visit them, and to give them a few books.

To send, as soon as possible, a sample from the print shop in Portuguese or another European language, so that the Society may have evidence of his skill in printing.

No. 58

A. W. Böhme to Seigneur de Ners
London, 2 February 1711

Our faithful God has abundantly blessed our efforts to support the Danish Mission. On the 26th of last month, Jonas Fincke, who has been assigned as a printer to Tranquebar to serve the mission, went to board ship at Portsmouth and commit himself to serving the missionaries and the Malabarians by printing edifying works . . . . May God draw us more and more to His love. Those who seek their sole rest in the center of love will not be struck by the floods of divine judgment, nor will they be harmed.

No. 59

A. W. Böhme to Seigneur de Ners
London, 22 March 1711

I am very grateful for the efforts undertaken out of love for the poor people of Malabar. Truly, our good God has visibly blessed the hard work of those who have made it their business to promote this labor of love. Mr. Clifford, a Presbyterian preacher, has collected £20 from his congregation and has shown great love to Jonas Fincke, who, for the spread of the gospel, has devoted himself to the mission as a printer. All kinds of people have contributed to it. What pleases me most in this matter is the inner principle and the integrity of heart, which has visibly manifested itself in this and that, and which has also moved those who are poor themselves to offer a hand to the Malabarians. The poor Palatines are coming back from Ireland in great numbers to return to their own homeland. About six hundred people have already embarked for Holland, and another sixty families have recently arrived to follow their compatriots. This affair has also prevented me from visiting the lady you mentioned in your letter, since I have been busy distributing the books and alms that a few friends have been sending me for the benefit of these woeful people. I now hear that Irish skippers have been ordered by the government not to take any more Palatines aboard, in an attempt to keep the rest of them in Ireland. I am afraid the Irish show little love to these poor people. I am just about to have Johann Arndt's *True Christianity* printed in English, through which so many thousands of souls have been converted in the Lutheran Church. As soon as I have the opportunity, I will send you proposals for this project, along with a sermon I preached on original sin. May the Lord help us by His grace in everything we do to the glory of God.

No. 60

A. W. Böhme to Mr. R., Merchant in Frankfurt am Main
London, 6 February 1711

The reason I am taking the liberty of writing to you is a curious rumor published in the newspapers here about the burning and reduction to ashes of the Juden-Straße in Frankfurt. Several people have recounted the circumstances surrounding this fire in different ways, and some have mentioned particular footprints of divine judgment. But, because the common newspapers cannot simply be trusted, and yet the Savior admonishes us to take into account and examine the signs of the times, I have wanted to send these lines to your lordship, partly on my own initiative, partly on behalf of some friends, to inquire more fully about the whole affair. To that end, please express your answer in such a way that I can also show it to others. Among other things, it has been said here that the fire was fanned and spread still further when water was poured on it; and that as soon as it reached the houses of the Christians, it stopped; and that the Jews in Frankfurt, by order of the authorities, are used before others for extinguishing a blazing fire, and are respected as the most adept at such work, but that they have now been put to shame with all their skills, and can do nothing. To say nothing of other unusual circumstances.

It appears that God is beginning to move in a very extraordinary way. Everything is in a state of disarray, and the bitter sectarian spirit, which is ever crying out that the temple of the Lord is with it, takes hold in such a way that even those souls who have hungered for righteousness are swept away in the current of nasty religious zeal. May the Lord make our hearts steadfast, and teach us to build our house upon the rock, that among all the disruptions around us, the inner spirit may be continually refreshed by the inspiration of divine light and peace. Please provide your answer as soon as possible and in as much detail as you are able. A printing press is now en route from here to the East Indies, along with a printer, to make the Word of God known among the Malabarians. There is a great desire among many to take to heart the salvation of pagans, more so than has previously been the case among Christians. All costs of the project were raised from the contributions of concerned people, and many are still working daily to finish the whole project.

No. 61

Mr. R. to A. W. Böhme
Frankfurt am Main, 12 April 1711

. . . The racket began just after 8:00 p.m. on January 14th, and soon it was reported that there was a fire on Juden-Gasse [the Jewish alley], and shortly thereafter that the rabbi's house and the school were in full flames. Initially, the Jews wanted to keep their alley—which is actually more properly called a city and is surrounded by a high wall—closed, and they even stationed stout guards at their gates, who beat back the people trying to force their way in with blows, until their plight got out of hand and they lost courage. Consequently, there was nothing left but to save their lives and goods, which were quite meager. God's great mercy is evident in the fact that the fire did not start an hour or two later, when the people would have been asleep. Perhaps half of such a large throng would not have been saved, because their number is so great that it is impossible to know actually how many there are. All the houses are made of wood; only the lower parts of their school were of stone. Everything was built very densely and enormously high; and every house that was built high up, including the rabbi's, burned down. The wind often changed the direction of the fire, which favored the city and the houses of the Christians, as one could see with the naked eye.

All reasonable Jews recognize the judgments of the Lord in this devastation, and some of them confess that their arrogance and pomp, which in recent years have become all too prevalent among them, are to blame for such ruin; but the appalling injustice may also have contributed to it. It is not true that the fire burned more from having had water poured on it; rather, because everything was built out of wood and too high and closely together, it was almost impossible to extinguish it. Although several houses were torn down to stop the fire, it did not help; rather, the fire seized the wood on the ground and consumed everything, so that not enough wood was left to make a knife handle. Judging from the burning embers left behind as a result of the horrible heat, an untold amount of property was burned, and the damage was estimated at several million Reichsthalers. A great deal was also robbed and stolen, although every precaution was taken to prevent it, and those who were caught were severely punished. A Jew saw a diamond ring and swallowed it, which was trapped for a long time inside him until it was recovered and returned to its original owner.

In the Christian neighborhood, no house was consumed, but some were badly damaged. Indeed, it is remarkable that two houses, which were built so close to the alley that they were separated only by a wooden wall, nevertheless remained standing, although quite ruined, and I saw with my own eyes how the wind drove the fire away from them. But there was also strong resistance, and the thick wall around the Jewish alley served very well, because one could fight the fire on top of it. Otherwise, the Jews often scoffed at the idea that the fire could burn in their vicinities, because they and their rabbis could pray; they also wanted to say that they fervently prayed about the recent fire and made it go out, but it fell from heaven again and reignited. Certainly, the Jews have always been extremely adept and industrious in the event of a fire, and because they are bound by a hard oath, they must not stay behind even on their Sabbath if a fire develops.

No. 62[20]

A. W. Böhme to Professor August Hermann Francke in Halle
London, 16 February 1711

On the 26th of last month, Jonas Fincke left for Portsmouth in order to board ship once the sailors to the East Indies had come together; however, it has not yet been dispatched. He has found immense love

20. AFSt/H C 229:49.

among the British because of his vibrant yet childlike nature. No father could have taken greater care of his son. May the Lord accompany him with blessing to the place where he is called! The day before Fincke left here, the Countess of Northampton sent £25, with the request that it be conveyed to the missionaries with this fleet, which was done.[21] The entire amount thus far collected is £500–£600, and more is still being brought in almost every week.

The latest edition of the East-Indian letters, augmented with a letter sent to Heinrich Ludolf, is now finished, and the project has been printed. We have been assured that this worthy undertaking shall also be channeled to Englishmen, in case a few of them are available and suitable for missionary work. Dr. John Sharp, Archbishop of York, has presented to the Queen a copy of the earlier edition of the Malabar letters, along with the whole project.[22] With regard to the Portuguese New Testament, the Gospel of Matthew has been printed in Amsterdam, and 250 copies of it have been sent to Fincke in Portsmouth, so he can take them to the East Indies to be used and tried out in their schools. It turns out to be a very clean edition. I sent two copies to Hamburg several days ago to be shipped from there to Halle. We will now proceed with printing the entire New Testament as soon as it can be conveniently done. I will see to both the dictionary and the lexicon in Portuguese, even though I know that Fincke, with great difficulty, was finally able to get a copy of an English-Portuguese dictionary from a bookseller who had only a few copies left in stock.

Regarding the Indian [Native American] Bible, a copy of which you recently said you obtained at an auction, I can report that the author of this translation is an Englishman named John Eliot.[23] It is not an East- but a West-Indian language; it is not printed in England but in America, in a city called Cambridge—American cities are commonly named after cities in (European) England. Cotton Mather, a New England preacher who published Eliot's biography—a third edition came out in 1694—wrote that *this book, the West Indian Bible, was the only Bible ever printed in*

---

21. Anne Finch, Countess of Nottingham (1668–1743), formerly Anne Hatton, second wife of Daniel Finch, 2nd Earl of Nottingham.

22. John Sharp (1645–1714), Archbishop of York from 1691 to 1714, supported a number of SPCK projects and was an advisor to Queen Anne.

23. John Eliot (1604–1690) was a Puritan missionary to the American Indians. He completed his translation of the Bible into the Massachusett Indian language in 1660.

America.²⁴ Certainly, Robert Boyle also had a hand in this matter, as can be seen, among other ways, from the biography of the well-known Richard Baxter (a book in folio, published in 1696 under the title: *Reliquiæ Baxterianæ*).²⁵ Baxter corresponded with Eliot, and some of his letters to him were inserted in the biography.²⁶ On page 290 [§149] it states that after Eliot had finished printing the Bible, he also produced various other practical writings in the Indian language, including *The Practice of Piety* by Lewis Bayly,²⁷ which Boyle had recommended for that purpose.²⁸ He also translated Richard Baxter's tract, *A Call to the Unconverted*, and dispersed it among the Indians.²⁹ He brought some Indians to the point where they were recognized for their ability to preach to their neighbors and to gather congregations here and there. Eliot did not die until 1690. A friend who knew him in America told me that Eliot (who was also an English preacher at Roxbury in New England) had such a love for the Indians that he would crawl into the huts where they lived and talk with them at some length. In turn, the Indians gained such a love for Eliot that when they saw him coming from far away, they ran to meet him and carried him through the mud.³⁰ There are quite a few fine recollections in the biography which are applicable to this time; I let Fincke take the whole book with him to East India. If you considered it worthwhile, I could translate the most important passages from the book, those that refer to the work of conversion, and send them to you in a letter, together with what I have collected from some oral accounts, should you wish to publish them.

---

24. Cotton Mather, *Life and Death of . . . John Eliot*, 105.

25. Richard Baxter (1615–1691), *Reliquiæ Baxterianæ*. Baxter, well-known among the Pietists, was an admired religious writer and pastor at Kidderminster, as well as one of the most influential Nonconformists following the Act of Uniformity in 1662. For more on Baxter, see Letter 70.

26. E.g., John Eliot to Richard Baxter, Roxbury, 6 May 1663, and Richard Baxter to John Eliot, Acton, near London, 30 November 1663, in Baxter, *Reliquiæ Baxterianæ*, 292–97.

27. Lewis Bayly (1575–1631), *Practise of Pietie*. Bayly was bishop of Bangor. In 1711, his classic text appeared in its fiftieth edition. On the reception of Bayly's work in Germany, see Sträter, *Sonthom, Bayly, Dyke und Hall*, 76–83.

28. Bayly, *Manitowompae Pomantamoonk*.

29. Baxter, *Wehkomaonganoo asquam peantogig*.

30. On the relationship between Native Americans and Pietists, particularly the Moravians, see Geyken, "Von Heiden und edlen Wilden."

No. 63

A. W. Böhme to Seigneur de Ners
London, 30 November 1711

    I am deeply grateful for the opportunity you afforded me to become acquainted with the two gracious ladies, Mrs. Howard and Mrs. Jones, with whom I spoke yesterday, and found with great pleasure that our good God had touched their hearts most tenderly, and with the knowledge of a thorough fear of God. As for the weekly paper, *The Silent Monitor*, rest assured that they do not know the author. Mrs. Jones herself does not know to whom the manuscript was sent by the Pensy Post to have such printed. The author seems to be well-meaning, judging by his knowledge, although his expressions are not vivid enough to stir the reader's heart. The books of T. in N. and another craftsman in F. are causing a stir in Germany. R., a preacher in H. who in the past greatly despised godliness, but is now touched by godly convictions, has left that evil life and will soon be dismissed by the consistory in H. He published a book in A., in which he speaks of great judgments that would soon erupt over Germany; however, he has been condemned to permanent imprisonment in H.

No. 64

A. W. Böhme to Mr. E. in the city of M. in Moscow
London, 20 April 1711

    Although I received your letter some time ago, in which you reported on the circumstances of your trip to Moscow, I have not had a suitable opportunity to answer it. I am also sending this message without knowing your whereabouts; but if it should reach you, it might be the beginning of a true and ongoing correspondence. Up to this point, the Lord has helped us in England. George Ruperti has now joined me as a colleague, and I hope that we will commit ourselves to a mutual appreciation. He has been retained by the German-speaking so-called Savoy Church, and Samuel Urlsperger has joined him. Of the poor Palatines sent to Ireland, over a thousand souls have returned at various times, and the last of them was sent back to Holland only 14 days ago. I have been overwhelmed by the number of them, but have been able to help only a very few of them in their misery. My perception of their situation was that they wanted to escape the judgments of God before it was time, which is why they have fallen all over again into more severe judgments, so that they would then be compelled to recognize the hour of their visitation.

I must report one more thing: our Jonas Fincke has been sent to East India by the local Society to offer a hand to the Danish missionaries in Malabar in the Lord's work, particularly as a printer—the art of which he had to learn here beforehand, as well as having to take a whole printing press with him—to print and distribute edifying tracts, and to be of assistance to them. It is a Latin printing press, which cost a considerable amount. Friends from Halle will provide them with a Malabar press, so that they may proceed all the more unhindered in spreading the gospel. People here have welcomed the affair with great interest, and I consider this small beginning to be a mustard seed from which in time a large tree can grow.

No. 65

A. W. Böhme to Miss Jane Slare
London, 27 July 1711

Next Tuesday, Lord willing, I am thinking of going to Windsor; if we are always on holy ground, it does not matter where we are. But for this reason, we must take off the shoes of our earthly desires, as Moses was commanded to do when, just off in the distance, he caught sight of and contemplated the marvelous working of God. Abraham did exactly the same when he prepared to sacrifice his beloved son: he left his servant with the donkey down the mountain and went alone with his son Isaac to carry out the sacred work of divine worship. All this gives us a picture of, and guides us to, the mystery of how it is with faith and love, since it encompasses all the duties of a Christian, and in which all the illustrations and figures of the Old Testament are fulfilled. But this is revealed only to the infants who follow the course of the historical mystery with a single-minded eye of faith, of which those who are called "Christians" know little or nothing at all.

If your present solitude, which you hopefully enjoy, serves to bring more stillness to the inner workings of your heart, you will have not undertaken this journey without benefit, and its advantages will be good not only for the body, but also for the soul. How many deceive themselves in this: by withdrawing from the outer temptations of the world, they imagine that they have also discarded their love for the world and their unruly attachment to it, since it is not the world outside us that distracts us, but our own inner desire that continually tempts the soul to eat of the forbidden fruit, and, having done so, to pick up and gather a handful of leaves to hide our nakedness from the all-seeing eye. The trees in the Garden of Eden, which before the fall had served along with the other creatures for discovering the goodness of God, were now used by fallen humanity as a hiding place; and out of leaves they wove a blanket to cover their shameful fallenness.

So it happens that corrupt people corrupt and misuse everything they can get their hands on; and the more devious they are, the more devious also are their contrivances to whitewash their vile nature. All this shows that you cannot expect anything extraordinary from an outward solitude, unless a higher power from within directs your love with an even greater desire for the Lord, and it is only for these people that everything works out for the best. On the other hand, nothing is pure to the unclean, because their minds and consciences are defiled and impure. But may the Lord teach us His divine wisdom, that we may be guided without harm through this crooked and perverse world.

No. 66

A. W. Böhme to Miss Jane Slare
London, 11 August 1711

Last Thursday I arrived back from Windsor, where I spent a whole week in solitude. Time will soon tell whether my presence there will have had any effect. I have done what I could, and must now leave everything to the supreme steward of all blessings, whose love and omnipotence are the two greatest pillars of a Christian's life, a double rock on which our faith must rest. Now we are living in a time when the weakness of humankind will likely be revealed more clearly than ever, and when those who have put flesh before fortitude and resorted to human wisdom will suffer great loss. Those who have grown accustomed to this way will harden themselves more and more; but those who fear God's Word will at such times hide themselves in the refuge of love, where wrath will not harm them, though it may affect them. If the smelter is our friend, as I have heard someone say, it will not let anything be burned up that is not of one's own making. But these things must be eradicated, since they are contrary to His holy will. By fiery trials the Lord burns away the stubble of selfishness, so that His own work may appear all the more beautiful and glorious in His children, and His grace may finally triumph over our natural dispositions, which have so many secret and hidden nooks and crannies, and are all too inclined to stick to the creature and to expect from it that which is to be sought only from the Creator.

It is obvious that some creatures cannot help themselves even if they wanted to, but others do not want to, even if they could to some extent do something. On the other hand, the love and power of God, as the unique attributes of our faith, are both willing and able to lead us through all inward and outward hardships, so that He may complete the work He Himself has begun. However, he wants to do everything when the time is right and pleasing to him. He created the world in six days, when He could have revealed it in an instant through his almighty word. And He still uses this process in creating us spiritually, which is the restoration of the divine image in our soul; first the grain or stalk appears, then the ear. Wherever even a beginning is made, we can also expect the continuation and growth of God's work, through the influence of His grace.

When I was in Windsor, I asked after the poor elderly man who lives about a mile from there, and whom we visited together before, and found him still alive. He said that his wicked dispositions were all rusted in him, which I understood to mean that they were so ingrained in him that he was unable to wash them away.

No. 67

A. W. Böhme to Georg Melchior Ludolf at Wetzlar[31]
London, 29 January 1712

Although I have enjoyed knowing the Ludolf name for many years, I have not had any personal acquaintance with anyone from this worthy family, except for the one about whom I must now report, with deep emotion, in this letter of sorrow. Namely, it pleased the Lord last Friday, January 25 (OS) at about two o'clock in the morning, to call home my best and first friend in England, Heinrich Wilhelm Ludolf; it was a blessed ending after a rather protracted illness. For me, though, this blessed passing is that much nearer to my soul, because I have lived with the blessed deceased in unwavering love and friendship from our first acquaintance, and in many ways I have benefited from his counsel and encouragement in both earthly and spiritual matters, especially since I had few friends when I first came to this country. Wherefore, may the Lord indeed allow him to find his portion and reward abundantly in eternity, where his soul has gone! I can call him my best friend all the more, because his friendship was always aimed at what is essential: the edification, improvement, purification, and perfection of the soul, which he most earnestly sought to promote in everyone he encountered.

But let me also address personal matters (although dangerous self-interest can easily creep in and render love insincere); nonetheless, in 1705, mostly if not totally by Ludolf's efforts, though without my knowledge or request, I was recommended to His Royal Highness, Prince George of Denmark, as court preacher, and was indeed subsequently appointed by him. I can also call him my first friend in England: as divine providence would have it, in 1701, when I was traveling to England for the first time, I met Ludolf in Rotterdam and sailed to England in the same ship in which he had reserved a place. As a result of these circumstances, our acquaintance and friendship, which were established outside of England, continued in England and never diminished, but only increased.

I trust your lordship can easily appreciate how the loss of such a friend so close to me would affect me even more deeply, if the lesson of self-denial, so highly praised by the blessed man himself, were not to be exercised in this matter as well. Apart from that, as far as the malady itself

---

31. Georg Melchior Ludolf (1667–1740), German judge and statesman, was half-brother to Heinrich Ludolf.

is concerned, it would be difficult to describe it in writing. It was not a single illness, but a complication of many symptoms, which eventually drained his spirit completely; in any case, he did not complain so much of pain as of an immense weariness.

No. 68

A. W. Böhme to Dr. Heinrich Lysius at Königsberg[32]
London, 29 January 1712

Some time ago, Professor Francke conveyed to me an extract of a letter sent to him by your most honorable sir, dated 21 August 1711. The subject matter, you may remember, was about how the Lord was beginning to open a door for the Word in Poland, Courland, Lithuania, and other neighboring countries, and how good it would be if more harvest workers were available to lend a hand to the Lord's work, while others, by providing material resources, were able to overcome the obstacles that arise from bodily need.

When I received your letter, our friend Heinrich Wilhelm Ludolf was ill; and because under such circumstances I wanted to uplift his spirit with Christian refreshment, I took the opportunity to read him the aforementioned excerpt; which, as he attested to me afterward, not only pleased him, but also caused him to bequeath £100 to Your Honor in his will and testament—for he passed away in the Lord here at 2 a.m. on the 25th of this month—for the purpose, he clarified, of helping to pay off the debts on your college.[33] I remember that the blessed man wished several times that your college would be set on firm footing, and thereby pave the way for the work of the Lord in Poland and other nearby lands suffering in darkness. He expected that in Poland and Moscow the gospel would find a home after the courts had heard about it and their hearts were somewhat prepared to accept the truth.

Moreover, our blessed Ludolf lay ill for quite some time, without it being possible to say exactly what illness he died of. It was rather a

---

32. Heinrich Lysius (1670–1731) was professor of theology and preacher in Königsberg and the first director of the prestigious Collegium Fridericianum there.

33. Ludolf, "Will of Henry William Ludolf." Ludolf's will was witnessed by Böhme, Samuel Urlsperger, Johann Christoph Martini, and Jacob DuBarry. Martini would become a reader at the German Lutheran Royal Chapel.

complication of many symptoms, which would take something supernatural to unearth; as he said to me several times: "The doctors don't know what my illness is . . ." And even though his pain became more and more severe, he complained little because he believed that Christians are called to suffer, not to complain. So, it was truly edifying for me when a few days before his death he told me that the very last thing he had read—that is, when he was healthier, since his illness prevented him from reading—were the closing words of the second book of Thomas à Kempis's *Imitation of Christ*: "For when all is done, this will be the Sum and Conclusion of the whole Matter, that, *Through much Tribulation we must enter into the Kingdom of God*."[34] Perhaps it was a hidden admonition of what he still had to endure. He had already told me earlier how, during his illness, he had found considerable refreshment in both the words from Romans 15:5: "the God of steadfastness and encouragement." And indeed, because it is one and the same God, so both are manifested in the one God of steadfastness and encouragement, and reveal themselves to the soul sometimes through steadfastness and sometimes through encouragement, depending on the circumstances. It must be equally pleasing to us that God reveals Himself as He wills: but the God of steadfastness goes before the God of encouragement, and steadfastness is the basis of encouragement. He has conquered, and left throughout London a lovely fragrance, through his blameless walk and particular gift of conversing with others.

No. 69[35]

A. W. Böhme to Professor August Hermann Francke in Halle
London, 21 March 1712

I recently reported the blessed death of Heinrich Ludolf. Soon afterward, I had the opportunity to inform our Queen of it, and to humbly request payment of his remaining bequest, which she indeed graciously promised, particularly since I assured her that the blessed Ludolf had dedicated this bequest only to works of love and had requested that I present it to Her Majesty movingly. The payment was made soon after,

---

34. Thomas à Kempis, *Christian's Pattern*, 119 [trans. Stanhope].
35. AFSt/H C 229:36.

and the money was handed over to Henry Hoare as executor of the will. The Halle orphanage will receive about £75, to be paid to Dr. Heinrich Lysius (in addition to the £100, about which he has already been notified).

Several Englishmen requested that I publish in English my funeral sermon for Ludolf on Matthew 25:21.[36] I have dedicated the publication to the Society for Promoting Christian Knowledge, and mentioned in the Dedication, among other things, that the establishment of an international seminary would be very beneficial to the growth of the Church universal, and that Mr. Ludolf had on several occasions wished to see such an institution among the Protestants, in which young people from all nations could be educated, and after being made fit for service of the Church, sent back to their homeland.

I would like some news from the Italian prelate. Mr. Ludolf has left him about £10, so that if he still wants to come to England, he will have something to live on when he arrives.[37] I do not know, however, whether coming here would be advisable after Ludolf's death, because he has no acquaintance here, and I have not been able to learn anything definite about the student to whom he previously had written. We have received news from the ship on which Jonas Fincke set sail to the East Indies, that it drifted very far west, and finally landed at the Portuguese port of Rio de Janeiro in Brazil. They were anchored in this harbor when French admiral René Duguay-Trouin stormed it, plundered it, and made off with everything, as well as setting fire to forty Portuguese merchant ships.[38] At this miserable sight, the English governor, who was on his way to the East Indies and was on the ship with Fincke, immediately surrendered to the French admiral, together with the captured ships, men, and goods, and thus wisely prevented his ship from being blown up along with the others. After the storm and fury of the enemies had passed, the governor ransomed his ship for £3,500, and last October set sail anew for the East Indies. And in this way our printing press and printer were saved and sailed off to East India. The French admiral has taken the English governor's son as a hostage to France, where he will remain until the ransom

---

36. Böhme, *Faithful Steward*.

37. The Italian prelate is almost certainly Francesco Bellisomi (1663–1741). Ludolf's will mentions leaving £10 to "Monsiour Buyon." Ludolf, "Will of Henry William Ludolf." On Bellisomi, see *Short Account of . . . Franciscus Bellisomus*; Malena, "Speranze, progetti e reti interconfessionali."

38. René Duguay-Trouin (1673–1736), renowned naval officer and privateer, captured Rio de Janeiro, then believed unconquerable, with twelve ships and six thousand men in September 1711.

money is paid by the English East India Company, although it is not yet known whether the company will agree to the exchange. Our Malabar chest had to contribute £150 as our part of the ransom for the equipment we had on board. However, the Society recognizes the finger of God in these circumstances and is glad that nothing further has inhibited the work.

No. 70

A. W. Böhme to Mr. S. S., a Preacher in E.
London, 11 April 1712

Both of your letters have arrived in good order, and I will now reply to both as needed. No payment is necessary for Richard Baxter's book, *Gildas Salvianus: The Reformed Pastor*, because I had an extra copy to give to a friend.[39] I acquired several of Baxter's writings when I came to England; however, in 1707 a few Presbyterian preachers—Baxter in his day was one of the leaders among those Presbyterians who did not want to fully conform to the Church of England—edited together in four large volumes many of his works which had previously come out individually, so I was advised to buy some of the individual writings and give them to good friends. Volume IV just includes Baxter's practical works and those originally written about an active Christianity; the editors, however, have omitted the controversial writings, which are available in large numbers, but have yet to appear in a new edition. In my opinion, they have acted wisely in this decision and thus avoided, through a new printing, renewing and stirring up old controversies in the minds of different factions; for we have had enough squabbles in this country without that, and so many new ones are coming to the fore that the old ones, with their authors, should all the sooner be put to rest and buried.

Baxter had a splendid gift of teaching the basics of true Christianity to the unsophisticated in a powerful and resounding way. This gift, however, was subsequently considerably eclipsed by a common vice, when he allowed himself to be drawn into the controversies of the time, and tried to settle the disputes between the Episcopalians and the Presbyterians. In

---

39. Baxter, *Gildas Salvianus*. *Gildas Salvianus* has been available in some form since it was first printed.

this labyrinth, this otherwise upright man lost himself somewhat, and in such clamoring forgot his calling, which was far nobler than to mingle in futile quarrels.

In 1704 a friend and I took a trip to Kidderminster, in the county of Worcester, where Baxter had been a pastor and had worked with immense blessing. We still found some characteristics bearing witness that Baxter had been there. For as we were walking through town on a Sunday evening, we heard people singing in many of the homes. The residents assured us that on Sunday afternoons in Baxter's day there was nothing but singing and praying in almost every home, of which now, however, there were only a few small footprints here and there. He practiced there what he wrote in *Gildas Salvianus*. In particular, he awakened many souls through his private visits, until he was finally dismissed from his ministry at the restoration of Charles II, along with many other ministers who did not endorse the so-called Uniformity Act. He wrote an account of his life himself, while in the same writing incorporating a history of his time. Matthew Sylvester, Baxter's friend, had his autobiography printed in a folio after the author's death in 1696 under the title *Reliquiae Baxterianæ*.[40]

No. 71

A. W. Böhme to his sister, Anna Elisabeth Böhme
London, 1 July 1712

I hope that you will continue to walk with each other along the path of life in blessing; and also pray for me, that the Lord will watch over me and keep me from all harm. Judgments are looming very darkly over England: only the one who sits under the umbrella of the Most High will the Lord preserve in this evil time. God is coming and visiting the people, so that we may know what is in us. Otherwise, a person remains in the dregs, and is not poured into another barrel; people continue on like this, until the Lord tests them by His visitations. May the Lord keep you in His name which is a mighty fortress!

---

40. Baxter, *Reliquiæ Baxterianæ*.

No. 72

A. W. Böhme to Bartholomäus Ziegenbalg, Missionary at Tranquebar in East India
London, 22 January 1713

I have received your various letters in good order one by one, of which I will answer the most urgent because the English fleet is about to depart, and I want to enclose what, to the best of my knowledge, would serve the mission.

Heinrich Plütschau arrived in London on November 4, 1712, having earlier spent several weeks in Holland, where he first landed. The Society for Promoting Christian Knowledge received him with particular honors; he stayed here until November 25th, when he departed with a gift for his travels. During his stay here, he compiled several sheets of a school or reading booklet in Portuguese, which is commonly spoken on the Malabar coast. The Society has had this printed from reserves previously collected for the Malabar Mission. With this fleet you will have received a packet for use in your Portuguese School.

In addition, since Johann Gottlieb Adler, a printer and typesetter, along with his brother, have now arrived to help with the work of producing the New Testament in the Malabar language, the Society has bought 75 reams of paper and donated them to this cause. By means of this lifeless paper and type, which we still need in this time of weakness, may the Lord prepare many living letters for Himself, and by His finger write the truth of the gospel into hearts in such a way that all paganism may be enlightened by it and freed from the wrongful ways of the carnal heart!

We hope that the printing press, which was given to Jonas Fincke in 1711, will have landed and is being kept in Madras, together with 100 reams of paper and all the related printing equipment. We ransomed it for £150 from the French, into whose hands it had fallen at Rio de Janeiro in Brazil. Thus, there is a total of 175 reams of paper, which can at least provide a good start toward printing the Malabar New Testament. Beloved brother, report just as soon as possible to what extent printing is found to be practical in the East Indies, and send back some samples of the printing, so that with the next fleet more paper can be sent over, and hopefully all the difficulties that tend to arise at the beginning of any enterprise can be cleared away.

Several weeks before Mr. Plütschau arrived here, I was visited by Johann Georg Bövingh, who had sailed via Bengal in an English ship. He had had a fast and fortunate passage. Because I already knew at the time that he had sent a very hostile letter against the remaining missionaries to one of his acquaintances, who then published it, causing great offense, I would have liked to have had an extensive heart-to-heart conversation with Mr. Bövingh, and to have addressed the given offense in good faith, in the hopes that it might deepen his understanding of the situation. With that in mind, I offered him my room and asked him to rest with me for a week or several; but once he left me, he never came back.

Mr. Plütschau has now traveled to Copenhagen to see if he can find an opportunity to present the missionaries' plight to the king and to seek some help. The consolation in all tribulation is that God is not bound to any person, nor does His work depend on human help or authority. In the midst of the cross, misery, and opposition, the seed of the kingdom takes deep root. It lies there completely hidden from human eyes. The winter of adversity that passes over it seems to lead everything to death and destruction. This must happen, so that all glory may be stripped from humanity and attributed to God alone, who through His almighty power can renew all things and, in His time, perfect His power in weakness. All the help that flows to us from others now and then, in doing the work of the Lord, is like tiny glimpses of spring that reveal from afar that an outflowing love is stirring in some hearts, and that the summer of the kingdom of God is approaching, although it is not yet here. The gospel of Christ will still have to pass through considerable bitter resistance before pagans will truly be able to share in it.

Mr. Plütschau wrote back to me from Holland that it was announced that a new commanding officer was to be sent to Tranquebar and the previous one recalled. This would be desirable, if the new commander had better Christian principles than the old one, or if he would at least be given better instructions around matters of the mission. However, I find almost everywhere that governors, when they are sent from Europe to the East or West Indies, get so absorbed in the love of worldly things that one can expect little help from them for the work of the Lord. Among the English there still tends to be some inclination to promote the good. I fear, however, that the present government in Madras has a very uncharitable impression of the work in Tranquebar; and perhaps they have allowed themselves to be taken in by the Danish commander's ranting and austerity measures against the missionaries. Here I cannot refrain

OUTREACH THROUGH THE SPCK AND BEYOND (1710–1714)

from enclosing a paragraph which is attached to the general letter of the governor and council at Fort St. George, and sent to the local East India Company as a warning, from which it is easy to see what the English opinion of the Danish mission is

Extract

From the General Letter of the Governor and Council at Fort St. George in East India,
dated 20 August and 1 September 1711,
and delivered on board the *Bouvery*:

> We have given permission to one of the Danish missionaries to embark on board the *Tankervill*, but have refused permission to another missionary, at the request of the governor at Tranquebar, rather than get involved in their disputes. We have good reason to report to Your Lordships that this mission is a fraud that is being perpetrated on gullible people who send money to missionaries in need. According to the best information we can gather, the money is being used differently than those who contributed it for good reasons intended. We do not mention this for any other purpose than to prevent more money from being collected in England for this cause; without doubt, it can be better spent at home than here.

You can easily understand that such an unsavory judgment of the matter has been very prejudicial. My advice is this: that you, dear Mr. Ziegenbalg, sincerely and truthfully present the details of the whole affair, and how it disintegrated with the Danish governor, to George Lewis, who has a good reputation everywhere here. Then in all humility, he should make inquiries about what might have caused the harsh judgment written by the English governors, and willingly offer to remedy everything that has been done, whenever and wherever, out of weakness and carelessness. Such an open-hearted statement—in which one must be careful, on the one hand, that nothing of the truth be left out for fear of others, but, on the other hand, that we never absolve ourselves of human weakness—should win back the trust of the most honest English and be quite favorable to the whole work.

We hear that Rev. Lewis will return to England with the next fleet. If this should happen, it would be that much more urgent to try to give him a true impression of this undertaking before his departure, and to put an end to the prejudices that he might have against it. You could also inform him in particular how the money previously sent from England has been used, so that he can in turn give an account of it to local benefactors. If more money is sent from England in the future, a detailed account of it could be kept, in order to show someone who might inquire after it. And in such a way, those uncharitable judgments, that the missionaries are misappropriating the designated money and using it for their own benefit, would be most emphatically prevented.

Moreover, you should also know that Mr. Plütschau was robbed shortly after landing in Hannover[?]; as a result, we lost many things that would have been useful for furthering the mission. Among other things, the account of Malabar paganism, which our dear brother in his letter had dedicated to his friends in England, has also been stolen. The thieves, no doubt, expected to find great treasures with Mr. Plütschau, because they knew that he had come from East India. I did not receive the copy of the Malabar New Testament, which our beloved brother mentioned in his letter from Pulicat (Palliacatta) on December 27, 1711. With the next fleet, perhaps a copy can be sent to the Society, along with a Latin letter. But may the Lord give us understanding in all things!

P.S.

When Johann Berlin completes his journey under the blessing of God, he will be able to tell us how the work of the Lord is now proceeding in Germany, and especially in Halle. Provost B. died at the end of last year in B., and the position was given back to Mr. P. A friend wrote me that the King, after he had confirmed the call, is supposed to have said to Mr. P.: "You can be sure that this calling is from God, because I was moved inwardly to give you this position, apart from any human counsel." On November 28, 1712, in the fortieth year of her life, A., a lovely rose, was broken off by the bridegroom and transplanted to another garden. Her posthumous manuscripts show that she had lived in intimate relationship with her bridegroom, by faith. Heinrich Ludolf, former secretary to His Royal Highness Prince George of Denmark, and a great friend of the East India Mission, passed into his rest on January 25, 1712. You will receive on this fleet £150 in Pieces of Eight, because it is very difficult to get hold of a note of exchange. The money has been added to the Company's treasury. The £150 comes from H.; use it also to supply with rations the three persons arriving with it and to shield them from the king of Denmark[?].

No. 73[41]

A. W. Böhme to Johann Ernst Gründler, Missionary to Tranquebar in East India
London, 23 January 1713

The last letter that I received from you, dated December 14, 1711, I am now sending to Halle to be included in the fifth volume of the Malabar Reports. I hope that when these three persons, under the keeping of the Lord, arrive among you, the whole enterprise, which has up to now lain somewhat asleep, will be newly reawakened. Hopefully, they will give themselves straightaway to the printing of the New Testament in the Malabar language. When this is done, by all accounts, there should be a strong stirring of hearts across Europe, and many a prejudice that some hold will fall away as a result of this proof of their work and zeal.

It is clear that, among some people, a shadow has been cast over the work by various unfair judgments and misunderstandings that have arisen around Europe, and especially in England. Many people have been preoccupied with: the harsh reflection of the English government at Fort St. George; Mr. Bövingh's uncharitable writing against the mission;[42] Dr. Lütkens'[?] death;[43] the war in which the king of Denmark is involved;[44] Mr. Fincke's death and the loss of the funds he had with him; your quarrel with the commander and other such occurrences which have for the most part become known in Europe. I am by no means writing this to devalue diligence you have demonstrated up to now, but only to awaken it more, so that the accusations that have been made against you may be

---

41. AFSt/II Nachlässe und Deposita ALMW/DHM 6/9:18.

42. On Bövingh's "uncharitable" writings, see Moritzen, "Bövingh Controversy," 3:1284–88; Brunner, "Collaboration and Conflict."

43. Most likely Franz Julius Lütkens (1650–1712), German theologian who in 1704 became court-preacher and professor of theology at Copenhagen. He was commissioned by King Frederick IV of Denmark and Norway (1671–1730) to find missionaries for Tranquebar. He remained an active supporter of the mission.

44. For much of his reign, King Frederick IV was engaged in the Great Northern War (1700–1721) against Sweden.

answered with deeds and genuine service rather than with words and written apologies, since this is always the most conclusive and emphatic way of refuting an opponent and repudiating other accusations. What is of God in a matter cannot be dampened. Even if it is oppressed, it will rise up again sooner or later. Here it holds true: *Crescit sub pondere virtus* [Strength increases under a burden]. But as for our own profession, which tends to attach itself to our best works, it must rightly be revealed and seared in the fire of testing. *Hora crucis, hora lucis* [An hour of the cross, an hour of light]. The cross of testing is like the pillar of fire that caused terror and darkness among the Egyptians, but gave light and comfort to God's people. God does not allow His own work to be destroyed, but He does allow it to be cleansed of human dross by every sort of trial through fire and water, and thus to be more exalted.

With all the adversities that the East India Mission has thus far encountered, is it not good to have discovered, among other things, that many people have been moved to consider whether it might not be possible to work with blessing and intention toward the conversion of the pagans? It has had such an effect on the English, among others, that they are now anxious to find someone who could be sent to Madras as a missionary, or at least as a schoolmaster, to train the English youth there. They have indeed found someone and are hopeful that he will be able to take over such a position; he is likely to leave here next year. If I find, as I hope, that he is fair-minded, then I would like to arrange for him to visit you at Tranquebar for several weeks to see what you are currently doing, so that he can give his supporters a detailed and impartial report, which would not be without blessing.

Timothy has impressed the English here, especially since they saw how he was so well versed in the New Testament and knew how to quote many verses from it.[45] I hope that the Portuguese New Testament, which the Society has had printed to support your Portuguese school and congregation, will have arrived by now and can be put to good use. Certainly, all of paganism in Malabar would be impacted if we selected five or six young leaders from among them to be prepared in Europe for the work of the Lord and then sent back to their homeland as leaven.

---

45. Timothy or Timotheus was one of two young Malabarian converts who accompanied the early missionaries to Europe. Timothy came with Plütschau in 1711; Peter Maleiappan traveled with Ziegenbalg in 1714. Grafe, "First Lutheran Indian Christians," 1:224–28.

Beloved brother, we have diligently pursued your request that the London directors of the East India Company turn the whole matter over to the English governors at Fort St. George and Fort St. David. However, I have let Bartholomäus Ziegenbalg know how much the present English administration, undoubtedly due to the Danish commander's insistence, is opposed to it, and how the missionaries must therefore take care to convey to the English there a better impression than they now have, so that in the future they may form a more favorable opinion than they did of those from the last ships. Then, on our side, we will spare neither effort nor expense in offering them a hand. It seems, however, that not one person in the whole Council at Fort St. George looks favorably on them; for I hear that the letter is signed by both Edward Harrison, the governor, and all the councilors. God alone can prepare a smooth way through such a desert! I myself am amazed that, in spite of the hostile judgment written against them here, the company has nevertheless given orders to make room for these three persons in their ships, along with the extensive equipment and goods they have with them, and to grant everything we have asked of them. I count this among God's providences which can serve to strengthen them.

Mr. Berlin[?] has brought a good supply of devotional books from Germany to take with them to the East Indies. To these I have added several copies of Arndt's *True Christianity* and a few other Latin tracts.

No. 74

A. W. Böhme to Zacharias Dezius, Lutheran Preacher in Rotterdam[46]
London, 26 February 1713

I have received your worthy letter, together with the title page of the Arndt's *True Christianity* in Dutch, and I am pleased with the hard work you have put into editing this book. After all, God has placed His seal on the book, so we can put it into the hands of others with all the more confidence and expect a blessing on its reading. I am happy to recommend such books to others for their use and edification, when I have been told

---

46. Zacharias Dezius (1678–1725), Lutheran pastor in Rotterdam from Pomerania, first published his Dutch edition of *True Christianity* in 1713. A previous Dutch edition was published in 1631. Matthias, "Translation of Johann Arndt's True Christianity."

of instances of numerous people being awakened by them and brought to true Christianity. Indeed, we would be hard pressed to find a book among Protestants from which there is evidence of such blessing and conversion of many souls as from Arndt's *True Christianity*. Since up to this point I have made it my business, as much as I am able, to make this book known to everyone, I am glad to hear that others are of the same mind and are trying to promote it in other countries as well.

But, to get to the matter at hand, namely your Dutch edition of the book: I promise, to the best of my ability, to recommend the book to those who are fluent in Dutch. The greatest difficulty is likely to be caused by the heavy duty that has been imposed on foreign paper and books here in the past year, since this makes a book printed out of the country almost twice as expensive as it would be if it were sold locally (especially if I include the freight).

No. 75[47]

A. W. Böhme to Professor August Hermann Francke in Halle
London, 3 March 1713

With the last post I wrote to Georg Heinrich Neubauer to disburse £1 to the orphanage. It was sent here, together with a package of small tracts, by Dr. Cotton Mather, a minister at Boston in New England in America, in order to be forwarded to you, as the enclosed letters demonstrate in more detail.[48] Both the package of books and the pieces of gold were addressed to Dr. Josiah Woodward (presumably because he had written a preface to *An Abstract of the Marvellous Footsteps of Divine Providence*); but because he has long since died, both the letter and package were handed over to me to be passed along.[49] At the first opportunity, I will pass along the small tract, which Dr. Mather himself wrote in English for the edification of his congregation. The small gift or piece of gold mentioned in the letter was a Spanish pistole wrapped in paper with this inscription: for the use of Francke's orphanage in Halle. The value

---

47. AFSt/H C 229:32b.
48. Cotton Mather (1663–1728) was a New England Puritan preacher, theologian, author, and Fellow of the Royal Society, who had correspondence with both Böhme and A. H. Francke.
49. Josiah Woodward, Preface to Francke, *Abstract of the Marvellous Footsteps*.

here amounts to 17 English shillings. When I related these details to Miss Jane Slare for her enjoyment, she threw in three more shillings to make it 20, or a pound sterling. It appears that *Pietas Hallensis* is making a good impression on many people around America, according to reports I have heard. And because these details can be edifying to many people, we do not want to forget to include them in the next historical Continuation, if there should be one someday. I trust you will send a Latin reply to Dr. Mather, even without my reminding you; and I will see to it that the letter is sent to him from here, and in duplicate, so that if one should be lost, the other will be preserved.[50] Indeed, I see from Dr. Mather's letters that he ordered two copies of both the letter and books sent to England, the first of which never came into my hands. Last February 23, Mr. B. left Deal with his companions, and since I have heard nothing further from them, they must, by all accounts, have now fully entered the ocean.

No. 76

A. W. Böhme to Miss Jane Slare
London, 12 May 1713

I am glad to hear of your favorable arrival in Bath, after overcoming many troublesome incidents. The pilgrim who has nothing but adversity to endure on the journey to blessed eternity must endure everything. The smallest tests of divine providence watching over us should leave a deep impression on our souls; for those who do not regard the small tests of it will hardly utilize a greater one to the end for which it was given. The world is full of great tasks, and yet we do not find people who are particularly concerned about them; for whoever is aware of the signs of the times regards the spiritual lethargy that overtakes people to be a very clear sign of divine punishment. And how can we notice and take advantage of those things which are perhaps still quite distant from us, when we do not take advantage of those things which are just outside our door? And why would we be concerned about what is outside of us, when we are unconcerned about what arises and proceeds from within us? The small world within us is in constant harmony with the big world

---

50. On Mather's correspondence with Francke, see Splitter, "Franckes Briefwechsel mit Cotton Mather."

outside us. A soul that has in some way gone through the path of repentance knows from experience what rigorous and reawakening means our loving God must use to soften one's nature, or rather to break it, so that it may be made responsive and humble by the gospel of Christ. And how should this great world be awakened without some means to awaken it, and without severe rods and whips to bring it back to its duty. The more we see people sleeping away in their carnal safety, the closer the Lord is to awakening them mightily.

And yet, at the same time, few people will give glory to God and declare that the Lord did it; instead, most will revert to this or that natural cause, forgetting the primary and supreme mover of all things. So stiff-necked is our nature to turn to God, and so inclined are we to idolize the creature, that we neglect our obligation to worship God in all His revelations, both of His wrath and His grace. It is a great grace when we keep our eyes open and thus become aware of a ray of light in the midst of the darkness that surrounds us everywhere. Blindness of heart, which the apostle attributes to the Gentiles (Eph 4:18), is, in my opinion, one of the greatest judgments that can befall poor mortals. And this impression often hovers in my mind in these times. What misery would it be for you in Bath if you and your companions were suddenly struck with physical blindness? Would you not fall over each other, or bump into each other, and not know what to do, or which way to go, with such a crowd of blind people? But what is all this compared to blindness of the heart? Where the heart is blind, how great must the darkness be? But I am writing more than I intended. I commend you to the Father of lights, and to Him who is the great light of the world.

No. 77

A. W. Böhme to Miss Jane Slare
London, 26 May 1713

You know, the blessed Heinrich Ludolf used to say: "It would not at all befit Him to live uselessly on earth." However, whenever we live solely in the will of God, we are not useless, even if we should have to endure constant suffering. Anything that breaks the impulse of our self-will is very salutary to us. And if others discern in our conduct our complete surrender to the will of God, they will be more edified than if they were to listen to innumerable ordinary sermons.

No. 78

A. W. Böhme to Miss Jane Slare
London, 1 June 1713

In the same letter, where he speaks of wanting to drink from the health springs at Hampstead, is the following passage: It is, he says, a great grace when, in the midst of such great darkness, we occasionally get a glimpse of a higher light and are convinced that God is still a fountain of living water. That said, God also uses troubled waters to foster the healing of all kinds of diseases, if only we have the courage to step into them when they are moved.

No. 79

A. W. Böhme to N. N.
N.p., [June 1713]

It is a great grace when, in the midst of such great darkness, a small ray of a higher light appears now and then, convincing us that God is still a fountain of living water, although He is accustomed to using troubled waters to heal all kinds of diseases, if we only have enough courage to enter them when they are moved (John 5:4).

No. 80

A. W. Böhme to Miss Jane Slare
London, 9 June 1713

I am pleased to see that you find so much pleasure in your relationship with Lady Mary Philipps; true friendship is to be valued all the higher, given that it is so rarely found.[51] Pilgrims traveling to a blessed eternity must indeed take delight in each other, since the way to Zion looks so desolate and so few travelers set foot on that path about which the eye of reason can detect nothing but the cross and misfortune. But the one who said, "I will guide you with my eyes," also knows the very depths through which Christian pilgrims must pass, and moreover is powerful and willing to support them in every adversity they may encounter on their pilgrimage. But we must leave the timing of that help to His wise guidance. Faith deals with things hidden from the natural eye. But God has given to each person a second eye, capable of beholding divine things. Blessed is the soul guided by that latter eye, for with it one clings to God as a child to its father. It is not easily distracted from its purpose by the agitations and noises of this world, and is a sure signpost through the howling desolation of this world, for it is guided by a light that has been kindled from above.

No. 81[52]

A. W. Böhme to Heinrich Plütschau
London, 9 June 1713

I have received your letters one after the other and now I will comment on them. I will send the latest shipment to Tranquebar at the first opportunity. I hope that now, under the blessing of God, the complaints directed to the Danish court by the missionaries will have been favorably settled, and that the court is pledging more help to carry on the work. *But I also hope that over time the missionaries will immerse themselves more deeply in the way of faith of the first apostles, and thus be able to avoid such complaints from the powerful in the world.* I confess that the letters from East India have always given me great refreshment when I read them; however, I cannot hide the fact that I have found little pleasure in the vehement complaints about their adversaries, because I believe that all truth must be refined by undergoing the way of the cross and all kinds of prolonged trials. In this way, the work that is of God is not hindered,

51. Mary Philipps (d. 1722), wife of Sir John Philipps (ca. 1666–1737) and daughter of Anthony Smith, an East India merchant. Sir John was one of the most active lay members of the SPCK.

52. AFSt/H C 229:30.

but is in fact advanced, and the one who works at it, and is faithful, is prepared for greater things.

But to come to the matter at hand: your catechetical reader or school booklet, which you drafted in Portuguese here for the use of the schools at Tranquebar, was immediately printed at the expense of the Society, and a considerable number of copies were transported to the East Indies with the last fleet. Beloved brother, you will find some copies in Halle, which I asked the Society to send for those who intend to study the Portuguese language there. And because you mentioned when you were here that you are willing to compile a Portuguese dictionary, if you could somehow be provided with the necessary books in Portuguese, the Society would be happy to help you in this as well, as it is able. To that end, you will receive seven Portuguese books, which you can keep until you have completed the dictionary; then you can return them here for others to use. The Society received them as a gift from a theologian who collected the books when he was an embassy preacher in Lisbon. He says that they mirror the language spoken at court, so they are suitable for your intended work. It occurred to me that if the dictionary were to be compiled, it would be most useful for furthering the mission if it were written in Latin and Portuguese, and so a Latin-Portuguese Lexicon could be published. For the English and other nations could also benefit from its use, and could thereby be all the more suitably prepared for these works.

As for the sermon which you preached here and which I was intending to publish in English, I need to tell you that I did not attempt to print it, because the small work lacked the necessary accuracy, especially since the Dedication to the Society was returned to me only after your departure from Harwich; one way or another, we should have conferred first for greater clarity. However, time constraints prevented you while you were here from putting everything down on paper with the required attention. Perhaps there will be another opportunity to do something similar and to thank the Society publicly for the services it has thus far rendered to the mission. Give Timothy my greetings in heartfelt love. I enjoyed his letter, and I pray that he may experience the power of the words of 1 Corinthians 6:11 in his heart, so that he may be vitally convinced of the truth of Christianity and its advantages over paganism.

No. 82[53]

A. W. Böhme to Mr. H. F.
London, 13 July 1713

Your letters witness the affection we share. They move me to provide you whatever advice I can give about the arduous study of theology—something you named—and to show you, in brief as you ask, the impediments and supports I have observed, so that you might avoid the former and embrace the latter more fully.

All our theology has Scripture as its first principle. This means that love of the Scriptures is not a small, preliminary step toward true theology, but must be understood as the constant means by which progress is made in such an excellent undertaking. The word of the gospel is not only the seed from which the new person must be born, but the pure milk which nourishes him until he grows into Christ's full stature. Here arises the question of how the Holy Scriptures are to be treated, and why they are to be treated so, in order that those who cultivate theology might arrive at that knowledge of truth which accords with godliness. For that is how the apostle describes theology in Titus 1:1. First, however, those things which precede the study of theology and the treatment of Scripture on which it is based are to be considered; when these are properly considered, they will help to open wide the door to theology's secrets.

Among those things which precede the study of theology, the principal ones are knowledge of the Hebrew and Greek languages. Some do not hesitate to place knowledge of these languages first in the cultivation of theology, at least so far as human and external aids to the same are concerned, and therefore they put it before all the rest. Not without reason: if we compare the support provided by languages to that of other things, it is easy to see that it wins the palm because of its many uses in all the elements of theology.

So far as the difference between Greek and Hebrew is concerned: it is easy to say that more time should be given to Greek, and that it should be cultivated before Hebrew; however, Hebrew should not be completely neglected while Greek is being attended to, and neither should what is done in that connection be superficial. There is a strong affinity between the original texts of the Old and New Testaments; the characteristics of Hebrew are often woven into the Greek of the New Testament so that the

---

53. Original letter written in Latin.

imprint of its character can be traced upon the New Testament's style. In this way, one language shares much with the other, so that in order to study its force and energy one looks in vain for help from other Greek writers.

So far as the actual reading of the Old and New Testaments is concerned, some distinguish between *cursory* reading and *attentive*, repeated reading. The former can be offered at any time and upon any occasion, and can be done in such a way as to develop understanding of the original languages, to which it is most conducive. For example: when I have been at public prayers or sermons, I have read through in the original the scriptural chapters or passages being read or adduced by the minister, and by following the reader's voice I have benefited in ways I do not regret. In the same way, when I traveled, the reading of the New Testament was at the very least my companion, as it still is. When I was a teacher, and would listen to the children reading in the vernacular, or would ask them to read scriptural passages during catechism, I would have the text of what they were reading in hand, and would follow the reader's footsteps in what was printed in another language. I recall several who used these and similar methods as a help so that they could, for a brief space and time, almost turn the vernacular into the Greek, so that later, even without book, they could recall the principal voices they had heard in the Holy Text which had been inscribed on their memories by attentive reading. My rule in this kind of reading was: *not quantity, but quality*. I would not counsel you to run through the various Greek authors unless you have first drunk more deeply of the style and diction of the New Testament itself. *Let other writers provide you hospitality for entertainment, but let Scripture alone be your home, the place where you dwell.*

There are portable editions of the New Testament available which are suitable to the purpose described. A small edition of the Hebrew books appeared in Amsterdam and Frankfurt, but it is without points and therefore not useful to novices in the language. Instead of the whole book, it is better to carry with you the Psalms of David, fully pointed, and, by reading and re-reading them as if they were sap to suck, make them into your bloodstream. I know, certainly, that the Psalter has many rare words which are difficult to understand; but I also know that if these are committed to memory the result is that the whole Old Testament becomes more intelligible—that is because the Psalter, with its peculiar abundance of words, is understood by some as the word-hoard of all Scripture. This Psalter was published separately in Amsterdam, with points but without a translation. The same appeared in London in 1688, with vowel points and with an added English translation.

I call this of which I am speaking a cursory reading, not because I at all wish such a tremendous and sacred work to be treated lightly or inattentively, but in light of external circumstances which do not permit us to sink into the reading of Scripture with proper and long-lasting attention. At the same time, readers should always and everywhere show holy reverence to these divine oracles, putting aside all perfunctoriness so long as they are concerned with them—for that is the habit of mind required of any who wish to treat Scripture in such a way as to be edified by it. Certainly, any who read Scripture to that end, as all should, in order to stimulate the growth of the new man, do not completely separate themselves from their goal even when they read cursorily. It is as with those, overwhelmed with business, who cannot always sit at a table set with many dishes, but must take food as prudently as they can, but who are nevertheless nourished and given strength; it is the same for those who read Scripture cursorily but sincerely find the inner flame of life fed in this way, and they gather from that something which faithfully remains from in the soul.

I should like you, therefore, to work on both languages of the Holy Book together, so that you make better progress in exegetical reading. That is the kind of reading which attends most closely to the text, so that you can more carefully uncover the literal sense intended by the Holy Spirit, and then, by diligently applying interpretive helps, so scrutinize what underlies it that you in the end arrive at the practice of internal application of the divine truth. This reading is to be undertaken with the most precise care. The purpose of each book is to be considered: the joints of the text are to be searched out; parallelisms, verbal and real, are to be looked for; implication and the understanding of voice are to be unearthed; the sacred phraseology of Scripture is to be investigated and elucidated by way of that selfsame text, as if out of its guts; and so on. By this method, properly practised, students will learn to look for the proper basis of each theological article in the scriptural book in which it is explicitly handed down, which is of great help in proving this or that matter of theological substance, and in rebutting the many tricks of adversaries.

If this course of action is not followed, readers wander through the Scriptures with no clear motive even if they are industrious; and not knowing where to stand they never see that heavenly analogy which provides the entire Christian religion coherence in all its articles—a quite admirable economy! It is a matter of great importance in theology that one should come to know this analogy of faith (Rom 12:6), neither in systematic fashion nor in an arrangement according to art, but by living and clear experience corroborated inwardly, so that one might proceed with this arduous business not apart from the proper divine order but rather according to it, the true order of things in the soul.

It is hard to credit how much damage neglect of this order and analogy does, particularly with respect to the practical use of law and gospel. This needs to be variously tempered and variously applied to souls moving toward conversion. This damage makes itself felt not only among the young, but through the entire course of the theological life in every part of the pastoral office. For what is absorbed in youth goes deep, and a defect suffered early is rarely completely corrected later (this is an axiom of natural scientists). For the church of God, together with the religion which belongs to it, is called a domicile (Eph 2:21ff; 1 Tim 3:15), in which neither should the lowest be exchanged with the highest, nor the highest with the lowest, but in which everything should be disposed decently and in good order.

I could give many examples to confirm this; one or two will suffice. The universal economy of salvation requires that the use of the law should precede that of the gospel in the conversion of sinners; i.e., that sinners be vividly affected by the spiritual sense of the law, by spiritual sadness, and by contrition; and then, according to the gospel's word of promise, be raised up again, and led, as if by the hand, to Christ, the restorer of the human race, to find life and salvation in him. And whenever a dispenser of the mysteries has to do with those entering, he speaks of these very things. But when the first use of the law is left behind, and the gospel is too soon announced to those willingly and confidently rushing toward sin, they are provided false comfort: and then sinners seeking grace are held captive by the law's bonds, so that they do not taste the freedom of the gospel. It is clear that conversion is greatly hindered by this topsy-turvy method. Equally, if someone zealously urges good works while neglecting to make the teaching of regeneration foundational, does this not clearly cut against the practical application of the analogy of faith and the harmonious order of salvation as a whole? To do that is to ask for good fruit before there is a good tree (Matt 12:33)—for spiritual works before people are imbued with the first principle of spiritual action. You will avoid these and other shipwrecks if you cultivate exegetical theology properly, investigate the truths of Scripture and the order that connects them one with another, and apply them particularly to yourself so that you may then be able to apply them securely to others who might have been placed under your care.

I have no doubt that systematic theology has some purpose here; I do not altogether condemn it by preferring those who studiously apply themselves to the business of salvation; but it is always better to draw the waters of heavenly truth from the source of the Scriptures themselves. I want this: that no system of theology should ever be simply accepted, but should rather serve as an avenue of approach to Scripture itself. If anyone knows how to use a system, or body of doctrine as they call it, to enter more deeply into good investigation of the Sacred Writings themselves, I would not at all dissuade them. In short: let systems be guides; they are not worth dying for, but one can go through them to arrive at something else. An impartial eye cannot avoid seeing how systems teem with prejudices on every side; when everyone bends the scriptural oracles to their own confession, it will be sufficiently difficult to discover the Christian system cleansed of human inventions and prejudices. Every sect has fabricated its own analogy of faith, to which it subjects all doctrines and by means of which it interprets the Scriptures themselves.

Others insist on a different way: they warn about the reading of commentaries, and say that those who cultivate theology should first familiarize themselves with Scripture by frequent reading, prayer, and meditation, and then subsequently consult other interpretations if they wish; and then that the same method be applied to this matter also: that they should read, repeat, and then work through the systems of others and judge them according to the light derived from Scripture as first principle. It is clear that systematic theology originated in part from scholastic theology, the fertile mother of inane distinctions and opinions and the offspring of Aristotelean philosophy. And so it happened that as the vices of the time increased, the simplicity of the Christian life and the golden age of the apostles, which were once evident everywhere, began gradually to vanish from the Christian schools. Theology itself put aside its chaste habit of innocence, and was then defiled by philosophical sophistries.

However that may be, since the greater part of the writings of theologians, at first in Latin, is full of scholastic terms, it is necessary to gain some knowledge of that theology if we want to understand their books easily. A middle way is necessary here: on the one hand we should not cling to the authority of the theologians with blind obedience (that is something close to the soul of papism); on the other, we should not superciliously reject gifts given to our neighbors, and, by relying more on our own judgments, fall into error and unproductive arguments. Relevant to this topic are the warnings provided by Gilbert Burnet in his book on pastoral care, third edition, p. 148.[54]

I will bring this letter to an end by adding just a few words on the topic of catechetical theology, which, as one who cultivates theology, I take to be very important for the Church's advancement. I greatly regret that only the slightest traces of this practice remain among Christian communities now. I openly declare that I found much benefit in this practice, which I once undertook for a time; I therefore always try to persuade my friends to be quick to undertake the work of examining the catechism as opportunity provides. In this connection, if solid foundations are laid, and heavenly teaching is instilled in unformed souls from their cradles onward, I think we would soon be able to leave polemical theology behind. For straight lines show both themselves and what is oblique to them. It may seem that a preceptor works fruitlessly for now to form the souls of children, but the time may come when the seeds of the word will take root because of the influx of grace, and will then appear more clearly, especially if both cross and affliction were to approach like an external teacher shaking off the mind's torpor, and making the will and the understanding more attentive to the word. And even if work with children seems greatly annoying, catechists do not at all lose the fruit of their work. They learn by teaching. For as they inculcate Christian learning in others by frequent examination, and prove it from the Scriptures, they become themselves more and more proficient in studying Scripture and prudently explaining it to others.

This, my dear friend, is what I wanted to propose to you about the elements of the hard work of theology as my experience of it has been. You can see that a proper treatment of the theology of Scripture is my first and last concern, the bow and stern of my enterprise. I grieve every time I recall the slackness and unpreparedness with which those who study theology treat the study of sacred literature! Believe me, this feeble study of the Scriptures is, if not the only cause then certainly not the least, of the Church's affairs continuously going from bad to worse unless timely remedies are applied to heal the Church's wounds—and these

---

54. Burnet, *Discourse of the Pastoral Care*.

remedies are best applied by imbuing the minds of the young from their very earliest age with the very form of Scripture's healing words.

You may be surprised that I have said nothing here about reading the Fathers. But you will cease to be so if I tell you that the reading of the Fathers has for a long time now been evident almost everywhere in theology, especially if you look at the English academies. There is an excessive number of writers who so immerse themselves in the reading of the Fathers that they permit the study of Scripture to seem worthless. It is from Scripture alone that divine convictions are generated in the mind, upon which faith can rest secure in time of trial; and since all human writings, which includes those of the Fathers, contain things other than what is godly, they lead in that direction and leave only human convictions behind them. I do not deny that some who turn with ardor to what the Fathers have written gather honey from there to nourish the spiritual life as if they were bees—as Francis Rous, once provost of your Eton College, did with the material he collected and published as a book in 1650 with the title *Mella patrum* [*Honey of the Fathers*].[55] There are those who read them in order to establish the scheme of external religion to which they are accustomed or to fabricate something new from them. And there are those who read in order to form this or that opinion for themselves from education, conversation, tradition, and so on, and then fortify and defend it. Reading of this kind, since it does not aim at theology (which is the restoration of the divine image in us and in others), and is too much concerned with ancillaries, is the basis and mother of the traditional theology of opinion which is everywhere so strong; examples of this are close at hand.

No. 83[56]

A. W. Böhme to Mr. R.
London, 24 July 1713

It is quite shocking how tardy I am in replying to your friendly letters handed on to me at the end of 1712. But here at last is a reply, late but

---

55. Francis Rous (1579–1659), *Mella patrum*. Rous was an English Puritan, known for his mystical theology and metrical version of the Psalms.

56. Original letter written in Latin.

perhaps not too late. I repeatedly looked for occasions to write to you, but whether from the hurry of my departure or because of my own tardiness, however involuntary, they slipped away. Now, at last, I pay the debt.

As for the pamphlets you wanted, I send you what I have to hand. No accurate biography of Michael Servetus has appeared here, but by way of the Collectanea some things about his life, his interrogation, his burning, and other circumstances not easily known up to this point and not unworthy of interest, have been published, as is evident from the bundle of papers attached here. The author, or rather the compiler of this work is Michel de La Roche from the French Protestants, who previously put out weekly, and now every other week, what are called new writings (and sometimes also records of old ones, as this story about Servetus shows), which makes known new books already published and about to be published in every part of Europe.[57]

As for the *Itinerarium* of Heinrich Ludolf, nothing of it has yet seen the light, and perhaps may never do so. And about the *Reliquiæ Ludolfianæ*, for example, please accept this copy from me as witness to my brotherly love.[58] That blessed man left me in his will the paraphernalia of his library, including his manuscripts, and particularly those having to do with the business of his travels; but when everything is heaped in confusion and is written in many languages (the author knew eleven), and some writings are too elliptical and imperfectly expressed, I would not venture to make public things that would need a great deal of editorial attention. You will find his plans for promoting religion in the Orient, particularly in Palestine, in these *Reliquiæ*, from which you will be able to see how he thinks. Would that others might undertake what he pointed to, as if with his index finger, even to the English Society for Promoting Christian Knowledge, to which in the end he proposed what he had conceived.[59] But we now lack such impartial lovers of wisdom, and will continue to do so unless they are being readied by heaven for work of such importance. The excessive zeal for religion which has pervaded the Anglican Church, to God's just judgment, is choking the very harvest sought. May God give better things, and yet by fiat bring into being a new creation out of the unformed and shadowy potentiality which will more

---

57. Michel de La Roche (ca. 1680–1742), journalist and translator, was a French Huguenot refugee and member of the Church of England. He reviewed books in his publication *Memoirs of Literature* (1711–1714).

58. Ludolf, *Reliquiæ Ludolfianæ*.

59. See Ludolf, "Proposal Relating to the Promotion of Religion."

perfectly show the impress of His image. May He also destroy more and more whatever remains in us of the old creation, so that the new might constantly be renewed and emerge into a better life.

As to the external circumstances of my own life, it would take too long to add anything about them here. Perhaps there will be another occasion more convenient to their discussion. I will be grateful, venerable one, if you will enter into an exchange of letters with me, and explain whether I can offer you any service here, which I am always ready to do. I often remember you, and especially when I open up, which I often do, the version of the New Testament in German which we have because of your work, several copies of which I have sent to the West Indies some time back at the request of friends in Germany.

No. 84

A. W. Böhme to Miss Jane Slare
London, 15 July 1713

I am enclosing an account of a poor Greek man's dream, which you can give to your brother, when it is convenient. Exceptional actions such as these can prompt us to reflect on His thoughts; they also give us reason to praise God for the more certain prophetic word, which is the guiding star that leads us to Christ. Dreams, prophecies and all other extraordinary gifts must finally all point to Christ, the hope of glory, and converge in Him. All gifts are like tiny stars that disappear as soon as the sun of righteousness rises.

P.S.

Just as the kingdom of light manifests itself in certain souls, so the kingdom of darkness is no less busy in its subjects, of which we had a pathetic example in our neighborhood last night. But as it was in the times of Noah, etc.

Mr. Rodokonakis's Dream of the blessed Heinrich W. Ludolf

Mr. Rodokonakis, a poor Greek man, who was generously supported by dear Heinrich Ludolf in his last years and was included in his will,[60] once had a dream in which Mr. Ludolf appeared to him and ordered him to go to Wapping, a suburb of London, and to enquire at a certain house, which he described, after two sick countrymen, who were in need of assistance. That kind of a vision was unusual for him, and even though it stayed on his mind all day, he regarded it as a natural part of his imagination, and so he did not go where the apparition had directed him. The following night he had the dream again, in which Mr. Ludolf chastised him for neglecting to serve his poor neighbor, and earnestly ordered him not to delay in visiting his countrymen and providing them with New Testaments from Bohemia. This made such a deep impression on him that he went out earlier than he was accustomed to, which even surprised his landlady. He went to the house that had been described to him and asked the maid if they had anyone staying in their house. "Oh yes," she said, "there are two foreigners upstairs who don't know a word of English and have no one to talk to." And she showed them up the stairs. As soon as he opened the door and addressed these poor people in Greek, one of them, lying in bed, said: "Thank God, now my dream has come true! Because two nights ago I had a dream about a distinguished man who encouraged me and said that I should not despair but trust in the living God, who would send me help and not abandon me." At this point Rodokonakis was even more convinced of the truth of his dream, and, having inquired about their circumstances, took leave of them and promised to come back soon. He came to me and told me their whole story; so I gave him two New Testaments and some money, which helped the poor men regain their strength and travel back to Greece.

Because of its similarity, the following dream was sent along with it.

The dream or apparition of a housekeeper of Richard, Earl of Cork, the eldest brother of the famous and godly Robert Boyle[61]

It is known throughout Great Britain that the Boyle family was particularly well-known for its godliness and charity toward the poor, and never let its left hand know what its right hand was doing. Before his death, the earl gave £500 to a minister in Dublin to distribute to the needy, especially those in poor houses where he would likely find true

---

60. In his will Ludolf left Rodokonakis £3 and fifty Greek New Testaments. Ludolf, "Will of Henry William Ludolf."

61. Richard Boyle (1612–1698), 1st Earl of Burlington and 2nd Earl of Cork

recipients of charity. However, after the unexpected death of the earl, the minister, who was in the process of building a new house and knew quite well that the earl liked to carry out his works of love in secret, appropriated the money and spent quite a bit of it on his building. So, it came to pass that the earl appeared in Dublin to his housekeeper, whom he had provided for generously in his will and who was spending her remaining years preparing for a blessed departure from this life into eternity; he admonished her to go to the minister, whom he named, and remind him that the £500 should be used for the purpose for which it had been given to him. The housekeeper was frightened by the apparition, but he told her not to be frightened and to follow his directive.

The next morning, the matter was still on her mind, but she was too afraid and allowed her reason to interfere to such an extent that she could not follow through with her master's order. Then the earl appeared to her again and reprimanded her for not having obeyed his directives. Now she was even more frightened and promised to do what she had been ordered to do. If she had had all manner of scruples after the first appearance, her reason and timidity now preyed on her all the more; she thought of a learned man from whom she wanted to ask for advice on how she should proceed, but for fear of being taken for a fool and dreamer by him, she delayed so long that she was still unable to come to a resolution. Then the earl appeared to her a third time, and not only chastised her severely, but also declared to her that it would not go well with her if she did not obey his command. This time, though, she promised, trembling, that she would not let reason interfere any longer, and that she would go in the name of God and follow his directive. She got up early, commended herself to God, and ventured over to the renowned learned man, who received her kindly and asked about her concern, because she seemed so upset. She implored him to pardon her, but he reassured her and persuaded her to tell him her concern freely and openly, and that he would listen to her patiently and assist her in word and deed to the best of his ability. When she revealed to him how the apparition unfolded, he paused briefly and then told her what she should do and how she should address the preacher.

After giving her these instructions, he asked her if she wanted him to accompany her and escort her to the preacher. She gladly accepted the proposal, and they both went to see him. The preacher received them very courteously, led them into his study, and asked the reason for such an extraordinary visit. The housekeeper asked him, as she had been directed, if he had not been entrusted with a certain sum of money that he was to distribute to the needy and poor. At that point the minister turned pale and said: Yes, shortly before his death, the Earl of Cork had given him £500 for the benefit of the poor, which he had used in part to build his house; however, with the help of God he wanted to restore the money and use it for the purpose for which it had been given. After she told the preacher that the earl himself had commissioned her to make this known to him, she and her companion took their leave, praising God for His providence. When they got to her home and the housekeeper was about to say goodbye, the learned man did not want to let her go, but asked her to go with him, because he still had something to say to her. When they arrived at his house, he told her that he would not have urged her to stay with him a little longer without a particular reason: he could not hide from her that when she came and told him what had happened, he was busy at the time writing a treatise against apparitions, all of which he had thought were fables. But since he had been convinced otherwise, he wanted her to see it, so he took what he had written and threw it into the fire. He discussed the matter still further with her and concluded that since her former master had appeared to her once, he believed that he would appear again now, since she had obeyed his command. And if he should appear to her again, the learned man asked if she could not summon up the courage to ask him whether he was blessed in the other world, and several more questions, which he wrote down for her, so that she could better commit them to memory. At first she told him that she did not know if she would ever see him again, and that she doubted whether she would be able to remember the questions and to put them to him if he came back. But he persuaded her to take the questions with her and to write them down. The earl indeed appeared to her again, and in the same kind, lovely form as he had appeared to her the first time, and expressed his pleasure at her obedience in carrying out his instructions; therefore, she took courage and asked him if he was in a blessed state. To this he answered in the affirmative, and said that he was blessed, but not as blessed as his brother Robert Boyle. But to the question, whether he had assumed his former body, because he had appeared in his former form, he answered in the negative. And to the third question, whether they could appear from the other world if they wanted to, he also answered in the negative, saying that they could not appear to their mortal friends unless heavenly wisdom deemed it good. And with that he disappeared.

No. 85

A. W. Böhme to Monsieur V. B. in H.
London, 15 July 1713

I was glad to receive your letters, because I see from them that your soul still perseveres in the love of the good and is strengthened rather than hindered in the good by the examples of the bad. That is how it should be. The examples of the wicked should drive us closer to God, but in no way hold us back from God and the heartfelt devotion that belongs to Him. Would you not guard a jewel if you have to travel with it through roads that are notorious for many thieves and highwaymen? And should we not try to guard our inner treasure and keep it close to us, since the whole world is full of soul robbers, who do not want to rob us of money, but of the blessedness and the jewel which the heavenly calling holds in store for us. Despite this, we carry *within us* our own enemy, which would like to rob us of our crown and deliver us into the hands of the world. We are never out of danger as long as we are carrying around our "selves," because selfishness dwells so close to us, and if we do not watch vigilantly, it hinders the growth of our inner foundation.

We are very pleased with your zeal, which you have shown in purchasing and distributing the spiritual books, for which we had given you two guineas. This can be a small seed out of which a glorious fruit can grow under the influence of divine blessing. A righteous beginning must be made. When a small light arises in a dark place, everyone gapes at it, and people do not know what to call it, because they have never seen anything like it. Hence it happens that the wicked often declare the true light to be a false light and a deception, which must be borne with in merciful love, until in time their eyes become clearer and accustomed to the light. Then they will realize for themselves that they have previously been children of darkness, and have never seen the sun of righteousness, which shines only by day, but not to those who want to remain in darkness. Furthermore, may you, my dear friend, be faithful to the Lord with the light you have received; may you walk, work, pray, read by the same faithfulness. In this way, the same light, which at first shines with limited effect, will spread more and more thoroughly, so that you will find the sure and straight path in the midst of the world's mixed-up ways.

God is still giving us one blessing after another here in London. The Lord's grace is particularly evident in young people, some of whom are called in the prime of life to serve a better master. Several of them have already left us. If they remain faithful, they will be salt by whose impact others can also be awakened. I am afraid, however, that some might come to love the world again. It is well known that many who receive the word with joy still fall away at the time of tribulation. The time of trial shows how deeply the seed is rooted. Before this happens, it is impossible to know which is a weed and which is healthy wheat. Our work to *care for the poor*, established in 1712, of which you were also a member, is still going on, and up to now many a poor person has benefited from it; others, too, have contributed to its maintenance. The *rules*, which we had just written down when you were here, are now printed in English and German, a few copies of which I have enclosed.

No. 86

A. W. Böhme to Mr. O. H. at R. near L. in H.
London, 3 August 1713

The reason why I am so slow in replying to your letter is that I first wanted to see the outcome of the last parliament here, so that I could report something certain about the French translation of Arndt's *True Christianity*.[62] As I recall, I previously explained what an immensely heavy tariff has been imposed for several years now on paper and books brought into this realm from other countries; as a result of which, books published outside the country are just as expensive, if not more expensive, than those published in country, where, apart from such special tariffs, both printing and paper are more expensive than in other countries. Now, during this last parliamentary session, some admirers of foreign books have been trying to get the parliament, which has the most to say in this matter, to lift this tariff, but it has not been able to come to a final decision; therefore, the aforementioned tariff remains in place and makes books printed outside the country extremely expensive. And this then is

---

62. The first French edition of Arndt's work, *Les quatre livres du vrai Christianisme*, was translated by Samuel de Beauval and published in Amsterdam in 1614.

the reason that I am waiting on the publication of the French edition of *True Christianity*, be it in Switzerland, Germany, or Holland, and cannot resolve anything for certain.

If dear Mr. Haferung can provide me with a copy of the French version, whoever may have it, I would like to pay the copyist—if it is written clearly and legibly—for the work of copying it.[63] It will serve my desire to show this manuscript to some well-meaning Frenchmen here who wish to see the book in their language, and to hear their opinion about it. So, I cannot absolutely promise that it will be printed, but I can promise that no effort will be spared. I do not see what reservations the translator could have with this particular collaboration, unless he wants to have his work paid for; however, I do not intend to get further involved in this kind of contract, especially since all the circumstances of the printing are so uncertain. My purpose is to serve the French nation by editing such a book, and to nourish the good desire that is arising in some people. The so-called mystics are badly received here by our French refugees; their taste for mystical authors has been spoiled and they are quite troubled by them.[64] But because Arndt converses diligently with the Scriptures, and the book is already known to some in Latin, one should be able to reach them more easily and do something good among them.

No. 87

A. W. Böhme to Monsieur V. B. at H.
London, 8 September 1713

Let me assure you once again that the diligence you have shown in distributing good books in Europe has made us very happy here. Who would not be moved by the misery, blindness, and ignorance of so many people? Yet, it cannot move in the heart of any but those who have first lamented and taken to heart their own condition, and have begun to save their souls from ruin by the grace of the Lord. Such people then desire that all people would be helped. For true Christians do not eat their bit alone, but share it so that others may also be satisfied with the bread of

---

63. Probably Johann Caspar Haferung (1669–1744), German Lutheran theologian, who revised de Beauval's translation and published it at Wittenberg in 1723.

64. See Laborie, "Huguenot Offensive."

life. But the taste for the spiritual gifts of God has so waned in many people that the Lord must awaken it again through grievous trials. And yet there are probably few who will thus allow Him to awaken them and to be helped from eternal ruin. Many are so hardened by a long habit of sinning that they only become harder when chastised, and more stubborn and godless by trials, an example of which is found in Revelation 16:9. Thus we have a reason to watch over our souls, lest our hearts be hardened, and thereby become poorly suited to hear God's voice. Not that God hardens people; but people harden themselves when they turn away from the chastening voice of the Lord, and think in their hearts what Pharaoh said that day with his mouth: "Who is the Lord whose voice I must hear?" And we are truly warned against such hardening of the heart (Heb 3:7–8), since it is a source of many other sins. Where it takes root, the seed of the gospel cannot sprout, much less bear fruit. May the Lord preserve us from this! God does not strike in judgment all at once, as He would be justified in doing; rather, He gradually lets His plagues work their way through, just as an approaching thunderstorm gradually gathers, turns the sky black, and finally breaks loose in fierce blows. And God does this so that a person may still have time to repent and turn back.

With regard to the current state of Germans in London, the Lord now and then makes us aware of a small blessing on our work. Most of them, however, harden themselves against the voice of the Lord and do not want Christ to be Lord of their lives, even though His lordship is gentle and mild. The Monday meeting still continues steadfastly; and because participants in it have the freedom to present their thoughts freely and unhindered, or to share their inner concerns and temptations openly without fear, I find that such simple conversation is often more beneficial than many sermons, which are generally listened to more out of habit than out of some inward desire. Our work to care for the poor is still going well, and many a poor person has enjoyed a material blessing from it. However, by the grace of God, we strive to set everything on such a footing that, in addition to the material gift, the poor and the sick also enjoy edifying encouragement aimed at the betterment of their souls, and thus the alms are truly sanctified.

No. 88

A. W. Böhme to Mr. T. in B.
London, 13 October 1713

At the end of last month, six French Protestants arrived here, who had previously been imprisoned in the galleys by order of the King. They were followed soon afterward by six others, out of a total number of 136, who, at the request of the Queen of Great Britain, were finally released from their bondage. These twelve have arrived here to give thanks to our Queen, on behalf of all those who were liberated. One would hope that those who were freed would be burning and shining lights among their compatriots and religious associates, among whom one finds but little of the power of a living Christianity; therefore, it is safe to assume that few leave their homeland because of the truth of the gospel and confession of the name of Christ, but that most of them have endured such hardships because of adherence to their sect and party. Perhaps the Lord has brought those who have experienced, as it were, a continual death in the galleys to a deeper sense of His hidden grace, or perhaps He has somewhat prepared them to enjoy it. It requires a great deal for one to be a true martyr, a witness and a confessor of the truth; therefore, we must not be too free with these names, for there are some who, virtually without any scrutiny, want to attach these precious names to the French released from the galleys. We are bound to thank God when we find them in such a state, because we can conclude that such chastisement has served them as an instrument of their true conversion to God; but we must also hope that in some of them these tribulations have sanctified them more deeply and have become a cross of Christ. The Marquis de Rochegude,[65] who is currently in London and has worked tirelessly at the Protestant courts in Europe to have these people released, asserts that there are still 178 souls in the galleys, not to mention others, both male and female, who are held in common prisons. It does not appear, however, that the King wants to listen to further appeals, since he has assured the government here, through his envoy, that there are none left who, on account of religion, are in galleys or prisons.

You will already be already aware of the latest harsh edict that the King issued against the refugees, thus cutting off all hope of their return

---

65. Le Marquis Jacques de Rochegude (ca. 1654–1718). Jaccard, *Marquis Jacques de Rochegude*.

to their homeland. These religious matters seem to be coming more and more to a crisis. Confusion is widespread, and nothing holds together any more. Everything pushes to the extremes. Another forty souls from the principality of S., along with a preacher, have arrived here to be sent to the West Indies, where they have been told they can work in the silver mines and earn their living in the process. However, up to now they have not been able to depart because they lack the necessary expenses for the crossing; I do not yet see how they will get away. So we see how the oppressed creature seeks rest, first in this place, then in another, which cannot be found in the world.

The so-called French Prophets, who for several years now have been causing a stir because of their inspirations and agitations, have recently received letters from the four they dispatched from their midst some years ago to Turkey, namely, as some have said, to the King of Sweden. They had then arrived in Belgrade, where they were promised sympathetic support. They must have endured considerable grief and misery, because the governor of Elbingen is said to have captured them as spies, taken their belongings from them, and maltreated them very severely. Maybe through such suffering they will be increasingly purified and kept safe from the dangerous cliffs (Rev 2:20–21), at which quite a few have suffered shipwreck. Recently, 12 of their colleagues arrived here, after the Swiss had indignantly evicted them. If one were to deal with these people in a spirit of gentleness, one would be more likely to obtain something from them. For this virulence, which has no place in Christianity, increasingly exposes the shame of the authorities, and eventually renders suspect all external worship as papist and anti-Christian.

No. 89

A. W. Böhme to Samuel Urlsperger
London, 6 November 1713

As for his first letter of Sept. 26, in which he requested protection from the French envoys here in order to be safe with his family from the enemy army standing on the Rhine, I promptly included it with the letters I had answered, because I could see that none of my English friends would interfere with such matters. The most honest people have refrained from dealing with the Duke of Aumont,[66] the French ambassador to London, since he has made the city to sin during his stay here, and has thereby provoked God's judgments against us. Because he resides in my neighborhood, I have had occasion, against my will, to hear many an abomination. He has revived the masquerades in this city that had lain dormant, as it were, since the time of Charles II, and has reintroduced them to the dismay of those who still have some sacred reverence for God. The unruliness of those who attended such shameful gatherings lasted all night long until break of day, when the spirit of worldliness had finally exhausted them in its service, for they slept during the day in the same spirit in which they had acted during the night. Many passed by my window in hideous shapes and disguises, and my mind repeatedly turned to Judith 5, especially vss. 17, 22, and 23; for I firmly believe that a nation becomes ripe for judgment when it first introduces all kinds of abominable vices and commits them with impunity. These things pave the way for judgment. And I wanted to mention this in passing, so that he would understand what we have dealt with here with this man. God must be our protection. People count for less than nothing, no matter how many of you there are!

I now come to his other letter of October 27th. What I promised to deliver to him concerning the *English State Church*, which he was still intending to edit, was, in my mind, a historical narrative of the Philadelphian Society. Richard Roach, who was one of its members—I say was, because now there is no longer a formal society and everyone has scattered—has long since promised to write such an essay for me, and now I will urge him to do so, the sooner the better.[67] I am glad to hear that an experienced theologian in W. wants to write about separatism. Such a subject is precisely what is *needed* in this time, when, according to all appearances, separatism is becoming increasingly widespread. To carry out such a project, mind you, requires a person who possesses exceptional openness, faithfulness, love, moderation, and theological wisdom. If these qualities are lacking, more harm than good is likely to result, especially since many and perhaps most of the separatists are basically honest people, and in many respects are right. If they were now to be treated too

---

66. Louis d'Aumont (1667–1723), the 3rd Duke, who married Olympe, daughter of Antoine de Brouilly, marquis de Piennes, and was French ambassador to London.

67. Richard Roach (1662–1730), Anglican priest with proclivities toward mysticism, who, along with Francis Lee, became a follower of Jane Lead and the leader of the Philadelphian Society after her death.

severely, and the obvious corruption of the clergy—which many cite as a main factor in separatism—were to be condoned too freely, they would be driven further and further into separatism, of which I am completely convinced from my own experience. He will remember from our previous discussions how I have often complained that the spiteful academic heretic-makers tend to mix the old so-called heretics with the new ones without any discretion, which one ought to distinguish carefully, if one otherwise intends to fulfill the commandment of love and truth. I have generally explained this with the example of present-day Anabaptists, who are very different from the old German Anabaptists, and on various points profess to be different from them. If now I were to throw both of them into one lump without distinction, then an unfair kind of heresy would ensue which would greatly exceed the bounds of love. This distinction would also be useful in the history of the old and new separatists, and would clear the way of many a misunderstanding. In the past few years, this matter has been examined pro and con here in England; the Episcopalians have accused the Presbyterians of separatism, while the Presbyterians have accused the Episcopalians of a papist coercion of conscience. However, little fruit has resulted because the parties lacked theological moderation and were more concerned about saving their party than about the glory of God. Therefore, the rift has only widened, and everyone has stuck to their opinions.

Something else to report from here: the day before yesterday, on the 4th, Johannes Edzardi,[68] Lutheran preacher in London, passed away, and thereby made room for another. Oh! that the successor would be a person after God's heart! Our efforts to *care for the poor* are still growing, praise God! God's providence grants us some refreshment now and then in such works of love: for example, the evening before last, at the regular meeting of all the members, my colleague Georg Ruperti brought £4, which had been collected by some well-meaning persons in Z. and sent here for this purpose. My colleague had sent the printed *rules* of our meeting, being something new, to a friend there, without any thought of soliciting a contribution by it. Since this gift came in so unexpectedly, it has refreshed the members present that much more, and encouraged us to consider expanding the work. On which topic, God willing, more in the future.

---

68. Johannes Esra Edzardi (1662–1713), German historian and pastor of Hamburg Lutheran Church on the site of Holy Trinity Church, Trinity Lane.

The correspondence he promised to send to the missionaries at Tranquebar will be very dear to them, for they have asked for news from Europe in several letters. At the end of the year, the fleet should leave here, especially now that the difficulties with the convoys after the negotiated peace have been solved. I am now working on an extract of the last letter sent from Tranquebar, which the Society has requested to be printed in English. You may know that at the request of the Queen of Great Britain 136 persons were freed from the French galleys. Twelve of them have arrived here to thank the Queen on behalf of the rest; indeed, about 14 days ago they knelt down before Her Majesty at Windsor and humbly requested that the rest of their brethren in the faith, who are still being held in galleys and prisons, may, through Her Majesty's intercession, also enjoy the same favor. Time will tell whether anything will come of this. It is clear, however, that the refugees are greatly hated at the French court and have been barred by new edicts from ever returning to their homeland. Claude Grostête de La Mothe,[69] whom I believe he saw when he was here, and whose name is also known from several tracts, died some weeks ago. He was one of the most distinguished French ministers in London.

No. 90

A. W. Böhme to Monsieur H. in P.
London, 31 December 1713

I duly received his letter from P. dated December 10. I am pleased to note that there is still a heartfelt desire and love for the good in him. May he continue to devote himself to the salvation of his soul with earnestness and zeal; and the more he sees that the world is in duress, the more he will strive to cling to his Savior, who overcame the world for him and wants to overcome it in him. I have already experienced several distressing examples of how some, after traveling from here, have lost what the Lord had given them. But let this make him and others all the more vigilant, and encourage him to watch and pray daily, that he may

---

69. Claude Grostête de La Mothe (1647–1713), conformed Huguenot pastor of the French Reformed Church in the Savoy, London, from 1694 to 1713.

not lose what he once received; for it is not the one who begins, but the one who perseveres, who shall be saved.

He will undoubtedly see a lot of idolatry and blindness in P., which should then awaken him to praise the God who will let him see something of the truth that lies hidden; such knowledge, even if it is only like a mustard seed, far exceeds all human tawdriness. How glorious it is when our hearts are firmly fixed in the grace of God and rightly rooted in the love of Christ! It is well worth the effort to do everything we can to find this precious pearl. As concerns our circumstances in London, God still allows us now and then to harvest a little fruit from the Word; but the weeds are so thick that what little good there is almost cannot grow up. But God will separate everything in His time and will know how to put each one into its proper container. Only let us be constant in sowing good seed, so that we, along with every servant of God from all corners of the earth, will one day come together bringing in our sheaves. The Monday *spiritual practice* carries on faithfully, and I consider it a great grace that the Lord still allows us the freedom to come together without fear, and to strengthen each other in the knowledge of the truth. I would enjoy getting a personal letter from him from time to time, especially if he has something to say about the kingdom of God and how it can be furthered.

No. 91[70]

A. W. Böhme to the missionaries in Tranquebar, Bartholomäus
 Ziegenbalg and Johann Ernst Gründler
London, 8 January 1714

Beloved brothers!

With the forthcoming departure of the English East Indies fleet, I will now, in God's name, answer your letters, which were written partly in January 1712, partly in September and October of the same year, and partly in January 1713; they have arrived safely on various ships. I am glad, along with others who seek the growth of Jerusalem, that the Lord has kept you so far and has added some blessing to the seed of the gospel scattered in the Malabar field. Everything depends on his blessing; for neither the one who plants nor the one who waters is anything, but it is

---

70. AFSt/H Nachlässe und Deposita ALMW/DHM 6/9:19.

God who makes things flourish; and yet both the one who plants and the one who waters must be faithful in their works, and in this order wait for the blessing that comes down from above.

Just as I hope that the work begun by your hand might be a tiny seed, with which in time some barren pagan fields will be sown, and perhaps harvested by others who join in their labors, so in England, where divine providence has thrown me, and thus far preserved me, I have made it my concern to promote the conversion of pagans. My meager efforts have not been without some blessing. Many are seeing the viability of such an undertaking right before their eyes, and are indeed lending a hand to assist the workers. Some are earnestly deliberating over the conversion of pagans. Some are making contributions from their earthly goods. Some are trying to find capable subjects who can be enlisted for this cause. Some are also seeking to stir other nations to a sacred emulation through verbal and written encouragement. Some are intent on planning how to remove the many obstacles, lower the hills, raise the valleys, and make a level path for pagans everywhere. From all of this you can clearly see that honest-minded people in Europe are serious about making a way for the blessed conversion of pagans and removing the veils covering their eyes.

Now, if you on your side will also beseech the Lord for the requisite wisdom and prudence, in time, by means of such concerted effort, a glorious breakthrough can take place, and the mountains of obstacles will become a plain. But who is capable of this without the grace of God working in everything! But since you are the first to be sent out for such work these years, you have all the more reason to conduct yourselves with godly wisdom, so that those who come after you in the same work may see in you an example of diligence, love, faithfulness, gentleness, and humility, and may follow your example, especially since so many eyes of both friends and enemies are fixed directly on you and the office you have received.

The thing that has particularly offended the Archbishop of Canterbury Thomas Tenison is that you have completely omitted the commandment against graven images from the small school booklet you printed at Tranquebar. From this it was assumed that you intended to introduce a crude or sectarian Lutheranism among the Malabarians. Some said: "The commandment against graven images is one of the most necessary for dealing with idolatrous and polytheistic paganism, since it is the one that most powerfully attacks polytheism and therefore addresses a particular danger." Some say: "You don't have to maim the Scriptures, or leave something out here and there." Quite a few said: "We do not want to help introduce either Lutheranism or Calvinism in India, and therefore we cannot offer any further support to the cause. Some believed that those who had benefited from studying under the professors in Halle should not be rigorously propagating Lutheranism, but should see for themselves what is best suited to the occasion, nature, and circumstances of each place, and follow it, etc."

You can easily see that by this unforeseen objection—especially since it was made by the most distinguished theologian in the whole country—a great deal of disruption and opposition has arisen, although I have not spared any effort on my part to calm emotions and to prevent further harmful consequences. The Archbishop went so far as to inform the Society that he would strongly advise clergy not to embrace in the least any mission aimed at promoting sectarian Lutheranism, or to support it in any way. I am, however, referring to the Society's own letter, in which it has presented to you its and the Archbishop's opinion along with several others. I never thought that such a commotion would arise over a small detail. Archbishop Tenison is otherwise a very well-meaning and honest man, as well as your friend and benefactor, as you can see explicitly from the preface to the Sixth Continuation of the Malabar Narratives. He has read with pleasure your letters, which I translated into English, and, before he became upset about this particular matter, he spoke very highly of the East India Mission.

So then, beloved brethren, you can see from this whole affair—which if it is not remedied in a timely manner is likely to have more dangerous consequences—how much caution is needed in the conduct of your office, if you wish otherwise to be supported in it by other nations. It is therefore my well-considered counsel that in the next edition of the booklet you include the entire commandment against graven images, whether it be attached immediately to the first commandment, or be turned into a separate commandment, as the Reformed Church traditionally divide them, a division that is also accepted by many Lutherans, in particular the churches at Strasbourg. Or you can print the commandments as they are listed in Exodus 20, without saying which is the first, which is the second, etc., especially since the numbering of the Ten Commandments is human; it can suffice, if we have the language of the commandments, and tell others that they are able to put them in whatever order they want. That is how I practiced it in the Prince of Denmark's chapel when he wanted to make use of several prayers and collects from the Church of England's liturgy. Among the books I have enclosed, you will find a copy of this prayerbook, compiled as it is partly from the Anglican liturgy, partly from other spiritual prayerbooks, and introduced into the Prince's Royal Chapel; you can see on pages 44–45 how the commandments are printed without any special designation of the first, the second, and so on.[71] And in this way, it seems to me, neither Lutherans nor the Reformed will find it easy to find fault with me, because I myself do not number the commandments, but leave it up to everyone to decide how they want to delineate them. For me it is enough that the ten words are presented to everyone. I do not know whether you can take anything from this idea for your lessons; at the very minimum, I did not want to keep from you what happened in the Society because of this matter, and how it might be remedied most simply.

But now that I have touched on this subject, I would like to add one or two other things that might help you going forward think carefully about the manner in which you carry out your office. One of them is that you abstain, as much as possible, from all human and partisan names, since they are likely to have dire consequences when planting the gospel among the Malabarians. You might move this way if you mention a Lutheran catechism in any book written for pagans, or should you do so in the future; or if you also incorporate into those books Luther's explanations of the catechism, using his name. On the title page of the *Explanation of Christian Doctrine*, you have referred directly to Luther's Catechism with these words: According to the Order of the Catechism of Martin Luther, etc. However, on reading through the tract, I have noted that not only the order of our Lutheran Catechism, but also Luther's entire explanation of the first and second main sections has been retained— which you have also done, no doubt, with the other three main sections, which I have not yet seen because the one you have sent only extends to the letter E—and thus it is a Lutheran Catechism, with the name, that has been edited. This now causes a reader, who, because of your sincere intention, has no satisfactory reason to believe thus, to think: "The people at Tranquebar are propagating Lutheranism among the Malabarians, and in time, instead of true Christians, they will produce mere Lutherans. But why should we help and encourage these people to spread Lutheranism?" This harm could be avoided if you maintained the truth that Luther testified to, but omitted his name, especially in printed books, particularly

---

71. Böhme, *Ein Gebeth-Büchlein*. On pages 44–47, the Ten Commandments are presented as a responsive litany, with the commandments themselves unnumbered.

since his name is of no use to the Malabarians, while, at the first sight of the book, it leaves an impression of sectarianism on the reader educated in Christianity.

So, in the same book (p. 79), the 107th question is: How does Luther describe faith? And the answer is taken from the well-known words of the preface to the Epistle to the Romans. But again, I cannot see what impact Luther's authority could have on pagans. Rather, I think that if Mr. Ziegenbalg or Mr. Gründler were to bear witness to the same truth, it would carry more weight with the Malabarians than Luther's name and reputation. Therefore, because the Malabarians deal with you daily, your faithfulness, love, and untiring zeal help them, in body and soul, to see, hear, feel, and experience; all of which, in the case of a beginner, are good vehicles to make Christianity initially appealing and enjoyable to them. Luther, on the other hand, is a completely unknown figure to them, unless the missionaries first tell them what good God has done through him, and how we therefore have reason to hold his teachings in high esteem as a confirmation of the known truth, and so on. But what purpose, dear brothers, do such human detours serve? *Since we ought to go straight ahead, and proclaim Christ as the author of blessedness to the Malabarians! Him who is indeed able to kindle and strengthen their faith*; and there need never have been a Luther in the world; or, at least to the pagan, he might have remained completely unknown! It is a different matter if you deal with German or Danish Lutherans and bear witness to the truth with them. In such a case, you may certainly reference Luther against their dead, erroneous belief, and bring shame on them with it (as indeed in Germany many righteous people regularly do, and to good advantage). For the name Lutheran has been instilled in such people from their youth, and because they practice such shameful idolatry under Luther's authority, but possess little or nothing of the truth that he taught, one can well bring one and the other argument from Luther to their shame. With all these things, however, one must act cautiously if one wants to present the order of salvation to the unconverted who know nothing of Luther. It is certain that the little good that Luther's name and testimonies may do them will be far outweighed by the harm associated with it; therefore, we have reason to beseech the Lord for sufficient wisdom in such a delicate matter.

I now recall that when this matter was being discussed in the Society, one of them said: "Missionaries should nevertheless have a catechism that they can use in their dealings with the Malabarians." Someone else answered: "The missionaries themselves are capable of preparing a catechism and of organizing it according to the nature and circumstances of paganism, better than anyone else can dictate to them. And with this kind of catechism, there is no need to introduce to the East Indies the sectarian-sounding names that will in time give birth to innumerable squabbles." Another said: "I have known Lutheran preachers in Hamburg who, when they were initially training their people in becoming disciples of Christ, referred to Luther ten times and presented him for discipleship as their father in the faith." Although someone replied that such papacy had leavened all Protestant parties, and that such papist fragments might be found in the Church of England as well as in any other, it was still decided: "Wherever it is found, it must be rejected; and because it is such a virulent plague, such evil must be counteracted at once, and, in particular, the poor Malabarians must be spared those things that contribute nothing to their salvation. Yes, one must not scatter even the slightest seed from which in time a Lutheranism or a Calvinism could grow in India. At the very least, we cannot lend a hand to those who pave the way for sectarian Lutheranism and spread such consequence-bearing names among the Malabarians." I have already noted that another said: I mean, these people have studied in Halle, where they present more general principles and are not so bound to human things, etc. In general, dear brothers, you can clearly see from this how your first books have been a source of offense to some, although in my heart I absolve you from any sinister or sectarian intentions. I willingly acknowledge that if I had had to put the Ten Commandments in an ABC book, I would have done it just the same way, unless someone had counseled me in advance, because that is how I learned them from the Lutheran Catechism when I was young. In the meantime, as much as possible, every effort has been made to bring the matter back on track after such a disruption. Accordingly, with this fleet you will receive £70 of what has been collected thus far, together with a gift of valuable books.

    I have counseled you to accept good advice and encouragement with gratitude, and to act on it as much as you are able. In your future letter to the Society, do not go into any detail about this matter, but keep it in general terms, with the cordial assurance that you will follow their *counsel as much as circumstances allow*, and that in the next edition of the school booklet you will include the commandment against graven images in its entirety. In this way, by and by, everything will be quietly settled and forgotten. You are the first Protestants who have been given the honor of preaching the riches of Christ among pagans in the East Indies. If the Lord grants you wisdom to lay a foundation, others will be able to build on it: for those English who were the first to take up the mission attest to such high esteem for your work among the Malabarians that they would not hesitate to send their own missionaries to you, in order to observe your whole way of life, methods, and manner of teaching among the pagans, before they themselves undertake the work. This would be a means of uniting your hearts most closely with the English, and of carrying on the missionary work with combined forces, as one person.

To say nothing at this point of the outward blessings that would thereby flow to you each year. But all these blessings will fall away completely as soon as you, by using suspect names, build a wall around you and make your gifts useless. Those specific names—as everywhere in Europe, but especially among the well-intentioned in England—are beginning to be hated because of the many nasty squabbles that have resulted from them. Should a seed be sown to this end in the East Indies, and over time more Lutherans, Reformed, and members of the Church of England be sent, I fear I foresee in my spirit that then the dance will begin in the East Indies, and all missionaries will seek to expand the interest of their party, and one will propagate Luther, the other Calvin, the third another Church tradition instead of the pure gospel. What miserable fruit will result from this, especially since disorderly adherence to a party eats away at everything around it like a cancer, and in time pours out like a torrent that no dam can stop. However, if one takes care at the start, many a disturbance can still be prevented under the blessing of God.

In all these dealings, beloved brethren, it is in no way my opinion that you should join another denomination, nor introduce some other church's liturgy or confession: for in a case like that, I would strenuously object that things would become worse, and I would rather let everything fall and sink, than consent to such a dangerous arrangement. So also I know well that God is not bound to England for the conversion of pagans, since He can raise children from stones and open another door when one closes. But the question is only whether or not it would be possible to find a *middle road* and teach Malabarians the way of salvation without those specific human names that have done so much harm in Europe. And here I frankly confess that if I were to work among pagans, I would, as much as possible, present general principles to them, or at least avoid all human names in doing so. The doctrine we have in the Lutheran

Church is as pure as any other Protestant Church, especially if we follow it in the same form as it has been presented in these latter years by Dr. Philipp Spener.[72] Therefore, I would gladly retain Dr. Spener's doctrine of faith and the foundational teaching of Johann Freylinghausen, which is based on Dr. Spener's teaching.[73] But I would never call such truths Lutheran doctrines, or cite Dr. Luther in the process, especially among pagans, whom I would refer directly to Christ and the more stable economy of blessedness that comes from him, without expanding into details.

Therefore, it seems to me that it would be sufficient in one's initial work among the Malabarians, if the five major sections were printed merely with scriptural words, without any human additions, and the tracts distributed among them. Regarding the Ten Commandments, I have already expressed my opinions above. The Apostles' Creed, as far as I know, is accepted by all Protestant churches, and therefore nothing need be mentioned about it. Nor is there any particular difficulty with the Lord's Prayer. As for the two sacraments, I would simply print the words of institution and have the youth memorize them. In the case of baptism, I would emphasize in particular the baptismal covenant and the renunciation that takes place, since the baptismal candidate is denying the world and idolatry and is being introduced into the spiritual life, and in general I would present it as a sacrament of initiation. In the case of the Lord's Supper, I would carefully emphasize that by its proper use the life of grace begun in baptism is to be strengthened and nourished, and how it is therefore a sacrament of confirmation, relating to the prior baptism. But I would by no means regulate the form, or presume to say how and in what way this sacrament nourishes the life of grace bestowed on the person, since regulating the form has previously been the cause of dispute between the Reformed and Lutherans. For, the efficacy of the sacrament depends neither on the Lutheran "in, with, and under," nor on the Reformed "signification," but, from God's side, on the Words of Institution, and, from the communicant's perspective, on his or her inner being, namely, on a penitent, believing, and grace-hungry heart. And in this way, I would strive to ensure that I would not be characterized by this or that opinion, nor that I would be confined to the kind of circle that others would not be able to share with me.

---

72. Philipp Jakob Spener (1635–1705) is regarded by many at the father of German Lutheran Pietism.

73. Johann Anastasius Freylinghausen (1670–1739) was a theologian, hymn writer, and administrator in Halle for Franckeschen Stiftungen.

When I myself have preached on such matters, I have proposed these general guidelines to my listeners, although there is clearly a difference between my circumstances (since I have been brought up in Christianity and know something about the letter of Christian doctrine) and yours (since you have to teach pagans who know nothing about that letter). I use a metaphor taken from nature to illustrate this process: A child, a farmer, and a simple person truly sense the vigor and nourishment that the Creator has put into bread, so that, after eating bread, the person is nourished to be able to work, walk, and labor. But neither the child nor the farmer has the knowledge to determine how the nourishment in the bread spreads through the body and all its limbs, or how it must go through the ways of digestion, myelopoiesis, etc. Nevertheless, by receiving the nourishment, they experience the end result, namely the preservation of their lives, which was the Creator's intention with the bread. How much more can this be said of the nourishment offered to those who are born again through the proper participation in the flesh and blood of Christ, especially since we assume that this is a mystery and a spiritual act that far exceeds any natural human understanding.

If I had to prepare a similar small catechism consisting of nothing but the words of Scripture, I would have no hesitation in using and following the catechetical explanations of Luther, Spener, and other righteous authors to good effect, but I would not print Luther's or any other theologian's name in the books without urgent need, lest I be seen as trying to propagate human opinions or systems among the pagans. Even if I were to quote purely divine and essential truths from a theologian—as, of course, is the description of faith, which you have quoted from Luther's preface to the Epistle to the Romans—I would not readily state a human name, but rather derive a divine truth from Scripture, and direct it back to its originator, God Himself. For since God is the ultimate source of all truth, and the human person is only a channel through which it flows, let us stick with the original and name everything after it, so that nothing is lacking in the channel and instruments by which the Lord makes known a truth. For the nature of the time, place, and other circumstances often requires that the names of our teachers be quietly omitted, since naming them might hinder the progress of the gospel.

But now I turn to some of the other matters you mention in your letters. The £150 for the printing press, which you had to repay at Madras[?], has been immediately reimbursed by the Society, so that you need not worry about it any further. You will receive a chest of books in the ship called Aurangzeb, which is being sent to you in part by the Society, in part by friends in Halle, and in part by me. The case is labeled "B. Z. n. 1." In Mr. Newman's enclosed letter, you will find a catalog of those books that come from the Society. The most prominent among them is Matthew Poole's *Synopsis criticorum aliorumque Sacrae Scripturae* consisting of five volumes.[74] There are also a few books in English enclosed, namely Robert Gell's works on the Old and New Testaments,[75] because we hope that the next missionary to be sent to you will be proficient in the English language. I have added 14 copies of Arndt's *True Christianity*, published in Dutch last year at Rotterdam; for since there are so many Dutch in the East Indies, you may on occasion be able to make a friend by the gift of that book, and help to promote good in that nation. To these I have added eight copies of the same book in Latin, and seven in German (the Lemgo edition), in order to distribute them in East India if the opportunity arises. In the same chest you will also find:

Francke's *Manuductio Ad Lectionem Scripturæ Sacræ* (12 copies)

Novum Testamentum Graece Vulgar (20 copies)

Johann Comenius's *De bono unitatis et ordinisi* (12 copies)[76]

Along with these are several Palatine prayer books and other small tracts that were close at hand.

And because in your letters you refer to the Armenian nation and especially to various merchants with whom you have become acquainted, I have enclosed an Armenian New Testament, so that you may honor a well-disposed Armenian. In the same case you will find *The Imitation of Christ* by Thomas à Kempis, together with an Armenian song book and Cardinal Bona's *Manuductio ad Coelum*,[77] which have been jointly published in the Armenian language in Amsterdam. The last one, Giovanni Bona's *Manuductio*, has long since been translated into Armenian by an Armenian Archbishop named Vartan Hunanyan, who resided at Leopoldstadt [Lviv] in Poland.[78] However, both this and all the other books that you will receive were printed with Armenian characters some years

---

74. Matthew Poole (1624–1679), *Synopsis criticorum aliorumque Sacrae Scripturae*.

75. Gell, *Gell's Remaines*.

76. Probably Johann Amos Comenius (1592–1670), *Historia fratrum Bohemorum*.

77. Giovanni Bona (1609–1674), *Manuductio ad coelum*.

78. Vartan Hunanyan (1681–1715), Archbishop of Lviv of the Armenian Catholic Church.

ago in Amsterdam by an Armenian archbishop named Thomas Sanctae Crucis.[79] This Thomas Sanctae Crucis was here with us in England in 1707, after he had been in Europe for thirty years and was now about eighty years old. He came here together with his nephew (a young man who knew Latin) to collect a financial contribution to cover his expenses for printing the books, and for which his own means were not sufficient. Our current sovereign, Queen Anne, paid him a hundred guineas for this purpose, besides other gifts that were given to him here and there.[80] That I am writing this in such cumbersome detail is due to the fact that I would like to have further news as to whether the Archbishop, or his nephew, together with the supply of books, from which he gave me the abovementioned texts, has arrived in Armenia again. For various newspapers here, soon after they left, were reporting that the old man had died at sea not long after his departure,[81] and that the whole ship and the books had fallen into the hands of the French, but I have not been able to get any reliable confirmation of this news. Perhaps the Armenian merchants who are on your coast would like to have some certainty about this.

The letter about Ispahan, which you mentioned, has finally arrived here, but much later than the English fleet. The first package I received was the historical narrative of the beginning and progress of the work at Tranquebar, which I then immediately sent by mail to Halle to be printed before the departure of the fleet; you will find several copies of it under the title *Continuation VI* in the case of books. I made extracts of your last letters as soon as I received them, and after translating them into English, submitted them to the Society, which then had them printed at their expense.

I hope that wherever these tracts become known, it might give a new awakening to the cause. May the Lord grant us the necessary prudence and wisdom in all our ways, so have no doubt that well-meaning Englishmen will continue to support the mission faithfully. You also need to take care that you do not use overly exaggerated words to describe the works, but candidly present it in its growth, obstacles, and whatever other footprints of divine providence are to be found in it; in that way

---

79. Thomas Vanandets'i, Archiepiscopal Sancta Cruces in the canton of Ghoghtan, in Nakhijevan in Perso-Armenia (ca. 1618–1708).

80. His nephew's name was Luke Nurigian. The SPCK gave him ten guineas. For an account of the Archbishop's visit to Oxford, see Macray, *Annals of the Bodleian*, 126–28.

81. According to Aslanian, "'Quintessential Locus of Brokerage,'" 656, the Archbishop died in Antwerp two months after his arrival in July 1708.

you will leave it up to the reader to decide what he or she will make of it. May the Lord bless us and the work of our hands to His praise and the salvation of many souls!

No. 92

A. W. Böhme to Mr. K.
London, 12 January 1714

I have received your kind letter from Lyons. I always find it gratifying when I hear from time to time that those who have once tasted the truth remain steadfastly devoted to the Lord with simple hearts, and do not go astray or wander off, as is not uncommon at this time. A lot is stirring in many people's hearts, but very little has come to maturity and purity. I appreciate the information you shared with me on matters of religion: If I should travel through France and stay for a while here and there, I would make a point to visit some trustworthy people and establish a Christian friendship and acquaintance with them. It is well established that the anti-Christian attitude is most pronounced in those circles in which a true heart-Christianity is transformed into outward ceremonies and human trappings, and poor souls, instead of being led to Christ, are duped with human pomp and inventions. That said, no party is so corrupt that God has not retained a holy seed within it. Such good souls, who are, as it were, salt in the midst of decay, are undoubtedly found most often among the simple and lowly crowd, those in whom the Spirit of God does not find as many obstacles for pressing and fixing the simple truth in the soul. I would seek out such souls as pearls, and rejoice with them in the hidden wisdom which the Lord has concealed from the wise of this world, and revealed to babes. For all disputes about these and other opinions and doctrinal positions, I would carefully guard against making myself useless in my dealings with others; *for love and humility always have the greatest power to win over other people's hearts* and to instill truth in them. I would abstain from commenting on the sacraments other than to say that they are a means to sanctify me more and more and to strengthen the inner life of grace. But since Catholics are not holier with seven sacraments than I and others are with two, I would not have much reason to support their opinion.

As for the question about the age of the Lord Jesus, we are told that he was 33½ years old and took on the lowly form of a servant. And because the whole life of Christ is full of wonders and mysteries, it is remarkable that the Savior spent His childhood years in such silence. After His birth almost nothing is recorded except what happened to Him in His twelfth year (Luke 2:42); after that nothing else is reported (except what is written in Luke 2:51) until he took up His teaching ministry.

No. 93

A. W. Böhme to Georg Heinrich Neubauer in Halle
London, 15 January 1714

I have some questions about the request for printing the Estonian Bible, which was sent to me by Professor Francke, and I would like to have them answered as soon as possible, if there is anyone able to do so. The reason I want to know in advance is that if I make the request known, I will be asked similar questions, which I cannot now answer. I'm also thinking about having the whole project printed, and distributing it here and there:

1. Are the Estonian and Livonian languages one and the same? If not, what are the differences between them?
2. Has not the Bible been printed in Livonian recently by Dr. Loth Fischer? Are there no more copies of it in print?
3. Is the Estonian language completely different from other European languages? With which language is it most closely related?
4. Does the language have special types or characters? Or, are German or Latin letters used?
5. Where should the Estonian Bible be printed?
6. Who are the main people promoting this cause?
7. Are there any theologians who are interested in printing the Bible, and who are they?
8. Can you describe more clearly the actual source or causes of the ignorance among the people?

9. What, in particular, are the causes on the part of the authorities?

10. Are there not enough churches in the country, because, according to the plan, people have to walk over two miles to get to a church?

11. Is the country, according to outward circumstances, very poor? And has it endured a lot, especially during the turmoil of war?

12. Are there not enough schools to fight against this ignorance over time?

No. 94

A. W. Böhme to Mr. H. in Halle
London, 26 January 1714

The package of letters together with the printed papers has been delivered to me by post. I was moved reading the historical account of the burning of the towns of Gartz and Wolgast,[82] and would like to have some advice on how those impoverished people could be helped in an active way by means of a collection. All hope does not appear to be lost for this purpose either, if those who are willing to be used in service of this emergency go right to work. The Society, to which you seem to be referring, cannot contribute as a society from its reserves—what people want to do privately is up to them and to God's good hand guiding them—because it is exclusively restricted by certain rules, as far as I am aware, to particular causes, namely the establishment and maintenance of charity schools, and the printing and issuing of edifying books.[83]

In the meantime, we shall see if Henry Newman will do anything after reading the letter, or at least offers some suggestion by which we can come closer to achieving the intended goal. But be that as it may, it will hardly pay for the collectors to make a trip here for that purpose; and they can definitely trust that if God should move some hearts to contribute personally and it should come into my hands, it will be handled in good faith and delivered over as quickly as possible. But were I to continue my reflections on such a work of love, it seems to me that in

82. Pomeranian towns devastated by Muscovites during the fighting of the Great Northern War (1700–1721).

83. On the relationships of the SPCK to persecuted European Protestants, see Nishikawa, "SPCK in Defence."

these kinds of matters, one must use procedures that others have used many times before with good results. This method involves obtaining a privilege to collect—called a "letter" here—at the court, and by virtue of it being authorized to take collections in the churches of London after the Queen's letter has been read from the pulpits. In order to obtain this license, however, you would have to call upon the Swedish minister in London to present such a request to the Queen, and to forward the "letter" to the Bishop of London, or in his absence, to the Archbishop of Canterbury. No private citizen can make a special presentation here. But if one approaches the matter in the above way, it would be more likely to receive some contributions. As I recall, several years ago a poor Protestant congregation in the Palatinate received a considerable collection, after the matter had first been presented at court by the then Prussian legate, Baron Ezekiel Spanheim, and the said royal order had been requested.[84] Other Protestant churches have also raised similar contributions here on various occasions.

You also mentioned the English translation of Luther's *Divine Discourses*, which were drawn from his Table Talks; they were published here in 1652, after Captain Henry Bell had translated them into this language as a result of an apparition.[85] The historical narrative is, by all accounts, prefixed to the book, from which it was subsequently repeated, albeit very imperfectly, by Dr. Christian Kortholt and Gottfried Arnold in their writings.[86] The book itself—*Table Talk* in English—is very rare, and I have never been able to get hold of it, but have only previously borrowed it from a good friend, in order to read through the above narrative.

The latest thing to happen here, and cause a great stir, is the publication last week of Captain Richard Steele's book, *The Crisis*; it contains the Acts of Parliament, together with other tracts, by which the succession in Great Britain is conferred upon the Electoral House of Hanover.[87] In this book he emphatically presents, from a human point of view, the great danger in which we are hovering. I hear that there are three thousand

---

84. Ezekiel, Freiherr von Spanheim (1629–1710), was a Genevan diplomat and scholar.

85. Martin Luther, *Colloquia mensalia*. In the introduction, Captain Henry Bell claims to have been motivated to translate Luther's table talk through the appearance in the middle of the night of "an ancient man, standing at my bedside, arrayed all in white, having a long and broad white beard hanging down to his girdle steed."

86. Christian Kortholt (1633–1694) was a German Protestant theologian and university professor.

87. Sir Richard Steele (1672–1729), *Crisis*.

subscriptions to the book—if it is only half that number, it is still a large subscription—so it is easy to see what kind of impact the book will have. But people are already beginning to make remarks and observations about it, and for a while the mischievous pamphleteers will find new material to work with, both pro and con. As for the new books that are being published here, you can find the most important ones reviewed in the Halle newspapers (if they happen to have been kept around), since Mr. M. sends a report on them to Halle every fortnight.

With regard to our Society, it continues to take up the missionary work in East India most earnestly. They sent £70 to the missionaries with the fleet that left this month, along with a gift of valuable books. They are also diligently searching for a capable English student, who will then join with one or a couple people who have studied at Halle or have otherwise adopted sound principles, and begin a similar work in the East Indian territories that are subject to the English Crown. A detailed account of what has been done here so far for the work of the mission, primarily written by Henry Newman, has been included in the 6th Continuation of the *Malabarische Nachrichten*, published in Halle.[88] Likewise, a further volume of the letters recently sent to the Society by the missionaries has been printed here in English at the expense of the Society, of which I will gladly provide several copies when the opportunity arises. The remaining part of Arndt's *True Christianity* in English is also now at the publisher.

No. 95

A. W. Böhme to Samuel Urlsperger
London, 29 January 1714

I turn straight away to answering the most important points of your latest letter, dated January 7th, which has just come into my hands. I have enclosed here the much sought-after essay on the Philadelphian Society, which was drafted by Richard Roach, one of its most distinguished members. If he had had available the writings which have previously been exchanged pro and con on the validity of Presbyterian baptism—which in this connection also includes Lutherans—he could have understood from them the current plight at the heart of the Church in England, and

---

88. *Der Königl. Dänischen Missionarien.*

how everything is falling more and more into ruin, and have added them to his book. Many of those who belong to the extreme or High-Church party set their sights so high that they want to make all other parties that do not entirely agree with them into outright un-Christians, which is common practice among the pseudo-orthodox. To achieve this aim, new formulations are always being devised, and recently the baptism of dissenters fell victim. Some say that many in the High-Church party consider Presbyterian baptism to be null and void, because they lack the proper ordination—which should be episcopal—as the basis of all Church functions. This alleged invalidity of baptism is asserted in several publications; therefore, some, who were lacking an adequate means of putting such a spirit to the test, have been induced by it to be rebaptized by the Episcopal party.

The most alarming incident, and the one that has caused the most sensation, occurred in the city of Exeter, where a ministerial candidate named Benjamin Reed, who had been a Presbyterian and had studied at their private academy for several years, was baptized again by the High-Church party. Having been taken in both by the shouting of the party and by reading their books, he was induced to be rebaptized. But because they declare the first baptism null and void, they will probably not want to call it rebaptism. Soon after this disturbance occurred, a Presbyterian preacher published a pamphlet under the title: *A Caveat against the New Sect of Anabaptists, Lately sprung up at Exon*.[89] In this pamphlet, which has already been published three times, he has demonstrated the folly of these procedures so plainly and reduced their supporters to such absurdity, that I do not see what one can say in response. But there is a greater hidden malice in all these things than one might find at first sight.

Thus religion, which should eliminate all obstinacy, hatred, and envy, can be used to mask all kinds of vicious and carnal passions! Having said that, it would take too long to list the most important arguments from both sides here. Michel de La Roche, who is known in this country for his *Memoirs of Literature*, noted in his review of the above book, among other things, that such rebaptizers surpass Henry Dodwell himself in zeal.[90] For since he desired that a person baptized by a Presbyterian should hold faithfully to the Church of England, and thus seek to recover by communion with the Episcopal Church what had been lost

---

89. James Peirce (ca. 1674–1726), *Caveat*.

90. Henry Dodwell (1641–1711), Anglo-Irish theologian, was one of the most vocal defenders of the nonjurors.

at baptism, so these new baptizers have pushed the matter even further, and even wanted to introduce rebaptism. But I cannot believe that this practice will continue to gain momentum, since such human inventions are like Jonah's plant or a certain kind of fungus that springs up in one night and then quickly dissolves again. What has not taken root in God then cannot draw strength from God for its preservation. Pope Clement XI's bull Unigenitus condemning Pasquier Quesnel's reflections on the New Testament has been published here in both Latin and English by a Catholic bookseller, but this has only made Quesnel's book itself more widely known.[91]

No. 96

A. W. Böhme to Henry Newman
London, 25 February 1714

The enclosed volume was recently sent to me from Halle; the Livonians, who have taken over the printing of this Bible, have expressly asked Professor Francke to send it to England, in the hope of receiving a grant for furthering this work.[92] As I do not know how to respond to their urgent request, but also do not want to miss something that would help spread the Word of God among such an illiterate people, I decided to communicate this project to the members of the Society, partly for their own satisfaction, partly so that they might see how the Lord reveals His mercy alongside judgment and awakens some to care for the spiritual welfare of certain benighted nations, and partly also to ask for good counsel in so pressing a need and to see if it might be possible to promote the welfare of souls in such an arid land. To this end, I ask you to read it to the gentlemen of the Society when you find a suitable opportunity to do so.

---

91. Pasquier Quesnel (1634–1719), *Nouveau Testament en françois*. Unigenitus Dei Filius, the bull issued by Pope Clement XI on 8 Sept 1713, condemned the doctrines of Jansenism. Quesnel was a French Jansenist theologian.

92. The Latvian Bible was translated by Ernst Glück (1652–1705), a Saxony-born pastor and missionary to Livonia, and published in 1694. The Estonian New Testament was published in 1715; it was a northern Estonian revision of the New Testament first translated and published by Johannes Gutslaff (d. 1657) in 1648. The full Estonian Bible, translated primarily by Anton thor Helle (1683–1743), pastor at Jüri, was finally printed in Tallinn in 1739. In it he united the two Estonian dialects.

OUTREACH THROUGH THE SPCK AND BEYOND (1710–1714)

A proposal for printing the Bible in the Estonian language

Since the Lord, out of His infinite mercy, has awakened many well-meaning souls in recent years, we must take to heart the miserable condition of the many people who either do not know the gospel of Christ at all, or who, apart from the name of Christianity, know little or nothing of the saving power of the gospel. Thus, it is hoped that the sad state of the Estonians will perhaps awaken a sympathetic consideration in some hearts.

The Estonians inhabit a strip of land in Livonia called Estonia, the upper part of which borders on the Finnish Sea.[93] People here get to be 20, 30, and more years old with almost no knowledge of the doctrine of salvation, much less do they have any taste of it from their own experience. The entire content of their instruction consists of a few forms of prayer, along with the mere letter of the catechism, which they learn from the local sacristan and through which they later consider themselves sufficiently qualified to be admitted to Holy Communion.

The preachers themselves are either simply uninformed or too negligent in administering the means of salvation. The only possible result of this, of course, is that people grow into adulthood and yet remain children in their understanding. For this reason, care has been taken to translate the most important points of Christian doctrine into Estonian, and to write them as much as possible in the simplest way, in question-and-answer form. Adding to the sad situation of these people is the fact that they have so few schools among them, and that the children have so little time to attend them. For they are only able to go to school in the winter; in the summer they have to take care of their houses, since their parents have to serve their rulers, especially in times of war or other hardships, all of which is enough to further the spiritual ruin of this illiterate people. Many pages would be insufficient to describe their pitiful condition.

It is true that some have already been stirred and made aware of the perilous condition of their immortal souls. But they are left little time to reflect further on the ideas that have been presented to them. Their slavery, especially in times of war, is almost unspeakable; and because they are impoverished by persistent levies, they do not have the means to maintain as many schoolmasters as would be necessary to advance the

---

93. In 1710, as a result of Russia's victory in the Great Northern War, the Swedish dominions Estonia and Livonia were integrated into the greater Russian Empire.

cause of religion over time. Some, who still desire to be instructed in the ways of God, must travel two German miles to church in order to listen to a sermon, and they are still forced to work for their rulers the same evening, or very early on Monday morning.

We have learned that one hundred years ago this country was graciously visited by God with the light of the gospel through an extraordinary movement to plant the knowledge of Christ in a more powerful way. But this good movement has now almost completely died out, and in its place such rampant ignorance has swept the land that one can hardly find a Bible or any other spiritual book in most families; consequently, it has become very difficult for those who are trying to restore a taste for religion to the starving people of this land.

Now, to remedy this rampant state of ignorance to some extent, it was decided last winter to start printing the New Testament in Estonian. And praise God—so far, they have reached the sixth chapter of Luke! But the problem is that only a few copies are able to be printed, and they have to be sold at such a high price that there is hardly one person in a hundred who would able to buy it.

Therefore, some who actually live there and are concerned for the spiritual well-being of the people, decided to put forward this proposal, in order to persuade their fellow Christians to make a loving contribution toward spreading the gospel more widely in a country that has been deprived of the written Word of God. These people, who for so many years have been starving for lack of spiritual nourishment, will be glad to glean even the crumbs of the gospel, and will perhaps be more grateful than many of those who for a long time have had the means of salvation at their fingertips, but have hardly used them to any real benefit.

The Bible will be printed promptly, as soon as there is some hope for meeting the necessary expenses. Meanwhile, those who lovingly promote this work can be assured that their contribution to the salvation of many souls from the path of destruction will be carefully used for the said purpose.

No. 97[94]

A. W. Böhme to Professor August Hermann Francke in Halle
London, 26 February 1714

I was surprised that the agitations of the so-called French Prophets, which have been known here since 1706, have also begun to creep up in Halle. Those who traveled to Turkey some years ago to deliver their inspirations to the King of Sweden returned through Italy a few weeks ago, after one of them, named Élie Marion, died in Livorno.[95] Two others, one of whom is Nicolas Fatio de Duillier, left here for Rome following an inspiration, and eventually made their way back to England.[96] One of the prophets told me that the whole description of the journey was now being printed in Holland, so that everything that happened to them could be seen in more detail. He also told me that four others from among them had been directed by inspiration to go to Switzerland to spread their "dispensation" (as they call it), knowing well that they would by no means be tolerated there. There are quite a few well-meaning people among them, who, if they get through the fierceness, should gain some good experience from it. Furthermore, since there is no shortage of adulterations, I would not advise anyone to join them.

Only a few days ago, one of our best people, having attended their sessions, was carried away into such frenzied agitations that almost no one (except the prophets themselves) would deal with him because of the frightful bodily abnormalities: some of them howl like a dog, others grunt like a sow. Some fall to the ground with such force that you would think their heads would burst into pieces, yet it does them no harm. Some become so constricted that they appear to be suffocating, and indeed there is an anxious sweat on their faces. Some move their hands and feet for a while before they speak. Others fall into a violent bellowing, sometimes also into loud unrestrained laughter or other similar partly disgusting, partly ridiculous gesticulations. Some have observed, in the

---

94. AFSt/H A 113, 169–72.

95. Élie Marion (1678–1713) was the founder of the French Prophets. He met with Francke and visited Halle on at least one occasion. He died on a mission to Italy.

96. Nicolas Fatio de Duillier (1664–1753) was a Huguenot, Fellow of the Royal Society in London, and friend of Sir Isaac Newton. Fatio became involved with the French Prophets in 1706 and helped with the publication of the prophecies of Marion. He visited Halle more than once. The other companion of Marion and Fatio was Jean Daudé (1651–ca. 1730), a lawyer from Nimtes.

case of women, that the intensity of the agitations has caused all their linen head coverings to fall off, exposing their heads and necks most annoyingly. When I happened to be among them some years ago, I asked such a woman, after she had returned to normal, how she had felt internally during those convulsions of the body, and she answered that she enjoyed many sweet sensations. When I urged her to call upon God for deliverance from such unruly compulsions, she said she was very comfortable with them and did not wish to be rid of them. But when I entered into a prolonged conversation with her about the cross and following Christ and other related matters, she understood as little of it as the common rabble.

A friend told me that the learned judge, Sir Richard Bulkeley, who quite blindly followed the Prophets' teachings and also wrote an Apology for them, eventually strayed into all sorts of unknown paths that shortened his life in no small way.[97] Even now, a French woman, who otherwise has a very honest heart and a great desire for the truth, was, according to her own testimony, so fiercely assailed by a spirit, that she would have suffocated if God, as she said, did not constrain and limit the spirit. For several weeks she slept very little and had to have someone watch over her every night to keep her company. She says that the spirit is called Asmoni, and that it is the same one that tormented Sarah in the book of Tobit.

In general, I have often observed that these good people build the whole of their Christianity on *perceptions* and feelings, and understand little of the plain and often hidden way of faith; therefore, perhaps, some of them shamefully surrender to such perceptions, in which flesh and blood find little refreshment. For those who have such perceptions, I like to cite a few passages from Catherine of Genoa's tract, especially what is written on pages 127 and following in the German edition.[98] One of the dangerous symptoms that happens with them is that they consider the agitations to be a new and special dispensation. Then it becomes very difficult to approach them with some Christian exhortation, especially since they set themselves above others in this kind of dispensation and regard the agitations and inspirations to be nothing other than divine powers and oracles. Not to mention that they confine themselves to a single

---

97. Bulkeley, *Impartial Account of the Prophets*; *Answer to Several Treatises*.

98. Catherine of Genoa (1447–1510), *Der Göttliche Liebes-Weeg*. Böhme used Pierre Poiret's (1646–1719) French translation of the original Italian to prepare his German edition. Sames, *Böhme*, 100–105.

party and sectarian circle, and therefore make themselves completely incapable of accepting anything good from others. In fact, it is common among them to hear: It is our dispensation. It is as if the agitations were introducing a new dispensation, and by this particular characteristic they had to distinguish themselves.

But there are other hypocrisies among them, some of which are obvious and some of which are still somewhat hidden. Among the latter, I count the libertinism that is beginning to creep in among some of them. Several among them—I say several, because others have also spoken out against such a practice—have not only approved of John Lacy's shameful dealings with the prophetess Elizabeth Gray, but also seek to justify them using the example of the prophet Hosea.[99] Another one of them, who has a wife, has tried to do the same with a young prostitute who is a member of the Prophets, but so far, this disgraceful scandal has been averted. Among the more obvious hypocrisies I include *refraining from physical labor*, in which some of those who come under their influence take part. The man mentioned above, who was seized by agitations only a few days ago, let it be known that he was now called to a *different kind of* (different from physical) *work*. In the meantime, while the husband follows the Prophets, the wife and children are in extreme poverty, which causes all kinds of hatred, envy, strife, and quarrels among them, along with other fruits of the flesh, while love is severely weakened. And even though the Prophets offer gifts to their new disciples—though not enough to sustain their families—a new hypocrisy is revealed in the process: for they do not offer gifts to him because they recognize him as a disciple of Christ, but because he has joined them and has become their disciple. Even if some of them lend a hand now and then and seem to be working, this only happens intermittently, so as long as they are free of the agitations; for as soon as they emerge, they drop everything in order to indulge them all the more unhindered.

Another and dangerous hypocrisy can be seen in the *extravagant praise* they give each other, thereby awakening spiritual pride among them. One is to hold this place of honor and the other that place of honor in the kingdom of God, and be great instruments in God's hand.

---

99. John Lacy (1664–1730) was a prominent Englishman among the French Prophets and a close friend of Sir Richard Bulkeley. In 1711 he left his wife and began an adulterous relationship with Elizabeth Gray. In a published letter, "Letter from John Lacy," Lacy stated that God directed him to do this, with "a supernatural outward Voice heard, that threaten'd me with Eternal Destruction and Hell-Fire if I disobey'd."

However, they do not appear to be doing more to spread the kingdom of God than others, whether they say so or not. Elizabeth Gray, who subsequently married John Lacy, has been called a morning star, a burning lamp in the house of God, etc. She was given the gifts of performing miracles, healing, speaking in tongues, etc. But this star has quickly fallen from heaven, and the lamp has become a false light.

Another hypocrisy can be seen in the fact that they have adopted the name "prophet," which is not appropriate for them, because they lack the true character of a prophet. For if a "prophet" is supposed to mean one who foretells things to come, their prophecies have been falsely fabricated because little or nothing of them has come to pass. This is so apparent that they themselves cannot deny it; therefore, they now resort to all sorts of pitiful excuses, and say that they have not been properly understood, although their prophecies concerning Dr. Thomas Emes are in print, in front of the eyes of anyone who can read.[100] But if a so-called prophet is someone who tills and opens up the prophetic Scriptures, then the name once again does not apply to them: the explanations and applications that they make of the Scriptures are quite offensive, for they use the Scriptures to glorify even the most shameful vices, as can be seen from the above-mentioned example of the prophet Hosea, which is often on their lips. They also wanted to excuse the galling things Lacy did by referring to the pilfering of Egyptian goods, which God Himself ordered the children of Israel to take. In this way, everyone could easily find an excuse for their sins in Scripture. However, the Scriptures are seldom read in their assemblies, and those who still read them do not seek by it to awaken the true foundation of faith and love, but to find something to illustrate their extraordinary actions, or, in their way of speaking, their dispensations, for which they often use the examples of the old prophets.

What strikes me as most suspect in the whole business of the Prophets is this: that in the six or seven years they have been here, I have not found a single example of anyone who has been truly converted to the Lord God by their so-called dispensation. For though I do not deny that there are some honest persons among them, neither can it be denied that those persons had at least a righteous beginning even before joining them. Some have indeed pointed out to me those who had known nothing of the agitations and inspirations beforehand, but now had both,

---

100. See Abraham Whitrow (fl. 1689–1714), *Warnings of the Eternal Spirit*. The preface was written by Richard Bulkeley. Whitrow was a wool-comber who became an important presence among the French Prophets.

and therefore must have been converted. But I have answered that these things are by no means the mark of a conversion which, according to the testimony of Scripture, should proceed from darkness to light. Therefore, they are lacking the seal that should bear witness to the truth, power, and blessing of their calling.

Although indeed I consider their activities dangerous because of these and other adulterations and confusions, I still love the good little seed that grows in several of them amid so many weeds. I cannot regard them all as impostors, as some have done here, and have written against them in such harsh terms; but I must speak with discernment, and separate the grain of gold from the dross. And it is surely true to say that deceivers have crept in among them, or have even emerged from them. Nor should I simply echo the opinion of Mr. P., who in 1709, when I was passing through Holland, used to call them nothing more than the devil's pickled herring, since there are some among them who have a good will and are simply naïve. The well-known mission, which tried to save them through writings from the harsh procedures of the French clergy, is now completely dormant. Blessed Heinrich Ludolf used to say of them: "Where there is fire, there is also smoke; however, smoke is not fire." By this, to the best of my knowledge, he meant to suggest that a supernatural power is present in these people, but that what is revealed in the frenzy is still highly adulterated, mere smoke or vapor.

I have often remembered in this connection the remarks of an old theologian named Jeremiah White,[101] who was Oliver Cromwell's chaplain and had witnessed many of the uncommon movements that were going on in England then. He liked to talk about these things. In 1704, before anyone knew anything about our Prophets, he told me that when he observed the extraordinary movements of so many high-flying spirits, he often thought of Mark 11:13. He would cite the various alternative interpretations of critics, with which they intended to remove the difficulties in the text; however, he would reject them and keep the plain interpretation. But he would point out that in the speeches of Christ there is generally something more than a mere historical meaning; and he thought that the tree of leaves without fruit depicted those souls who, before it was time, wanted to ascend to a higher dispensation. Such people,

---

101. Jeremiah White (1629–1707) was a seventeenth-century Nonconformist minister and Puritan chaplain to Oliver Cromwell. After White's death, Josiah Woodward published White's *Perswasive to Moderation and Forbearance*. It was later edited and reissued by Richard Roach as *Persuasive to Mutual Love and Charity*.

instead of healthy and ripe fruit, would generally produce only leaves with all their efforts, while the fruits that would only grow in one of the following dispensations could not ripen in the present one, because the time of the figs had not yet arrived. Therefore, he thought that it was better to bear fruit in the present, albeit weak, dispensation than to rise to a higher order before its time and produce nothing but leaves. I confess that this memory, whether well founded or not, affects my mind very much, and has shed light on many occasions.

The matters surrounding the Prophets, as they have thus far unfolded here, have been to me, as it were, an example of that rule, in that I have found little fruit, but many leaves. Indeed, one of the most distinguished among them has withered away, as it were, and, in spite of all those prophetic inspirations, has been put to shame before the world.

The strongest objection that some well-meaning people have made to me is this: These people nonetheless say so many good things; why then should it not be from the Spirit of God? To which I have answered from 1 John 4:1: "Test the spirits to see whether they are from God." For if people speak and teach evil, that spirit would be evident and would not need to be tested further. But since John requires testing and careful investigation, it must be a spirit that is hidden under a false covering, and cannot be identified other than by a thorough examination, and therefore cannot be accepted or rejected until after such an examination. But because few have received that gift of testing in sufficient measure, I try as much as I can to keep well-meaning people from such untrodden paths, so that they do not fall into them and, because of the good words they hear, accept everything without discernment. But on to other things.

No. 98

A. W. Böhme to Henry Newman
London, [March 1714]

The enclosed extract of a letter that I recently received from Copenhagen will acquaint you with the good effect that the Malabar Reports, printed in Halle, have had in Denmark, but especially what a blessing the historical account of the British nation's efforts to promote this work has produced. The Society itself prepared this narrative and it was included in the 6th part of the Malabar letters printed in German. This ought to be an edifying example, by which not only individuals, but also whole nations and public bodies, might encourage one another to promote those undertakings which are directed toward a true and universal purpose. I hope that in the future there will be more examples of these undertakings than there are in the present, because the general selfishness of human hearts prevents people from extending their horizon beyond the borders of their own land, nation, sect, party, or any other such border that the spirit of selfishness has set for itself in these times. We have every reason to rejoice in the little sparks of divine mercy that now and then break through the thick clouds of judgment. Be so kind as to communicate the enclosed extract to the members of the Special Committee, and at the same time ask them for their good advice on how the money transferred over from Denmark can be sent to Tranquebar.

Extract of a letter received from Copenhagen, dated March 6, 1714

There has been a great movement recently with regards to the Malabar Mission, which has not happened since it was established. His Royal Majesty of Denmark, Frederick IV, has ordered the East India Company to send new instructions to its governor at Tranquebar. He is to comply with these instructions in his conduct toward the mission, which he is in no way to hinder, but should rather promote and protect by all possible means. A copy of these instructions has been sent to the missionaries, along with a letter to encourage them in the work so happily begun. His Majesty has also added a gift of 2000 Reichsthaler to the annual allowance granted to the mission, in order to extend the missionaries' undertaking. This royal benevolence has also favorably influenced other people to contribute to so worthwhile a work. Prince Carl[102] not only wrote to the missionaries and answered their letters, but also presented them with 500 Reichsthaler for their encouragement. Princess Sophia Hedwig[103] added 55 ducats, and the royal widow[104] likewise added another contribution. All these funds were entrusted to the ship Dansburg bound for the East Indies, which sailed on February 10th. A few days later, however, we received the tragic news that the Dansburg had been wrecked in a

---

102. Prince Charles of Denmark and Norway (1680–1729).
103. Princess Sophia Hedwig of Denmark and Norway (1677–1735).
104. Queen Charlotte Amalie of Denmark and Norway (1650–1714).

storm off the coast of Jutland, taking with it all its goods and people, with the exception of two sailors who had saved themselves by the skin of their teeth only to be the sad messengers of this misfortune. Prince Carl had his money insured, but the King and the other aforementioned benefactors, who had not taken such good precautions, immediately replaced their money, so that the missionaries would not be adversely affected by this unfortunate incident.

Through divine providence, the King has been uncommonly inspired by the historical account of what happened in England with regard to the Malabar Mission, which is prefaced to the 6th Continuation recently printed in Halle.

Given these circumstances, and the fact that there is no hope of a Danish ship going to the East Indies this year, I am hoping that, at your request, the illustrious Society for Promoting Christian Knowledge will assist us with good and prompt counsel as to whether or not this generous contribution can still be sent to Tranquebar on an English ship. One thing I almost forgot to tell you is that the King has granted the missionaries the liberty to address their complaints directly to him, together with their proposals for the advancement of the mission. All these funds have been transferred to London, where they can be collected as soon as requested.

No. 99

A. W. Böhme to Christopher Wendt at Copenhagen[105]
London, 30 March 1714

I was very pleased to hear of the good effect that the report on the work of the East India mission has had at the Royal Danish Court. I have immediately translated into English an extract from my Lord's letter and had it read to the Society, which has up to now shown such pleasure in the Danish-East Indian Mission. Indeed, all the members of the Society

---

105. Christopher Wendt was the secretary of the Missions College in Copenhagen, the mission's official governing body established by King Frederick IV "with a full and unlimited Power to transact, manage, and determine all such things as relate to the Mission." See "Abstract of the Kings Instructions," 13. Since Wendt's relationship with the German missionaries was uneasy and tense, Böhme had to walk a fine line in his correspondence with him. See Letters 111 and 119.

present at that time expressed great pleasure at His Majesty's gracious decision to support the mission so earnestly, and in particular that he gave the missionaries the freedom to present their complaints and other information about the progress and obstacles of the work directly to His Majesty, since this will give a swift and effective response to any difficulty (of which there will undoubtedly always be several). Just as there are all kinds of good developments in Denmark for the advancement of such a Christian undertaking, so we can also report with good reason that the renewal that has arisen here since 1709, when the first letters of the missionaries appeared in English, is still going on and has not been hindered at all by the hard times that are also beginning to affect this country. All of which convinces me in no small measure that the Lord God must have a hand in this matter. Only a fortnight ago, a certain nobleman sent a sum of £40 to the Society for this purpose, after he had seen the Extract of the latest East Indian letters, which were recently published in English at the request of the Society. Similarly, a former friend of the mission, who died recently in the country, dedicated £20 annually as a permanent income to this work. To say nothing of other donations. Through these and other edifying circumstances, of which we have witnessed many, the English have been very much awakened to consider their own plantations, factories, and fortresses, and to emulate the Danish nation in missionary work. Indeed, they have taken great pains to enlist qualified people to promote Christianity among their own people in the East Indies, as well as to endeavor to convert the Malabarians. However, until now there has been a lack of people who could be used for such an important work. And even if the Society would not be averse to assigning some students from Halle to such work, they would still first have to learn English thoroughly, in order to safeguard the stated purpose. To say nothing of other obstacles.

As for the money that was to be forwarded to Tranquebar via England, when the Society learned of it, they immediately sent the matter to the East India Company. However, they were told that it was too late at this point, since all the ships bound for Madras had already been dispatched; therefore, it would have to wait until the departure of the next fleet (which usually sails in December). They promised to do all they could to help. In the meantime, the package of letters sent from Copenhagen has been forwarded in an envelope to a ship that has already departed for Deal, and I have informed the missionaries of the donation that had been given them from Denmark, but which could not yet be delivered. I have no doubt that they will be able to get credit and borrow some money until the next fleet arrives.

It is always my pleasure to offer a hand with a Christian cause like this. Going forward, care should be taken that the letters, parcels, or whatever else are to be sent to the East Indies via England, are provided several weeks before the departure of the fleet, so that the East India Company can be notified promptly and the necessary clearance requested.

No. 100

A. W. Böhme to Mr. K.
London, 30 April 1714

In response to your recent inquiry, I am pleased to inform you that only a few pages remain to be translated of the book on the considerable miracle cures that occurred in England; they can therefore be completed in a few days.[106] They shall be forwarded to you as soon as Mr. Fr. has secured a publisher to take over the printing. Since my colleague[107] has translated most of it, he will finish translating the rest as soon as I can assure him that the printing of what has already been sent has begun; therefore, please include a sample of the first sheet in a letter and send it to me. It is a pity that such examples, which are so well attested—as are in particular the cures wrought by the Irishman Valentine Greatrakes[108]—and so gloriously testify that the Lord God has at all times still left some extraordinary gifts to His Church, even in the midst of corruption, should not be spread further, thus making known the finger of God in this matter as well.

If one had found only a few such genuine characteristics of miraculous works, and especially miraculous cures, among the so-called *French Prophets* here, to which the first and most prominent among them aspired, then their dispensation, as they like to call their work, would have been at least somewhat recognized. However, nothing like this has been

---

106. It is unclear what book Böhme is referring to. On the revival of interest in miracles in the eighteenth century, see Butler, "Spiritual Importance," 105–6.

107. Most likely Johann Christian Jacobi (1670–1750); see Introduction, xxviii.

108. Valentine Greatrakes (1628–1682) was a faith healer from Ireland who toured England in 1666.

found, although a number of people have diligently inquired about it. Otherwise, there is hardly any more mention of these people, who caused quite a stir here some years ago, even though they still have their meetings here and there. I attribute this mainly to two things: the first is the reported resurrection of Dr. Thomas Emes, about which they had several inspirations printed publicly, although it came to nothing. The other is John Lacy's galling affair with an uninhibited woman named Elizabeth Grey, who was embraced as a prophetess among them and crowned with extravagant praises, even though she eventually married Lacy, whose own wife was still alive. The failed resurrection of Dr. Emes did not affect me—although there is much in it that makes this so-called dispensation suspicious—as much as this shameful example of Mr. Lacy, which paves the way to libertinism in such a way that in time, under the cover of Christianity and spiritual inspiration, one will be able to justify doing the most disturbing things. I confess that I was appalled by this, and from that time on I have had a negative opinion of the Prophets.

The worst thing is that most of their followers approved of that disturbing act, and sanctioned under a solemn inspiration, and continue even now to whitewash the scandal and to misuse the precious Word of God for this purpose. Since then, my friends, some of whom followed them, have sternly warned against this spirit and the dangerous cliffs of libertinism to which it leads. We must await the righteous judgment of God for such things at the end of time; however, we must also be on our guard, so that we will not be deceived on the right or on the left. And more and more I find that spiritual defilements penetrate deeper than those that arise from mere natural reason; for the deeper the vitality of the soul that is defiled by an error, the deeper the error itself penetrates, and the more difficult it is to be persuaded of the error.

I have finally come across Richard Baxter's book, *The Certainty of the Worlds of Spirits*, at a bookseller who sells nothing but old books, and I am taken aback by it.[109] The English say that Baxter was too gullible in his narration of several histories, and therefore his book should be read with proper caution. In it, he passed judgment on a number of unprecedented events that he had not seen, and as a result his judgment went beyond the scope of his ability to discern people's spirits. This includes the examples of Jacob Böhme and John Pordage, whom he described as dangerous, but without sufficient proof. Furthermore, this work by Baxter—who not only asserts ghosts, apparitions, and other such extraordinary things, but

---

109. Baxter, *Certainty of the Worlds of Spirits*.

also often put too much credence in them—could serve to reinforce the convictions of the Reformed in Germany, since many of them flatly deny such spiritual powers, and thereby open the door to a Sadduceeism that is gaining considerable momentum.

No. 101

A. W. Böhme to Professor Joachim Lange in Halle
London, 28 May 1714

Now that the holidays are over, *Medicina Mentis* is ready to go to press; therefore, please send the rest of the material as soon as possible, so that printing will not be delayed.[110] What we have learned previously shall be taken carefully into account; your book will be printed in the same format as Arndt's Latin edition of *True Christianity* (1708). Allow me now to be so bold as to add one or two other reminders that may help in the reception of the book.

1. The copperplate set on the front of the book will be neatly copied by an engraver. It occurred to me that it might be useful to add a short explanation of the book, in as many lines as would fit on one sheet. The English like to read well-crafted poems, only in a clean style that is light and flowing, and avoids any extravagant touches which often make the words difficult to understand. Just as several years ago a German theologian, who is still alive, composed a poem on the deeds of the Duke of Marlborough, which, however, was only read by a few people because its pompous and fanciful style required a lot of brainwork (although others might have thought it very appropriate for the subject).

2. Given the current state of affairs, we cannot advise dedicating the book to any particular person, because of the antagonism between the parties that has arisen in the Church of England over the years. These parties are so hostile that they have almost no contact with each other, and even detest the books written by scholars of the other party. For this reason, little is written now that does not flow into the circle of these heated controversies. Even those who see through such miserable matters, and have no desire whatsoever to meddle

---

110. Joachim Lange (1670–1744), *Medicina Mentis*.

in them, cannot remain free from such labels; thus, it would appear that a great crisis of the present church system is approaching, and that the Lord is about to sweep his threshing-floor in England with great zeal. So, if in these times a book is dedicated to a certain person or society, the dedication itself is sufficient to make the book partisan; and it is understood that by means of the dedication the author wants to declare himself for one party, or to favor one over the other. It is thus best to let it go freely into the British world, awaiting better times, and take note of what its fate will be.

3. It would appear that the title of the book is too long, or too detailed, for the taste of local scholars; therefore, it would be advisable either to omit some lines or to arrange them differently.

4. Because the Scotsman Sir George Mackenzie's essay on the weakness of human reason is not obtainable as a tract, I am willing to have the entire small tract reprinted here.[111] However, since it is not available here in Latin, I assume that someone else must have translated it from English or Scots into Latin and had it printed outside of England. If you, dear brother, would help me obtain a copy in Latin, I would publish it, together with another treatise on the same subject, immediately after *Medicina Mentis*, in the hope that it would be useful here and illuminate *Medicina Mentis* in some way.

No. 102

A. W. Böhme to Heinrich Plütschau
London, 30 June 1714

The letter from Copenhagen has duly come into my hands; it is with sorrow that I have seen how bad the change in Tranquebar is, from whom many well-meaning Englishmen had taken such good hope. In the process, however, we have learned that probably the best counsel is that a missionary seminary be established in East India itself, rather than that the youth be dragged from there to Europe in the hope of preparing them here for service among the pagans. In Europe, there are many tempting trees that grow before the eyes of youths and tempt the untrained to eat

---

111. Sir George Mackenzie (1636–1691), *Essays upon Several Moral Subjects*.

from them; once they have tasted the forbidden fruit, it is not so easy to get them out of the habit. But God Himself must equip workers for such a ministry; for human help and wisdom are not sufficient here.

Otherwise, matters surrounding the mission are still well-regarded here among the best of the English. On May 20th, John Robinson, the current Bishop of London, preached to a large assembly of London youth who were being educated in the charity schools.[112] This happens once a year under the auspices of the Society for Promoting Christian Knowledge, so that the people of London may be moved by the sight of so many children to give more generously, being convinced of their good education. After the sermon, fifty copies of an account of the mission, which had been excerpted from recent missionary letters and printed in English, were distributed to many prominent people, and thus the whole cause was renewed in some and made known to others who did not yet know about it. In the attached short preface, I have addressed the objection that many have previously made, that the Malabarians only accepted Christianity externally for a time, for the sake of temporal gain, but in the absence of it, quickly fell back again.[113]

Johann Berlin who, together with Johann Adler and his brother, sailed here in January 1713, having brought the Malabar printing press with him, has now arrived in the East Indies together with his companions, as is confirmed by a letter dated September 1713 from Madras. It was written by an Englishman, who also referred to other ships, with the assurance that there would be more reports from them, but these have not yet arrived. Otherwise, we have not as yet been able to find an Englishman who would be willing and able to go to the East Indies as a schoolmaster or missionary; nor do the directors of the East India Company here, nor the governors in the East Indies, appear to consider the matter significant enough to promote it and offer a hand in it. Whoever does not dare to trust God here will soon get tired and lose courage. Your Latin letter, in which you answered the objection about the first commandment that was omitted in the catechism printed at Tranquebar, and about which there was considerable controversy here, was read to the Society, in order to assuage any troubled minds. But we must learn with time that when one storm blows over, another begins to rise again,

---

112. John Robinson (1650–1723), *Benefits and Duty of the Members of Christ's Kingdom.*

113. *Propagation of the Gospel in the East.*

so that we might always be on our guard and prepare ourselves in these times.

No. 103

A. W. Böhme to Loth Fischer in Utrecht
London, 20 July 1714

The recent report about the so-called Prophets horrified me, and I hope to become more and more wary of such unusual movements. The Prophets here are a bit more proper than those in Holland, even if they do occasionally step out of line. Up till now, a number of marriages have been performed among them that were arranged through inspirations in which the bride and groom were named. And because they believe that what is given them—through the action of the Spirit, as they say—are truly divine oracles, they proceed without any further examination and imagine that they are relying solely on divine authority and decree. These things seem somewhat dangerous to me, especially when one tries to arrange by inspiration marriage-related and similar delicate matters in which the flesh likes to meddle. You cannot confront these people in almost any way; for since they hold their own sayings in such high esteem, they hold those who want to encourage them doubt their own oracles to be ignorant of the ways of God.

Last month, the second volume of Arndt's *True Christianity* appeared in English, after the first one, edited earlier in 1712, had had some good effect here and there, mostly among the lower classes. *Surgunt Indocti et Coelum rapiunt* (The unknowing rise up and seize heaven). The edition of Bromley's theological writings has still not come to fruition.[114] The manuscripts and especially the letters Bromley left behind have been handed over to Dr. Francis Lee by his heirs; however, thus far he has not taken the trouble to put them into some order, despite the encouragement he has received to do so. Dr. Robert Gell's single sermon on astronomy could be hard to find here.[115]

---

114. Bromley, *Way to the Sabbath of Rest . . . To Which Are Now Added*.
115. Gell, *Stella Nova*.

From Queen Anne to George I (1714–1716)

Letters 104–130

No. 104

A. W. Böhme to Johann Gottfried Seelig[?] in Pennsylvania[1]
London, 18 August 1714

Both of your kind letters arrived a few weeks ago, one after the other. Praise be to the Lord who has sustained us thus far—you, my beloved brother, in the American wilderness and me in the English wilderness—and has watered our gardens in times of drought. The Lord will know how to save those who obey His voice and flee from the fields of creaturely servitude along with some of Pharaoh's servants. Because of King Charles XII of Sweden and the important transactions in which he is supposed to be instrumental—partly according to prophecy, partly conjecture—everything still remains quiet now; and nothing of the well-known prophecies by Johannes Daut has yet to come true.[2] What the Lord has determined in his hidden counsel, and whether any of Daut's prophecies will be fulfilled, only time will tell. Since 1709, when his army was defeated by the Muscovites, King Charles has stayed in Turkish territories and has been subjected personally to almost unspeakable physical sufferings; his country is in large part at war and what still remains of it is exhausted, and it is not yet clear what effect it will have on him.

1. Possibly Seelig, as in Letter 28.
2. Johannes Daut (1656–1736), *Approaching Judgments of God*.

It cannot be denied that in this matter both true and false Christians draw all kinds of inferences, though for different reasons. Our local Prophets, under the direction of the Spirit, have dispatched three people to Turkey out of their own resources, to address the King of Sweden with their inspirations. They have already returned, and it is reported that they were not granted a personal audience with the king. Now they are having an account of their journey and the events that took place printed in Holland, so that everything can be seen in more detail.[3] And while I am thinking about the Prophets, I must add a few other things about them.

Ever since John Lacy took Elizabeth Gray as his wife, even though his first wife was still living, the reputation of the Prophets has been visibly damaged. Most of the Prophets have approved of such shameful deeds, claiming, in fact, the influence of the Spirit, as they like to say; a few, however, have spoken out against such actions and have denounced them as wicked, from which it is clear that the spirit that moves them is not itself united. Some have sought deep mystery in such insolence, and have wanted to present him as a symbol and image of Babylonian ecclesiasticism; in doing so, they also know how to cite various examples from the Scriptures, which, after all, can be misused to cover all kinds of disgrace and folly. Those, however, are truly the wisest who hold that he has simply revealed his own motives and has opened the door for others to libertinism, which I fear is likely to become all too common in these latter times. But if he is a symbol of a corrupt Church, it seems to me that none is more fitting than the church at Thyatira, which participated in the same kind of defilement. But what need is there to look for figures and pictures of the corrupted ecclesiasticism, seeing that, alas, the originals in their false underpinnings are clearly hovering everywhere before our eyes? The innocent among them, who follow these things with good intentions and regard them as a new dispensation, which is what they call this movement of the spirit, distress me the most. But God will also know how to spare them, so that in the end they will still gain much good experience from it.

Those who traveled to Turkey some years ago, as mentioned above, stayed for a while in Halle and prepared their fellow French brethren who had fled there for the same dispensation. They were very eager for

---

3. Four French Prophets went to Constantinople: Jean Allut, Élie Marion, Nicholas Fatio de Duillier, and Charles Portalès. Marion died in Italy. Portalès and Allut returned directly to England, while Fatio stayed in Holland to see to the printing of Allut et al., *Plan de la justice de Dieu* and *Quand vous aurez saccagé*. Schwartz, *French Prophets*, 178–81.

these new things, basing their hope on a prophecy to that effect from their brethren in England. They also joined together in prayer and fasting to plead for this gift; then, after some time, their bodies began to show signs of being moved or agitated. They called these physical stirrings the first fruits of the Spirit, in the hope that the gift of prophecy would soon follow. However, it took some time before the gift of prophecy was given to them.

At the same time, a German maid was overtaken in the orphanage and began to speak through the Spirit; she was then immediately pulled by the French into their meetings, and her utterances were accepted and recorded as genuine oracles. At this point, the clamor in Halle really took off. Many of the students there emulated this spirit in the maid, being intent, like the Athenians, only on something new, in spite of the fact that their utterances were rather insubstantial, and had little of the anointing and balm of life in them. The maid herself, Maria Elisabeth Mathisin, was about 22 years old, and notorious for lying and scheming, so no significant oracle could be expected from her. Subsequently, she could be found daily in the meetings of the French, and was honored and respected by them as a prophetess.

Before long, during their initial gatherings, the spirit in the maid instructed those present not go out on Sundays, not even to church. This immediately struck some as suspicious, and they began to doubt that this was the voice of the Savior, since he would hardly keep people away from the true path of repentance and faith that is proclaimed there. After this, the theology professors gathered together in order to examine more closely, after fervent prayer and supplication, the whole affair that was causing so much unrest. They declared that they could not find any divine sign in the matter, but they did discover some things from which the opposite could reasonably be deduced. Professor Francke then had the maid and her father come to him, demanded the reason for her new behavior, and asked what kind of spirit it was that drove her to such talk. To which she answered that a spirit was indeed speaking through her, but she did not know whether or not it was from God, and, after a stern rebuke, she began to waver somewhat in what she thought about prophecy. But this admonition, warning them against seduction, was of little avail. For as soon as the French and other followers received word of it, they confronted the maid and reproached her that her wavering was a serious matter. Soon afterward, the Spirit began to speak through her again, which she had supposedly renounced in obedience to Professor Franke's admonition. From then on, she relentlessly prophesied against Professor Franke, calling him a wayward star who had blasphemed the Spirit of the Lord; she foretold the downfall of the orphanage and the other institutions connected with it, and made other frightening insinuations. All these things were attributed to Jehovah speaking through the maid. And this was the beginning of the so-called prophetic dispensation in Halle.

In February of this year, the commotion grew even larger. Students ran wild and caused all kinds of mischief, particularly since the Spirit had given orders that their meetings should now be held in the evening and at night. They also held so-called love feasts at night, including the washing of feet and other similar acts prompted by the Spirit. In view of these and other circumstances, the matter could not remain hidden for long.

Professor Francke warned the students in their academies, and sought to draw them away from the Prophets' gatherings and from their attachment to such extraordinary behaviors, contending that they were following a spirit that they had not yet tested, and that perhaps they were not yet equipped to test whether it was of God. He told them about the failure of those who prophesied in England that a dead man would be raised, but was not. And since the agitations of the prophets in Halle came from the English, or from the Camisards who had fled to England, it would be reasonable to assume that their prophesies were based on the same false grounds. He insisted that he would not be ashamed to publicly assert that this was a work of God, if he felt a conviction of its godliness in his soul. But since he had more and more doubts about whether he could attribute it to the Lord God, he often let these or similar words come from his lips: "It is not my Savior who is speaking, and I have not the slightest fear of all the distortions that this spirit utters."

On the Feast of the Presentation of Jesus Christ, he preached a sermon on prophetic movements (which will be published later), in which he touched briefly on the matter of the inspired Prophets and pointed out their incorrectness.[4] He also admonished the people, in part for rashly following the prophets and in part for judging them uncharitably and disdainfully; instead, they should pray for their betterment. Some students, who had been attending the table at the orphanage but were now following the prophets, were dismissed from the table and its teaching. The same thing happened to the inspired maid's father, who was a teaching assistant; when he was serving the young noblemen, he told them all sorts of things about his daughter's visions.

4. Francke, *Jesus Christus als das Licht der Heyden*.

The other preachers in the city now thought they had found a way to discredit the so-called Pietists at court, and to blame them for the disturbance caused by the prophets. However, they were quite embarrassed when they saw that Professor Francke publicly declared himself against these people and contradicted their novelties in sermons and in their academies. Nevertheless, he confined himself to verbal statements and did not in any way want the matter reported to the government, so that it would not raise the slightest hint of an intended persecution. The French preachers who had settled in Halle, however, had a commission appointed by the court to inquire into the matter of the prophets, to which in April two physicians, Dr. Hofmann and Dr. Stiffer, together with a preacher from Halle and Professor Francke's colleague Johann Freylinghausen, were appointed. However, an order has already arrived from the court that if the people would not listen to reason, they should then leave; the order also stated that Professor Francke should first be heard about the causes of the matter. Professor Francke replied that if the people were to be dismissed straightaway, there would be no use in establishing grounds for it. In addition, he assured them that he did not wish to exact revenge on them, although they had already caused him a great deal of irritation in fulfilling his duties. He did not want to help to make them leave, but rather to wait patiently for their improvement. He also sketched out his thoughts on this matter and sent them to the government. In the meantime, the inspired maid has now declared that her own prophecies were false and cannot be persuaded by her father or anyone else to return to the prophets' meetings.

The most important reasons Professor Francke gave for opposing the agitations and inspirations that some regarded as divine—which he also submitted to the government—are as follows: (1) Because of the lack of proper scriptural evidence, by which such violent agitations in particular could be proved. It is true that the gift of languages, among other gifts, is found in the early church, but not such bodily convulsions. (2) Because of the Scriptures (see Deut 18:22) that bear witness against these prophets. This is seen especially in the reported but failed resurrection of Dr. Emes in England and some other predictions that were found to be false. (3) Because of the bad fruit which can be found among these people. The example of John Lacy in England can be cited, who, while his wife was still alive, married Elizabeth Gray and tried to defend in print such an obviously offensive act.[5] Other prophets as well have

5. Lacy, "Letter from John Lacy."

subsequently approved this behavior. (4) Thus, especially in the case of M. E. Mathisin, many things are found to be unworthy of God's majesty. (5) If prophecies have a divine character, one should at least find in them inner traces of an awakening to the works of faith, although this is still far from sufficient for an adequate examination. But this is not found in the sayings of the inspired maid, for her sayings only extend as far as what was already in her mind, and she could not reveal anything that she did not already know, whether true or false. (6) Those who claim to be prophets must be certain of it themselves; otherwise, how can they persuade others of what they themselves do not believe? Now, according to M. E. Mathisin, when she was questioned by the ministry at Glauche about these matters, she answered quite honestly that she did not know whether it was from God.

This is a brief summary of the most important details I wanted to convey to you of what happened in Halle in connection with the Prophets. In Holland, where they have also left behind a seed, many troublesome things are said to be going on, and those who are inspired are compelled by the Spirit to stand on their heads and strike all sorts of ridiculous postures. Here in England, where they still have full freedom, their number has been growing, since several have fled here from Switzerland, where they are not tolerated, in order to enjoy freedom. I also hear that for the same reason quite a few of the French will be arriving here from Halle. May the Lord have mercy on this lot, and preserve the few among them that are still upstanding, and purify them from the deceit and confusions of the corrupt nature and from other deceptive influences here in England, that they may yet lead markedly pure lives. But it seems to me somewhat dangerous that they have been arranging various marriages among their followers by means of their customary inspirations, in which the Spirit has named the persons who are to marry; then, in accordance with that command, the marriages have been consummated. It seems to me that these are bad signs of a prophet's character and do not correspond to the gravity that should be found in extraordinary witnesses to the truth; much less should it accord with the purpose of a prophet and messenger of God. And one may well wish that even more dangerous symptoms of such things do not occur.

But as far as other movements in Church and religious matters are concerned, both in and outside England, almost everything is going to extremes, and a bitter sectarian spirit is bent on seizing the throne of every party and subduing others under it. This unseemly upheaval I regard as a harbinger of the approaching downfall of the corrupt state of the Church among all parties. *Nullum Violentum diuturnum.* [May the violence not last.] It will be unnecessary to add anything about the High and Low Church parties into which the Church of England is now divided, and which are constantly at war with each other, since the rumor of it, and perhaps also its spirit and practice, will undoubtedly have penetrated as far as the West Indies. The saddest thing is that neither party is concerned for the glory of God, but only for its own interest, with the exception, perhaps, that the leaders of the moderate party have a little more natural honesty, and are better patriots than their opponents. They even show a little more sympathy and leniency against the Dissenters, and do not condemn out of hand everything that is not within their circle of opinion and practice. Here is an example from the High-Church Party Procedures, from which one can easily deduce what the other articles of faith of High-Church theology are about: The adherents to this party have now wanted to prove in numerous books that baptism which was not conferred by a bishop or an episcopally ordained priest, but by a lay person—by which they mean all those who did not receive their ordination from a bishop—is null and void.

Therefore, all other Protestant Churches, especially the large bodies of Lutherans and Calvinists, would essentially be made un-Christian by these extremists; moreover, if it were in their power, these zealots would undoubtedly deprive the Protestants of all the outward privileges they have as Christians—the inward motive for baptism seems to be hidden from them. It is also very difficult to establish the validity of baptism with a party that exhibits so little evidence of death to the world and the crucifixion of the flesh, which should be the clearest sign of the power of baptism. Although this absurd proposition finds little acceptance among those with common sense, some irrational souls have been so taken in by the thoughtless ranting that they allow themselves to be rebaptized or baptized again by Episcopal priests, regardless of the fact that they had previously been baptized by a Presbyterian. In this way a young Presbyterian and candidate for theology named Benjamin Reed was misled and rebaptized by an Episcopal priest near Exeter. Some laughed at this ridiculous act, while others showed compassion and looked with pity upon both the baptizer and the baptized. But what will this irrational sectarian spirit not do when it is left to its own devices and driven to greater extremes by carnal desires?

In neighboring France, there are just as many subversives among the so-called clergy. Several years ago, Father Pasquier Quesnel edited the New Testament in French, adding moral reflections to each verse to make the book all the more appealing for the reader, and also to provide guidance for devotional meditation.[6] The notes are taken in good part from Augustine. But because the Roman See found several passages in these notes that violated the interests of the Church, the author and his book fell under severe censorship in Rome, and the current Pope, Clement XI, banned the book last year by means of a solemn bull. From those notes, 101 propositions were extracted and condemned as heretical, many of which contain the true essence of Christ's teachings; a sensible person, therefore, can conclude from such a condemnation how little those in Rome understand about the teachings and life of Christ. In the meantime, many French bishops and clergy have refused to submit absolutely to the Papal Bull, but have requested that they be given a more detailed explanation of some of the points on which they have scruples. However, since the Pope and the King have refused them and are insisting on absolute submission, the entire clergy has been stirred up and is divided over it. Those who wanted to let the matter rest submitted to the Pope's dictatorial authority without reserve; the others, however, who saw a bit further, asked for more reasons and explanations in the matter. This division and disruption of the clergy has now nearly reached its peak, and one cannot see at present where and how this conflict will end. The Jesuits carry on like Jehu, and know no measure, so long as they have power on their side, which, however, the sensible regard as a prelude to their approaching ruin in France, where, except for the kings themselves, they have few friends. The author himself retired to Holland just before the storm surrounding him could reach its peak; there, he is trying to redeem himself and his book with written defenses against the Pope's thunder and charges of heresy. From this whole depiction, dear brother, you can clearly see that the Church and religious affairs of the most important countries in Europe are in great ferment and disruption.

I cannot fail to mention another graphic example of the bitter spirit of sectarianism and persecution that has recently taken place in Switzerland among the Reformed, and which has aroused in other nations indignation against the persecutors and compassion for the persecuted. Several years ago, the authorities in the Canton of Bern ordered the Anabaptists, or Mennonites as they are called there, to leave the land.

---

6. Quesnel, *Explication Apologétique*.

Consequently, many set out on a journey to Holland, and from Holland to England, in order to sail from there to the West Indies. Some stayed here and there in Holland, staying with their fellow believers and supporting themselves with the labor of their own hands. I visited those who were going to the West Indies, while they were waiting here for passage, and gave them a word of admonition, as best I could, with heartfelt love; they welcomed my words and expressed their appreciation of them. In the meantime, the States of Holland, in the year 1710, sent a very moving appeal to the lords of Bern, in which they emphatically represented these Mennonites, and informed the Swiss authorities that they, the States of Holland, from many years of experience, were well convinced of the quiet and obedient conduct of the Mennonites, and therefore had no hesitation in approaching the Bernese authorities with a letter of intercession in favor of these people. They also answered the objections and accusations that commonly caused these people to be hated by others. In fact, the Swiss had requested the help of the Dutch, and especially ships for transporting these people to America; the Dutch, however, refused to assist them, so that they would not give the slightest appearance of endorsing this kind of severity in religious matters, and thereby approving the practice of the papists themselves. However, neither these nor other appeals had the intended effect: rather, the spirit of persecution was given even more room, and these people suffered imprisonment and other punishments. Some time ago, six of those who had previously been expelled returned to their homeland, hoping to remain in hiding in some of the villages, and to make a living in silence. They were, however, discovered and reported to the authorities, who, to the consternation and grief of all fair-minded people, handed them over to the king in France, who condemned them to the galleys and thus to a perpetual death.

Tantum Religio potuit suadere Malorum! [Only religion can induce this evil!]

No. 105

A. W. Böhme to N. N.
London, 30 September 1714

So, it has pleased the Lord to transfer Queen Anne, who has ruled over these dominions until now, from time to eternity on the first of

FROM QUEEN ANNE TO GEORGE I (1714–1716)

August, the tenth Sunday after Trinity, between seven and eight o'clock in the morning, and to bring an end to her reign. It was on March 8, 1702, when her predecessor King William died, also on a Sunday and at almost the same hour, that in the afternoon the then Princess Anne was proclaimed Queen with great pomp in London. Thus, one rises when the other falls, and in the dominions of this world there is nothing more constant than constant change. *Blessed is the one whose protection is the God of Jacob, and blessed is the one who does not rely on rulers, but on the living God, Who does not waver, but is a rock in time of trouble!* How often then I am refreshed in spirit over these two attributes of God: His *mercy* and His *omnipotence*, in both of which our faith must rest with childlike trust. For since the Lord *can* help according to His omnipotence, and *wants* to help according to mercy, faith grasps hold of this with heartfelt desire, and flees to this twofold attribute—which, since it is not found in any mere creature, we have all the less reason to cling to it idolatrously—as to an insurmountable fortress.

But to return to the passing of our Queen: the people were in considerable consternation, because of the poor state in which the Empire found itself, to make a defense in case France and the Pretender Prince of Wales should attempt a landing. Our soldiers had disbanded, and were begging in droves in the streets; the warships, which constitute the most important power of this country, were scattered here and there, and, after the Peace of Utrecht made with France, were considered unusable. In Ireland, the Pretender had long since recruited soldiers, and had them transported to France for his benefit, even daring to do the same in England itself, and was otherwise perpetrating all manner of insolence. The city of London—not to mention the surrounding countryside, since the situation was probably the same there—was full of Jesuits and Catholic priests, who made converts here and there, and on occasion let it be known that they hoped to establish a firm foothold here and to see the old religion reestablished. The English nation was divided, and many expressed great displeasure with the peace made with France. The differences of opinion were so widespread and pervasive that the Church of England was divided into two houses, the High- and Low-Church parties, which hated and envied each other to such an extent that husbands and wives often fell out with each other, and even menservants and maidservants, and the children themselves, could say which party they wanted to belong to. If one were to name a bishop or a preacher, one would know instantly to which party he was loyal, and whether or not he could be promoted by the present government, which favored the High-Church party. Thus it is easy to determine how the hirelings will have invaded; for since they only care about the belly and its fullness, and sail according to the wind that blows from the court, it is all the same to them which party they join, as long as they can achieve their purpose by doing so.

These unchristian divisions were not only instilled into an unwitting multitude in the pulpits, but were also propagated in innumerable writings and caricatures, so that posterity might see how far people, having been handed over by divine judgment to their own devices, can sink. Each party wanted to make the other unchristian, and even deprive them of their general privileges, by which they at least belong to the external church community. Which work they could have spared themselves, since Christian hearts were fully convinced from their works that both parties were concerned not so much with Church and Christianity, as with worldly honor and advancement that needed religion only as a tool to achieve this main purpose. How little there is of the truth of Christianity in both parties, and therefore they have no right to quarrel over something they do not have, although in the Low-Church party there is generally a little more natural honesty and more earnestness in resisting the gathering momentum of the papacy. But thus far they have been narrowly restricted by the ruling party, and have been deprived of any power, to such an extent that they can do little or nothing. Now the papists, who have previously been ensconced in our country, are beginning to leave in droves and to go over to France; indeed, there is news from Dover that since the Queen's death more than three thousand papists, Jesuits, and priests have already been transported from there to France.

In Ireland, where the danger of the encroaching papacy was obvious, and where the Catholics flattered themselves that their religion would be the first to take root—for which many in the present government gave them considerable encouragement—the tide has suddenly turned, and the Catholic-centered party has been humiliated to such an extent that it seems as though the weather will not break in from there. A party of soldiers, from those still left in Flanders, was sent to Scotland to keep the disaffected party in check; meanwhile, in England, Scotland, and Ireland, the Elector of Hanover was proclaimed king with immense pomp and universal joy.[7] Anyone who has learned to examine the signs of this time must easily recognize the hand of the Lord governing everything. But

7. King George I of Great Britain and Ireland and ruler of the Electorate of Hanover (1660–1727).

only time will tell whether this wonderful and unexpected deliverance of these countries and the nation will be a blessing. Those parties that have been previously excluded are beginning to raise their heads and rejoice, but I do not see them rejoicing in the hope that the kingdom of God will gain more room, but only that their party has found more protection and support.

Time will tell how this change will affect my own humble self and whether this new king will grant us the previous royal chapel for further use. Some people strongly suspect this to be the case, because the king has such a large retinue of German servants around him—some say around five hundred—who do not know the English language, and therefore cannot listen to English preaching. These past Sundays, the chapel was so full that no apple could fall to the ground, and many were forced to leave for lack of space. I have committed the whole matter into the hands of God, and leave it to His all-wise guidance whether or not He will continue to use me and my humble witness in this place. For just as I did not move a finger to come into this chapel, neither will I move one to hold onto the teaching office in it, especially with such a noticeable increase in it.

No. 106

A. W. Böhme to Georg Heinrich Neubauer in Halle
London, 23 November 1714

My colleague and I have been preaching in the Royal Chapel every Sunday until now, without being told whether or not we are to be retained at the chapel. I had free access in the previous sovereigns, so that I could come not only to the Prince of Denmark, but also, if I wished, to Queen Anne; indeed, she approached me most graciously more than once to come and have a good conversation with her. Since I almost never asked for anything from her that she did not immediately grant, whether interceding for the poor or for other matters, I have sought such access only to promote the general good, and, I hope, not without every blessing. How lamentable it is that eminent persons often know and experience very little of what they should first know and experience; which is why many a good work, which could otherwise be accomplished, is left undone.

The example of the Frenchmen released from the galleys last year often comes to my mind. For when the peace negotiations at Utrecht were in progress, I took the opportunity to propose to the Queen that she address the plight of those poor people. She responded by asking whether I had reason to believe that such people still remained, since she had been told that not a single one was still imprisoned or in the galleys on account of religion. But when I presented her with irrefutable confirmation, she took such an interest in the matter that soon after 136 of them were released, and some of them were sent here to thank the Queen. So seldom do our leaders learn of things in which they might otherwise help, and thereby bring blessing upon themselves and their government.

Some have been persuaded that there is no difference between the English and Lutheran ecclesial constitutions. Indeed, many English people are quite convinced of this, and have asked me before: Why do you not come to our Church, since there is no difference at all? But to these I have answered: If there is no difference, then I will stay where I am; for what would move me, in such circumstances, to run from one church to the other, and thereby incur all kinds of needless censures? And with that answer, I have, without undue rambling, answered their request, so that now I have no further disputes about it, and am also assured that I have more credibility among the most well intentioned than I would have had if I had immediately made my way over to their Church. For if I had made that choice, I would have attracted attention, as though I were seeking promotion in their Church, or a fat offer, or the favor of some people, and the like. But since I have not given the slightest appearance of such a desire, but have stood steadfast at my post, I have thereby made myself more useful among them than by all manner of conformities, which are always subject to manifold misunderstandings.

Moreover, we know that some preachers in Germany have affirmed the same thing and have given complete freedom to conform solely to the Church of England, because they do not see any difference. I ask myself, what kind of Lutherans are these! If a so-called "Pietist" had said such a thing, whole books would likely be written against him, painting him as a destroyer of Lutheranism. However, those writers, because they want to please people, are at the same time most shamefully hypocritical, because they approve of everything to which the powerful seem to have taken a liking. It is certainly true that the doctrines of the Church of England on the subjects of the Lord's Supper and predestination are more favorable to the Reformed in Holland and Germany than to the Lutherans, though

I do not deny that theologians here are very free in their explanations, and that many of them agree more with the Lutheran than with the Reformed confession. Nevertheless, it is customary to evaluate a Church not according to the opinions of some individual scholars, but according to its public confessions.

So, looking at the matter as I do, especially at this time, I do not think that such changes in religion are advisable, since I do not foresee any good in them, but rather many bad outcomes. The party to which one belongs—especially those among the priests who are more interested in expanding their party than in the growth of the Church of Christ, or who otherwise envision a worldly interest in doing so—is in general inclined to flatter those who cross over to them, and by undue praise to put them in danger, of which I have seen many an example here. But this would only last as long as the situation is new and is deemed important; but it would stop as soon as they think that their fellow believer has settled into their new church and could not so easily go back again. I have heard that our princess is praised by preachers around her and is still being praised for her conformity. We have had to grant her our chapel, where the court preachers read the prayers from the English Liturgy for her every day (except Sunday).

In other matters, I had held out some hope that the English Table, the costs of which Queen Anne had paid for a number of years, might be retained by the present government, so that that small charity for the relief of a few poor students might be continued; but it seems, since it is so difficult to gain an audience with the government, that there is little hope of this happening, and therefore that Table might come to an end this year; unless, in the course of time, God were to provide us the opportunity to do some other good for that work. When the King arrived here, his own preacher traveled with him, and we have had to alternate preaching with him in the chapel. He has already tried several times to change a few things in the chapel, and in particular to do away with the Halle hymn book that I had introduced here; however, we received a royal order the day before yesterday from the King's German ministers, to whom the said preacher had submitted a memorial, and, among other points, it made clear that His Majesty's *order and will is that the Halle hymn book be retained as it was before.* As a result, the preacher has been quieted, and now we hope to continue doing the Lord's work with more calm, as long as it is pleasing to the Lord.

No. 107

A. W. Böhme to Samuel Urlsperger
London, 26 November 1714

Let me get straightaway to the main matter: the package sent the other day that included the dedication that Chancellor Jäger has prefaced to a manuscript that is to be dedicated to the King of Great Britain. My colleague himself will report whether he can obtain permission to do so (in general, it is customary to ask about this). I doubt, however, that he will be able to do anything in this matter, especially since none of us has so far been able to gain access to the King, despite my having sought such access on several occasions. Even my colleague, though he is acquainted with all the German ministers, has not been able to obtain an introduction to the King. The same difficulty is also found with the Prince and Princess of Wales, with whom none of us has yet spoken.

But concerning the religious affairs themselves here, the clashes now are more alarming than they have been in the last few years. The Tory or High-Church party, or at least many in it, of whom one believed—and perhaps not without good reason—that they favored Popery and sought in secret to build a bridge for it in England, has now suddenly turned around and wants to be regarded as a pillar of Protestantism. Conversely, they accuse the poor Lutherans in the ugliest way, and portray them to the people in public writings as half-papists. It is easy to see the purpose of these accusations and the resulting hatred against Lutherans. Among others, Dr. Thomas Brett,[8] who has previously written books arguing for episcopal baptism,[9] attacked the Lutherans and charged them with many vulgar things. The title of the publication is *A Review of the Lutheran Principles*.[10] He accuses the Lutherans of removing various books from the canon of the New Testament, and of still having relics among them that they allow the people to kiss, etc. In particular, he draws attention to the fiction of consubstantiation, trying to make the Lutherans hated by it. Throughout his work, he has taken particular issue with Samuel Freiherr von Pufendorf's tract, *The Divine Feudal Law*,[11] and zealously

---

8. Thomas Brett (1667-1744) was a controversialist and bishop in the nonjuring Church of England after the accession of King George I in 1714.

9. Brett, *Extent of Christ's Commission; Enquiry into the Judgment; Further Enquiry*.

10. Brett, *Review of the Lutheran Principles*.

11. Samuel Freiherr von Pufendorf (1632-1694), *Divine Feudal Law*. Pufendorf was

seeks to prove that there is no hope of uniting the Lutherans and the Church of England, primarily because the Lutherans have no bishops and are opposed to episcopal church governance. There are many other similar things that he attributes to them, too numerous to recount here.

Dr. Peter Allix brought me Brett's inflammatory writing and suggested that one of the local Lutheran preachers confront the man and expose the falsehoods in his accounts. Although it would not require any great art or learnedness, since one would only need to present the facts as they are, I have thus far been reluctant to get involved in these kinds of disputes, which are rooted in nothing but hatred or envy on the part of the opponents. For I could easily be diverted from edifying things and involved in all kinds of ramblings.

Meanwhile, an English priest[12] from the moderate party has approached me and asked me to give him some materials pertaining to Dr. Brett's histories, which I have indeed promised to do. In this way I will only watch from a distance such wars of the pen, within which there is little to be found of the wars of Jehovah. This priest has already edited two tracts and addressed them to Secretary of State Townshend, in which he critiques the many dangerous caricatures that have come out against the new government, and presents in general terms the far-reaching consequences that can be expected from such writings and especially from Dr. Brett's anti-Lutheran book.[13] Now in particular he wants to take up this last work by Dr. Brett in a new epistle and demonstrate its wicked intention. However, it will probably do little to ease the controversy, which is not based on the love of truth, but on the hatred of certain persons. Furthermore, one can see from such things the kind of chaos the Church and religion in this country have fallen into.

I still remember that Chancellor Jäger told me when he was here that he supported the High-Church party in England; if he still thinks that that party comes closest to the desired objective, he should say a few words in favor of it. Such a book, however, would not be very welcome at the present Court, because, as you can probably see in the newspapers, all the ministers of the more vehement Tory party are being deprived of their offices and the moderates are again being promoted. If there

---

a German jurist, political philosopher, and historian, who was often quarreling with clergy and theologians over his ideas for Church union.

12. Robert Watts (1683–1726) of St. John's College, Oxford.

13. Watts, *Two Letters; Answer to Two Letters*.

should be in the Chancellor's book any irenic proposals related to religious unions, it would not have any credibility whatsoever within the High-Church party, which does not want to hear anything about unions with the Lutheran Church, but ignominiously dismisses them. In sum: no matter how I look at Church and State here, the priests seem to me to be "men stirred by a particular theological furor" [*viri, furore quodam theologico perciti*]; it is not easy to deal with those who have such a state of mind about theological matters.

Should the frenzy pass with time, and some halcyon days ensue, one might be more likely to gain an audience with them. They do not want to listen to any argument or peace proposal; rather, they want to raise up and establish the Episcopal Church as the bride of Christ, to the exclusion of all others. In such confusions, I often think of the description that an old English lexicographer gave of a fanatic: Fanaticism (says he) is peculiar to priests, because they seemed to be insane, or furious, when they were giving answers from their temples. It is well known how despised a name has been attributed to those who insist on inward Christianity and on more than just a literal understanding. I think one could also rightly ascribe it to those who get into a furor over theology, as has happened to Dr. Henry Sacheverell, Dr. Brett, and others in our country, and want to force everything authoritatively, under the guise of the Church and orthodoxy.

As for myself, in the face of such dissension, I readily acknowledge more and more that all thoughts of unification between the parties are dissolving, and all efforts aimed at it seem to me to be in vain. How would the kingdom of God be served by driving people into a so-called union with human or magisterial restraints and convictions, while the evil root of self-love, pride, self-interest, fear of others, and people-pleasing maintained its dominion in the soul? After all, it is quite evident that people in the party system squirm, bend, and turn after being dragged by their passions, interests, pride, and selfishness. And since such deplorable things are often observed in the theological community, it is easy to see how it must be in other professions.

From Queen Anne to George I (1714–1716)

No. 108[14]

A. W. Böhme to Dr. Johann Georg Pritius, Senior Minister of Frankfurt am Main[15]
London, 24 December 1714

Happily, a friend in Belgium sent me your first replies to my letters in response to yours of 22 November. I have known for a while that you are in charge of the ministry in Frankfurt, and Christian charity obliges me to beseech the Holy Spirit for you that you might carry out worthily such a difficult task—that of reviving with the help of divine grace and the proclaimed word the seeds once scattered in the field of the Church in Frankfurt by your predecessors, and subsequently bringing them to maturity.

I am fortunate, most reverend one, in the exchange of letters to which your letters kindly invite me. You may trust me to be prepared to offer you any help I can if there is anything you would like me to do for you here in Britain; I take myself to be all the more obliged in this connection because I am sure of your sincere interest in referring everything to the glory of the divine name as the final goal. Neither have I forgotten your presence here in England, for at that time I was in charge of the school which I had begun to put together the people of our country: I say that I had begun, but progress was lacking because certain ministers of the Lutheran Church who should have promoted such work stood in its way as much as they could by suggesting to a credulous crowd that my orthodoxy was insufficient. But this is by way of introduction, for since both of them have been called to the supreme tribunal, neither you nor I need spend more time with them.

As for the state of England, and especially its ecclesiastical condition: you know that everything is so shaken by theological battles (would that they were Jehovah's!) that many, as if maddened by theological delirium, suffer because the magistrates provide few constraints to defend them from extremes. This theological plague has gained new force from the succession of the Elector of Brunswick to this realm. That is because the common people fear theologians because this one, whom they believe to be imbued with Lutheran principles, might be less favorable to

---

14. Original letter written in Latin.

15. Johann Georg Pritius (1662–1732) studied at Leipzig, traveled to England in 1705, was professor of theology at Griefswald, and was appointed senior of the Lutheran Ministrium in Frankfurt am Main in 1711.

the Anglican Church and more favorable to others. This fear increased when the King announced in public that he intended to grant the free exercise of religion to followers of any sect. A few weeks ago a certain turbulent theologian published *A Review of Lutheran Principles* which, since it was written in the language of the people, has been taken up everywhere with such energy that it has already come out in public for the second time.[16] This book stitches together a patchwork of fictions and frivolous accusations sufficient to excite the people's hatred of those belonging to the Lutheran Church. Thomas Brett, which is the author's name, is angry with, among others, the celebrated Samuel von Pufendorf concerning a treatise (*The Divine Feudal Law*) recently published in England, because of the irenic counsels proposed in it. He does not at all wish that these counsels be extended to the Anglican Church, whose agreement with Lutheran principles he takes to be quite impossible, and this for the principal reason that Lutherans reject episcopal government, or, according to the way the writer puts it, they have bishops only in name (that is, none) and not in reality. To these he adds fictions about consubstantiation, the crass ubiquity of the flesh of Christ, relics, the canon of the New Testament (from which, the author alleges, Lutherans exclude some works), and other things of the same kind, all of which are presented by the author as pleasing to the Lutheran Church—all this in an attempt to show the absolute incapacity of Lutheran principles to be reconciled with the doctrines of his own Church. To all this he adds, as if crowning it, a story about a certain placard which he says was hung in a public house in Leipzig, and on which were images of Calvin and Jesuits and suchlike demons, with the legend: Enemies of the Church.

By this little story, whether or not it is true, the author intends to indicate the spirit of enmity which inflames Lutherans against Calvinists. Our joint friend, Dr. Pierre Allix (who mentions you in complimentary fashion from time to time), first pointed out to me this book against the Lutherans, with the warning that it might be outside our scope to rebut this elaborate piece of poetry, or in any honest way to vindicate the truth against so many calumnies. So far, I have not been able to persuade myself to take up such a task, for which what is needed is not so much erudition as a plain statement of the truth; indeed, I fear that I would become more deeply embroiled than I would like in unproductive polemic, and

---

16. Brett, *Review of the Lutheran Principles*; *Review of the Lutheran Principles, Second Edition.*

would as a result gradually withdraw from more solid work; that is the usual unfortunate but natural result of controversy. However, I hear that a minister of the Anglican Church of moderate views is considering an apologia for the Lutheran Church,[17] and I will offer him my labor for the more successful completion of his. I remain silent about other books of the same kind written up to this point about Lutherans. About such matters everything goes from bad to worse, and the Churches which seemed still somewhat united are everywhere separated and will remain so until they are once again firmly and divinely bound.

Furthermore, if I can help you, most reverend one, by procuring books and suchlike, I am always ready to do so: please name a merchant in London to whom your business in Frankfurt can be handed over, and who will take care of its transmission.

You will find attached a list of authors from Boyle's Testament who, up to the year 1712, delivered sermons, of which some have been published, against atheists, Jews, pagans, deists, and other opponents of Christianity. You may trust that I would always be most grateful for Philipp Spener's book on nature and grace, together with its preface, reprinted; and for others edited or to be edited by you;[18] and if you were to send two or three copies I will share them with our German colleagues throughout the West and East Indies, for access to them is easy from here, and they are very happy to get such small gifts.

Farewell in the Lord . . .

No. 109[19]

A. W. Böhme to Bartholomäus Ziegenbalg and Johann Ernst Gründler
  in East India
London, 31 December 1714

Your letters, manuscripts, and tracts, many of which were sent in English ships, have all safely come into my hands, as far as I can tell from comparing the letters with each other. Both the packages and letters were expediently forwarded to Halle, and the enclosed replies have been

---

17. Robert Watts (see Letter 107).
18. E.g., Spener, *Catechismus-Tabellen*; *Gerechter Eifer*.
19. AFSt/H A 185:80.

received back from there. Enclosed you will also find a number of books and tracts, some of which have been sent to me from Halle and some of which have been purchased by the Society. As for the things from Halle, our friends there will undoubtedly provide the necessary details themselves in the enclosed letters. The Society has donated the remaining items for the promotion of the work. There are some rare descriptions of journeys made by Catholics to East India; likewise, you will also find enclosed some Arabic, Armenian, and other valuable books. However, we have found little to nothing of those writings from the catalog you included in your last letter, despite diligent inquiries in local bookstores. Should any of these come to our attention in the future, they shall be most diligently added for your use. And because in one of your letters you mentioned some Armenians with whom you have some dealings, I was persuaded to propose that the Society include some of the Armenian books that can be found here as a helpful part of the gift of books donated to you. At the very least, in case you do not need to learn the language, you will be able to strengthen your ties with a friend or two among the Armenians. The same thing is intended with the Arabic and other similar books.

All these things, however, and whatever else does not properly belong to your work, you must not regard as anything other than a secondary work, so that you may by no means let yourselves be distracted from the main purpose of the mission. Your task is to work for the conversion of the Malabar people. The more closely this or that project fits into such a purpose, the more highly you can regard it; but the more it deviates from it, even though it might otherwise be inherently good and praiseworthy, the more reason you have to avoid it and leave it to someone else whose vocation is more suited to it. This is perhaps the reason for Rev. George Lewis's proposal to the Society regarding your Portuguese school and printing press: the costs would be far better spent and more in keeping with our main objective if you directed your work in school, church, and printing directly to the Malabarians, since the Malabar youth understand little more of Portuguese than they do of other European languages, and must therefore first learn the language in which they are to understand your message. He asserts that very few of the Malabarians—namely, those who trade with Europeans—know anything of the Portuguese language, and what they know consists mainly in those terms and idioms of buying and selling which they have learned through diligent interaction with Europeans.

By this proposal (by which, I hope, he did not intend you any harm), some people have come to think that the money spent on the Portuguese school and church, and especially, from the Society's perspective, on the acquisition of the expensive printing press and the entire edition of the Portuguese New Testament, has not been administered and expended with proper care. I could not answer this intimation other than in very general terms, for I could not well imagine that you would waste the least penny unnecessarily, and thereby make your burden heavier, given the kind of harsh duress and scarcity in which you have so far found yourselves. But I could not give a specific answer to the Society, because I could not presume to understand the situation in East India better than Rev. Lewis. You will be able to answer this objection by corresponding with the Society and presenting your explanations with such caution that, on the one hand, Rev. Lewis is not offended, but on the other hand, you divert from yourselves any blame for not having handled the contribution of good friends in a proper manner.

At present, Rev. Lewis has done you no harm in this nation; we are also hopeful that from now on he will restrain himself, so that no one will be taken in by him against you. He will now also be of some benefit to you, because the letter you wrote to him and had printed will be translated from Portuguese into English at the request of the Society, and will be printed here along with the testimony of Rev. Lewis—who, having recently arrived from the East Indies, is to some degree considered an eyewitness who can give the best account of the necessity of the mission in general, and of your circumstances in particular—which is likely to find its way into the hands of many.

In the meantime, there are still many obstacles that must be overcome by the end of the year, when the fleet is being outfitted and the mission is being renewed in the hearts of the people. One of the most serious obstacles is the opinion that many people have that you intend to introduce a sectarian Lutheranism among the Malabarians, instead of a true Christianity. I have written about this objection and the clamor stirred up by it in a letter dated 8 January 1714. In it I offered my thoughts in detail, and also made a few non-binding suggestions as to how any dire consequences could be effectively prevented. I hope that the letter will now have come into your hands; I subsequently sent a copy of it to Halle, so that friends there, in case they have something to remind you of, may make you aware of it or offer you further good suggestions. It seems, however, that they are of the same mind as I am. Among others, Professor Joachim Lange wrote to me on 1 June 1714. *I must say that I was very much pleased by what he wrote about matters in Malabar:* "When I thought about what you wrote, I found nothing that I would omit, add, or rewrite. To be honest, my appreciation for your work, as well as my confidence in you, only increased. My faith in you was renewed." I refer, however, to the aforementioned letter, because this year, when you sent over copies of Luther's Explanation of the Catechism (*Explicaçao do Catecismo do B. Luthero*[20]), new people raised the same objection, and because the commandment against graven images was omitted, things became considerably more complicated. So, we have had to do a lot of work to keep the mission in reasonably good repute; you should not be surprised, then, that under such circumstances the zeal of the English is beginning to wane somewhat, as you yourselves report.

I remember reading a fine expression from your letter of 13 September 1713, regarding the Latin language: "One should not expect good Latin from India; rather, one should expect good news, about whether Jesus has come alive in pagan hearts. In eager pursuit of the latter, the other is more left behind." It is a golden truth! But you can also put Luther's name among the things to be left behind, as something we do not expect to be propagated in India, especially since it hinders more than it promotes the main work to which you are called. You have recently obtained some freedom in these matters, after responsibility for the mission was taken away from the theologians in Denmark and entrusted to a skilled politician: which one has to regard as a remarkable providence. For since faithful people must do a lot to legitimize themselves with Orthodox theologians, it is easier to get along with politicians and, under their supervision, to proclaim God's plan of salvation with greater peace and freedom. The same precaution concerning human and sectarian names, which I expressed in previous letters and am now repeating, is also useful with regard to Holland; in time, some blessings may spring from there, if you are careful not to put obstacles in your way by using unnecessary particular names.

But now let me turn to several other points that arise from your letter. The Queen of Great Britain, to whom you wrote about the cause of the mission, died last August 1st, and the Elector of Hanover, George

---

20. *A Explicaçao da Doutrina Christaã Segundo a Ordem do Catecismo, do B. Luthero* (Tranquebar, 1713).

Ludwig, was elevated to the crown of these realms. But because it appears that with the present government I have little access to the King and the royal house, and therefore have little opportunity to present the cause of the mission to them, my advice would be that you write to the King of Denmark or to the Inspectors, and express sincerely what blessings have already accrued to England from this work and could continue to accrue, if the mission were to be recommended by an influential person to the King of Great Britain (who, as far as I know, is on good terms with the King of Denmark). In the meantime, I will at least do my best to make the matter known at court here with the help of certain Englishmen and pave the way for further help. But may the Lord Himself, who alone has the key of David, incline people's hearts in love and mercy toward the poor Malabarians! However, if you think that theological faculties in Europe will take on such a work, I, for my part, fear that we are more likely to encounter obstacles from those places than to expect any real help in carrying out the Lord's work.

To have a capable person available to translate and publish your tracts here in English would be useful and would serve to keep the work in good stead with the English; so far, however, I have not come across anyone with the necessary qualifications. I have already mentioned in one of my previous letters, if I remember correctly, how it was reported here from Madras that you had written several troubling letters to the English government concerning a certain Jew: I have done what I could to prevent any worrisome consequences. When you have reprinted the little booklet with the Ten Commandments, including the entire wording of the commandment against graven images, you can send several copies to us. And may the Lord further the work of our hands! To whose grace, faithfulness, and care I most sincerely commit you . . .

P.S.

I have mentioned in my previous letters that the English would like to establish Malabarian schools for the poor at both Fort St. George and Fort St. David, and to use some of your young Malabarians as schoolmasters, if there were one or more in your school who would be capable of doing so.

No. 110

A. W. Böhme to Mr. F. at Edinburgh in Scotland
London, 27 January 1715

...I was delighted by your proposal to publish a new English translation of Arndt's *True Christianity* and to have it printed in Scotland, and I thank God for putting such good intentions into your heart. Several Englishmen have already lamented that the earlier publication is more a paraphrase than an accurate translation of Arndt's work—something also noted in the printed proposal. Therefore, I would prefer a translation that follows the author's footsteps and is thus worthy of being called a translation. As for the subscriptions that one might want to collect in England for printing, it might be a bit difficult, because most of my acquaintances already have the London edition, and will therefore be unlikely to incur new costs. I do intend, however, to contribute £10 toward the copies, although I will not be able to pay for them until the King reestablishes our chapel, or until he restores what is left of our salary. It is said that this will happen at the session of Parliament scheduled for next March. In the meantime, let me know whether the printing is proceeding; I can recommend it all the more confidently when I am assured that the work is progressing. I would like to kindly remind the translator to use a pure English style as much as possible, and not to mix in idioms unique to the Scots, so that the book may find its way into England more easily.

I hope that the Latin copy which I sent recently has arrived.

At Copenhagen, the King of Denmark recently established a special Mission College, composed of various well-meaning persons, whose main purpose is to ensure that in the conferences—that is, the directives issued by the King—the gospel of Christ is proclaimed and spread among the Gentiles, that souls are brought to Christ our Savior, and that the Danish mission in particular, which has been established for this purpose, is promoted in the best possible way. In Moscow there are still many Swedish officers, who, after the Battle of Poltava, were brought there as prisoners to be dispersed throughout Siberia, Kazan, and other lands. Among them there is a tremendous awakening to true repentance and change of heart, for which great poverty has prepared them. We have taken up a collection for them here, so that through such a labor of love the flickering spark may be all the better kindled.

FROM QUEEN ANNE TO GEORGE I (1714–1716)

No. 111

A. W. Böhme to Christopher Wendt in Copenhagen
London, 14 February 1715

I am finally responding in some detail to your kind letter of December 22nd last year, in which you requested a report on the organization of the Society here—which has been active for several years and has by necessity gained considerable experience in establishing good institutions—in order to see whether something might perhaps be utilized in the Mission College. I have decided to provide the established Rules of the Society, translated into German, from which you will be able to understand most clearly the most important aspects both of the structure of the whole work, as well as of the function of each particular member. The Society has translated into English and published a letter from the missionaries at Tranquebar to George Lewis, then chaplain to the East India Company at Fort St. George, and has also requested of Rev. Lewis, who has since returned to England, that his testimony of how he views the whole matter be placed before this epistle instead of a preface; I have enclosed a copy of his testimony translated into German (see attachment A). It is hoped that through this publication the entire work will be reawakened among the English, especially when they read that the authenticity of the mission is attested to by one of their own countrymen, a preacher who has been in the East Indies for many years.

Finally, I have also enclosed an extract from the Society's letters to the missionaries, sent in this last fleet, in the hope that the Inspectors will welcome hearing about what was done in England last year for the sake of the Danish mission. We still receive contributions from time to time for the furtherance of the mission; in the case of the fleet which recently set sail to Tranquebar, we sent £30, together with a valuable gift of writing and printing paper and other necessities. Those who left for the East Indies in 1713 under Royal Danish protection and were employed as printers wrote me, asking in particular that I send them some European beer for their refreshment, because they were not used to drinking water and were particularly weakened by it, given the great heat and heavy work. I immediately proposed this to the Society, which quickly ordered that they be provided with a case of beer; but because we did not have enough space in the ship, with so much other equipment being sent, we were only able to send one case of beer, containing 13 dozen bottles, to Tranquebar to be distributed among the missionaries and printers. I am writing this with the aim of finding out whether that shortage could be supplied from Denmark if ships were to go out from there this year.

Attachment A

Rev. George Lewis [to the SPCK]
London, 26 January 1715

To the reader:
The purpose of the following letter is to describe the method used by the Protestant missionaries at Tranquebar in converting Malabarians to the Christian faith, and the progress they have made so far in this work. That the letter was addressed specifically to me—I was then a preacher at Fort St. George—was done for no other reason than that the world might the sooner be convinced of the truth of what they write; for since Tranquebar and Madras are so near to each other that I could easily myself have inquired into the truth of these things, it should by no means be presumed that the missionaries would represent the matter to me differently than it actually is. It is easy to see from the entire letter with what zeal and diligence these people are doing the work they have taken on. And when one considers the way youth are taught in our Western countries, it could easily be thought that the missionaries are doing too much rather than too little, and that by consistently instilling the good, they require responsibilities from their students that one cannot expect from so young an age. However, in these particular circumstances, we must readily admit that those who are there can themselves be the best judge of these things. Besides, it is also known that Indians, in the instruction of their children, use a stricter discipline than is found here among us, and also train them in a certain manner much sooner than we are accustomed to do.

The most alarming thing in the letter, however, concerns the expenses incurred by the missionaries in maintaining so many schools and feeding so many children, since they have little to support them except the contributions sent to them from Europe; but even these are not sufficient to pay their large daily expenses. It is to be hoped indeed that those whom God has blessed with both material means and a willingness to use them for the right ends, would have a thorough knowledge of this

FROM QUEEN ANNE TO GEORGE I (1714–1716)

important and Christian undertaking. Perhaps they might then consider that at least a part of what they have devoted to Christian works of love would bring no less of a blessing in this work of love than in another that they might come across.

No. 112[21]

A. W. Böhme to Dr. Cotton Mather in New England
London, 21 February 1715

Please accept at last Francke's reply to your letter, which reached my hands some years ago. Dr. Josiah Woodward, a man of godly memory, was charged with sending it to Halle in Saxony. But when he had already exchanged this life for a better one, your bundle of letters was brought me by friends of the deceased, together with the money he had attached so that I might take care of sending it on. I did that as soon as I could, but it was not until long afterward that I received the reply enclosed here. It is in this way that his reply has come at last, very late; and yet I trust that the delay imposed by its passage across land and sea will be to some extent compensated by the lengthy account of what is being argued about in the European tracts.

If, reverend one, you ask why I was impelled to give you these, I would like you to know that it is because of continued literary exchange with Mr. Francke, under whose guidance I began my theological studies in the Academy at Halle. Toward the end of the year 1701, having left Germany, my birthplace, I came to England, in part to open a German school for my countrymen, and in part so that I might become more proficient in the study of theology and its various ancillaries by consulting with the better-known theologians here. Divine providence, beyond any expectation I had, called me to another task, which was nothing less than to undertake a pastoral office in the court of George, the Prince of Denmark and the consort of Anne, Queen of England. And so I have been in England for a number of years now, for the aforementioned Queen graciously gave over the Queen's chapel which was previously dedicated to the administration of the sacred rites, to our German people for the same use; she continued this even after the death of her husband, until the end

21. Original letter written in Latin.

of her life. You can see, then, reverend one, how it is that Francke's bundle of letters conveyed to me is sent to you—sent with the greatest eagerness to serve you, and with constant readiness to do so, if in either England or Germany I can show you what Christian love is capable of.

For while I am on the way I am eager to help however I can others who are also striving toward the fatherland.

Ecclesiastical affairs in Europe appear lacerated and miserable. For although the habits of sin flourish in full measure, the just judgment of God, which always falls upon sin, looms on the horizon, and in this dangerous and doubtful state of things people do not know where to turn. Everything which lacks a divine basis and rests only on human power and authority will collapse. Many among those—and this is the principal source of the evils!—who are confident that they dispense the mysteries of God are as if stirred up by theological madness; they divide into dissenting groups, and in place of the mysteries of God, which they do not know themselves, they exhibit to others the figments of their own minds. How vast and deep the darkness will be when those who should have served as the eyes of the church's body have themselves become darkened and are children of darkness!

However, we do see that divine grace does not cease in the present to raise up good people here and there who, setting aside partisan pursuits and urging the Lord's work with united strength of soul, encourage the weightier matters of the law and treat more lightly the precept to tithe mint, dill, and cumin. It can be gathered from your letters, reverend one, that you are yourself among these, for they breathe with a most generous love, with which you concern yourself with inquiry into what has to do with religion in the most remote countries. May the same grace which rules you grant that all those who work for the Lord's harvest, bearing the burden and heat of the day, might become more and more unified; and that hope might lighten the evils of their present condition.

Farewell, very reverend one, and may you do the Lord's work faithfully.

P.S.

Please accept the gift of this collection of books, which is sent in duplicate: Johann Arndt's *True Christianity*, published in London in Latin some years ago by my efforts;[22] Joachim Lange's *Medicina Mentis*; August Hermann Francke's *Manuductio Ad Lectionem Scripturæ Sacræ*; and my

---

22. Johann Arndt, *De vero Christianismo*.

own *Enchiridion Precum*, with some sermons published in English; Comenius's *Parænesis*.[23]

No. 113

A. W. Böhme to Seigneur de Ners
London, 23 April 1715

I am always quite pleased when I receive a good report of your health, both in spirit and in body. In striving to preserve the latter, we must also not neglect the care and preservation of the former, which is eternal and the fruits of which we will be able to enjoy in the life to come. True, it cannot be denied that God alone gives the growth, and all blessing comes down from above; but the same God who bestows flourishing also commands Paul to plant and Apollos to water. The gardener does not neglect to cultivate the soil, to clear it and to take care of it, even though he knows that his efforts would be in vain if heaven were to withdraw its influence toward fruitfulness. It is evident that our progress in the way of life would be improved if we would follow the orderly movements of nature, the workings of which, to some extent, represent for us the workings of grace.

P.S.

I do not know if you have read the enclosed letter that the missionaries wrote to the English preacher in Madras, George Lewis. The King of Denmark has established a Mission College at Copenhagen, specifically to take care of and promote the mission, and whose members have invited the English Society here to a correspondence.

No. 114

A. W. Böhme to Professor C. S. in L.
London, 1 March 1715

I did not want to wait any longer for a favorable opportunity, but without further delay, in response to your letter from the end of last year,

---

23. Comenius, *Historia fratrum Bohemorum*.

I wanted to assure both you, esteemed professor, and your beloved wife of my heartfelt thanks for the confidence you placed in me out of your fatherly regard for your child. I was also very pleased that I am to join such a devoted Christian and my beloved friend in the Lord of many years, Mrs. S., whom you chose to be a co-godparent with me. Her conduct, which I particularly recall on this occasion, can serve to revive me, since she was in Christ before I was. May the Lord bestow His blessing on the child, and fill him from his youth with the spirit of power, love, and godly discipline, so that he may be fortified against the troubles of the world, and may keep a good and gentle conscience until the end! I wish for him, since we share the same name, Anton, that he may bloom as a fragrant flower in Christ's garden—as some explain the Greek meaning of the name—and that he may be preserved in it, unfaded, until the end. Now, as for the name Wilhelm, may the Lord make him a "willing" fighter to lead the wars of Jehovah against the world and sin, and arm him in battle with the "helmet"—the hope of salvation—until he is given complete victory and a crown on the day of retribution.

If the Lord preserves both of us and I am able to extend some love to him, I will be mindful of my particular duty in this, by the grace of God.

No. 115[24]

A. W. Böhme to Dr. Johann Georg Pritius[?][25]
London, 8 March 1715

... Since you wanted to be sent biographies of good men published since 1705, I attach here Richard Ward's life of the most illustrious Henry More, published in 1710.[26] All Dr. More's works, the principal of which treat the mysteries of godliness and of wickedness, were published in 1707. The life of a certain Robert Nelson, whose name has become known from some books of ascetical theology, is soon to be published, and I will send it in due time.[27] The well-known Oxford theologian Thomas Haywood

---

24. Original letter written in Latin.

25. Probably Pritius again (see Letter 108), given Pritius's interest in the works of Macarius.

26. Richard Ward (ca. 1657–1723), *Life of... Henry More*. Henry More (1614–1687), theologian and philosopher, is usually associated with the Cambridge Platonists.

27. Robert Nelson (1656–1715), *Practice of True Devotion*. Nelson was a nonjuring

has for some time been working at digesting and annotating Macarius's shorter works, which he will send to press shortly after Easter.[28] He asked me through a friend to let him know whether I or my friends in Germany had anything which might shed light on Macarius, so that he might add material in the proper place. I have no doubt that, as is the custom of the English, he will add scholia, notes, variants, readings, and suchlike, ornaments admired here. But I have not yet been able to find anything like this; if you, most illustrious one, have anything to hand which could shed light on this work, I am sure that this would be supererogatory on your part. As regards William Penn: he is still living (if it is right to say of someone deprived of the light of his mind that he lives), but he has mastery of his mind only for short intervals. Apoplexy has afflicted him for a long time, and made him quite incapable of business.

A few months ago, a certain German of Pennsylvania, to which he had earlier migrated and bought land, returned here to plead his cause against some Quakers of Pennsylvania whom he believed to have done him an injury, according to what Mr. Penn has said; however, because of his illness Penn has done nothing until now. When I inquired into the state of things in America, especially among our Germans, who were among the first to cultivate that part of the world, he replied, among other things, that he was not very surprised at the negligence on the part of the Frankfurt Company (commonly, *die Franckfurtische Compagnie*), which, after purchasing so much American land, has now permitted it all to be scattered or divided without taking account of its owners. But this is by the way: it is not our concern.

Every month there is published here a catalog of all the books and tracts which have appeared in London during the preceding month; most also show their price. If you think this would be of use, it can be sent to you from now on. It will show you at a glance the entire business of literature as now practiced here. Also, a few weeks ago, the celebrated Jacque Abbadie came here from Ireland to give information about his writings on Christ's divinity and the truth of the Christian religion (these were published at Rotterdam in 1690 and 1701, in French, for the fourth time) to foreigners.[29] He has been the Dean at Dublin. He really came to

---

philanthropist and religious writer.

28. Macarius (ca. 300–391), *Primitive Morality*. This is the edition John Wesley would read and include in his Christian Library.

29. Jacque Abbadie (1654–1727), *Vindication of the Truth*; *Vindication of the Truth II*. Abbadie was a French Protestant preacher, apologist, and writer, upon whom the deanery of Killaloe, Ireland, was conferred by King William III in 1699.

England to communicate his new analysis of the Apocalypse (it is apocalyptic through and through) to the learned for their approval. I have not yet discovered whether and to what extent his calculations agree with those of Pierre Allix, who states confidently that Rome will be burned by the Protestants two years from now. I have not heard whether he met with William Whiston, the famous renewer of Arianism among the English, who has himself also devised an apocalyptic system which he has imposed on others with an air of infallibility, which is the common disease of such people.[30] It is regrettable (as I have observed before, directly and more than once) that good people are often so immersed in apocalyptic studies that these constitute, as it were, the bow and stern of their work, so that they treat everything else lightly, which are the weightier matters of the law. This is not without reason: for while they direct their minds more than is proper to the future dispensations of the Church, they necessarily neglect things of greater importance which are directly in front of them, so that in the end they are all the same in seeming to present for sale something great, which is a patchwork of opinions rather than the truth—to say nothing worse. In this way the common enemy of souls imposes upon us and carries us away from the smooth path of essential truths to an extreme and deviant one, unless divine moderation should govern the mind and provide us protection from the reefs which are found at the farthest extremes.

No. 116

A. W. Böhme to Carl Hildebrand von Canstein
London, 26 April 1715

In terms of my own situation, we are told that the present government wants to retain the German Royal Chapel, where I have been working until now, for the benefit of the Germans. This much is certain: because there will always be some German ministers and other servants here, there should also be a German chapel for their use. However, up to now it has not been rightly established, nor has any of the pension that

---

30. William Whiston (1667–1752), Anglican priest, historian, mathematician, and popularizer of Sir Isaac Newton's thinking.

we previously received been given to us. But word has it that this is to happen soon.

The English Table, which until now has been maintained from here to feed a number of poor students in Halle, is now likely to be discontinued. I would receive 100 guineas every year from Queen Anne for the foreign poor, and distribute them wherever and however I wished, to say nothing of what was given to me for the local poor. Whether divine providence will one day present me with the opportunity to ask for such things at the present court, I will quietly wait. The costs for the English Table in Halle were deducted from the 100 guineas, and the remainder was distributed among other foreigners. When I made some Englishmen aware of this after the Queen's death, they wanted me to present this matter to the Crown Princess, for she would undoubtedly continue this labor of love. I will therefore see if in time I may find opportunity, through those around her, to bring the matter to her, or through their assistance, to gain some access myself.

About seven weeks ago, the Arab Solomon Negri, who stayed several years ago at the orphanage in Halle, arrived here, hoping to find Heinrich Ludolf, whom he had known before, still alive; but since Mr. Ludolf has died, he sought to settle here where he could enjoy freedom of conscience. However, there was nothing to be found for him in this country, where Oriental studies have now completely disappeared. And because such freedom is now being curtailed more and more in France, where he has many friends, I advised him to go back to Halle and spend his remaining days there peacefully. After leaving Halle, he was in the entourage of the Venetian envoy to Constantinople, and mastered the Turkish and (to some extent) Persian languages. After his return from Turkey, he served in Rome as a reader of Arabic; he stayed there for four years, as long as he could enjoy a certain degree of freedom. However, when they tried to force him to submit to papal authority, he escaped, although with the pope's approval, boarded an English ship at Livorno, and came here. The man has walked along many different paths, but he has thus far withstood all the temptations of the papacy that have befallen him, to the point of risking his outward well-being and promotion. I am well aware, though, that this is not in itself a sufficient indication of a genuine Christianity. He could perhaps be used in Halle to revise the Turkish New Testament, which has recently been translated into Turkish here by William Seaman, at the instigation of the honorable Robert

Boyle, but may well be in need of improvement.[31] Besides that, the book is in quarto and in a very awkward format. And since the New Testament has recently been published in several languages, it is certainly worthwhile to have it published in Turkish as well. But in Halle one would have to acquire the necessary characters.

No. 117[32]

A. W. Böhme to Mr. P. F.
London, 31 May 1715

A week ago, one Solomon Negri left England for Holland and will go from there to Halle in Saxony, where he previously taught Oriental languages for some years. Mr. Negri was born in Damascus, and from there was taken to France at the age of seventeen by Jesuits for literary studies so that he might then devote himself to propagating papism among the peoples of the East. The Jesuits did not, however, achieve their goal. When threatened by papists in Paris, Negri moved to England, where he became friends with Heinrich Ludolf, who was at that time secretary in Prince George of Denmark's court; he remained in London until, persuaded by his friend, he left for Halle. Leaving Germany, he came to Venice, where, having joined that Republic's legate to the Turkish Empire, he remained at Constantinople for some years; eventually, for various reasons, he was brought to Rome, where he taught Arabic and other languages as long as he was allowed to. I say allowed to: Once again threatened with harm by the papists, he took ship at the Port of Livorno for England, which after some weeks brought him to our coasts.

I have done what I could to find him some support here, so that not only might he live, but might also find opportunity, given his linguistic skill, to teach Arabic, Turkish, and other languages of interest—especially since the libraries here are well stocked with books in Arabic, which in Germany he might have looked for in vain. However, I was able to obtain nothing here in these turbulent times; he says himself, however, that in the Academy at Halle, where I know that many assemble to study, he could bring talented students to a better understanding of Oriental

---

31. *Testamentum Novum, Turcice redditum*. The translator, William Seaman (1606–1680), was an orientalist who graduated from Balliol College, Oxford.

32. Original letter written in Latin.

languages—and certainly, since providence has now opened the door to the treatment of these languages, I think that there would be great benefit for the propagation of the gospel. Clearly, if this man from Damascus could now translate the New Testament into Arabic or Turkish, or could thoroughly amend by his own work the editions which already exist, his time would be well spent. For he says himself that the Turkish version of the New Testament made by William Seaman here in England, and printed in Arabic characters in 1666, teems with errors, and that it stands in great need of revision if it is to serve in any way to promote the gospel.

Well, most illustrious one, the reason for my detaining you with this story is that the aforementioned Mr. Negri, before he left London, had decided to see your F., unless unexpected obstacles in Belgium should prevent him. He asked me to write to arrange a meeting with someone among the learned with whom he could converse freely, so that he could act on that person's advice about the matter. I want to make good this request, feeling sure that you will be refreshed rather than annoyed by theological conversation with this traveler, who is of a kind rare in Europe. Should you grant me this, you may be sure that I am ready to serve you in turn in any way I can.

Now to other things. There was no sermon at Gilbert Burnet's funeral. Theologians opposed to him thought him unworthy of the honor; his friends, perhaps out of fear of the Jews, did not dare to provide one. I gave Negri a book to hand over to you which contains Burnet's will; it was printed in the public press after his death. They say that a manuscript containing some of Burnet's moral meditations has already been sent to press. That is close to certain. His sermons are all compressed into a single body, which is why they are very rarely found separately or individually.[33] Isaac Barrow's *Theological Works* are published again.[34] He was an outstanding preacher, entirely scriptural, and as a result his works are more sinewy than modern ones, which for the most part present nothing but sterile moralizing elegantly wrapped in sophistry.

I return to Burnet. A little before his death he published the third volume of his *History of the Reformation*, in which, in addition to the matter of the book, he responds now and then to a certain Jeremy Collier.[35] Collier wrote a history of the British church from the beginning

---

33. Possibly Burnet, *Collection of Sermons.*

34. Isaac Barrow (1630–1677), *Works of Isaac Barrow.* Barrow was a mathematician, who resigned his professorship to Sir Isaac Newton in order to pursue a calling to theology.

35. Burnet, *Answer to Some Exceptions.*

of Christianity to the death of Charles II.[36] In this work, which takes up two folio volumes, he freely criticizes Burnet's history, often more than is just, and impugns the author's many historical errors—which Burnet attempted to remove in the work mentioned, but was again refuted in the new writings recently published by Collier.

In Scotland, some lovers of true godliness have inevitably begun to prepare a new, Scottish version of Johann Arndt's *True Christianity*. The same book was published in English in London, but since the author of that version often went beyond what should constrain a good interpreter, the Scots, not pleased with this, are considering another version which will follow the author's footsteps more closely throughout.

No. 118

A. W. Böhme to Professor August Hermann Francke
London, 14 June 1715

Several weeks ago, an American named Moses Bartlett arrived, who resides in Rhode Island, New England, in the seaside town of Providence, and is a blacksmith by trade.[37] He was born of Anabaptist parents, and was powerfully drawn by the Lord even in his youth. He describes very movingly the miserable condition of the American provinces, as far as Christianity is concerned, and desires to do his utmost, even to dare everything, to see the country helped. About five or six years ago, the account of the Halle orphanage came to his attention, which not only personally inspired him, but also prompted him to write to Old England and inquire whether one or a few capable students, either from London or Halle, would come to Rhode Island, establish schools, and preach the pure gospel in New England. I saw his letters from several years ago, but because I did not see any help from the people here, his request slipped from my mind, and the whole thing was eventually forgotten.

In the meantime, his desire increased so much that his conscience could not rest until he set out on his own and, after much expense, suffering, and hardship, visited us here. His purpose, as I already mentioned,

---

36. Collier, *Ecclesiastical History of Great Britain*; *Answer to Some Exceptions*. Collier denounced the excesses of theater (see Letter 7) and was a bishop of the nonjuring Church of England.

37. Moses Bartlett (1672–1753) of Glocester in Providence, Rhode Island.

was to seek out some devout people here and bring them along with him; or, in their absence, to inquire of you, my esteemed professor, if a few Halle students would follow him to Providence and help the inhabitants there by preaching the Word. He promised that initially he would support them faithfully in external things, until a richer harvest would be granted to them from God's hand. "I have now traveled three thousand English miles, by sea and land, in considerable adversity," he said. "I have been sorely mocked on board ship, despite the fact that I have paid for everything. I have nothing else to do in Old England but to seek to accomplish this purpose during my lifetime. But should God take me away before a trustworthy person comes, I will make provision in my will, so that he may find some support when he arrives and not have to worry about food."[38] He hoped that any student who would come to them would be skilled in the art of instrumental music, which would give him a greater reception in the region. Regarding the state of religion, he said that the whole city was full of Quakers and Anabaptists. The Anabaptists have divided themselves into five different branches and have such ill will against each other that they do not intermarry. Apart from that, there is complete freedom to do good, and he has now learned from experience that the people in America are much more likely to be receptive of spiritual influences than Christians in Europe. It is a healthy and lovely land in appearance, can feed its inhabitants quite well, and has a steady trade with Old England.

Dr. Cotton Mather, the preacher at Boston (about 45 miles from Providence), whom he knows very well, gave him this public recommendation:

> Boston, New England, January 12, 1715.
>
> The bearer of this letter, Moses Bartlett, is an honest, sincere, and well-meaning man, and is worthy of being received kindly by good people on his journey. I might have wished that he had received better treatment than has been the case so far from the people of Providence, where, I am told, he has been a zealous witness against the disorderliness that has been going on there.

And this is what I was obliged to write to you, most honorable professor, at the urgent request of this man, who is traveling back tomorrow. And now I leave it to the good hand of God whether and how something

---

38. An abstract of Bartlett's will, dated 25 Dec 1752, can be found in Beaman, *Rhode Island Genealogical Register Rhode Island*, 3:54.

might be done in this matter, for I have promised to report back to him as soon as I have received some answer from Halle.

Another thing: Solomon Negri, the well-known Damascene, left here on May 24th and returned to Halle on the advice of several friends. He has given great pleasure to several well-meaning individuals, and some wish to have kept him here, had there been some hope of doing so in these troubled times. However, almost all good projects are now at a standstill until the Lord opens a new door, for which there still seems to be some hope. It seems to me that Mr. Negri is a little more settled in his heart than he was several years ago, and that he can therefore be used with great blessing. And since he spent four years in Constantinople and has mastered the Turkish language, I would like him to revise the existing Turkish and Arabic versions of the New Testament and to prepare them for printing in a befitting edition. Such a book could be useful not only in Turkish territories proper, but could also be distributed with blessing in East India, where the Mohammedans, according to the missionaries' report, use the Arabic language. But since this would require new costs, and an Arabic printing press would have to be purchased, have no doubt that the project will be supported from here, in case anyone ventures to do something about it.

No. 119

A. W. Böhme to Christopher Wendt
London, 30 June 1715

I have duly received both the report on the establishment of the Mission College and your last letter of June 15th. There is nothing that needs to be answered in your letter, but I was able to translate the report into English when my circumstances permitted, and gave it to the secretary, Henry Newman. However, since the Society is dealing with many different matters, and the matter of the mission is only dealt with at certain times, I will report to you when something relevant to the mission comes up for discussion.

Apart from that, the Mission College will by now have already been informed of the intended arrival of Bartholomäus Ziegenbalg; he reached the Cape of Good Hope in February 1715 on a Danish ship.

He wrote several letters from there, which he sent on an English ship; however, he did not report when he would set out again and continue his voyage to Denmark. He also sent nine copies of the first part of the New Testament, printed in Malabarian Tamil, with the request that they be distributed here among the foremost benefactors and friends of the mission. Furthermore, his journey here has raised a number of concerns among some Englishmen, who have concluded that the missionaries will not find the necessary protection and support at Tranquebar to carry out and expand their work, and may therefore soon be at liberty to settle elsewhere and, under the protection of other nations, to use their gifts for the conversion of the Malabarians.

I remember now that in previous letters you wanted to know how native peoples and slaves were treated with regard to baptism and similar matters in the English plantations in the East and West Indies; so, I have included here some passages from a sermon published by an English bishop named Dr. William Fleetwood on this subject.[39] He preached this sermon on Acts 26:18 in 1711 at the request of the Society for the Propagation of the Gospel in Foreign Parts.[40] And since the English have up to now taken very bad care of their slaves in the West Indies, the bishop took it upon himself in the sermon to answer the most notable objections that are generally made against the conversion of pagans to Christianity, objections based, it must be said, only on shameful self-interest. Among other things, he spoke of the conversion of pagans:[41]

> What do these People, [who are educated in Christianity and baptized apart from their slaves,] think of *Christ*? . . . That He who came from Heaven, to purchase to Himself a Church, with His own precious Blood, should sit contented, and behold with unconcern, those who profess themselves his Servants, excluding from its Gates those who would gladly enter if they might, and exercising no less Cruelty to their Souls (as far as they are able) than to their Bodies? . . . For if they would consider Him in any Quality or Capacity whatever, as *Saviour, Law-giver, Head of His Church*, or *Judge*, they would no more venture to lay an

---

39. William Fleetwood (1656–1723) was Bishop of St. Asaph. Not only was he regarded as a fine preacher, but economists note that he was the first to construct a price index. Many of his sermons dealt with economics and finances.

40. Fleetwood, *Sermon Preached*.

41. Translator's note: Because the sermon was published in English, the original text is cited here, except those few places where Böhme made slight emendations in his German translation, noted by brackets.

Impediment in any one's way to Conversion, than they would throw themselves into the Fire deliberately.

It would be as hard for them, to give an Account of what they think of those unhappy *Creatures*, whom they use thus cruelly: They see them equally the Workmanship of God, with themselves; endued with the same Faculties, and intellectual Powers; Bodies of the same Flesh and Blood, and Souls as certainly Immortal: These People were made to be as Happy as themselves, and are as capable of being so; and however hard their Condition be in this World, with respect to their Captivity and Subjection, they were to be as Just and Honest, as Chaste and Virtuous, as Godly and Religious as themselves: They were bought with the same Price, purchased with the same Blood of Christ, their common Saviour and Redeemer; and in order to [do] all this, they were to have the Means of Salvation put into their Hands, they were to be instructed in the Faith of *Christ*, to have the Terms and Conditions fairly offered and proposed to them. Let any of these cruel Masters tell us, what part of all these Blessings were not intended for their unhappy Slaves by God, purchased for them by the Blood of Christ, and which they are not equally capable of enjoying with themselves? What Account then will these Masters give of *themselves*, who are the Occasion and the Instruments of bringing these unhappy People, from a Country where the *Name of Christ* is never heard, or call'd upon, into a Country where *Christians* govern all, and *Christ* is call'd their *Lord and Master*, and yet will not permit these Slaves to be Instructed, and become the Servants of this Heavenly *Master*? Who bring them, as it were, into Sight of *the Waters of Life*, and then with-hold them from receiving any Benefit from them! They hope, 'tis likely, *God* will be merciful to these unhappy Creatures, tho' *they* themselves will not be so: Their Hope is good; but they have Reason to fear, God may deny that Mercy to themselves, which they deny to others. . . . If these Men ever read the Scriptures, and meet with such a question as this—*Lord, are there few that be saved?* What a strange puzzle must they beat to make an Answer? I for my own particular part hinder, as much as I possibly can, some Fifty or an Hundred, it may be many more, from being Saved. I can be certain only of the Salvation of *Christians*, and therefore am my self a *Christian*: I know 'tis impossible for any one to become a *Christian*, without being instructed in the Knowledge of Christ, and being afterwards *Baptized* with Water, in the Manner and Form prescribed by Christ himself; and I know I hinder all these People that are under me, from being Instructed and Baptized; Go on—Therefore I know I hinder them, as much as in me lies, from being *Saved*....

To these and other heavy Objections that lye to this inhumane Practice, there are but Two or Three poor Pretences that must answer, which I will now consider in a few Words. The *First* is, that were their Slaves *Christians*, they would immediately, upon their Baptism, become *Free*. The *Second* is, that were their Slaves *Christians*, and still to continue Slaves, yet they should be oblig'd to treat them with more Humanity and Mercy, than the nature and necessity of their Service would admit of, to make their Masters Gainers. And the *Third* is much of the same kind, that were their Slaves *Christians*, they could not sell them; it being Unlawful, they say, to *sell Christians*.

To the *First* of these Pretences, Namely—That should they suffer their Slaves to be Baptized, they would immediately become *Free*—We may answer, that were this true, the Mischief of it would be no greater in our *Plantations* abroad, than it is at home, where there is no such things as *Slavery*, but all our Work is done by *hired* Servants.... But allowing this would be some Inconvenience to the Civil Government, with respect to Trade, is there any Question, whether the Blessing of God upon their Piety and good Designs in furtherance of his Glory, in the Salvation of Mens Souls, would make an ample Compensation for all the Inconveniences and Loss it might sustain, by making their Slaves, or letting them be made *Christians*? But after all, what considering Man would run the Hazard of being under God's Displeasure, by hindring [sic] others from becoming Christians, for all the Profit, Honour, and Advantage in the World? But *Secondly*, there is no fear of losing the Service and Profit of their Slaves, by letting them become *Christians*: Their Avarice and Cruelty are grounded on a certain Mistake: They are neither prohibited by the Laws of *God*, nor those of the *Land*, from Keeping *Christian Slaves*; their Slaves are no more at Liberty after they are Baptized, than they were before. There were People in St. *Paul*'s time, that imagin'd they were freed from all former Engagements by becoming *Christians*; but St. *Paul* tells them, this was not the meaning of *Christian Liberty*; the Liberty wherewith *Christ* had made them Free, was Freedom from their Sins, Freedom from the Fears of Death, and everlasting Misery, and not from any State of Life, in which they had either voluntarily engaged themselves, or were fallen into through their Misfortune. *Let every Man* (says he, 1 Cor 7:20) *abide in the same Calling, wherein he was called.* Let every Man know, that his being called to the Faith of Christ, does not exempt him from continuing in the same State of Life he was before; it makes no alteration of his Condition in this World; the Liberty of Christianity is entirely Spiritual. *Art thou called, being a Servant? care not for it; but if thou mayst be made free, use it rather.* Are thou Baptized and made a Christian, being a Slave? mind it not; be not much concerned at it; but if thou canst obtain thy Liberty, by fair and honest Means, *use it rather*, take the Opportunity: If Liberty comes legally, or by the Favour of thy Patron, accept of it by all Means; thou mayst thereby be better enabled to serve God, when thou art at thine own Disposal. *Brethren, let everyone wherein he is called, therein abide with God.* In a Word, the *Law of Christ* made no changes of this Nature, but left Men under all the Obligations and Engagements that it found them, with respect to *Liberty* or *Bondage*: Nor do *the Laws of the Land* hinder people from being Slaves when they become *Christians*. . . .

The *Second* Pretence is this: That should their Slaves continue Slaves after Baptism, yet they should be oblig'd to use them with *less Rigour*, than the nature and necessity of their Service will admit, if their Masters must be Gainers by them. . . . But 'tis a strangely cruel and most wicked Absurdity that is built on this Mistake: I may not use a *Christian* Unmercifully; therefore I will not let this *Savage* be a Christian, for fear I may not use him afterwards unmercifully. What a Mockery would it be, to pretend that I cannot relieve a Man, because he is not qualified for my Charity, when I know at the same time, that I hinder him from being qualified, least I should find my self obliged to relieve him? What is this but to hinder him, as much as in you lies, from being happy *for ever*, for fear he should be a little more at Ease in *this Life*? . . .

The *Third* and last Pretence, is built upon the same Bottom, i.e., that of Interest. For since they bought their Slaves for Money, they should be Losers by permitting them to be made Christians, since after that, they could not part with them for Money; it being, they say, Unlawful to sell *Christians*.

Away with all these Honours, that are so hurtful to our Lord! I dare engage He parts most freely with them: He well remembers, how he who betrayed Him, gave Him first a *Kiss*; and could never since endure, that a seeming Respect should do Him Mischief, and debar Him of a real Advantage. A *Christian* must not, it seems, be Sold; but then he shall not be a *Christian*, because he may not afterwards be Sold. This is too like to—*Hail King of the Jews*, and Buffeting Him, *bowing the Knee before Him*, and then Spitting at Him. If *Christ* might be the Advocate for these poor people, He would consent, He would intreat they might be Sold, condemn'd to Bonds, to Stripes, Imprisonment, and Death, rather than live the Slaves of Sin and Unbelievers, the freest and most arbitrary Princes of their Country. He was Himself both Sold and Bound, and loves a virtuous and religious Slave, rather the better for his Chains or Clog. Let but the Soul be free from Sin, and the Hands clean from all Unrighteousness, and He regards not how the Body is encumbred with its Weights, nor how those Hands are worn with Bonds and Labours.

But after all, 'tis far from certain, that the Laws forbid a *Christian* to be Sold: If Men had truly a Propriety in their Slaves before they were Baptized, and could dispose of them as they do of other Goods and Cattel for Money, or its worth, I dare be positive, the *Laws of Christ* will not deprive them of this Property; and I am very sure, the *Laws of the Kingdom* take not away the Right of such a Sale, upon receiving Baptism, if it were justifiable before.

But did the Laws indeed pretend, in such a sort, to honour *Christ's Religion*, it could be no hard matter to convince our Lawgivers, how prejudicial all such Favours were to Christianity; and to desire them no longer to honor *Christians* already, with such Privileges as put a Stop to the Propagation, and farther growth of *Christianity*; but let the Christians (as was said above) be Sold, and Bound, and Scourg'd, condemn'd to Bonds and Imprisonment, to endure all Hardships and Disgrace, *and to enter into Heaven, Blind, and Halt, and Maimed*, rather than having Two Eyes, and Hands, and Feet entire, to perish miserably.... And all that can consider seriously these Things, will certainly consent, nay, and be glad, that Slaves, tho' *Christians*, might be Bought and Sold, and used like Slaves, rather than still be Bought and Sold, and used like Slaves, and not permitted to be *Christians*. And one may wonder how a *Christian Government* can look upon it self as unconcerned in this Affair; and only consider these unhappy Wretches, as Creatures that save the Kingdom the Charge of transporting Horses, and Beasts of Carriage, for the *Islands* Service, without reflecting on their Shape and Form, and intellectual Powers, and without looking up to *Christ*, their common Master, the Saviour and Redeemer of us all.

This unconcernedness of the Publick it is, most probably, that encourages a great many private People at home amongst our selves, to keep these *Africans*, or *Indians*, in their native Ignorance and Blindness, and to continue them *Infidels* in the midst of a *Christian Kingdom*. These People ought to think what answer they will make to *Christ*, when He shall ask them, why they would not help to increase His Kingdom, and to make their Fellow Creatures as Happy, as they hoped themselves to be, by being *called by His Name?* ...

But that which chiefly inclined me to speak to this particular Case, at this Time, was—That it is really, now, *our own Case*; a thing, in which we are all of us here, that belong to *this Society*, so personally concerned, that it behoves us, every one of us to think of it. We are now, by the Munificence of a truly *Honourable Gentleman* [Codrington], our Selves become the *Patrons* of at least *Three Hundred Slaves*, who are to Cultivate, and be Maintain'd upon the *Two Plantations* he hath left to *this Society*, for the Promoting Learning and Religion. ...

That if all the Slaves throughout *America* ... were to continue Infidels for ever, yet *ours alone must needs be Christians*: We must instruct them in the Faith of Christ, bring them to Baptism, and put them in the Way that leads to everlasting Life. This will be preaching by *Example*, the most effectual way of recommending Doctrines, to a hard and unbelieving World, blinded by Interest, and other Prepossessions.[42]

That is the excerpt from Dr. Fleetwood's sermon. The nobleman who assigned three hundred slaves to the Society [SPG] is a general named Christopher Codrington, who at his death bequeathed in his will two whole plantations on the island of Barbados and a piece of an island called Barbuda.[43] At least three hundred negroes or black slaves are being kept on these plantations. The trade that the English do with these slaves is extensive, in that they are shipped on entire fleets from Africa to America, and sold there. However, so far, little effort has been made to convert them. Some years ago, the matter was examined in some depth, but they lacked capable persons who could be used for this purpose. Now a Scottish theologian, Dr. Sharp, who was a preacher in the American province of New York, has put forward a new project in which he once again urges the conversion of slaves to Christianity and presents how it is possible. However, when it comes to pagans in America, no reasonable effort up to now has been made to convert them to Christianity. One reason why the work is arduous is the diversity and difficulty of the languages, which few people have the necessary skill or energy to learn. It is true that in some

---

42. Fleetwood, *Sermon Preached*, 13–25.

43. Christopher Codrington (ca. 1668–1710), educated at Oxford, was an English army officer and governor general of the Leeward Islands. Simmons, "Towards a Biography of Codrington."

places people have begun to interact with them through interpreters, in an attempt to see if by this means the most essential parts of Christianity could be taught to them; but others have demonstrated from experience that that method is insufficient for instructing them.

No. 120

A. W. Böhme to Miss Jane Slare
London, [July 1715]

I thought the dreadful newspaper about the Pretender's arrival would have brought you straight back to London, but I see you still have plenty of courage to endure it. Who knows if this storm will soon pass? If we just had Job's disposition and submission to God's will, we would surely be content, even though one tragic messenger should follow another while the first was still talking. But this lesson is not learned all at once; rather, it must be spelled out in the school of wisdom, until we finally learn with the great apostle to be content with whatever state we find ourselves in. This much I have learned: As long as my will is not serene, I have no rest, neither in the city nor in the country; whereas a Christian, in serenity of will, necessarily enjoys heaven and blessedness, peace and quiet, joy and contentment. Blessed is the soul that is like the mountain whose top reaches above the clouds, elevated above the thunderstorm in the depths below. We know that the whole world is in trouble, so no place is free from its grievous effects. I leave you to the never-ending goodness, love, and protection of our great God.

No. 121

A. W. Böhme to Mr. N. N.
London, 28 July 1715

... It would seem that the judgments of God are pouring out almost everywhere, chastising the excessive wickedness of Christians. About fourteen days ago, news arrived here that Indians in South Carolina had suddenly attacked the English settlers there and slain more than two hundred of them before they could mount any resistance.[44] As soon as the English received news of these savage raids, they sent several agents among them to listen to their demands and to come to an amicable agreement with them. But all of the agents were strangled and executed without mercy. Among others, they killed a captain, who had been commanded to make an accord with them, in a rather barbaric and inhuman way: they stabbed him with many wooden stakes, all over his body, and thus slowly drained the life out of him. These wooden stakes are said to burn almost like our European torches, and to be sharpened or pointed at one end in such a way that they can easily be pushed through a person's skin deep into the flesh; hence the English call them "touch wood," or sticking wood. The body of the miserable person whom they deem deserving of death, is staked over and over with these sharpened pieces of wood, while the other end is lit like a torch; in this way, the poor person is gradually burned up in unspeakable torment and literally roasted by the many torches from every side.

But returning to the above account: the remaining settlers, about 1,500 of them, retreated to Charleston, the most principal place in this region, to wait there patiently for the successor to the throne of England, to whom they have made a plaintive appeal. There are said to be eight Indian chiefs who joined together and consulted how and by what means they would most effectively exterminate the English. But when, after careful deliberation, two of the chiefs broke from the others and would not consent to the attack, they are said to have suffered the same fate as the English themselves, and to have been slain on the spot. Whether this fury of the Indians will continue to spread, even to other American provinces, only time will tell. For not without reason do the wise fear these things, and regard this cruelty as a harbinger of more severe judgments on those Christians who have been scattered among the pagans. This much is certain, these Indian raids should be regarded as something unparalleled, since they are not in accord with their nature, which is kind-hearted, gentle, and tolerant.

At about the same time that the above tragic event became known in London, a member of the Society received a letter from Jean-Frédéric Ostervald, preacher at Neuchâtel,[45] informing the Society of Bartholomäus

---

44. On the Yamasee War (1715–1717), see Ramsey, *Yamasee War*.

45. Jean-Frédéric Ostervald (1663–1747) was a Protestant pastor from Neuchâtel and leader of the liberal Swiss divines; some of his writings were distributed by the SPCK.

Ziegenbalg's presumed death; he had received information from Venice that the Malabarians had flayed him alive or skinned him. His words, in which he counted Mr. Ziegenbalg among the martyrs, are alarming:

> Last week I received letters from Venice, informing me that Mr. Ziegenbalg, Danish missionary in Malabar, was flayed alive by the Malabarians, and that this was done at the instigation of jealous Jesuits. In one sense, this event is very sorrowful, but it is also fortunate and glorious for this zealous servant of God, who was honored with the crown of martyrdom. I have seen with singular pleasure the German letters he sent to Europe during his lifetime.

May God prosper this work, inspired by Mr. Ziegenbalg, and may we continue the works he has begun with even more zeal.

No. 122

A. W. Böhme to Monsieur V. B. in H.
London, 31 August 1715

I spoke to Johann Georg Gichtel[?] in Amsterdam during my return trip to England,[46] and talked to him in particular about marriage, his views of which had become broadly known. I had already read many of his letters, for several of my friends had maintained an ongoing correspondence with him, which, I hope, was not without benefit and encouragement. Several of my acquaintances have told me that they have been awakened and strengthened in goodness by the man's words of encouragement. It would be deep joy for me, if you, my dear friend, by reading these letters, have also been strengthened in a living faith, the love of God and neighbor, following Christ, and other essentials of Christianity, since I heartily desire the growth of your soul in the grace of life. And all the more so, because so few remain faithful to the Lord and use the godly zeal they once received to be drawn powerfully by the Father into the kingdom of the Son, in order to find pasture and abundance there.

---

46. If Böhme is indicating his 1709 return trip to England, then he would likely be referring to Johann Georg Gichtel (1638–1710), German theosophical mystic, proponent of Jacob Böhme, and advocate of a form of ascetical celibacy.

Nevertheless, I cannot deny that I noticed something in his writing that I did not like, because it could easily lead to all kinds of opinions that contribute little to the central issue. Something I have learned from experience and to my own detriment is that we tend to embrace devout persons' opinions rather than their sound fundamental principles, and prefer the latter more than the former for discipleship. Certainly, there lies hidden in this the subtle hand of the universal enemy of the soul, who likes to allow us to go from one opinion to another, even to drift around in a circle of opinions, rather than to break into the essence of true Christianity, I mean, the new birth, self-denial, and those other necessary things by which we diminish the kingdom of darkness.

Because I now know that Mr. Gichtel has spoken quite harshly against marriage and has extolled the unmarried state very highly, it seems to me that you, my dear friend, have adopted this position and seem to be seeking something special and sacred in it. But this is another example of a bad human habit: to engage in various physical exercises and think that one has found something special in them, which can easily lead to all kinds of dangerous temptations. Among those physical and outward practices, I include abstinence from marriage, as well as abstinence from various kinds of food, and the like. If a person does such things in freedom, and keeps the mind free from any dangerous attachment, no mature Christian is likely to have anything further to say about it. But as soon as a person engages in such outward practices, and ascribes something special to them, all kinds of dangerous and indeed spiritual defilements can arise, which bring so much greater danger with them the more they touch the heart and the inner powers of the soul. Such persons are prone to think of themselves more highly than others, to evaluate themselves through their physical practices, to be pleased with themselves, and whatever other similar dangerous inclinations there may be. This is likely to be followed by an uncharitable and unfounded judgment of others who do not have the same outward form or practice, even if they are mature in the inner foundation of their faith and are more concerned with inward than with outward practices.

This dangerous judgmentalism can be seen when you, dear friend, think that Mr. A. abandoned true wisdom after he got married, and that he died miserably or half-crazed because of it. It is not our place to judge other servants, and especially not according to such outward circumstances, which may arise for reasons other than we imagine. I remember something a devout man once said: there are more saints in Bedlam than in many a university. I can all the more readily believe his words, because I know how oblivious our reason is in the hidden and obscure ways of faith. He knew that Bedlam is the large insane asylum here in London and that it is filled with such people. I must say that I have walked through this very place several times, and have had spiritual conversations with several such persons, and I cannot deny that I have observed in some of them the kind of holy effects and powerful expressions of the ways of God that one would have looked for in vain in many other, even devout, souls; and yet their natural reason is deemed foolish. God's ways, however, transcend reason, and he often does his work inwardly, while outwardly there is nothing but folly. We do well to remember often that such souls come to a most blessed end, and that they leave the abode of the body with nothing but triumph and joyful affirmations; and at their departures they know how to speak of nothing but the virtues of that world. Now far be it from me that I should in the least judge such persons, or suspect their sensibilities, especially in such cases where one can reasonably be assured that they are furthest removed from pretense and hypocrisy.

In addition, I do not intend to pass unkind judgment on those who, in the face of persistent temptations, in fear and anxiety, persevere in their struggle until their last breath. It is said here: The harder the war, the nobler the victory! Even if such persons should leave this world half-raving in their minds, I would by no means judge that divine wisdom has perished in them. I am writing in such detail, my dear friend, because I gather from your letter that you are in danger of running into this or that cliff and getting hurt. And out of love for your soul, I wanted to give you a word of advice and warn you against various divergences and detours that we can easily take. What good is all our knowledge if it causes us to abandon humility and spiritual poverty, and makes us judge others.

And because I conclude from your letter that you have a good opinion of me because I am still unmarried and not bound to a wife, I can assure you that I care little about such external things and do not assume anything about others who are married. I know many instruments of God who are in deep communion with true wisdom, and who are far ahead of me in sanctification, and yet are married. In this God shows the mighty power of faith, by which a sincere soul, in the midst of such temporal bonds, nevertheless knows how to preserve its inner freedom in such a way that it can make use of the creaturely without idolatrous attachments. We are living in a dangerous time, when everything is going to extremes, and therefore we have to be even more careful not to adopt all kinds of opinions instead of what is essential.

You know how we like to sing: On the right hand and on the left hand, help me offer strong resistance. Embrace nothing from human authority, but wait until the Lord, through His Spirit, seals your heart in the truth. We often abandon, on the one hand, the external defilements of the flesh, while we let ourselves, on the other hand, be carried away unnoticed by the defilements of the spirit; we attach ourselves to this or that person, we fall for new opinions, we judge others who do not agree with them. We exalt human giftedness above the desired goal, delight ourselves in the appearance of great knowledge, and read all kinds of books in a fervent urge, which we cannot test. And the increase of such impulses draws the heart away from the simple path of faith and weaves it into self-chosen paths. Once the craving for knowledge awakens in people, they are gradually weaned away from the divine and simple testimony of the Holy Scriptures, and the way is paved for new temptations. But may the Lord give us a measure of his divine wisdom in these times, when so many spirits are stirring and so many voices are sounding, so that we will not miss the straight way, but will keep our treasure steadfast to the end.

No. 123

A. W. Böhme to Carl Hildebrand von Canstein
London, 12 September 1715

I will come straightaway to the question that Your Honorable Grace put to me in your last letter: Do I still have scruples about being ordained and giving absolution? To this, I can briefly respond that whatever small blessing I have found in my work so far has stemmed partly from the preaching of the Word and partly from the preparation and translation of some edifying writings. Thus, I can only conclude that this is the post that divine providence has assigned to me, in order to use my few gifts in this way for the common good. Not only have I found such blessings in England, but I have also seen some fruit from my small labor here and there in the West Indies, where I have established a correspondence in several provinces, and have continued it with no small blessing. Since we have so far had no shortage of persons to administer the sacraments, I have gladly left that responsibility to them, and have not considered it advisable to take unnecessary leave of the freedom given me, or to spend my time on such functions, since others have fewer reservations, and therefore take them on more willingly. Furthermore, I acknowledge that since the Lord, as I hope, has given me a richer measure of merciful love toward my neighbor, the scruples I have had up to now have been largely resolved by such a principle.

For I consider merciful love for one's neighbor to be a better reason for resolving such difficulties than all kinds of rational ideas by which one would seek to ease one's mind. Although I could indeed from such reasoning agree to absolution and such things, I prefer to use my freedom where and as long as I may have it.

In the present state of affairs, I do not regard ordination as anything other than a civil act, to which I could also be moved if I were to be forbidden to preach the Word because of a lack of ordination. However, I have not noticed among the Prince of Denmark's remaining attendants—for until now I have only had to focus on them—that they have shown less love and trust in me for lack of ordination; rather, they have had good cause to believe that my reluctance to enter fully the office of preacher has been founded on the dictates of my conscience, disregarding temporal interests. For when, in 1705, I alone was offered the position of court preacher to His Royal Highness Prince George of Denmark, with the full salary, I volunteered to share the salary with a colleague and to be satisfied with half of it, which hopefully left a good impression on many people. What the future arrangement will be with this new government, time will tell.

Regarding the New Testament that has been printed at Halle in vernacular Greek, I can say that I would be very pleased if about a hundred copies (or even more) could be made available. A Greek archbishop from Thebes stayed here for a while and was seeking a contribution for his church. He has several priests around him who perform the weekly rites according to the model of the Greek Church; it is a sight one cannot look upon without compassion. I had a copy of the vernacular Greek New Testament, which Heinrich Ludolf had printed here in 1703, shown to him, and told him that he could have quite a number of copies to distribute in his church, which is why they were published. However, he sent the copy straight back to me; he explained that the Greek Church had put a curse on those who read the book, but if I wanted to give him a few copies of the Halle edition for his people to use, he would gratefully accept them. However, I had only one copy on hand, which I sent to him. The curse was probably caused by an offensive preface, inserted by a Greek archbishop, Seraphim, in which he ridiculed the ignorance of Greek Church prelates and thereby provoked the Greek clergy to forbid the reading of the book to their people. Although this infuriating preface was subsequently removed and an exhortation to read the Bible faithfully was printed in its place, the book is so detested among the Greeks that those who know about it hardly want to touch it. However, in order that the book does not remain here, completely useless, I distribute remaining copies among those poor Greeks who regularly come to this region as servants on English ships and do not know about the fierce bellowing of the clergy.

In the future, I will try to have several of Philipp Jakob Spener's treatises translated into English. *The Spiritual Priesthood* should be printed here before long.[47] Someone wanted to translate the treatise *Nature and Grace* into English;[48] however, I have recommended postponing it until the Latin version appears, since it might shed light on how to express some passages clearly. I would like that the blessed Dr. Spener's biography, as it was presented by Your Excellency in your last volume of reflections, would be published in Latin, as it would give strangers a general taste of this theologian's gifts and work.[49] One could indeed expand it here and there and include several useful passages on the administration of his office, the application and handling of the Scriptures, and other pertinent matters, which might attract foreigners to discipleship. This would gradually pave the way for foreign nations to read his writings, and his gift would be more widely recognized.

---

47. Spener, *Geistliche Priesterthum*. The work does not seem to have been published in English until much later, as Spener, *Spiritual Priesthood*, translated by Voigt.

48. Spener, *Natur und Gnade*.

49. Canstein, *Das Muster Eines rechtschaffenen Lehrers*.

No. 124

A. W. Böhme to Miss Jane Slare
London, 12 October 1715

I am very much obliged for the kind invitation to Windsor, and I assure you that nothing would be more pleasant to me than a retreat among such friends, whose faces are turned toward the Jerusalem above, the mother of all those who have been born again through the Spirit of Jesus, and who have received a living hope of an unfading inheritance. But the present circumstances do not allow me to leave London. I wish I could tell you that our German Chapel has been reestablished, but everything remains in the status quo, which serves to convince us more and more of the complexity and uncertainty of temporal things, and to wean us from the love of transitory goods. When we believe that everything that comes our way is directed by God's providence, we find peace in the midst of the tides and waves of this world-sea. For we can therefore believe that everything will turn out for the best and make our return to our good God all the easier. The undisciplined love of the creaturely is one of the greatest obstacles to progress in the inner life, and it is extremely difficult to possess temporal goods without loving them.

I am grateful for those who have subscribed to the printing of the English edition of *The Garden of Paradise*.[50] As soon as there are enough subscriptions, it will be printed, although the distress and chaos of these times are hindering good projects for promoting Christianity, which is why so few persons are interested. The Society is now in the process of publishing Jean-Frédéric Ostervald's remarks and observations on the Old Testament, which John Chamberlayne has translated.[51] Bartholomäus Ziegenbalg, the Danish missionary, is determined to spend the remaining days of his life among the Malabarians, which so pleased the King of Denmark that he said it was by the Spirit of God that he was willing to risk his life so often for the sake of others.

---

50. Arndt, *Garden of Paradise*.
51. Ostervald, *Arguments of the Books*.

No. 125[52]

A. W. Böhme to Bartholomäus Ziegenbalg
London, 31 October 1715

... At last, the East India Company has given you freedom to sail to Malabar on one of its ships. And because the company's comments on this matter have come into my hands, I will include them here:

> The directors of the East India Company, having been informed that the Society for Promoting Christian Knowledge is requesting that a German named Mr. Ziegenbalg, who has previously been useful in promoting the Protestant mission in the East Indies, be allowed to return there again in a ship belonging to the Company, together with his family, have resolved that said Mr. Ziegenbalg, together with his wife, a maid, and a servant, be at liberty to cross over to the East Indies on a ship belonging to the Company, free of charge, insofar as the Company has anything to do with it. On 27 October 1715

We have also given the Company a copy of what has so far been printed of the Malabar New Testament, neatly bound in several bundles, which they have placed among their curiosities to keep as a lasting reminder. A copy, very beautifully bound, has also been offered to King George, the Crown Prince and Princess,[53] each by three different bishops, along with the VI Continuation in German,[54] and an abstract of the latter printed here in English. At least we have tried to make the whole work somewhat known at court. Whether it will have some effect in promoting the mission, only time will tell, although in the current state of affairs there seems to be little hope for it.

---

52. AFSt/H C 229:20.

53. George August, Prince of Wales (1683–1760), and Caroline of Ansbach, Princess of Wales (1683–1727).

54. *Königl. Dänischen Missionarien.*

FROM QUEEN ANNE TO GEORGE I (1714–1716)

No. 126

A. W. Böhme to Mr. C. V. in W.
London, 26 November 1715

I have long kept your name and person in fond remembrance, but it has been renewed all the more by your letter of October 18th. It is always a source of great refreshment to me when various testimonials of the constant faithfulness of God's servants stream in from all corners of the earth and awaken me to show the same faithfulness in the service of the Lord.

In the first part of the letter, you asked whether, under the protection of the present King of Great Britain, a chapel for the benefit of the Protestants in W. could be established and supplied with an upright man. After receiving the letter, I promptly presented the whole matter to Baron von Bernsdorf,[55] and earnestly asked him to offer his hand in this Christian matter, and also to ask His Majesty for his most gracious consent. He replied that he had recently been looking into the matter, but that previously, due to all kinds of obstacles, it had not been possible to investigate or respond to it. However, he now wanted to present the matter in the appropriate place, and so the written resolution should be signed over to the Baron von = =, with whom one could make inquiries. I sincerely hope that the matter will be brought to a good end, and that a blessing will be created in those places that will also illuminate the surrounding lands with its light. For if the light of the gospel first penetrates large cities with greater power, then there is no doubt that the good will also break through in other places and, like a mustard seed, reveal its inner spiciness. We have an example of this very thing here in London, where almost nothing good arises that is not quickly spread throughout the whole country and to some extent imitated. The religious societies established in London are particularly diligent in this respect.

The Danish missionary Bartholomäus Ziegenbalg is expected to return here next month in order to sail with the English fleet to the East Indies. Such work is still applauded in this country, although the current rebellious times stifle many a good undertaking in its first bloom. It is undoubtedly one of the greatest judgments when a society is divided and disunited, and tries to whitewash an evil matter with the name of church and religion. How great then the corruption must be, when that which

---

55. Andreas Gottlieb Freiherr von Bernstorff (1649–1726).

should control the corruption is used as a tool to make the corruption only that much greater!

No. 127

A. W. Böhme to Mr. U. in W.
London, 6 December 1715

I thank God, who has put it into your heart to embrace so faithfully the East India Mission in region of W. For example, yesterday a merchant from F. visited me and brought news that he had received £300 from W. via F. for the benefit of the Malabar Mission. Your example can inspire many others in Germany and arouse them to the same zeal. It can also actively refute the useless scoffers who stand in the way and condemn other works, which is invariably the most compelling and best way to argue. Here in England as well this undertaking receives ongoing approval, which convinces me in no small measure that the Lord must have a hand in it. Last November, a woman, quite unknown to me, came to me, and we engaged in an extensive conversation about the East India Mission; and after I answered her questions as best I could, she presented me with £30 to expand this work among the Malabarians. When you report to me in more detail the most salient circumstances surrounding the W. collection, they can be recounted here to others all the more emphatically.

But coming back to England, a lady from the country, who recently died, left £200 in her will for furthering this mission. Such gifts from the country are still sent in now and then. Thus, the mustard seed of the kingdom of God pushes through all hindrances, and Jerusalem is built, although at a pitiful time. Both the East and West Indies will finally be made fragrant with the blessed knowledge of Christ, of which some faint signs are to be seen here and there.

FROM QUEEN ANNE TO GEORGE I (1714–1716)

No. 128

A. W. Böhme to Mr. K. in S.
London, 7 December 1715

I am glad that God has preserved you, and I hope that he will continue to watch over you in his mercy, and especially that He will preserve your soul from every danger. Many things have changed here in England since your departure. Most of the good people you knew here have moved away and been scattered here and there. And oh, that they may all remain faithful to the Lord; then we would meet again on the day of the great harvest, bringing in our sheaves with joy.

Caspar Leutbecker has moved to Pennsylvania in America, and yesterday I received a letter from him in which he reports that after many sufferings and storms, he has almost reached the end of his journey.[56] Everyone who has tasted the truth of the gospel must strive to be light and salt wherever the Lord's providence places them. Here and there one still finds a neglected soul in which a spark of divine desire smolders, but which, because it is not awakened, sighs in anguish until it tastes and grasps the power of the Savior. A man who is now quite old and who has sought God in the American wilderness from his youth, came to England some time ago to seek out some devout souls whom he could take with him to America, in order to proclaim Christ there with power and to begin doing so by establishing good schools. However, he had to return without achieving his purpose, since no one could be found who was qualified for this work. Underneath it all, one sees how fervent the desire is to come to know Christ among his members and to praise his glory to others. If you were to go to Jerusalem, you could have the tomb of our Savior pointed out to you, remembering however that it is not the physical sight of the tomb, but beholding Jesus and His death in faith that would save your soul.

---

56. According to Henry Muhlenberg, *Journals*, 1:170 (6–7 July 1742), Caspar Leutbecker (or Leitbecker) (d. 1738) was a tailor who had been "awakened" by Böhme and even "alleged" that Böhme had ordained him in London before coming to America.

No. 129

A. W. Böhme to Georg Heinrich Neubauer
London, 9 December 1715

I recently sent over a bill of exchange for £5 for the benefit of the Halle orphanage, to which I am adding a few details. These gifts were collected by some American friends, who settled in New England and have a particular love for the Halle orphanage, and were sent to me to further its growth. The gifts were enclosed in three envelopes, and the names were added of those persons who, by reading the historical account of the orphanage, were inspired to make such a gift of love. Because this money, which is mostly in Portuguese coins, cannot be sent without complaints or long delivery times, I had it converted to English coins by a moneychanger, in order to be able to send it by bill of exchange sooner and more conveniently. I have, however, enclosed the three original envelopes in which the money was wrapped, and which bear the names of the benefactors, so that they may be kept with the correspondence of the orphanage, but also so that others, at this sight, will be all the more inspired to praise God for such an unexpected American favor. The particulars of the gifts in each envelope were as follows:

In the first envelope, which is marked N. 1. and bears this inscription, *D. Colmanni donum Orphanotropheo Franckiano* [Benjamin Colman's gift to Francke's orphanage], was a Portuguese gold coin, which, according to the moneychanger, amounts to 20 shillings, 6p in English money. There was also half a French pistole, which here amounts to 8s, 6p. In the next envelope, N. 2, which has the inscription *Dilectissimi Iuventis Dr. Samuelis Greenwoodi donum* [Dr. Samuel Greenwood's gift for the dear youth], was a large Portuguese gold coin, called a moidore, which converts here to £1, 7s, 6p.[57] In the third envelope, N. 3, there was enclosed another Portuguese moidore of the same value and half an English Guinea, with the words: *Cotton Matheri munusculum Orphanotropheo Francke* [Cotton Mather's donation to Francke's orphanage]. Lastly, all of it was placed inside a single envelope, on which is written: *Orphanotropheo Francke Munuscula Americana* [American Donations for Francke's Orphanage]. And these various gifts together, according to the bill of exchange, amount to £4, 14s, 9p in English currency, to which another person added 5s, 3p, to make it an even number.

---

57. Probably Samuel Greenwood (1662–1721), a silversmith married to Elizabeth Bronsdon.

Additionally, Dr. Mather, a preacher in Boston, New England, who expresses great pleasure with the institutions in Halle, has sent a large package containing all kinds of spiritual tracts to be forwarded to Halle. He has also had a short account of the orphanage and the other institutions connected with it printed in New England and distributed here and there.[58]

No. 130

A. W. Böhme to Mr. B. on the C.
London, 26 December 1715

... The current state of affairs in this country will be quite familiar to you from the public newspapers. It appears that God has an indictment against the inhabitants of this country (as Hos 4:1 puts it), which is nonetheless connected with exceptional signs of grace. It is said to have been a moving sight—for I myself was unable to witness it—when on the 9th of this month 218 rebels were led through the city of London and put into various prisons. Time will tell what further will be done with them. I confess that I was quite surprised when I was told that one James Cuninghame was among the rebels taken prisoner in the city of Preston; for I knew that he had previously been associated with the so-called French Prophets here, and in the year 1712 had published a whole book of prophetic pronouncements under the title *Warnings of the Eternal Spirit*.[59] Undoubtedly, he joined this rebellious crowd at the command and impulse of a special inspiration, and thereby plunged himself into this misery. I hear that he is to be imprisoned with others at Chester; and now that he has time to reflect, I hope that he will come to a thorough awareness of his inner condition and learn the danger of such works. It may also reveal to us the grave consequences of a false enthusiasm, in which more people are involved at this time than one would think. Indeed, many who are zealously writing again are often ill; so, one who wants to care for souls rightly has plenty to do to portray it correctly in its origin, growth, and fatal consequences, and to warn them about it.

False flattery and delusional belief, mere outward lip-service and works righteousness, arise from such false enthusiasm, since those

---

58. Mather, *Orphanotrophium*.
59. Cuninghame, *Fifteen Warnings of the Eternal Spirit*.

persons, disregarding the sound and apostolic depiction of it we find in the Scriptures, want to practice faith and worship according to their own impulses. And perhaps this is how the aforementioned prophet went wrong, when he gave in to all kinds of dangerous impulses that tempted him to take up arms against the authorities, preferring them to the will of God that is clearly revealed in Scripture. And because I hear that these people still have followers here and there in Germany, I hope that such an example will catch the eye of all honest persons, so that they will be all the more thoroughly convinced of the danger of such ways.

In other matters, on December 14th the former Archbishop of Canterbury, Dr. Thomas Tenison, having suffered for several years from gout and other related ailments, was taken into eternity. And our king has already appointed Dr. William Wake, formerly Bishop of Lincoln, to this important position.[60] He will not lack for work, if he intends to bring the current clergy into an order pleasing to God, and to develop them through his teaching and life. He is one of their ablest people, and has, among other things, translated into English several portions of the *Apostolic Fathers*, for the use of the common person.[61] Therefore, one would hope that he has also imbibed something of the spirit of these early witnesses. On the same day the elderly George Hickes died, who was one of the most prominent of those who are called nonjurors.[62] While King James II was still living, they recognized no one but him as the rightful king, and after his death they held, and still hold, a very favorable opinion of the Pretender, the Prince of Wales,[63] and therefore would never swear an oath of allegiance to anyone else.

On the 22nd of this month, the Danish missionary, Bartholomäus Ziegenbalg, arrived here to continue his journey to the East Indies on English ships. He will be introduced next Thursday to the Society for Promoting Christian Knowledge, of which he is a member.

---

60. William Wake (1657–1737) was Archbishop of Canterbury from 1716 until his death in 1737.

61. *Genuine Epistles of the Apostolical Fathers*.

62. George Hickes (1642–1715) was a nonjuring Anglican divine and scholar.

63. James Francis Edward Stuart (1688–1766) was the son of King James II and his second wife, Mary of Modena. He was nicknamed the "Pretender" by Whigs and was technically only Prince of Wales for a few months until his father was deposed in the Glorious Revolution of 1688.

Later Years (1717–1721)

Letters 131–152

No. 131

A. W. Böhme to Seigneur de Ners
London, 10 April 1717

For your edification, dear friend, I am sending you a tract by Daniel de Superville about the new creation, which you will surely enjoy.[1] To me it is all the more pleasing, because such discourses, which deal with inward Christianity, are very rare, and one would have to have remarkable courage to reissue such books, which are old-fashioned and would hardly be approved by our present barren and conformist world. May our faithful God grant us to grow more and more in His grace and true godliness, so that we may be preserved blameless until the coming of our Savior Jesus Christ.

---

1. Superville (1657–1728), *Christian a New Creature*. Superville was a Huguenot pastor and theologian who, on fleeing France, became the minister of the Walloon church in Rotterdam.

No. 132

A. W. Böhme to Seigneur de Ners
N.p., [1717]

I have received £5 from Mr. D. M., of which £3 is dedicated to the mission in East India and the remaining £2 to the orphanage in Halle. Since I have not been able to provide anything to Halle from England for a long time, I am all the happier for this loving contribution. . . . May the Lord unite our hearts more and more in His heavenly love, which is the source and origin of all good actions, and without which all the things of this world are just a foretaste of the hells that will torment a soul deprived of this divine principle. The East India Mission is still carrying on by the grace of God, but because the number of workers is still very small, they cannot extend their enterprise among the Malabarians as far as they would like. The prayer that our Savior has commanded in Matthew 9:38 is imperative. For the laborers whom the Lord Himself calls and then sends out to work in his vineyards are also well equipped for these great works. But those who undertake this work solely out of their own will and intent, for temporal gain, will contribute little to this spiritual temple that is being erected among the Malabarians. The eye is the light of the body and of all that it does, but wherever it deviates from singleness of heart in Christ, it dissipates into many things and moves further and further away from its source, which is God Himself. It is this singleness of heart on which the main work of our spiritual growth rests. It also draws us away from the love of the world and unites our heart with the true object and only center of our soul. I commend you and those dear to you to this holy love.

No. 133

A. W. Böhme to Seigneur de Ners
London, 7 May 1717

I did not read *The Life and Last Hours of Mr. Rivet* before Mr. Fraser left, so I kept it until now.[2] However, I do indeed remember the expres-

---

2. *Dernières Heures de Monsieur Rivet*. André Rivet (1572–1651) was a French Huguenot theologian.

sion he used at his death, which some German authors are said to have used against the false intellectuals, in order to confound them further in their dry speculations and knowledge: "You are God, the spiritual Doctor. I have learned more theology in the last ten days, during which you have visited me, than in the previous fifty years." This is an exquisite passage of a theology of the heart, by which the Spirit of God instructs His children, giving them a far more powerful conviction than the vast store of human science can impart. This small book would be well worth translating into English, especially at this time, when the rationalists and free thinkers go to great lengths to ridicule the most profound truths, and to scoff at everything that transcends the horizon of their foolish reason.

I hope as soon as possible to send you an extract of the East Indian letters from Tranquebar, which will no doubt please you and give you hope that the work among the Malabarians will spread more and more. Bartholomäus Ziegenbalg has arrived there happily with his wife after a journey of five months. I am also sending my sermon in German on the true and false Christian.[3] Here is the reason: A God-fearing journeyman tailor works for a Frenchman; one of his fellow journeymen who knows a little German lent him this sermon, which he liked so much that he wanted to see it translated into French and promised that he would gladly contribute something from his daily wages. Now I know of no one among all my acquaintances who would be capable of translating it; therefore, I am taking the liberty of asking you to undertake such a task. Should circumstances otherwise permit, if you were to devote only half an hour to it every day, it would soon be possible to translate it. It is not necessary to be bound by the literal words; a translation must be free to express in the best way the sense and emphases of the author.

There are already three hundred Palatines who have arrived, intending to go to Pennsylvania. Now I am trying to get a subscription of £50 per year for the salary of a preacher who can care for the spiritual as well as the physical interests of these poor lost sheep. I have already found a capable person who is willing to go if the said salary can be obtained, without which a preacher will hardly be able to manage in this West Indian wasteland and fulfill his profession.

---

3. Böhme, *Wahre und Falsche Christ*.

No. 134

A. W. Böhme to Seigneur de Ners
London, 26 June 1717

I have not yet been able to achieve my goal of obtaining a preacher for the Palatines. I entrusted the matter of the subscriptions to some persons who are in a position to deal with the government; however, the project will not proceed any further, because projects of this sort involve considerable difficulties. Charitable work, which is sufficiently "warm" one year, gradually begins to grow cold in the following year, especially among those people who practice charitable works only out of natural motives; indeed, the natural love in people almost disappears if it is not based on the love of God, which should be its origin and foundation. I can assure you that the Duchess of Kendal[4] is not a papist, but steadfastly attends our chapel, where she also receives Holy Communion from my colleague.

No. 135

A. W. Böhme to Seigneur de Ners
London, 12 October 1717

Having recently published a volume of my sermons in English,[5] I take the liberty of giving it to you, dear friend, which I pray you will accept with love. Perhaps providence will accompany its reading with some edifying suggestions for the growth of the good desires that it senses in your heart. Whoever does not continue on the path of life is in danger of going backward and losing the first traces of grace. But whoever endeavors to make good use of the initial invitation of God's love, and to open the door of the heart as soon as the grace of the gospel begins to knock, will in time taste the Lord's Supper, and thereby be drawn closer to eternal life. It is very difficult to hold onto sparks of the heavenly fire in the midst of the darkness and coldness with which we are surrounded,

---

4. Ehrengard Melusine von der Schulenburg, Duchess of Kendal, Duchess of Munster (1667–1743), was a longtime mistress to King George I.

5. Böhme, *Several Discourses*.

and not to die under so many spiritual corpses and invalids, but it is not impossible to hold onto this fire and this life. For He who commanded us to let our light shine before others has also promised us His Spirit to abide with us and in us.

Recently, a society was established here for the care of poor proselytes who turn to the Protestant religion.[6] However, I am afraid that more care is taken to nourish the body than to edify the soul. Mr. Ziegenbalg has sent a letter, no doubt concerning the mission, to our King, which the King has also graciously had answered. This gives us some hope that the court will in time take steps to help promote the cause. But one must always keep one's eyes fixed on God, the prime mover, who must set in motion the good desires that will further His kingdom on earth. May the Lord keep you and yours in His constant care . . .

No. 136

A. W. Böhme to Anna Elisabeth Böhme
London, 14 October 1717

So, it pleased Him who is Lord over the dead and the living to carry our dear mother[7] into eternity, thereby making us utter orphans. Now we have all the more reason to hold on to Him whom we do not see, as if we did see Him, and to cast our concern on Him who alone wants to be and remain our father, mother, shepherd, caretaker, protector, and shield, yes, all in all. But such a faith, which longs to seek and find everything in God alone, must be a true *orphan faith*, which no longer seeks in the creature what it can find in the Creator alone. To the extent that we still cling to certain creatures, we are lacking our true *standing as orphans*, and so we forfeit the fatherly provision that is promised to the destitute, the poor, the abandoned, and true orphans. However, we have reason to rejoice in the hope that at the end of days, after our dear mother has rested in her chamber, we will see her again at the right hand of the Chief Shepherd, and we will be inseparable from her in the presence of the Lord.

---

6. The Commission for the Relief of Poor Proselytes. Austen-Leigh, "Commission for the Relief."

7. Anna Catharina Oynhausen (ca. 1640–1717).

No. 137

A. W. Böhme to Henry Newman
London, 29 January 1718

By order of the Society, I have looked through the book, *Wisdom from Above*,[8] and find it a lovely collection of many sayings—spiritual, practical, and drawn from experience—which relate to an inward life of grace and the manifold effects that flow from it. Some of them are of such a lofty nature that they will hardly remain uncensored should they fall into the hands of supercilious readers, who routinely attach the label of enthusiasm to anything that exceeds the ideas or model they have formed of religion. In many places, the book makes a precise distinction between a spiritual Christianity and a pagan moral doctrine, something much needed in this our time, when these two great principles are so often confused and so unhappily mixed with each other. The author presents the latter principle as entirely inadequate for reaching the true spiritual nature called for by the gospel, and according to which all virtues must be tested, not by human strength and skill, but by Christ Himself, the great Redeemer of our fallen nature.

Just as our Society is named not for the promotion of some set of pagan morals, but for the knowledge of Christ Himself, in whom there is eternal life, we should also, in the choice of our books, always keep an eye on this honorable title which we have adopted, and by no means deviate from the purpose of promoting the knowledge of Christ, to which we have committed ourselves.

While reading in particular the first part of this book, it occurred to me that two or three years ago the Society had intended to have printed a collection of the most important and necessary pieces of Christian faith and life, so that it could be posted in people's homes and read for everyone's edification. But there was no final decision at that time. If, however, the Society wanted to set the same work in motion now, I should think it would not be difficult to draw a stately collection of select sayings from this book, and to arrange them, *mutatis mutandis*, in such a way that the intended purpose could be maintained.

---

8. John Mapletoft (1631–1721), *Wisdom from Above*.

No. 138

A. W. Böhme to Miss Jane Slare
Amsterdam[?], 25 January 1719

After my safe arrival in this place, under the protection of the Most High, I am delighted and obliged to let my friends know how dependable and gratifying the guidance has been that I have enjoyed through divine goodness and that I hope will accompany me to the end of my journey. At Harwich I met several of my old friends, although others had already gone to their eternal rest. We crossed the sea safely in 24 hours with fair wind and weather. In Rotterdam, I heard of the passing of elderly Mr. P., whom I had planned to visit during my travels, but arrived 14 days too late. However, I visited his company, which is located in his house in Rotterdam, and which will publish the manuscript he left behind for the general benefit and edification of everyone. Some of his last words before his departure were, "Jesus all in all"—whose love and grace he commended to those around him. I hope that you will continue your reflections on the works of creation, from which you were kind enough to read to me some time ago. They will serve both for your own sweet refreshment and for the edification of others who may read them.

No. 139

A. W. Böhme to Miss Jane Slare
Amsterdam[?], [1719]

I thank God that I have arrived safely in Holland, although I have been making slow progress, partly because of an attack of kidney stones which befell me in Rotterdam, and partly because of some friends who kept me longer than I had hoped. I do not doubt that you are accompanying me with your prayer and good wishes. I was thinking of you that day with particular fondness, and the hope came into my heart that God would anoint you with the oil of gladness. This oil transcends everything, and all fellow believers are anointed with it as truly as was Christ, according to His human nature. The difference is only in the measure. He, as our head, was anointed without measure, whereas each of His living members receives but a certain measure of this divine anointing. May the Lord graciously gladden our souls throughout the days of our pilgrimage, until we finally reach the end of our journey.

No. 140

A. W. Böhme to Miss Jane Slare
Rotterdam, 3 September 1719

Traveling, thank God, is quite beneficial to my health, and I can spend three or four nights on the carriages without much discomfort, as long as my typical symptoms, namely the kidney stone pains, do not trouble me. But all our pleasures should be tempered, so that we do not fall too much in love with anything; for our desires should be entirely directed to that great passage we must make from time into eternity. It is incumbent upon us to eat our bread, and even the paschal lamb itself, with bitter salts, hastening away from the slavery of our sins and from the bondage of this corrupt world. The locusts and other like worms, which serve as God's armies, have devoured much fruit in Germany. And wherever people do not repent, there is the fear that other armies will come and devour what is left. For wherever the root of all evil, namely sin, becomes rampant and spreads, the result that infallibly accompanies it cannot be far off. Still, the Lord will build an ark for Noah and his family, and His kingdom will flourish despite all the misery that will come upon those who call themselves Christians and yet do not have the anointing by which they are named.

No. 141

A. W. Böhme to a preacher in the country
London, 24 December 1719

At long last I am replying to your letter, which has taken me some time to answer; I hope that the delay will be taken in the best possible way, especially since such exchanges are often the best means by which each of us can encourage the other in the knowledge of the truth. To make my answers as clear as possible, I will summarize his misgivings about cards and other games in several questions, and direct my answer to them.

1. Why can't the game of cards and similar variations come from a Christian motive in the same way as the games of bowling, skittles, etc.?

Answer: (a) I do not think that bowling and skittles are permissible, except under many important and strict conditions; and I believe that if the bowlers and skittles players were obliged to follow them, the bowling and skittles places would be rarely visited.

(b) I do not consider such practices permissible at all, unless it is to preserve the health of those who have to sit a lot in their way of life. Where the same end can be served by a less troublesome or more useful exercise, I would gladly abandon all such pastimes, which, regardless of whatever precautions one might take, give the person the occasion for all manner of temptations. It is a pity that the praiseworthy custom, which used to be popular among the learned Jews, is now largely forgotten: that those who were to study, in addition to their regular studies, also had to learn a craft or other useful art. And some expositors demonstrate these things, along with many other examples from history, with the trades of the apostle Paul himself (Acts 18), who practiced them not only when he sat at the feet of Gamaliel, but also afterward, when he was an apostle to the Gentiles. If our students today would do the same, they would have an honest activity to refresh themselves after spending a few hours on their more important and serious studies.

I recently saw this custom revived at the Halle orphanage during my last trip to Germany, where the young people who were sent to school there used their recreation hours to learn something useful, while at the same time exercising and refreshing their bodies. They have a rather spacious room, adapted for this purpose and equipped with all kinds of apparatuses. Some practice glass-grinding, while others make microscopes, field glasses, or similar things. In this way, the health of young people is promoted, and they are directed to the knowledge of mechanical sciences, which will be of great benefit to them as they grow older. I have also known a distinguished theologian who, when he was tired from his studies, went and sawed or turned wood, thus trying to guard against the negative consequences of a sedentary body. If such activities were practiced more at this time, there would be no need to consider bowling and other such games, which can be so easily abused, and which, in the corrupt world we are living in, can hardly be practiced without confusion, or at least without partaking to some extent in other people's vices, especially in those places full of so many tempting conditions. In a word: just as Christians can use medicine, so they can also move their bodies by bowling or playing skittles; however, just as the best medicine can harm rather than heal a patient, so any exercise of the body, if it does not remain within Christian bounds, may cause all kinds of trouble. For this sole reason I consider it unacceptable. Should you, however, wish to place card and dice games in the same class, you must first prove that they are just as beneficial to the body as the other games.

2. The structure and constitution of people are such that their minds cannot always be focused on important and serious things, so they must at times have a more enjoyable change.

Response: We must make a distinction between a person who is born again and one who is not, a distinction that is essential for a minister of souls to observe. With regard to those who are idle and disorderly, they do as they please, but it is all sin, and so their pastimes cannot be anything else. They play and pray with unregenerate hearts, and therefore both pursuits are ruined, because both come from an evil motive. For just as converted souls are instilled with a constant and single motive for everything they do, so also the unconverted have a single motive: they seek *themselves* in all things and not God, for whose honor and service they were created. There is no reason at all to allow these unfortunate people the slightest freedom, for they already have too much freedom of their own. If the mental refreshment brought from the card game is applied to those souls who are in the process of conversion, I would think that they do not need such mental refreshment at all.

If one were to consider service of God and works of love toward one's neighbor as the important and weighty activities for which one would need refreshment, I cannot regard them as the kind of burdensome tasks that would require refreshment with cards and dice. If we look at the matter in the right light, we must acknowledge that service of God is a perfect freedom, and if this is true, how can this service be burdensome or tiring for anyone? The yoke of Christ is not an iron yoke, and its burden is not Egyptian slavery. A godly theologian has said: the burden of Christ is like a burden of cinnamon or other spices, which refreshes those who carry it.

3. Our bodies cannot be constantly worked without occasionally resting and enjoying pastimes.

    Response: This is indisputably true, but did not God soon after the fall, in His infinite wisdom, provide a suitable means by which people can renew their weakened faculties. Has He not ordained the day for work and the night for rest, and has He not provided daily food and sustenance for the preservation of the body, the blessings of which are all the greater when they are sanctified by prayer and the Word of God?

4. Why can't devout and born-again people enjoy playing cards or backgammon, as well as bowling or skittles, especially if they consider them more beneficial to their health and well-being?

    Response: I have never heard of playing cards being prescribed as a remedy for health; at the very least, it cannot be a suitable cure for those unhealthy effects caused by excessive sitting, since such games are usually played while sitting, and thus are more likely to increase the symptoms than to reduce them. As for the favorable cleansing or encouragement of the disposition, which you are so keen to commend, I would only point out that *joyfulness* is either *natural*, and arises from the temperament or physical constitution of a person, and must therefore be sanctified by grace and purified from the mannerisms associated with it; or it is *carnal*, and therefore must be put to death, as well as other sinful inclinations of the flesh; or it is *spiritual*, and arises from a grace-filled sense of the love of God, which is poured out in a believing soul. Which of these three types you are now trying to serve by playing cards must be clearly explained; otherwise, the licentious and ungodly gamblers will soon come here and believe that you are giving them complete freedom to indulge in their carnal and unholy revelry. And consider what harm could come from such an unrestrained way of speaking, especially if the pen of a preacher encourages them to do so.

5. So you say: "Everyone follows their own pleasures." (Virgil)

    Response: It would be preferable to draw on Cicero's words when he says: "Mortals are caught by pleasure, like fish with a hook." And again:

"Pleasure is the greatest enemy of virtue." And the same author says: "Pleasure is not worthy of a learned person." And a greater pagan than he says: "Despise pleasures; pleasure hurts when purchased by pain." But to come closer to the point, pleasures or desires are either *spiritual* or *carnal*. The first are wrought by the good Spirit of God, by which a born-again soul is drawn to Him as the chief source of all good affections. The latter are workings of the flesh and nature as they are now, after the fall and apostasy from God, so that the lusts of the flesh always drag the soul down to pursue its sinful appetites. These two are always opposed to each other, and therefore the spiritual struggle arises in a born-again soul, about which the unconverted, worldly person knows nothing at all.

Now you will surely admit that the flesh with all its evil desires must be crucified and killed, and thus cannot at all be coddled when it tempts a person, for fear that it would give birth to sin (Jas 1:14–15) and become mother to many evil children. You should determine fairly beforehand to which kind of pleasure you want to reckon board and card games. If you want to include them among the spiritual delights, you must certainly practice them; but if you choose to include them among the carnal delights, it is up to everyone, especially a preacher of the gospel, to tell people how to restrain the temptations of the flesh and thus fulfill the main purpose of the incarnation of Christ, who appeared in the world so that we should renounce worldly pleasures (Titus 2:12) and avoid everything that would be contrary to this holy ultimate aim.

You know that a devout bishop of the Church of England has written a remarkable treatise in which he demonstrates that the restoration of humankind to true inward righteousness and holiness is the foremost and highest ultimate aim of our Savior's coming into the world, and the highest purpose of the blessed gospel. In his Dedication to the Archbishop of Canterbury, he says that it is a very sad thing to consider how alarmingly the ultimate aim of the gospel is being abused by its confessors. He says that the doctrine, discipline, and liturgy of the Church do not give the slightest opportunity for a reprobate and ungodly life, but that they all aim at building us up in our most holy faith and purifying us through it from every defilement of the flesh and spirit. And because you want to make people cheerful, and draw on board-, card-, and I know not what other games for help, I want you to ponder what this theologian said in chapter 10, section 2, page 109. For there he demonstrates that no pleasures can be compared to those that arise directly from a holy and virtuous life, and that those who live holy lives act in a way that is most consistent with the nature and character of their souls and, consequently, most natural.

Furthermore, since he is so keen on encouraging the lively disposition and cheerful humor that are particularly promoted by playing cards, etc., he should well consider whether the present state of religion would and could encourage or permit such a merry disposition. Do not all honorable people complain about the blatant liberty that is increasing everywhere, and from which such a godless life arises that no earthly remedies are able to control it? And this overflowing wickedness is all the more dangerous the more common it becomes. All parties are infected with it, as with a hellish plague, even those parties that advocate, more than others, for leading stricter lives. For these and other reasons, it would be more fitting for a preacher and minister of the gospel to pray and plead with tears: "O Lord spare your people, etc." Even the least concession in this innocent pastime—supposing that it could in some way be preserved innocent and harmless in every instance—is very dangerous in this our time, since people are only too willing to cross the line or go out of bounds, and abuse the least hint of permission to enjoy the world's pleasures to the fullest.

6. Playing cards is in itself something indifferent, etc.

Response: (a) This is precisely the question, and who should decide the matter? (b) If the player is unconverted, all his deeds are defiled and sinful. *For that which is born of the flesh is flesh.* (c) In my previous letter, as a parenthetical argument, I cited a passage from Bishop Hopkins in which he asserts that the prayer of the unconverted—including their pastimes and everything they do—is entirely sinful. (d) Assuming they are innocent or indifferent things, they must be limited and delineated with great care and caution. Where this is neglected, I do not see how one can avoid the outcome that all vanity and godlessness shall be justified under the pretext of this indifferentism. (e) Those who live in a state of grace have a general rule from the apostle Paul, by which they govern their life and walk (1 Cor 10:31; Col 3:17). In my first letter I made a distinction between the natural, social, and spiritual actions of people; accordingly, the apostle's rule must be applied consistently to all of them. I am not sure to which category playing cards belongs.

7. Playing cards is a pleasant diversion and refreshment for the body. It is an amusement that makes us better able to do our work, promotes health, and makes us feel happy. It is pleasant and refreshing to those whose bodies have been worn out all day long working in their profession. Those who are born again find it very beneficial for prolonging their health, and need it, so that through the benefits of their health they may all the more be able to serve God and promote His glory and the salvation of others. It encourages and refreshes their frame of mind, etc.

Response: I do not believe that there has ever lived a single person in the world who has found as many advantages in the game of cards as the one, who has even made it a general panacea to cure, or at least to relieve, diseases of both the soul and the body. You say it is a pleasant diversion. I confess (a) that it could be so for those whose discernment has been spoiled by a prolonged gambling habit. (b) I have already mentioned above some things that are both refreshing and satisfying, and consequently far preferable to playing cards, which often gives occasion for much mischief. We should never promote something as broadly useful, when it is only beneficial to me or perhaps to a few others who have the same temperament and understanding as I do.

You say: An entertainment makes a person all the more disposed to attend to their profession.
Response: (a) Your profession is to preach the gospel and lead souls to Christ. I cannot imagine how playing cards should or could be necessary for you to do such a remarkable work. (b) You speak so broadly and without qualification, as if playing cards had the same effect on everyone without exception. And that when I know that playing cards would only make an innumerable number of people less adept at administering the office entrusted to them. So, playing cards has quite different effects, according to the different circumstances and characters of the players.

You say: It promotes the temperament's vivacity and cheerfulness, and prolongs life and health, etc.
Response: (a) After the fall, the happiness or merry temperament of all people is corrupt and sinful. For it arises from self-love, the original root of all vices, and therefore, according to the precepts of the gospel, must not be coddled at all but put to death. (b) Spiritual joyfulness of heart arises from experiencing the fatherly love of God, after our natural

enmity has been removed and the soul has been reconciled by the blood of Christ. Does he think that playing cards can promote this lasting kind of joyfulness? (c) As for health, I have never read or heard of a single person (other than yourself) whose health has been improved by playing cards. But I could well name a few who have developed a sickly physique as a result of such play. But here you would say: Yes, these people play too long; one should choose a suitable time and place for it, and use it leisurely and judiciously. But I beg you, sir, tell me, what time and place would be suitable? Who should prescribe all these conditions? The time that appears suitable for you may not be suitable for someone else. And what does playing judiciously mean? What are the rules of a judicious cautiousness in this game? The greatest gambler will undoubtedly say that he plays both with cautiousness and at a suitable time. Who should decide this matter? It would therefore be necessary to draft a set of reasonable and moderate rules for this purpose. But who would draw them up, those of spiritual or secular authority? So, my lord, you see what endless complications we get into when we talk about such bad and frivolous pleasures.

As for prolonging health, I'm quite willing to admit that I don't know the exact time when playing cards appeared in the world. But don't you think that our forebears, who knew nothing about this pastime, were as strong and healthy as those who live in our time? Speaking for myself, I definitely believe that the people of our time are unhealthier than those who lived in previous centuries. And yet there have never been so many gamblers as in this present time. So, I don't think you are proposing the right means for prolonging life. (d) And even as these things are insufficient for that purpose, so also the glory of God, which you want to build on such a paltry foundation, cannot possibly be upheld by playing board games and cards. So again, this counsel is very unbecoming to the integrity of someone who is an ordained minister.

But he goes on to say that it is good for the one whose body has been wearied all day in the duties of his profession.

Response: Solomon says: Sleep is sweet to the laborer (Eccl 5:12). And when our Savior, in the low estate of His humanity, was weary from His journey, he sat down, and asked for a drink of water to refresh Himself (John 4:6). And why then do we not follow these virtuous means for the rest and refreshment which divine providence provides and are most fitting to our human constitution? But we have already discussed this above.

He goes on to say: It animates and delights the heart.

Response: When Solomon recounts all his entertainments and pleasures, along with all the ways he sought to promote them, he finally confesses that it is all vanity and a weariness of the spirit. True, he does not mention card games or similar pastimes, of which nothing was known at that time, but he does mention other kinds of entertainments, which were undoubtedly even more enjoyable and attractive than your board and card games. Just read in the next chapter, Ecclesiastes 5:4–8. But in the end—see 5:11 (in Poli's paraphrase)—when he surveyed and pondered all his previous works and labors, and whether or not he had found in them the pleasure he sought and expected, behold, he said, all was vanity, etc. He soon found himself deceived and dissatisfied: The pleasure had disappeared, and he was none the better for it, but was as empty as before, and had nothing of it left but a sorrowful memory. He found none of those lavish benefits which my lord has discovered in card playing, and which I hold to be entirely imaginary, having no gambling experience whatsoever. But to avoid making this too long, I hasten to the last objection, which was included in the postscript.

> I readily confess that to a penitent, sorrowful, and broken heart, and to a born-again, holy, and heavenly minded soul, the above-mentioned pleasures seem like hollow and unsavory travails, as long as they remain in such a state. But who can live so happily, and constantly hold such a spiritual and heavenly outlook, as long as we are here in the body?

Response: It seems that his conscience struck him as he was closing his letter, convincing him that he had written too carelessly for a preacher and theologian. He admits that to a penitent and believing soul, cards and such pastimes seem like unsavory travails, but he doubts whether it is possible to hold such a spiritual and heavenly outlook all the time. From this it is clear that he himself admits that it is not at all suitable to play cards in front of devout people when they are heavenly minded, and therefore he instructs them in playing cards when they are unspiritual or at least not so heavenly minded. I confess that this distinction disturbed me more than all the previous objections in his entire letter. (a) I hope he will acknowledge that a born-again person is always spiritual day and night, sleeping or waking, eating and drinking; faith in Christ is, as it were, the soul of new birth, and the living source from which all spiritual actions flow. What the circulation of the blood is in the physical body, that is the effect of faith in the spiritual body. Just as blood circulates through the entire human body by means of a constant and orderly movement, so faith flows through all of a person's powers and faculties. These workings of the spiritual life are orderly, uninterrupted, and constant; should they move only occasionally, when the person gets a sudden impulse, it would soon deteriorate into a fanatical enthusiasm, so that one would be spiritual one hour and unspiritual the next. This would inevitably lead to very dangerous consequences. (b) I do not think it is advisable to play cards or to indulge in other games when people are in a cold or unspiritual state. Such dissolute actions will certainly make a person colder and less inclined to spiritual things, and finally even snuff out and extinguish the divine flame that should burn steadily on the altar of the heart. (c) Therefore, it would be much more advisable, at just such a time of deadness, to implore the Lord earnestly to awaken the spiritual life in us again when it lies, as it were, floundering or languishing under the temptations of this life. (d) By such holy practices as praying, singing, reading, and meditating, the spiritual life will be newly reawakened and regain its former strength and splendor. (e) The question of whether it is possible to remain in a spiritual and heavenly consciousness at all times is one that I will not presume to answer. My own experience is quite limited. I firmly believe that many other souls have attained those qualities that I can only see from afar. We must never make our own experience a rule and guide for deciding matters of spirit or conscience.

No. 142

A. W. Böhme to Monsieur Williams
London, 14 February 1720

The stronger our temptations are, the more glorious will be the victory; and this will unfailingly occur, if only we remain faithful under those trials which our beloved God allows to come upon us for our testing and growth. They are not signs of God's wrath, but God's discipline, by which we are prepared more and more for greater things. Where is there a child whom a father does not discipline (Heb 12)? True warriors of Jesus Christ have a twofold character: the first is that they must fight under the banner of their Lord; the other is that they must suffer hardships from the enemy of the soul, to unsettle the soul, when it is not possible to bring it back under his diabolical rule. But precisely this inward struggle and strife, if rightly considered, give us an opportunity for great consolation, for it is a clear sign that God has begun his work of grace in our souls. If there were no light in us, why would the enemy stir up such storms and temptations to extinguish it? And if there were no grace, why should nature rise up and oppose it? All this turmoil and inner uproar and rebellion can be sufficient to assure us that sin is alarmed in its mighty fortress, and that a stronger power has come into the soul to cast out the tyrant and depose him from his dominion. At this point you can only recall your former sense of security, when you felt nothing of all these disturbances, and sin ruled quite placidly and undisturbed. In my opinion, if you seriously consider the state you were in and weigh it against your present state, you will find enough reason to praise God for His marvelous goodness, which I wish you from the bottom of my heart.

No. 143

A. W. Böhme to Henry Newman
London, 2 June 1720

I have read through the collection of letters between Theophilus and Eugenio.[9] They deal mainly with the love of God, which Theophilus, as someone more experienced in religious matters, strives to instill in the heart of Eugenio, as a beginner in the Christian walk. The second letter (pp. 9–15) contains a particularly impassioned exhortation to the love of God, which could almost put one into a poetic rapture or enthusiastic paroxysm of devotion for a while, but which would not last long, because what is motivating this love is in large part taken from natural ideas and reflections. Our blessed Savior Jesus Christ, in whom the love of God is made manifest beyond our comprehension, is mentioned only twice in the whole collection (pp. 7 and 22). After the author touched on the works of creation and preservation (p. 12), he also finally mentioned redemption, but apart from the word redemption, nothing else is mentioned of it in the whole book. The most beautiful paragraph of

---

9. These letters were written by Sir Richard Blackmore (1654–1729), an English poet, physician, and theologian.

all is found on page 24, where there is a whole sentence about the Holy Spirit and its influence on the human heart. And it is the only thing, in my opinion, that has the flavor of true Christianity in the whole book.

The other arguments which are meant to inspire the love of God are taken from nature, or from the notion of God as a creator, benefactor, loving father, etc. But not a single word is mentioned about what our Savior did to bring this love of God back to us again. Nothing of His incarnation or mission to the world, nothing of His cross and suffering, nor of His death, resurrection, and ascension into heaven, nor of other great deeds that one encounters in the life of Christ, and which are the true and proper sources from which God's love is poured out toward us, and from which there arises in us a love in return for Him who loved us in the first place. I hope that no one will doubt that this is the clear, simple, straightforward, and, in a word, right apostolic way to preach the love of God, and therefore I will refrain from citing various texts of Scripture to support it. In a word, Theophilus makes too much of natural reason and too little of that which is spiritual and Christian. And therefore, I do not see how his letters would be compatible with the purpose of a Society whose endeavors are to promote the knowledge of Christ on the basis of Christian, scriptural, and spiritual principles.

We live in a time when Jesus Christ's person and merit, and all the effects they should have in our souls, are being utterly destroyed and rejected. Why then should a Society that seeks to promote the knowledge of Christ promote religion only through natural reason, casting aside those arguments that in fact conform directly to its purpose? Will not an unwary reader get the idea that these letters were expressly written to promote Christian principles, because they were recommended by a Society which is dedicated to promoting the knowledge of Christ?

But if these letters were to be distributed by the Society, I would like all three collections—the last of which is still to be published—to be bound together, and that those members who have recommended these letters to the Society would see to it that the last collection be written in a more Christian and spiritual way, so that the last one might shed light on the two preceding ones and resolve everything in Jesus Christ, the author and perfecter of our faith. For if we were to continue with collections such as these, then we would eventually also get the point of recommending *Senecae Moralia*[10] to promote the knowledge of Christ.

---

10. Seneca (ca. 4 BCE–65 CE), *Tomus primus*.

[Original editor's note:] The last part of this collection was compiled in accordance with this proposal, and since then, all three parts have been distributed at the same time.[11]

No. 144

A. W. Böhme's reflections on the love of God (not included in the previous letters)

The highest and most perfect revelation of God's love for humankind can be seen in the mission of Jesus Christ to the world. This can be clearly seen in the words of our Savior (John 3:16): "For God so loved the world that He gave His only Son." And from 1 John 4:9: "God's love was revealed among us in this way: God sent His only Son into the world..."

1. The work of creation, which was known for several thousand years before Christ's mission to the world, does not give rise to such a glorious image of God's love.

The greatest revelation of this love happened in Christ and His blessed incarnation. And that is why the greatness of this love is expressed by "so": *so* wonderful, *so* extravagant, *so* high. Where this revelation of God's exalted love is indeed experienced and applied, it will guide the heart and make it able to use the lesser revelations of God's love toward a good end: such as, the work of creation and all the unique and particular footprints of divine providence that everyone has experienced in their own person, family, and elsewhere.

2. The love of God, which is poured into the heart and justifies it by faith (Rom 5:1, 5)—so that He may love us—stirs the heart to a tender, blessed love for God.

This love of God for humankind is now revealed in diverse outpourings. The first immediate and natural effect that arises from this love is that we love God in return (1 John 4:19). Paul ascribes such divine power

---

11. It is unclear how the letters were "distributed." They were not published until the American statesman Benjamin Franklin (1705–1790) did so in 1747. Blackmore, *Letters Between Theophilus and Eugenio.*

to this love that he maintains that a whole swarm of the very strongest temptations would not be enough to hold back love's very nature. Who shall separate us, he says, from the love of Christ? He then defies all the combined or concerted powers of the ungodly, however they might, to separate him from the love of Jesus, and finally concludes: "In all these things we are more than conquerors through him who loved us." But when he exalts the love of God in this way, he always means the love that is in Christ Jesus our Lord (Rom 8:36, 37, 39). No other love can produce such steadfastness of character, not even the works of creation and its preservation, which cannot properly be called the love of God in Christ. It has often brought me considerable consolation that the apostle speaks in the plural: "Can we be separated?" And with these words he includes all those Christians who are not as mature as he is, so that no one may think that the depth of God's love of which he speaks can only be realized in an apostle. Elsewhere he attributes a compelling power to this love: The love of Christ (with which he loved us) urges us on (2 Cor 5:14), as if he wanted to say: Love is a strong impetus to practice every Christian virtue with sincerity and without the oppressive bondage of the law and its dreadful threats; rather, love is a pleasant yet potent bondage.

3. The work of creation is only a secondary cause that can move us to love God again.

To love God with a spiritual and evangelical love is a work of the gospel alone, which has revealed how the work of redemption is the great source of God's love for humankind. Through it, the flame of loving God in return is kindled. For God, viewed only as a creator without Christ the mediator, cannot be the real object of our love; however, God in Christ is. The reason is clear: God, viewed without Christ, is a consuming fire, and is so far from being the object of our love that He causes everyone to flee from Him, and to withdraw from Him, as the people did at Mount Sinai (Exod 20). On the contrary, God, having been reconciled to us through the all-sufficient sacrifice that Christ made for us, has now become the pleasing, sweet, and loving object of our blessed love. Moreover, the capacity of our soul to love God has been so terribly corrupted by sin and made incapable of loving God, that instead it harbors an innate hatred and enmity toward God (Rom 8:7). How then can it be possible to love God whom we hate? Therefore, whoever wants to love God must truly experience a change of heart and must have, at least to some degree, recovered the divine righteousness to be able to love God. But this spiritual restoration does not come from creation, or from its influence, as some people might think, but solely from Jesus Christ and His office as mediator, by which He took away the enmity and endowed the soul with His own complete righteousness. And then the Father loves it, and looks upon it with fatherly grace and affection. He also gives it the Holy Spirit, as a pledge of its future inheritance. The Holy Spirit enlightens the soul's understanding more and more, sanctifies the will, and purifies its desires, so that it can love God first and foremost and through love be united with Him as its real and true object. All this is brought about by the power of Christ's redemption, but not by creation. Nevertheless, it cannot be denied that a careful contemplation of creation could pave the way for some people to listen to the gospel sooner. I say "some people" advisedly: Many of those who spend too much time contemplating the visible creation and the wonderful variety that is expressed in it become so preoccupied with it that they care little about the work of salvation. Here it is worth noting that the greatest mathematicians are often the greatest atheists, who lead the most profligate and dissolute lives. A little philosophical morality, which they form out of their own speculation, is enough for them.

4. The love with which we love God does not consist of an extraordinary feeling of elation, rapture, or other such emotional states, but in a humble recognition of one's own insignificance and in a childlike obedience to God's precepts (John 14:21; 1 John 2:5 and 5:3).

It is true that divine love gladly manifests itself to a soul that is prepared to receive it. However, it is rarely manifested in outbursts of exceptional joy. A humble soul that loves God deeply does not desire such things personally, nor does it urge others to chase after them. When true lovers of God occasionally receive a foretaste of the world to come, they then sink all the more into their own misery. Lofty inspirations and rapturous movements put people in greater danger than the denial and renunciation of themselves. And this is the reason why holy souls in every age have desired the latter more than the former. One of them has said that he would rather see his own misery than an angel in all its glory, and he gives this reason: because the vision of my misery, he says, can increasingly humble me, while the appearance of an angel would stir a feeling of pride and self-importance in me.

5. Those souls who have experienced the lower practices of the spiritual life are quite capable of tasting and partaking in the love of God.

By these lower or preparatory practices, we are referring to repentance, contrition of spirit, breaking or shattering of the heart, the knowledge of sin through the law, godly sorrow, and the like. The love of God is the true mark and essence of the gospel, but it is only reserved for and imparted to those who have been faithful under the prior discipline of the law. This discipline of the law in its manifold effects prepares and guides the heart, but it is the revelation or working of the gospel that truly applies and imparts the benefits for which the law has prepared us. Now where this work of preparation is deficient or has not been done at all, we may rightly doubt the goodness of any virtue that we think we have. So, if people purport to have experienced extraordinary feelings of God's love, and yet have experienced nothing or very little of repentance, self-denial, divine sorrow, etc., we have good reason to distrust the goodness and authenticity of their love. No matter how well people think of their heavenly raptures and divine feelings, all these exhilarating movements are nothing but the effects of one's own imagination, when kindled by one or another coincidental cause. Does it not often happen that weak men and women are wholly enraptured by watching a moving tragedy, but as soon as the actor has finished the performance, all such soulless emotions dissipate?

6. Ordinary natural philosophers, no matter how intelligent they may be in other matters, cannot give a living and personally experienced description of God's love.

This is inherently self-evident. For an ordinary philosopher does not recognize the primary means by which God has revealed His love, namely the blessed incarnation of His Son, as mentioned above. By force of eloquence, high oratory skills, and other inventions, the philosopher may well bring a person into powerful stirrings and even into a philosophical enthusiasm: But what is all this froth in comparison with the love of God. Archimedes was so absorbed with and full of his circles that he neither heard nor saw what was going on outside of them. All that time, however, he was oblivious to the love of God. The most learned discourse only hinders hungry souls, produces many words, and arouses people's desires, but in the end gives nothing to satisfy the longing of the heart.

No. 145

A. W. Böhme to Monsieur Williams
London, 13 October 1720

    I am glad that you continue in your pursuit of the greatest cause of all: the blessedness of your immortal soul. Your description of the present state of your soul gives me hope that the work of conversion has really begun in your soul, and that it will go from one stage to another until you are established on a rock that is immovable. When we have an unfeigned loathing of the sin within us, and a firm resolve to uncover it more and more—as you now assure me you are doing—then God has truly begun His work of grace. Satan does not give us this abhorrence at all, but rather uses all his powers to keep us in the love of our spiritual bondage and to prevent the hand that wants to break it. So, it is not our evil corrupt nature, but God Himself and His Spirit, who first shows us how deeply we have sunk into ruin through sin, and who then uses His blessed hand to heal our wounds. But this does not happen in a day, not even in a year. Being born again and renewed to a godly life is a work that requires time. And often, when we think we have overcome a sin, before we know it, it may reappear with greater ferocity than before, producing great turmoil in our hearts. However, as long as we restrain ourselves from following the temptations of sin, it cannot cause us great harm, although we may have occasion to humble ourselves and recognize the odious corruption of our nature, which has penetrated deeply into all the powers of the soul.

    I am only telling you this so that you will not be surprised if you should encounter something like it in the future. A relapse into sin happens only when I wholly indulge in the temptations of sin and surrender myself to its rule. But as long as I resist and fight, groan and pray, and thus resist as much as I am able, it is a sign that sin has not yet gained dominion over me, and in such a case we can certainly rely on the goodness of God, who will help us in His time and will not let us be tempted beyond our ability. As for the hardening of the heart that you are lamenting, it is God who makes you feel these things; and since it is His work, He will guide you in time along a sweet path, which is the path of love. And then the heart will be softened and melted in delight of God's love. But we must persevere to the end through the initial process of uncovering our hardness of heart and odious corruption. And the more we realize this reality, the more we will experience the redeeming power of Christ; for since he came to save sinners, and indeed those who acknowledge their corruption, he will also give us rest under his yoke. I earnestly hope that you will experience these things at the time God chooses.

P.S.

With your father you must act in sincere submission and obedience in those things which are not contrary to your conscience. But since you do not mention any particular circumstances that might make this or that seem right to you, I cannot give you any further advice. Truly we must never do or consent to anything that is contrary to God. For the love of our neighbor is subject to the love of God.

No. 146

A. W. Böhme to Monsieur Williams
London, 1 November 1720

You do well never to trust your own heart and to remain suspicious of the manifold stirrings within it. For we carry the greatest deceiver in our own bosom, who is always ready to lead us into manifold delusions and falsehoods, which are rampant everywhere, even in matters of the greatest importance that concern our eternal salvation. I am very pleased that you are beginning to discover the disordered movements of your heart and its evil dispositions toward the world. In truth, this work is done by the grace of God through the action of His Holy Spirit, which you should receive with the deepest gratitude. A true sense of the absence of God's grace is indeed an effect of the very grace we long to enjoy. The evil spirit, the greatest enemy of our souls, is not at all interested in letting us know too much about ourselves, for fear that we might escape his cruel service and surrender to the guidance of a better master. That is why he tries to cover over our bad habits, to diminish them, to hide them from us, and to portray them only as minor faults or as small blemishes that can easily be wiped away. On the other hand, when the gracious Spirit of God begins working in the soul, He removes these veils that hang before our eyes and prevent us from receiving a true understanding of the corrupt state of our heart and of the real defilements that flow from this poisoned well.

But these realizations happen step by step. At first, we see only a little of our spiritual poverty, but as we strive to purify ourselves of that which might hinder our growth, we daily receive greater light, and finally reach the point where we learn to discern not only the defilements of the flesh, but also the inward defilements of the spirit. And I was willing to touch on this here because you are beginning to see the dearth of grace that we all lack by nature. Be heartily grateful for this beginning. The same God who shows you your lack will also supply it. This self-knowledge should make you poor in spirit, so that you may become rich in grace. It should make you weary and burdened, so that you may learn all the better to savor Christ, the author of our salvation. It should make you lowly in your own eyes, so that you may more deeply embrace Christ in his sufficiency. If only you are faithful with what you have, you will get more in time and will have abundance. Hardness of heart is certainly a work of Satan, but awareness of this hardness is a gift of God, who is both able and willing to remove it. To whose gracious care I commend your soul . . .

P.S.

I cannot now mention anything about the duty of prayer. But you will find this subject in Arndt's *True Christianity* and especially in the latter sections.

No. 147

A. W. Böhme to Monsieur Williams
N.p., [1720]

The penitent woman of Luke 7 gives us a vivid image of the contrite heart and spiritual sorrow that precedes a justifying faith and prepares a person for an extraordinary blessing. She had an exceedingly great sense both of the righteousness of God that condemned her and of the grace of Christ that swiftly sustained her after she had been utterly crushed by fear and sorrow over her prior transgression. We must not assume that such a great change occurred in her suddenly at one time, since God's way is to carry on His work through many stages of trials and difficulties. Doubtless the gracious Spirit of God had prepared her beforehand to receive the consolation of the gospel, which poured into her heart so abundantly as she drew nearer to Christ. We can be sure that the deeper we sink into a sense of our own misery, the more we are lifted up to a sense of God's love and goodness. But we must not tear ourselves away from the preparatory works of the law before it is time, lest we hinder our growth in the life of grace through premature effort and action. How often has God knocked at the door of our heart, so that He might be let in and delight us with his gracious presence. And why should we grow weary of asking, seeking, and knocking, since we are all beggars at the door of His grace and can do nothing without Him? We have the promise that the door will be opened to us and our soul will be admitted to the throne of grace. For after God has humbled us and stripped us entirely of all false pretenses, He will then clothe us again with garments of righteousness.

And then we will set foot on the consoling footpath of the promises of the gospel. We must not doubt the hour that will surely follow, in which we will find rest for our souls. And just as God's gracious Spirit will pour His love into our hearts (Rom 5:5), so we must entrust to Him the time and hour when it will please Him to delight us with the sweet enjoyment of His love. Nevertheless, when we feel some spiritual consolation rising in our hearts, we must apply all these crumbs of consolation to a greater measure of humility, patience, and surrender to the divine will, and be willing and ready to forego any consolation we have received, if the supreme giver of all our joy should deem it more beneficial to our souls. The most certain legacy that our Savior has left us is the daily cross. And this cross is not forced on us, but we are to take it upon ourselves voluntarily, and embrace it as a singular sign of His grace, and entrust our joy to that world where we shall enjoy it in undefiled purity, since here we are in danger of defiling it with the sin that always clings to us and makes us lethargic. With this, I commend you to the all-wise guidance of our blessed Savior.

P.S.

The use of a good prayerbook does not hinder the ministry of the Holy Spirit in any way (as some have indeed tried to teach you), since the Spirit of God Himself is the author of all spiritual prayer, both in us and in others. Thus, how can the Spirit of God be against the use of His own gifts? Even so, I can use the gift of another to awaken the same gift in me. Johann Arndt's *The Garden of Paradise* contains several prayers which have been and continue to be of great benefit to many souls.[12]

---

12. Arndt, *Garden of Paradise*.

No. 148

A. W. Böhme to Monsieur Williams
London, 9 December 1720

I do not remember a single word in my letter that should have given you occasion to think that your correspondence was burdensome to me, for it is not. It is no small satisfaction for me to be able to impart the slightest good to a soul that unashamedly seeks the knowledge of the truth, and indeed at a time when the paths to Zion do not appear to be paved, and the number of those who walk on them has grown ever smaller. I always read your letters with pleasure, but I cannot promise you an answer the next day; however, you may well expect it the next week, as soon as I can spare an hour to answer your queries, and especially when I realize that my little experience in the ways of God will be of some benefit to you in furthering the eternal welfare of your soul.

No. 149

A. W. Böhme to Monsieur Williams
London, 24 December 1720

When we feel our failures and the manifold temptations to commit former sins, it should indeed constrain us and drive us to an unfeigned repentance, which is the daily cross and discipline of those who decide to live a Christian life. The devil tempts us to sin, but the object of his hellish arrows resides in our own breast, giving us the opportunity for humility and repentance every day. This is the inherited cause of our corruption, which ceaselessly stirs up all kinds of disorderly desires, and is ready to break out into any number of worldly deeds, were they not restrained by a higher and mightier hand. However, the more this sin is busy tempting us, the more the grace of God will powerfully protect us, if only we ask, seek, and knock. We must completely despair of our own natural abilities, so that the power of Christ may be manifested gloriously in our weakness, which will unfailingly happen if we only continue steadfastly in the work to which we have been called. We are tempted in many ways at the beginning of our conversion; many begin to respond to the invitations of grace, but many falter and regress as soon as their faithfulness is tested by inward and outward temptations. In this way, many a conversion gets stuck and is fruitless because it does not faithfully endure the trials that divine providence sends us. But here we should bear in mind that none of our spiritual gifts of grace can grow significantly without manifold trials, by which they are made mature, as it were, and secure a divine goodness. This consideration will sweeten all God's chastisements and make the way of the cross more and more bearable. For this cross is what must differentiate a true disciple of Christ from a haughty person of the world. If you take up this cross joyfully, in time it will produce a priceless effect that you will never regret.

No. 150

A. W. Böhme to Dr. Isaac Watts[13]
London, 9 August 1721

Thank you very much for the thoughtful letter you were kind enough to send me, and for the undeserved expression of gratitude for the several small printed gifts I gave you. Thank you for the various similar items you sent me, and especially for the volume of sermons that I have been reading with an inward delight.[14] I am planning to take the last one about prayer into the country with me. I hold in high regard those books that set forth Jesus Christ and the order of salvation established by Him, that is, those books that derive the whole of religion, its roots, fibers, branches, etc., from Christ, the true and proper foundation. If ever it has been necessary to restore fundamental Christian truths, in the midst of so-called Christians, it is truly ours, since worldly and Christian principles are so woefully interwoven and mixed, and the author of our religion is so often set aside and forgotten.

I am glad that you enjoyed *Enchiridion Precum*, and even to such a degree that I have rarely seen before. Some members of the Church of England have commended the prayers and expressed their appreciation, but have not mentioned the Introduction at all. You understand my

---

13. Isaac Watts (1674–1748), renowned dissenting minister, theologian, correspondent, poet, and hymn writer.

14. Watts, *Sermons on Various Subjects*.

meaning quite well when you say: I try to find a true middle road with regard to prescribed prayer forms. I know that some parties or sects, especially the smaller ones that have only arisen within the last few years, originated primarily in extremes. For, imagining that they were trying to improve matters and to avoid one extreme, they have unwittingly slipped into a different one; and having thus gone too far, they have unfortunately given rise to new forms of religion, and have increased the number of sects, instead of reducing them. I thank God that I am above the fog in this matter, and thus can see the aberrations of those who are still in it.

Whether the *Enchiridion* will one day be translated into English, as you kindly suggest, I cannot say. The usual translators of various newspapers, or of other books and materials that have little to offer, are generally not very good at translating spiritual books, unless they themselves have a taste for the things they are translating. And so, I commend you to the care of our Father's providence, who will graciously watch over you in the midst of your bodily infirmity, and I remain your friend and co-worker.

[Original editor's note:] The esteemed Watts took the opportunity to use this letter for the dialogue he included in his miscellaneous thoughts, in which he describes two stubborn leaders who cling to their opinions: one zealously defends the liturgical form of the Church of England, and the other zealously upholds the Presbyterian form of extemporaneous prayer from the heart.[15] In the midst of these zealous quarrelers he introduces the impartial Boehm, who juxtaposes the good arguments of both parties as well as their flaws, and shows where both are right and also wrong. He therefore admonishes them to avoid the extremes of partisanship, because the blessed Holy Spirit, who cannot contradict Himself and is the author of true prayer, can use and still uses daily forms of prayer other than those flowing from the heart to further His kingdom. Therefore, neither party has reason to take offense at the other, but rather should allow the Author of our true life the freedom to decide how and in what way He wants to edify souls. By such an authoritative account, he encouraged both parties not only to abandon their previous stubborn opinions, but also to pass judgment more leniently, and to better use and practice both those forms of prayer penned by other spiritual writers and the prayers flowing from the heart through the good Spirit of God in the fear of the Lord. Praise be to the Lord for every glimpse of His revealed truth, and may He teach us all to pray aright!

15. "Sect. II. Of Forms of Prayer, of Free or Conceived Prayer, and Praying Extempore," in Watts, *Guide to Prayer*.

No. 151

A. W. Böhme to Mr. B.
N.p., [1721]

I hear that you are happily continuing in the condition in which God's providence has placed you. It is certainly true that a Christian's pleasure should not be derived from any other cause than the testimony of a good conscience, and this can be called good when we fulfill both the main purpose of our creation and our particular vocation. Since the supreme Steward of our persons and gifts will not reward us according to our office and status, but according to the faithfulness with which we have stewarded our office, we therefore have good reason to take good heed of this part of our Christian life. For this faithfulness is the crown of all our efforts, and should flow through our whole life and its conduct. Therefore, take great pleasure in cultivating this principal virtue when instructing the youth entrusted to your care. Wherever a common love between teachers and students is built on a solid foundation, God has a hand in it. For just as a method that is solely rooted in the law tends only to embitter hearts and draw them away from the One who is love itself, so, on the other hand, a method rooted in the gospel reassures hearts and conforms them to their divine Origin, as the infallible precept of our life and conduct. May the Lord make us increasingly aware of His holy will and, through His gracious support, make us capable of carrying it out.

P.S.

Since your native country borders Estonia, I should inform you of a recent initiative: I have been asked to raise some money for printing a Bible in the Estonian language for the benefit of the poor who are in need of this spiritual food; some well-meaning students have actually begun to produce it, and have reached the Gospel of Luke, but are unable to continue for lack of funds. I have translated the proposal into English and shown it to a few people, but I doubt if I will be able to provide any help, since we live in a time when love has become very cold. Farewell...

Extract of a letter [by Johann Bernhard van Dieren] sent from New York, the capital of the North American territory of New York, to the author, dated 26 May 1721[16]

Last May I went from the city of New York to the region of Schoharie with the books I had with me. It is located 180 English miles from New York in the wilderness, isolated from all other people. I thought it would be most needed there, since others who are near New York have already received books; but since they are remote and isolated, no one has taken the trouble to bring them some books. So, with God's help, I set out to bring them the books, and I also gave them spiritual resources that the gracious God has given me.

The people had written that they wanted me to preach the Word of God to them, without knowing whether I was a teacher nor what they should make of me. This winter two men from Schoharie saw me working at my craft in New York, and afterward they told the people that I was a tailor, although my manner was unusual, and it seemed that I was a priest in the guise of a tailor. Therefore, they came with one accord—two hundred people old and young—to hear the tailor preach. I, poor worm, did not know a single word of what I should say to the people; I should and had to preach, even though I had not studied for preaching. I will omit here what the old Adam thought. But the devil laughed and asked me: "Where is your God now?" I answered by the power of God that he would soon know. I went into the assembly in the power of the Lord Jesus, who, by His all-sufficiency, unlocked the mysteries of His knowledge on 2 Corinthians 5:20–21, the text that the Most High God Himself provided.

After the sermon was over, I witnessed in others the power of God, which I myself had also felt. There were people present who had previously been living in great anger and discord; but when they came away

---

16. Almost certainly Johann Bernhard van Dieren (d. ca. 1753). Muhlenberg, *Journals of Muhlenberg*, 1:237 (February 1750), wrote that van Dören [Dieren], "a tailor by profession, was sent with good intentions, to the province of New York by the late Court Preacher Böhm, who gave him books to take along. The man's awakened condition, his edifying speech, the high regard in which the Germans held Court Preacher Böhm, the lack of preachers, the free American air, and the man's inner desire and aspiration to attain to the difficult office of the ministry—all these things worked together to foster a desire that he should be ordained." Whether van Dieren was actually ever *officially* ordained is unclear. Scholars are divided over his legacy in American religious history. Williams, *Journey of Justus Falckner*, 75–79; Jacobsen, "Johann Bernhard van Dieren."

from the sermon, they fell on each other's necks and with tears begged for forgiveness. Some even came to me, praising God that by His word He had bestowed such power, not only on their hearts, but also on the hearts of others who had gone home weeping, people who themselves had been quite spiteful and whom they had never before seen weeping. Oh, how can I thank the Lord for all His benefits!

I can also say that I have preached several times since then in Schoharie, solely by the power of God; and He who does not let His word be proclaimed by the wisdom of the world has put His word into my mouth, even though I have difficulty speaking. Now the people of Schoharie, namely the whole Lutheran community around here, have asked me, for the sake of the eternal love of God and the blood of Christ, to remain with them and teach them the way of Christ, which I can in no way refuse them. Indeed, I told them that I was not a preacher, but a tailor, and that, because I was 180 miles from the city, I could not practice my trade, which would be my intent in order to serve them voluntarily and free of charge. But nothing I said could change their minds: the whole congregation promised to give me a salary from their meager means. They have also said that they want to lead better lives from now on, with God's help. I hope that God will accomplish everything according to His holy will, so that it may be to His divine honor.

I delivered all the books that were given to me.[17] At Schoharie I distributed one hundred copies of *True Christianity* and twenty-four prayer books. I also left two copies of Philipp J. Spener's book of sermons for a congregation that did not have a single book.[18] At Löbesteinland I left August H. Francke's book of sermons in two parts.[19] I also left one part of Dr. Francke's sermons for the congregation in Denderhofe, which did not have a book. The other part I gave to a family in Königslande, and to another large family I gave a copy of Dr. Spener's sermons. Another copy of Dr. Spener's sermons I gave to the silver mine in New England, where there are many Germans and they have neither a book nor a preacher. They have promised me to be more diligent in encouraging one another to listen to the divine Word.

---

17. In a letter to A. H. Francke, Leipzig, 9 Oct 1721 (AFSt/H A 175:160), Heinrich Julius Elers describes the large number of Bibles and devotional books that the Halle bookshop had sent to America with van Dieren.

18. Likely the first volume of Spener, *Lauterkeit Des Evangelischen Christenthums*.

19. Francke, *Buß-Predigten*.

The other prayer books have been handed out at your request. The short sermons have also been delivered. I sold three small Bibles in New York, and gave one away. I borrowed the English books I found in the chest to read. In summary, with God's help, I have distributed and delivered everything well. God grant that many souls may be won through this. I am enclosing a list of books that the people in each village want for their own use.

No. 152

A. W. Böhme to Johann Bernhard van Dieren in New York in America
N.p., n.d.

I have duly received the letter from May, in which you reported the events that happened to you in the region of Schoharie. It was very gratifying to me to hear that the books that were entrusted to you were received here and there with such eagerness, and that many more are still desired for further edification.

I have actually written to various friends in Germany and presented to them the concern of our Germans in the American provinces; and now I hope that well-meaning people both here and in Germany will make contributions, so that the price of the books will be all the more affordable for our friends in New York. I will be glad if I can play a part in furthering edification among them, and in helping to build the kingdom of God in the West Indian wilderness.

The good movement that was evident in many people at his arrival in Schoharie shows us the finger of God, which pursues souls in all corners and in every wilderness, to save from corruption those who still want to be saved. We have every reason to beseech the Lord to nourish and multiply such mustard seeds with a constant influx of His grace, so that in time they may grow into a great tree. In the meantime, we must not put too much trust in such a first movement, but see if it will last. I fear that with some people, their seemingly good desire was nothing more than a curiosity; although with others, and I hope with many, it may have flowed from an inner hunger. For since they hear few sermons in such a remote wilderness and have not previously been able to have a proper preacher, a hunger has clearly arisen in many due to such a great lack of good teaching. Whether this was a pure hunger for the Word of God or only due to the habit of hearing a sermon, time will tell.

I will admit that when you told me of you desire to travel to the West Indies, I had not the least thought that you would serve as a preacher among our fellow compatriots, but only that you might foster the salvation of their souls by establishing a school and through edifying fellowship. But if the all-wise God should intend otherwise and appoint you a preacher instead of a schoolmaster, I hope that he will confer upon you the necessary gifts from above, that you may be a burning and shining light among them, as it is written of John the Baptist, who also preached in the wilderness and prepared the way for Christ (John 5:35). I am also very glad that you have not in the least forced yourself on them, but allowed yourself to be called and persuaded by them; for in such circumstances, it is worthwhile to consider the apostle's reminder in James 3:1. Friends here now very much want to know if your ordination is still moving forward, for in your letter you report only that the congregation has unanimously desired you as a preacher, but that you have not yet been ordained.

But whether or not the matter is moving forward, you should be confident and not lose heart; you can still serve the Lord God and edify your neighbor. You might recall the meetings you had here in London on Sunday evenings with some young people, which were not without blessing and which continued after your departure. It may be that the preachers there have reservations about ordaining you and presenting you to the congregation as a proper preacher. Perhaps they have important reasons that prevent them from doing so under the present circumstances. Whatever happens, may you accept everything and submit to God's will with childlike equanimity, and everything will work out for the best. Nor should you in any way oppose the local ministers if they should refuse to allow you a preaching ministry. You can then assume that it was not God's will to use you in this way.

As for myself, I readily confess that I would have no hesitation in appointing a pious artisan, experienced in the Scriptures, to a public teaching position; indeed, I would prefer him to all those scholars who have experienced little of a true conversion of heart. There are also various examples of those who, though not having studied academically, have not only been recognized by others as distinguished teachers, but have also worked with great blessing. You yourself may have heard of the English teacher John Bunyan and the edifying books he wrote. He was an ordinary craftsman who nevertheless won many souls for the Lord Christ through his sermons and writings. His tract, *Pilgrim's Progress, or a Christian's journey to blessed eternity*, has been translated into French, High German, and Low German, and has to date been read with considerable edification.[20] It was one of the first books through which God worked on my heart and persuaded me of the nature of a living Christianity. And, if necessary, I could cite several such examples of unstudied men who have served as teachers.

Such examples can serve to encourage you to use the gift you have received with confidence in the name of the Lord, whether in public office or in your private life and affairs, and to let your light shine in the American wilderness, being assured that in his time God will shine His truth on that region as well. Your friends here wish you many blessings. Others who hear about such a good movement will not fail to beseech the Lord for constant growth; meanwhile, may you seek to fortify yourself more and more in the poverty of the Spirit and the humility of Christ. Every profession has its special trials, and every new way of life gives birth to new temptations. Humility and lowliness of mind form the best fortress in which we can be safe and guard against the dangerous courses of evil.

Perhaps the Lord will provide you with one or several good friends there, so that you can join with others and work together in unity. If in time I can send you one or two others from here to help you gather in the American net, it will be my pleasure. There is a package of books arriving on this ship, along with several Bibles that I had on hand; the others will follow as soon as I can collect them from Germany. You can serve Lutherans and Reformed, who desire the books irrespective of their differences, and can thereby help to promote edification throughout the region. Of all the books that come into your hands, you can keep a few copies with you to lend them to those who have no books at all, even if they do not have the means to buy any.

---

20. Bunyan, *Pilgrim's Progress*.

Bibliography (Pre-1800)

Abbadie, Jacque. *A Vindication of the Truth of Christian Religion Against the Objections of All Modern Opposers.* Translated by Henry Lussan. London, 1694.

———. *A Vindication of the Truth of Christian Religion, Against the Objections of All Modern Opposers. Part II.* Translated by Henry Lussan. London, 1698.

"An Abstract of the Kings Instructions to the College, or Incorporated Society." In *A Brief Account of the Measures Taken in Denmark, for the Conversion of the Heathen in the East-Indies,* edited by A. W. Böhme, 7–18. London, 1715.

Alleine, Joseph. *An Alarm to Unconverted Sinners. In a Serious Treatise: Shewing, I. What Conversion Is Not, and Correcting Some Mistakes About It. II. What Conversation Is, and Wherein It Consisteth. III. The Necessity of Conversion. IV. The Marks of the Unconverted. V. The Miseries of the Unconverted. VI. Directions for Conversion. VII. Motives to Conversion. Whereunto Are Annexed Divers Practical Cases of Conscience Judiciously Resolved.* London, 1703.

Allut, Jean, et al. *Plan de la justice de Dieux sur la terre, dans ces derniers jours, et de relèvement de la chute de l'homme par son péché.* N.p., 1714.

———. *Quand vous aurez saccagé, vous serez saccagés: car la lumière est apparue dans les ténèbres, pour les détruire.* N.p., 1714.

Arndt, Johann. *The Garden of Paradise or, Holy Prayers and Exercises; Whereby the Christian Graces and Virtues May Be Planted and Improved in Man, the Divine Image Renew'd, True Christianity Promoted, the Kingdom of God Established, and a Heavenly Life Raised up in the Spirit.* Translated by Anton W. Böhme. London, 1716.

———. *De vero Christianismo libri quatuor ob præstantiam suam olim latine redditi. Nunc autem revisi ac emendati, cura et studio Antonii Wilhelmi Boemi. Accedit huic editioni nova præfatio de vita et scriptis Arndtianis.* London, 1708.

Arnold, Gottfried, ed. "Das Leben des vortrefflichen Dieners Jesu Christi, Hn. Joseph Allein, weyland Predigers bey dere Kirchen zu Taunton in der Grafschaft Tomersetshire in England." In *Das Leben der Gläubigen: Oder Beschreibung solcher Gottseligen Personen, welche in denen letzten 200. Jahren sonderlich bekandt worden,* 708–26. Halle, 1701.

Barrow, Isaac. *The Works of the Learned Isaac Barrow, DD, Late Master of Trinity-College in Cambridge.* 3 vols. London, 1716.

Baxter, Richard. *The Certainty of the Worlds of Spirits: Fully Evinced by the Unquestionable Histories of Apparitions, Operations, Witchcrafts, Voices, &c. Proving the Immortality of Souls, the Malice and Misery of the Devils, and the Damned, and the Blessedness of the Justified.* London, 1691.

BIBLIOGRAPHY (PRE-1800)

———. *Gildas Salvianus; The Reformed Pastor.* London, 1656.

———. *Reliquiæ Baxterianæ, or, Mr. Richard Baxters Narrative of the Most Memorable Passages of His Life and Times. Faithfully Publish'd from His Own Original Manuscript.* Edited by Matthew Sylvester. London, 1696.

———. *Wehkomaonganoo asquam peantogig kah asquam quinnuppegig, tokonogque mahche woskeche peantamwog. Onk woh sampwutteahae peantamwog. Wutanakausuonk wunneetou noh nohtompeantog.* Translated by John Eliot. Cambridge, MA, 1688.

Baxter, Richard, et al. *The Life and Death of That Excellent Minister of Christ Mr. Joseph Alleine.* London, 1822.

Bayly, Lewis. *Manitowompae Pomantamoonk: Sampwshanau Christianoh Uttoh woh an Pomantog Wnssikkitteahonat [sic] God.* Translated by John Eliot. Cambridge, MA, 1686.

———. *The Practise of Pietie Directing a Christian How to Walke that He May Please God.* 3rd ed. London, 1613.

Bernier, François. *Histoire de la derniere revolution des Etats du Grand Mogol.* La Haye, 1671.

Blackmore, Richard. *Letters Between Theophilus and Eugenio, on the Moral Pravity of Man, and the Means of His Restoration. Wrote in the East-Indies, and Now First Published from the Original Manuscript.* Edited by Benjamin Franklin. Philadelphia, 1747.

Böhme, Anton Wilhelm. *Acht Bücher von der Reformation der Kirche in England: und was von dem 1526ten Jahre an, unter Henrico VIII. und folgenden Königen bis zu Caroli II. Regierung bey derselben merckwürdiges sich zugetragen. Jetzo zuerst and Licht gegeben.* Preface by Johann Albert Fabricius. Altona, 1734.

———. *Enchiridion precum: ad promovendum solidioris pietatis studium collectum. Cum introductione, de natura orationis.* London, 1707.

———. *The Faithful Steward Set Forth in a Sermon Preach'd at St. James's, the Third Day of Feb. 1712. On Occasion of the Funeral of Mr. Hen. Will. Ludolf. . . . Dedicated to the Honourable Society for Promoting Christian Knowledge.* London, 1712.

———, ed. *Ein Gebeth-Büchlein: theils aus der englischen Liturgie, theils aus andern geistreichen Gebeth-Büchern zusammengetragen; und zum Gebrauch der Capelle Ihrer Konigl. Hoheit, Printz Georgens von Danemarck, eingerichtet.* London, 1707.

———. *The Life of a Christian: A Sermon on the Occasion of the Death of His Royal Highness Prince George of Denmark.* London, 1709.

———. *Sämtliche erbauliche Schriften: anfänglich eintzeln, nunmehr aber zusammen, Theils in Teutscher, Theils in englischer Sprache, aus welcher sie mit Fleiss in Teutsche übersetzet worden.* Translated and Preface by Johann Jacob Rambach. Altona, 1731–33.

———. *Several Discourses and Tracts for Promoting the Common Interest of True Christianity.* London, 1717.

———. *Universal Love the Surest Way to Advance the Interest of Religion, and Unite the Several Contending Parties About It.* London, 1709.

———. *Das verlangte nicht erlangte Canaan bey den Lust-Gräbern, oder, Ausführliche Beschreibung von der unglücklichen Reise: derer jüngsthin aus Teutschland nach dem Engelländischen in America gelegenen Carolina und Pensylvanien wallenden Pilgrim: absonderlich dem einseitigen übelgegründeten Kochenthalerischen Bericht wohlbedächtig entgegen gesetzt.* London, 1711.

BIBLIOGRAPHY (PRE-1800)

———. *Der Wahre und Falsche Christ: In einer Predigt am Sonntage Rogate 1711. aufs 2 Tim. III. 5.* London, 1715.

Böhme, Jacob. *Der für die Einfältigen epitomirte, nicht tunckel, sondern klar und deutlich, redende hocherleuchtete Jacob Böhme: Oder Seraphinisch Blumen-Gärtlein.* Amsterdam, 1700.

Bona, Giovanni. *Manuductio ad coelum: Medullam continens sanctorum patrum & veterum philosophorum.* Munich, 1663.

Brett, Thomas. *An Enquiry into the Judgment and Practice of the Primitive Church, in Relation to Persons Being Baptized by Lay-men.* London, 1713.

———. *The Extent of Christ's Commission to Baptize: A Sermon Shewing the Capacity of Infants to Receive, and the Utter Incapacity of Our Dissenting Teachers to Administer Christian Baptism.* London, 1712.

———. *A Further Enquiry into the Judgment and Practice of the Primitive Church, in Relation to Persons Being Baptized by Lay-men.* London, 1714.

———. *A Review of the Lutheran Principles; Shewing, How They Differ from the Church of England, and That Baron Puffendorf's Essay for Uniting of Protestants, Was Not Design'd to Procure an Union Between the Lutherans and the Church of England.* London, 1714.

———. *A Review of the Lutheran Principles.... The Second Edition. To Which Is Added, a Postscript, Containing Some Transient Remarks on a Late Virulent Pamphlet, Entituled, Two Letters to the Right Honourable the Lord Viscount Townsend, &c.* London, 1714.

Bromley, Thomas. "On the Necessity of Mortification and Self Denial." Excerpted from: "An Account of the various Ways of God's Manifesting Himself to Man. With Observations on those Dispensations call'd Extraording." N.p., n.d. *PasstheWORD*, Dec. 25, 2017. http://www.passtheword.org/gospel-rediscovery/bromley-selfdenial.htm.

———. *The Way to the Sabbath of Rest; or, the Souls Progresse in the Work of Regeneration. By a Lover of Truth, and a Member of the True Church.* London, 1655.

———. *The Way to the Sabbath of Rest or the Soul's Progress in the Work of the New-Birth to which Are Now Added, Two Discourses of the Author.... The Journeys of the Children of Israel, as in Their Names and Historical Passages, They Comprise the Great and Gradual Work of Regeneration. and a Treatise of Extraordinary Divine Dispensations, Under the Jewish and Gospel Administrations.* London, 1710.

———. *Der Weg zum Sabbat der Ruhe oder der Seele Fortgang in der neuen Geburt.* Amsterdam, 1709.

Browne, Thomas. *Pseudodoxia Epidemica, or, Enquiries into Very Many Received Tenents and Commonly Presumed Truths.* London, 1646.

Bulkeley, Richard. *An Answer to Several Treatises Lately Publish'd on the Subject of the Prophets. The First Part.* London, 1708.

———. *An Impartial Account of the Prophets: In a Letter to a Friend.* London, 1707.

Bunyan, John. *The Pilgrim's Progress from This World, to That Which Is to Come Delivered Under the Similitude of a Dream, Wherein Is Discovered the Manner of His Setting Out, His Dangerous Journey, and Safe Arrival at the Desired Country.* 2nd ed. London, 1678.

———. *The Works of That Eminent Servant of Christ, Mr. John Bunyan, Late Minister of the Gospel and Pastor of the Congregation at Bedford Containing Ten of His Excellent*

BIBLIOGRAPHY (PRE-1800)

Manuscripts Prepared for the Press before His Death, Never Before Printed, and Ten of His Choyce Books Formerly Printed. London, 1692.

Burnet, Gilbert. *An Answer to Some Exceptions in Bishop Burnet's Third Part of the History of the Reformation, &c. Against Mr. Collier's Ecclesiastical History.* London, 1715.

———. *A Collection of Sermons Preached by the Right Reverend Dr. Gilbert Burnet, Lord Bishop of Sarum.* London, 1704.

———. *A Discourse of the Pastoral Care, the Third Edition, with a New Preface Suited to the Present Time; and Some Other Additions.* London, 1713.

Canstein, Carl Hildebrand von. *Das Muster Eines rechtschaffenen Lehrers In der erbaulichen Lebens-Beschreibung Des Um die gantze Evangelische Kirche hochverdienten Theologi, D. Phil. Jacob Speners, Kön. Preuß. und Chur-Brand. Consistorial-Raths und Probstes zu Berlin, Von dem seligen Herrn Carl Hildebrand Freyherrn von Canstein Verfasset, und dem letztern Theile der Theologischen Bedencken vorgesetzet: Und Wegen seines ungemeinen Nutzens auf besondere Veranlassung Mit Anmerckungen und angehengtem Lebens-Lauf des gedachten Herrn Barons zum Druck befördert von D. Joachim Langen.* Halle, 1740.

Catherine of Genoa. *Der Göttliche Liebes-Weeg Unter dem Creutz.* Translated by A. W. Böhme. Halle, 1701.

Collier, Jeremy. *An Answer to Some Exceptions in Bishop Burnet's Third Part of the History of the Reformation, &c. Against Mr. Collier's Ecclesiastical History.* London, 1715.

———. *A Defence of the Short View of the Profaneness and Immorality of the English Stage: Being a Reply to Mr. Congreve's Amendments.* London, 1699.

———. *An Ecclesiastical History of Great Britain, Chiefly of England.* 2 vols. London, 1708.

———. *A Short View of the Immorality and Profaneness of the English Stage.* London, 1698.

Comenius, Johann Amos. *Historia fratrum Bohemorum: eorum ordo et disciplina ecclesiastica, ad ecclesiae recte constituendae exemplar, cum Ecclesiae Bohem. ad Anglicanam parænesi. Accedit eiusdem auctoris Panegersia, siue Excitatorium vniuersale.* Halle, 1702.

Congreve, William. *Amendments of Mr. Collier's False and Imperfect Citations.* London, 1698.

Cuninghame, James. *Fifteen Warnings of the Eternal Spirit, Pronounc'd by the Mouth of James Cuninghame, Being Mostly Explications of Scripture.* London, 1712.

Daut, Johannes. *The Approaching Judgments of God Upon the Roman Empire, and Whole False and Impenitent Christendom; with the Fall of Babylon, and the Redemption of Sion.* Translated by Benjamin Furly. London, 1711.

Les Dernières Heures de Monsieur Rivet vivant Docteur et Professeur honoraire en l'Université de Leyden, et Curateur de l'Eschole Illustre, et Collège d'Orange à Bréda. Breda, 1651.

Domini nostri Iesu Christi Testamentum Novum, Turcice redditum. Translated by William Seaman. Oxford, 1666.

Falckner, Justus. *Grondlycke onderricht van sekere voorname hoofd-stucken, der waren loutern, saligmakenden, Christelycken Leere, gegrondet op den grondt van de apostelen en propheten, daer Jesus Christus de hoeck-steen.* New York, 1708.

BIBLIOGRAPHY (PRE-1800)

Flavel, John. *Husbandry Spiritualized or, the Heavenly Use of Earthly Things and Navigation Spiritualized; or a New Compass for Seamen. Together with a Saint Indeed, or the Great Work of a Christian Opened and Pressed. The Touchstone of Sincerity and a Token for Mourners*. London, 1669.

Fleetwood, William. *A Sermon Preached Before the Society for the Propagation of the Gospel in Foreign Parts: At the Parish-Church of St. Mary-Le-Bow, on Friday the 16th of February, 1710/11. Being the Day of Their Anniversary Meeting*. London, 1711.

Francke, August Hermann. *An Abstract of the Marvellous Footsteps of Divine Providence*. Edited and translated by A. W. Böhme. London, 1706.

———. *Buß-Predigten: Darinn Aus verschiedenen Texten H. Schrifft deutlich gezeiget wird, Wie nicht nur Unbekehrte zur wahren Buße gelangen, sondern auch die, so bekehret sind, in täglicher Buße und Gottseligkeit leben und wandeln sollen*. 2 vols. Halle, 1706.

———. *Christus der Kern Heiliger Schrifft Oder einfältige Anweisung, Wie man Christum, als den Kern der gantzen H. Schrifft, recht suchen, finden, schmäcken, und damit seine Seele nähren, sättigen, und zum ewigen Leben erhalten sole, Worinnen vornemlich der Anfang des Evangelii Johannis durch neun unterschiedene Betrachtungen erläutert, und die wahre wesentliche Gottheit unsers Herrn Jesu Christi mit klaren Gründen erwiesen wird*. Halle, 1702.

———. *Jesus Christus als das Licht der Heyden, und der Preiß Israels: Nach Anleitung des Evangel. Textes Luc. II, 22–32. Am Tage der Reinigung Mariä Anno 1714*. Halle, 1723.

———. *Manuductio Ad Lectionem Scripturæ Sacræ. Omnibus Theologiæ Sacræ Cultoribus Commendata, A. Petro Allix, STP Cum Nova Præfatione, De Impedimentis Studii Theologici, Et Appendice, Exhibente Aliquot Ecclesiae Anglicanae Scriptorum Loca, and Illustrationem Opusculi Facientia*. London, 1706.

———. *Pietas Hallensis; or, a Publick Demonstration of the Foot-Steps of a Divine Being Yet in the World: In an Historical Narration of the Orphan-House, and Other Charitable Institutions, at Glaucha near Hall in Saxony. . . . with a Preface Bringing It Down to the Present Time; Together with a Short History of Pietism*. Translated by A. W. Böhme. London, 1705.

———. *Pietas Hallensis; or, an Abstract of the Marvellous Footsteps of Divine Providence, Attending the Management and of the Orphan-House at Glaucha near Hall. . . . Part II. For the Year 1707 and 1708*. Translated and edited by A. W. Böhme. London, 1710.

Gell, Robert. *Aggelokratia Theon or a Sermon Touching Gods Government of the World by Angels: Preached Before the Learned Societie of Artists or Astrologers, August 8. 1650*. London: John Legatt, 1650.

———. *Gell's Remaines, or, Several Select Scriptures of the New Testament Opened and Explained Wherein Jesus Christ, as Yesterday, to Day, and the Same for Ever, Is Illustrated, in Sundry Pious and Learned Notes and Observations Thereupon*. Edited by Robert Bacon. 2 vols. London, 1676.

———. *Stella Nova, a New Starre, Leading Wisemen Unto Christ, or, a Sermon Preached Before the Society of Astrologers*. London, 1649.

The Genuine Epistles of the Apostolical Fathers: S. Barnabas, S. Ignatius, S. Clement, S. Polycarp. . . . Translated and Publish'd, with a Large Preliminary Discourse Relating

BIBLIOGRAPHY (PRE-1800)

to the Several Treatises Here Put Together. Translated and edited by William Wake. 2nd ed. London, 1710.

Goodwin, Thomas. *The Works of Thomas Goodwin, DD, Sometime President of Magdalene Colledge in Oxford*. 5 vols. London, 1681–1704.

Hopkins, Ezekiel. *A Discourse on the Great Duty of Mortification*. London, 1701.

Jäger, Johann Wolfgang. *Historia Ecclesiastica Cum Parallelismo Profanæ: In qua Conclavia Pontificum Romanorum Fideliter Aperiuntur Et Sectæ Omnes Recensentur. . . . Cum Societate Philadelphica Et Novellis Prophetis Sevennensibus Sistuntur*. 2 vols. Hamburg, 1709.

Kempis, Thomas à. *The Christians Pattern; or a Divine Treatise of the Imitation of Christ*. Translated by John Worthington. London, 1663.

———. *The Christian's Pattern: or, a Treatise of the Imitation of Jesus Christ*. Translated by George Stanhope. London, 1708.

Der Königl. Dänischen Missionarien aus Ost-Indien eingesandter ausführlichen Berichten. 9 vols. Halle, 1718–72.

Lacy, John. "A Letter from John Lacy, to Thomas Dutton, Being Reasons Why the Former Left His Wife, and Took E. Gray a Prophetess to His Bed." N.p.

Lange, Joachim. *Medicina Mentis, Quae, Praemissa Historia Mentis Medica, Seu Philosophica, Detectaque Ac Rejecta Philomoria*. London, 1715.

Lead, Jane. *The Heavenly Cloud Now Breaking the Lord Christ's Ascension-Ladder Sent Down to Shew the Way to Reach the Ascension and Glorification Through the Death and Resurrection*. London, 1681.

Ludolf, Heinrich Wilhelm. "Proposal Relating to the Promotion of Religion in the Oriental Churches; Offered in the Year 1700, to the Honourable Society for Propagating [sic] Christian Knowledge." In *Reliquiæ Ludolfianæ: The Pious Remains of Mr. Hen. Will. Ludolf*, 145–52. London, 1712.

———. *Reliquiæ Ludolfianæ: The Pious Remains of Mr. Hen. Will. Ludolf*. Edited by A. W. Böhme. London, 1712.

———. "Will of Henry William Ludolf, Gentleman of Saint Andrew Holborn, Middlesex." National Archives, Kew, March 3, 1712. PROB 11/526/17.

Luther, Martin. *Colloquia Mensalia: or, Dr. Martin Luther's Divine Discourses at His Table*. Edited by Anton Lauterbach and Johann Aurifaber. Translated by Henry Bell. London, 1652.

———. *A Explicaçao da Doutrina Christaã Segundo a Ordem do Catecismo, do B. Luthero*. Tranquebar, 1713.

Macarius. *Primitive Morality: or, the Spiritual Homilies of St. Macarius the Egyptian*. Edited and translated by Thomas Haywood. London, 1721.

Mackenzie, George. *Essays upon Several Moral Subjects: Viz. The Religious Stoic. Solitude Preferr'd to Publick Employment. Moral Gallantry. The Moral History of Frugality: with Its Opposite Vices. An Essay on Reason*. London, 1713.

Mapletoft, John. *Wisdom from Above: or, Considerations Tending to Explain, Establish, and Promote the Christian Life*. London, 1717.

Mather, Cotton. *The Life and Death of the Reverend Mr. John Eliot*. 3rd ed. London, 1694.

———. *Orphanotrophium. or, Orphans Well-Provided for an Essay, on the Care Taken in the Divine Providence for Children When Their Parents Forsake Them. with Proper Advice to Both Parents and Children, That the Care of Heaven May Be the*

More Conspicuously & Comfortably Obtained for Them. Offered in a Sermon, on a Day of Prayer, Kept with a Religious Family (28 Jan 1711). Boston, 1711.
Neander, Joachim. *Glaub und Liebes Ubung Aufgemuntert Durch Einfältige Bundes Lieder Und Danck Psalmen*. Bremen, 1680.
Nelson, Robert. *The Practice of True Devotion, in Relation to the End, as Well as the Means of Religion; with an Office for the Holy Communion; the Third Edition corrected to Which Is Added, the Character of the Author*. London, 1716.
Ners, Peter Anthony Delon Seigneur de. "Will of Peter Anthony Delon Seigneur of Ners or de Ners of New Windsor, Berkshire." National Archives, Kew, February 7, 1752. PROB 11/792/302.
Ostervald, Jean Frédéric. *The Arguments of the Books and Chapters of the Old (and New) Testament, with Practical Observations*. Translated by John Chamberlayne. London, 1716.
Peirce, James. *A Caveat Against the New Sect of Anabaptists, Lately Sprung Up at Exon*. London, 1714.
Piety and Bounty of the Queen of Great Britain. London, 1709.
Poole, Matthew. *Synopsis criticorum aliorumque Sacrae Scripturae interpretum et commentatorum*. 5 vols. Frankfurt am Main, 1694.
Propagation of the Gospel in the East: Being a Farther Account of the Success of the Danish Missionaries, Sent to the East-Indies, for the Conversion of the Heathens in Malabar. Translated and Preface by Anton Wilhelm Böhme. London, 1714.
Pufendorf, Samuel von. *The Divine Feudal Law: or, Covenants with Mankind, Represented. Together with Means for the Uniting of Protestants*. Translated by Theophilus Dorrington. London, 1703.
Quesnel, Pasquier. *Explication Apologétique Des Sentimens Du Père Quesnel Dans Ses Reflexions Sur Le Nouveau Testament*. N.p., 1712.
———. *Le Nouveau Testament en françois, avec des reflexions morales sur chaque verset, pour en rendre la lecture plus utile, & la meditation plus aisée*. Paris, 1699.
Rambach, Johann Jacob. *Memoirs of the Life and Death of the Late Reverend Mr. Anthony William Boehm*. Translated by J. C. Jacobi. London, 1735.
Robinson, John. *The Benefits and Duty of the Members of Christ's Kingdom. a Sermon Preach'd in the Parish-Church of St. Sepulchre, May 20. MDCCXIV . . . at the Anniversary Meeting of the Children Educated in the Charity-Schools, in and About the Cities of London and Westminster*. London, 1714.
Rosenroth, Christian Knorr von. *Neuer Helicon mit seinem neun Musen. Das ist: Geistliche Sitten-Lieder, von Erkäntnisz der wahren Glückseligkeit*. Nürnberg, 1684.
Rous, Francis. *Mella patrum: Nempe, omnium, quorum per prima nascentis & patientis Ecclesiæ tria secula, usque ad pacem sub Constantino divinitùs datam, scripta prodierunt, atque adhuc minus dubiæ fidei supersunt*. London, 1650.
Rules and Orders for a Charitable Society, Set Up by some Germans at London in the Year MDCCXII. London, 1713.
Sacheverell, Henry. *The Communication of Sin: A Sermon Preach'd at the Assizes Held at Derby, August 15th, 1709*. London, 1709.
———. *The Perils of False Brethren Both in Church and State: Set Forth in a Sermon, Preach'd . . . on the 5th of November, 1709*. London, 1709.
Seneca, Lucius Annaeus. *Tomus primus continens opuscula moralia*. N.p., 1713.
Sentimens désintéressez de divers théologiens Protestans; sur les agitations, et sur les autres particularitez de l'état des Prophetes. London, 1710.

BIBLIOGRAPHY (PRE-1800)

A Short Account of the Many Extraordinary Mercies . . . Conferred upon Franciscus Bellisomus. N.p., 1712.

Society for the Propagation of the Gospel (SPG). "20 December 1706." *Lambeth Palace Library.* https://archives.lambethpalacelibrary.org.uk/CalmView/Record.aspx?src=CalmView.Catalog&id=SPG%2f1&pos=1.

———. "No. 85: Frideni [Friedrich] Bonet to Secretary, Suffolk St., 9 December 1706." *Lambeth Palace Library.* https://archives.lambethpalacelibrary.org.uk/CalmView/Record.aspx?src=CalmView.Catalog&id=SPG%2f9&pos=2.

———. "Nos. 195–96: Account of Lubomirsky [not Lubominsky]." *Lambeth Palace Library.* https://archives.lambethpalacelibrary.org.uk/CalmView/Record.aspx?src=CalmView.Catalog&id=SPG%2f9&pos=2.

Spener, Philipp Jakob. *Catechismus-Tabellen: Darinnen der gantze Catechismus D. Martin Luthers Deutlich und gründlich erkläret, aber auch zugleich Der Kern der Gottesgelehrsamkeit erbaulich vorgestellet wird, Aus dem Lateinischen ins Teutsche getreulich übersetzet, und mit einigen Einleitungs-Tabellen Vermehret.* Edited by Johann Georg Pritius. Frankfurt, 1713.

———. *Das Geistliche Priesterthum, Auß Göttlichem Wort Kürtzlich beschrieben, und mit einstimmenden Zeugnüssen Gottseliger Lehrer bekräfftiget.* Frankfurt, 1677.

———. *Gerechter Eifer wider das antichristische Pabstthum, welchen er bey unterschiedlicher Gelegenheit in seinen Predigten und sonst gezeiget.* Edited and Introduction by Johann Georg Pritius. Frankfurt, 1713.

———. *Lauterkeit Des Evangelischen Christenthums: In auserlesenen Predigten, verfasset, So von demselben an verschiedenen Orten, als Franckfurt am Mayn, Dreßden, Berlin und anderswo Uber die ordentlichen Sonn- und Fest-Tags-Evanglia . . . gehalten.* 2 vols. Halle, 1706–9.

———. *Natur und Gnade, Oder der Unterscheid der Wercke, so aus natürlichen kräfften und aus den gnaden-würckungen des H. Geistes herkommmen und also eines eusserlich erbarn und warhafftig Christlichen gottseligen lebens nach der regel Göttlichen Worts einfältig aber gründlich Untersucht.* Frankfurt am Main, 1687.

Steele, Richard. *The Crisis, or, a Discourse Representing, from the Most Authentick Records, the Just Causes of the Late Happy Revolution.* London, 1714.

Strandiger, Otto Lorentzen. *Bekänntnüs von dem Kirchlichen, so genannten, Gottesdienst im Lutherthum.* Flemsburg, 1708.

Superville, Daniel de. *The Christian a New Creature: Being the Substance of a Discourse of Mons. Superville, Deliver'd on a New-Year's-Day. with a Preface to the Reader Concerning Regeneration.* London, 1739.

Tauler, Johann. *Medulla Animae, Das ist, Von Vollkommenheit aller Tugenden.* Franckfurt am Main, 1644.

Walton, Brian, ed. *Biblia Sacra Polyglotta.* 6 vols. London, 1657.

Ward, Richard. *The Life of the Learned and Pious Dr. Henry More, Late Fellow of Christ's College in Cambridge: To Which Are Annex'd Divers of His Useful and Excellent Letters.* London, 1710.

Watts, Isaac. *A Guide to Prayer: or, a Free and Rational Account of the Gift, Grace, and Spirit of Prayer.* London, 1715.

———. *Sermons on Various Subjects Viz. I. II. III. The Inward Witness of Christianity. IV. Flesh and Spirit; Sin and Holiness. V. Drawing Nigh to God in Prayer. VI Sins and Sorrows Spread before God. Vii. Viii. A Lovely Youth Perishing in Sin. IX. X. The Hidden Life of a Christian. XI. Nearness to God the Felicity of Creatures. XII.*

BIBLIOGRAPHY (PRE-1800)

The Scale of Blessedness; or, Blessed Saints Blessed Saviour, and Blessed Trinity. XIII. XIV. Appearing before God. Wherein Many Things Relating to Christian Experience, and the Future State, Are Set in a Fair and Easy Light. Together with a Sacred Hymn Annexed to Each Subject. London, 1721.

Watts, Robert. *An Answer to Two Letters to the Right Honourable the Ld Viscount Townshend, So Far as They Relate to a Letter to the Author of the History of the Lutheran Church, from a Country School-Boy; in a Letter to the Author.* London, 1715.

———. *Two Letters to the Right Honourable the Lord Viscount Townshend: Shewing the Seditious Tendency of Several Late Pamphlets; More Particularly of, a Review of the Lutheran Principles, by Tho. Brett, LLD, Rector of Betteshanger in Kent; and of, a Letter to the Author of the Lutheran Church, from a Country School-Boy.* London, 1714.

White, Jeremiah. *A Persuasive to Mutual Love and Charity Among Christians Who Differ in Opinion.* Edited by Richard Roach. N.p., 1739.

———. *A Perswasive to Moderation and Forbearance in Love Among the Divided Forms of Christians ... with the Effigies of Mr White.* London, 1708.

Whitrow, Abraham. *Warnings of the Eternal Spirit, Spoken by the Mouth of the Servant of God, Abraham Whitro. Faithfully Taken in Writing When They Were Spoken.* London, 1709.

Woodward, Josiah. *An Account of the Rise and Progress of the Religious Societies: In the City of London, &c. And of Their Endeavours for Reformation of Manners.* 3rd ed. Enlarged. London, 1701.

Worthington, John. *The Great Duty of Self-Resignation to the Divine Will.* London, 1675.

Bibliography

Ansorge, Catherine. "The Revd George Lewis: His Life and Collection." *Journal of the History of Collections* 32 (2020) 143–56.

Aslanian, Sebouh David. "The 'Quintessential Locus of Brokerage': Letters of Recommendation, Networks, and Mobility in the Life of Thomas Vanandets'i, an Armenian Printer in Amsterdam, 1677–1707." *Journal of World History* 31 (2020) 655–92.

Austen-Leigh, R. A. "The Commission for the Relief of Poor Proselytes 1717–1730." *Proceedings of the Huguenot Society* 15 (1936) 4–9.

Beaman, Alden G., ed. *Rhode Island Genealogical Register*. Princeton, MA: Rhode Island Families Association, 1976.

Bebbington, David W. *Evangelicalism in Modern Britain: A History from the 1730s to the 1980s*. London: Unwin Hyman, 1989.

Bebbington, David, and David Ceri Jones, eds. *Evangelicalism and Fundamentalism in the United Kingdom During the Twentieth Century*. New York: Oxford University Press, 2013.

Brecht, Martin. "Einleitung." In *Der Pietismus vom siebzehnten bis zum frühen achtzehnten Jahrhundert*, by Johannes van den Berg and Martin Brecht, 1–10. Geschichte des Pietismus 1. Göttingen: Vandenhoeck & Ruprecht, 1993.

Brunner, Daniel L. "Anglican Perceptions of Lutheranism in Early Hanoverian England." *Lutheran Quarterly* 20 (2006) 63–82.

———. "Collaboration and Conflict in Europe Around the Early Tranquebar Mission." *Covenant Quarterly* 65 (2007) 3–15.

———. "The 'Evangelical' Heart of Pietist Anthony William Boehm." In *Heart Religion: Evangelical Piety in England and Ireland, 1690–1850*, edited by John Coffey, 72–92. New York: Oxford University Press, 2016.

———. *Halle Pietists in England: Anthony William Boehm and the Society for Promoting Christian Knowledge*. Arbeiten zur Geschichte des Pietismus 29. Göttingen: Vandenhoeck & Ruprecht, 1993.

———. "Luther's Mysticism, Pietism, and Contemplative Spirituality." *Word and World* 40 (2020) 20–28.

Bultmann, William A. "A Layman Proposes Protestant Union: Robert Hales and the Helvetic Churches, 1700–1705." *Church History* 27 (1958) 32–45.

Butler, Jon. "The Spiritual Importance of the Eighteenth Century." In *In Search of Peace and Prosperity: New German Settlements in Eighteenth-Century Europe and America*, edited by Hartmut Lehmann et al., 101–14. University Park, PA: Pennsylvania State University Press, 2000.

BIBLIOGRAPHY

Campbell, Ted A. *The Religion of the Heart: A Study of European Religious Life in the Seventeenth and Eighteenth Centuries.* Columbia, SC: University of South Carolina Press, 1991.

Clifton-Soderstrom, Michelle A. *Angels, Worms, and Bogeys: The Christian Ethic of Pietism.* Eugene, OR: Cascade, 2010.

Collins Winn, Christian T., et al., eds. *The Pietist Impulse in Christianity.* Princeton Theological Monograph Series 155. Eugene, OR: Pickwick, 2011.

Cowie, Leonard W. *Henry Newman: An American in London, 1708-1743.* London: SPCK, 1956.

Cox, Jeffrey. *The British Missionary Enterprise Since 1700.* New York: Routledge, 2008.

Diffenderffer, Frank Reid. "The German Exodus to England in 1709." In *The Pennsylvania-German Society: Proceedings and Addresses at Philadelphia, Oct. 25, 1896,* 7:257-414. Lancaster, PA: Society, 1897.

Falckner, Justus. *Fundamental Instruction: Justus Falckner's Catechism.* Translated and edited by Martin Kessler. Delhi, NY: ALPB, 2003.

Fengar, J. F. *History of the Tranquebar Mission.* Translated by Emil Francke. Tranquebar: Evangelical Lutheran, 1863.

Gehrz, Christopher, and Mark Pattie III. *The Pietist Option: Hope for the Renewal of Christianity.* Downers Grove, IL: IVP Academic, 2017.

Geyken, Frauke. "Von Heiden und edlen Wilden—Die Indianermission und die Erforschung indianischer Kulturen und Lebensräume." In *Freiheit, Fortschritt und Verheißung: Blickwechsel zwischen Europa und Nordamerika seit frühen Neuzeit,* edited by Claus Verlmann et al., 131-43. Halle: Franckeschen Stiftungen, 2012.

Grafe, Hugald. "The First Lutheran Indian Christians in Tranquebar." In *Halle and the Beginning of Protestant Christianity in India,* edited by Andreas Gross et al., 1:209-28. Halle: Franckeschen Stiftungen, 2006.

Gross, Andreas, et al., eds. *Halle and the Beginning of Protestant Christianity in India.* 3 vols. Halle: Franckeschen Stiftungen, 2006.

Hall, Marie Boas. "Frederick Slare, F. R. S. (1648-1727)." *Notes and Records: The Royal Society Journal of the History of Science* 46 (1992) 23-41.

Hamm, Berndt. *The Early Luther.* Translated by Martin J. Lohrmann. Grand Rapids, MI: Eerdmans, 2014.

Haykin, Michael A. G., and Kenneth Stewart, eds. *The Emergence of Evangelicalism: Exploring Historical Continuities.* Nottingham: Apollos, 2008.

Hessayon, Ariel, ed. *Jane Lead and Her Transnational Legacy.* London: Palgrave Macmillan, 2016.

Hoffman, Bengt R. *Theology of the Heart: The Role of Mysticism in the Theology of Martin Luther.* Edited by Pearl Willemssen Hoffman. Minneapolis: Kirk, 1998.

Jaccard, Emile. *Le marquis Jacques de Rochegude et les protestants sur les galères.* Lausanne: Georges Bridel & Cie, 1898.

Jacobsen, Douglas. "Johann Bernhard van Dieren: Peasant Preacher at Hackensack, New Jersey." *New Jersey History* 100 (1982) 15-29.

Jeyaraj, Daniel. *Inkulturation in Tranquebar: Der Beitrag der frühen dänisch-halleschen Mission zum Werden einere indisch-einheimischen Kirche (1706-1730).* Erlangen: Ev.-Luth. Mission, 1996.

Kisker, Scott Thomas. *Foundation for Revival: Anthony Horneck, the Religious Societies, and the Construction of an Anglican Pietism.* Lanham, MD: Scarecrow, 2008.

BIBLIOGRAPHY

Laborie, Lionel. "The Huguenot Offensive Against the Camisard Prophets in the English Refuge." In *The Huguenots: France, Exile and Diaspora*, edited by Jane McKee and Randolph Vigne, 125–33. Brighton: Sussex Academic, 2013.

Lehmann, Arno. *It Began at Tranquebar: The Story of the Tranquebar Mission and the Beginning of Protestant Christianity in India*. Translated by M. J. Lutz. 1956. 2nd ed. Chennai: Christian Literature Society, 2006.

Lehmann, Hartmut. "The Communities of Pietists as Challenge and Opportunity in the Old World and the New." In *Pietism and Community in Europe and North America, 1650–1850*, edited by Jonathan Strom, 351–58. Brill Series Church History 45. Religious History and Culture 4. Leiden: Brill, 2010.

———. "Pietism in the World of Transatlantic Religious Revivals." In *Pietism in Germany and North America 1680–1820*, edited by Jonathan Strom et al., 13–22. Burlington, VT: Ashgate, 2009.

Lindberg, Carter. *The Third Reformation: Charismatic Movements and the Lutheran Tradition*. Macon, GA: Mercer University Press, 1983.

Lothrop, Samuel Kirkland. *A History of the Church in Brattle Street, Boston*. Boston: Wm. Crosby and H. P. Nichols, 1851.

Lund, Eric. "Johann Arndt and the Development of a Lutheran Spiritual Tradition." PhD diss., Yale University, 1979.

Macray, William Dunn. *Annals of the Bodleian Library, Oxford, AD 1598–AD 1867*. London: Rivingtons, 1868.

Malena, Adelisa. "Confessional Impartiality in Europe at the Turn of the Eighteenth Century: Projects, Networks, and Cultural Transfers." *Bulletin annuel de l'Institut d'histoire de la Réformation* 41 (2020) 31–44.

———. "Speranze, progetti e reti interconfessionali in Europa fra Sei e Settecento. Heinrich Wilhelm Ludolf e Francesco Bellisomi." *Rivista Storica Italiana* 135 (2023) 11–54.

Martin, Lucinda. "'God's Strange Providence': Jane Lead in the Correspondence of Johann Georg Gichtel." In *Jane Lead and Her Transnational Legacy*, edited by Ariel Hessayon, 187–212. London: Palgrave Macmillan, 2016.

Matthias, Markus A. "The Translation of Johann Arndt's True Christianity into Dutch and the Distribution of His Books in the Dutch Republic." *Quaerendo* 53 (2023) 121–59.

McKenzie, Edgar C. *A Catalog of British Devotional and Religious Books in German Translation from the Reformation to 1750*. New York: de Gruyter, 1997.

Moritzen, Niels-Peter. "The Bövingh Controversy." In *Halle and the Beginning of Protestant Christianity in India*, edited by Andreas Gross et al., 3:1283–89. Halle: Franckeschen Stiftungen, 2006.

Muhlenberg, Henry. *The Journals of Henry Melchior Muhlenberg*. Translated by T. G. Tappert and J. W. Doberstein. 3 vols. Philadelphia: Muhlenberg, 1942.

Nishikawa, Sugiko. "The SPCK in Defence of Protestant Minorities in Early Eighteenth-Century Europe." *Journal of Ecclesiastical History* 56 (2005) 730–48.

Noll, Mark A. *America's God: From Jonathan Edwards to Abraham Lincoln*. New York: Oxford University Press, 2002.

———. *The Rise of Evangelicalism: The Age of Edwards, Whitefield and the Wesleys*. Downers Grove, IL: InterVarsity, 2003.

Nuttall, Geoffrey F. "Methodism and the Older Dissent: Some Perspectives." *Journal of the United Reformed Church History Society* 2 (1981) 259–74.

O'Connor, Daniel. "Lutherans and Anglicans in South India." In *Halle and the Beginning of Protestant Christianity in India*, edited by Andreas Gross et al., 2:767–82. Halle: Franckeschen Stiftungen, 2006.

Olson, Alison G. "Huguenots and Palatines." *Historian* 63 (2001) 269–85.

Olson, Roger E. "Pietism: Myths and Realities." In *The Pietist Impulse in Christianity*, edited by Christian T. Collins Winn et al., 3–16. Princeton Theological Monograph Series 155. Eugene, OR: Pickwick, 2011.

Olson, Roger E., and Christian T. Collins Winn. *Reclaiming Pietism: Retrieving an Evangelical Tradition*. Grand Rapids, MI: Eerdmans, 2015.

Otterness, Philip. *Becoming German: The 1709 Palatine Migration to New York*. Ithaca, NY: Cornell University Press, 2004.

Pardoe, Elizabeth Lewis. "Confessional Spaces and Religious Places: Lutherans in America, 1698–1748." In *Religion, Space, and the Atlantic World*, edited by John Corrigan, 246–66. Carolina Lowcountry and the Atlantic World. Columbia, SC: University of South Carolina Press, 2017.

Phillips, Charlie, ed. "Roundtable: Re-Examining David Bebbington's 'Quadrilateral Thesis.'" *Fides et Historia* 47 (2015) 44–96.

Porterfield, Amanda. "Bebbington's Approach to Evangelical Christianity as a Pioneering Effort in Lived Religion." *Fides et Historia* 47 (2015) 58.

Ramsey, William L. *The Yamasee War: A Study of Culture, Economy, and Conflict in the Colonial South*. Lincoln, NE: University of Nebraska Press, 2008.

Roeber, A. Gregg. "The Problem of the Eighteenth Century in Transatlantic Religious History." In *In Search of Peace and Prosperity: New German Settlements in Eighteenth-Century Europe and America*, edited by Hartmut Lehmann et al., 115–38. University Park, PA: Pennsylvania State University Press, 2000.

Sachse, Julius F. *German Pietists of Provincial Pennsylvania, 1694–1705*. Philadelphia: American Philosophical Society, 1895.

Sames, Arno. *Anton Wilhelm Böhme (1673–1722): Studien zum ökumenischen Denken und Handeln eines Halleschen Pietisten*. Arbeiten zur Geschichte des Pietismus 26. Göttingen: Vandenhoeck & Ruprecht, 1989.

Schunka, Alexander. *Ein neuer Blick nach Westen: Deutsche Protestanten und Großbritannien (1688–1740)*. Jabloniana: Quellen und Forschungen zur europäischen Kulturgeschichte der Frühen Neuzeit 10. Wiesbaden: Harrassowitz, 2019.

———. "Zwischen Kontingenz und Providenz: Frühe Englandkontakte der Halleschen Pietisten und protestantische Irenik." *Pietismus und Neuzeit* 34 (2008) 82–114.

Schwartz, Hillel. *The French Prophets*. Berkeley: University of California Press, 1980.

Simmons, George C. "Towards a Biography of Christopher Codrington the Younger." *Caribbean Studies* 12 (1972) 32–50.

Söderblom, Nathan. *Tre livsformer [Three Patterns of Life]*. Stockholm: Hugo Gebers, 1922.

Spener, Philipp Jacob. *The Spiritual Priesthood*. Translated by A. G. Voigt. Philadelphia: Lutheran Publication Society, 1917.

Splitter, Wolfgang. "August Hermann Franckes Briefwechsel mit Cotton Mather und seine Sicht auf Amerika." In *Freiheit, Fortschritt und Verheißung: Blickwechsel zwischen Europa und Nordamerika seit frühen Neuzeit*, edited by Claus Verlmann et al., 61–69. Halle: Franckeschen Stiftungen, 2012.

BIBLIOGRAPHY

Stein, Stephen J. "Some Thoughts on Pietism in American Religious History." In *Pietism in Germany and North America 1680-1820*, edited by Jonathan Strom et al., 23-32. Burlington, VT: Ashgate, 2009.

Stoeffler, F. Ernest, ed. *Continental Pietism and Early American Christianity*. Grand Rapids, MI: Eerdmans, 1976.

———. *The Rise of Evangelical Pietism*. Studies in the History of Religions 9. Leiden: Brill, 1965.

Sträter, Udo. *Sonthom, Bayly, Dyke und Hall: Studien zur Rezeption der englischen Erbauungsliteratur in Deutschland im 17. Jahrhundert*. Beiträge zur historischen Theologie 71. Tübingen: JCB Mohr, 1987.

Strom, Jonathan. "Problems and Promises of Pietism Research." *Church History* 71 (2002) 536-54.

United Society Partners in the Gospel (USPG). "Renewal and Reconciliation: Codrington Reparations Project." N.d. https://www.codringtonproject.org/.

Wallmann, Johannes. *Der Pietismus*. Die Kirche in ihrer Geschichte 4. Göttingen: Vandenhoeck & Ruprecht, 1990.

Ward, W. R. *Christianity Under the Ancien Régime, 1648-1789*. Cambridge: Cambridge University Press, 1999.

———. *Early Evangelicalism: A Global Intellectual History, 1670-1789*. Cambridge: Cambridge University Press, 2006.

———. *The Protestant Evangelical Awakening*. Cambridge: Cambridge University Press, 1992.

Williams, Kim-Eric. *The Journey of Justus Falckner (1672-1723)*. Delhi, NY: ALPB Books, 2003.

Yoder, Peter James. "Rendered 'Odious' as Pietists: Anton Wilhelm Böhme's Conception of Pietism and the Possibilities of Prototype Theory." In *The Pietist Impulse in Christianity*, edited by Christian T. Collins Winn et al., 17-26. Princeton Theological Monograph Series 155. Eugene, OR: Pickwick, 2011.

Zaunstöck, Holger, et al., eds. *London und das Hallesche Waisenhaus: Eine Kommunikationsgeschichte im 18. Jahrhundert*. Hallesche Forschungen 39. Halle: Franckeschen Stiftungen, 2014.

Index

(page numbers in *italics* refer to footnotes)

Abbadie, Jacque, 237
Adler, Johann, 137, 204
Alleine, Joseph, xxiv, 50
Allix, Pierre, 50, 71, 221, 224, 238
Allut, Jean, *207*
Anderson, William Owen, 115
Anne, Queen of Great Britain, 16, 18, 34–36, 39, 42, *50*, 69–70, 73, 80, 86, 91–92, 95, 109, 125, 133, 166, 170, 181, 185, 206, 214–19, 228, 233, 239
Ansorge, Catherine, *115*
Arndt, Johann, xix, xxii–xxiv, 28, 38, 52, 62, 72, 104, 109, 119, 122, 125, 143–44, 163–64, 180, 186, 202, 205, 230, 234, 242, *259*, 292–93
Arnold, Gottfried, 51, 185
Aslanian, Sebouh David, *181*
Augustine of Hippo, 213
Austen-Leigh, R. A., *271*

Barozzi, Pietro, 91
Barrow, Isaac, 241
Barth, Karl, xxii
Bartlett, Moses, 242–43
Baxter, Richard, xxiv, xxvi, 126, 135–36, 201–2
Bayly, Lewis, xxiv, xxvi, 126
Beaman, Alden G., *243*
Beauval, Samuel de, *163*
Bebbington, David W., xxi
Bell, Henry, 185

Bellisomi, Francesco, 134
Bengel, Johann Albrecht, xviii
Berlin, Johann, 140, 143, 204
Bernier, François, 99
Bernstorff, Andreas Gottlieb Freiherr von, 261
Blackmore, Sir Richard, *284*, *286*
Böhme, Anna Elisabeth, 15, 17, 19, 136, 271
Böhme, Anton Wilhelm, *passim*
Böhme, Jacob, xxv, 48, *71*, *107*, 201, *253*
Bona, Giovanni, 180
Bövingh, Johann Georg, 104, 138, 141
Boyle, Robert, xxvi, 16, 30, 126, 159, 161, 225, 239–40
Boyle, Richard, 1st Earl of Burlington and 2nd Earl of Cork, 159–61
Brecht, Martin, xix
Brett, Thomas, 220–22, 224
Bridges, Charles, 24
Bromley, Thomas, xxv, 48, 66, 110, 205
Bronsdon, Elizabeth, *264*
Brouilly, Antoine de, *167*
Browne, Thomas, 105
Browne, Anne, *105*
Brunner, Daniel L., *xvii*, *xxi*, *xxiii*–*xxiv*, *xxvi*, 24, *141*
Bulkeley, Richard, xxv, 54–55, 192, *194*
Bultmann, William A., 24
Bunyan, John, xxiv, 61, 301–2
Burnet, Gilbert, *50*, 51, 155, 241

INDEX

Butler, Jon, *xvii*, 200

Caesar, Johann Jakob, 36
Calvin, John, 177, 224
Campbell, Ted, xix
Canstein, Carl Hildebrand von, 34, 98, 238, 256, *258*
Caroline of Ansbach, Princess of Wales, 220, 239, 260
Carteret, John, 2nd Earl Granville, 7th Seigneur of Sark, 74, 78
Casamajor, Rachel, *97*
Casotti, 24
Chamberlayne, John, 96, 101, 259
Charles, Prince of Denmark and Norway, 197–98
Charles II, King of Great Britain, 77, 136, 168, 242
Charles XII, King of Sweden, 191, 206–7
Charlotte Amalie, Queen of Denmark and Norway, 197
Churches or Denominations
    Anabaptist, 44, 169, 187, 213–14, 242
    Anglican, xii, xxv–xxvii, 24, 37, 62, 66, 69, 71, 93, 100, *103*, *106*, 135, 157, 168, 169, 174, 177, 186–87, 212, 215–16, 218, 220–25, 278, 295
    Baptist, 44–45, 61
    Catholic / Jesuits, xii, 24, 33, 89, 98–99, 102, 120, 169, 182, 188, 213, 215–16, 220, 224, 226, 253, 270
    dissenting / nonconforming, xii, 36, *126*, 187, *195*, 212
    Lutheran, xii, xviii–xx, xxii–xxiv, xxvi, 26, 36–37, 44, 52–53, 70, 88, 94, *104*, *109*, 120, 122, 143, *164*, 169, 172–78, 186, 212, 218–25, 227–28, 299, 302
    Presbyterian / Reformed / Calvinist, xx, 26, 36, 52–53, 65, 72, 88, 121, 135, 169, 173–74, 176–78, 186–87, 202, 212–13, 218–19, 224, 296, 302
    Quaker, 59, *93*, 237, 243
Cicero, Marcus Tullius, 277–78
Clement XI, Pope, 188, 213
Clifford, Mr., 121
Clifton-Soderstrom, Michelle A., *xxi*
Codrington, Christopher, xxvii, 250
Codrington Reparations Project, xxviii
Collier, Jeremy, 18–19, 241–42
Collins Winn, Christian T., *xx–xxii*
Colman, Benjamin, 72, 264
Comenius, Johann Amos, 180, 235
Congreve, William, 19
Cowie, Leonard W., 30
Cox, Jeffrey, *xxvi*, xxvii
Craven, William, 2nd Baron Craven, 78
Cromwell, Oliver, 51, 96, 195
Cuninghame, James, 265

d'Aumont, Louis, 168
d'Aumont, Olympe, *168*
Daudé, Jean, *191*
Daut, Johannes, 206
Dezius, Zacharias, 143
Dieren, Johann Bernhard van, xxiii, 298, *299*, 300
Diffenderffer, Frank Reid, 37
Dodwell, Henry, 187
DuBarry, Jacob, *132*
Duguay-Trouin, René, 134
Duillier, Nicolas Fatio de, 191, *207*

East India Mission, xi, xxvii, 47, *97*, 101–6, 108, 116–18, 121, 125, 128, 134–35, 137–43, 148–49, 170–82, 186, 196–200, 203–5, 225–33, 235, 244–45, 259–62, 266, 268–69
Edward VI, King of Great Britain, 40
Edzardi, Johannes Esra, 169
Elers, Heinrich Julius, 96, *299*
Eliot, John, xxiv, xxvi–xxvii, 125–26

318

INDEX

Elizabeth I, Queen of Great Britain, 40
Emes, Thomas, 194, 201, 210
Epicurus, 278
Ernest Heinrich George, Count of Waldeck, 12
Erskine, Frances (Fairfax), *105*

Fabricius, Johann Albert, xxviii
Falckner, Justus, 51, 56, *109*
Fengar, Johannes Ferdinand, xxvii
Finch, Anne, Countess of Nottingham, 125
Finch, Daniel, 2nd Earl of Nottingham, 125
Fincke, Jonas, 111, 116–19, 121, 124–26, 128, 134, 137
Fischer, Loth, 47, 66, 110, 183, 205
Flavel, John, 30
Fleetwood, William, xxvii, 245
Fleming, Robert, 72
Fortescue, Sir Hugh, 71–72
Francke, August Hermann, xi–xix, xxvi, 15, *28*, 30, 42, 46, 50, *58*, 64, 71, 90, 94–95, *96*, 103, 105, 111, 124, 132–33, 144–45, 180, 183, 188, 191, 208–10, 233–34, 242, 264, 299
Franklin, Benjamin, *286*
Fraser, Mr., 268
Frederick I, King of Prussia, 31, *47*
Frederick IV, King of Denmark and Norway, 141, 197–98, 229–30, 235, 259
French Prophets, xi, xxv, 43–44, 54, 71, 90, 167, 191–96, 200–201, 205, 207–11, 265–66
Freylinghausen, Johann, 178, 210

Gehrz, Christopher, *xxi*
Gell, Robert, 47–49, 64, 66, 180, 205
Genoa, Catherine of, xxv, 192
George, Prince of Denmark, 3, 49–50, 70, 92, 95, 131, 140, 217, 233, 240, 257
George August, Prince of Wales, 220, 260

George I, King of Great Britain, xxvi, 216, 219, 223, 228–30, 260–61, 271
German Lutheran Royal Chapel, xvii, xxviii, 36, *50*, 62, 92, *132*, 173–74, 217, 219, 230, 233, 238, 259
Geyken, Frauke, *126*
Gichtel, Johann Georg, 69, 253–54
Glück, Ernst, *188*
Goodwin, Thomas, xxiv, 96, 98
Grafe, Hugald, *142*
Gray, Elizabeth, 193–94, 201, 207, 210
Greatrakes, Valentine, 200
Greenwood, Samuel, 264
Griffiths, Paul, xxix
Gross, Andreas, *xxiv*
Gründler, Johann Ernst, 104, 141, 171, 175, 225
Gutslaff, Johannes, *188*

Haak, Theodore, *16*
Haferung, Johann Caspar, 164
Hales, Robert, *24*
Hall, Marie Boas, *16*
Hamm, Berndt, xxii, *xxiii*
Harrison, Edward, 116, 143
Harrsch, Josua (see Joshua Kocherthal)
Haykin, Michael A. G., *xxi*
Haywood, Thomas, *236*
Helle, Anton thor, *188*
Hessayon, Ariel, *71*
Hickes, George, 266
Hoare, Henry, 134
Hoffman, Bengt R., *xxiii*
Hofmann, Dr., 210
Hopkins, Ezekiel, xxiv, 106, 279
Howard, Mrs., 127
Hunanyan, Vartan, 180

Jaccard, E., *166*
Jacobi, Johann Christian, xxvi, xxviii, 5, *96*, 200
Jacobsen, Douglas, *298*
Jäger, Johann Wolfgang, 65, 220–22
James II, King of England, 70, *266*

319

INDEX

Jeyaraj, Daniel, *xxvi*
Jones, Mrs., 127
Jones, David Ceri, *xxi*
Jordan, Polycarpus, 104

Keith, George, 93
Kelpius, Johannes, xxv, 59, 70
Kempis, Thomas à, xxv, 133, 180
Kisker, Scott Thomas, *113*
Knyphausen, Baron Ernst von, 47
Kocherthal, Joshua, 52, 109
Kock, Andreas, 90
Korholt, Christian, 185

Laborie, Lionel, *164*
Lacy, John, 193–94, 201, 207, 210
Lange, Joachim, 202, 228, 234
Lead, Jane, 47, 66, 69, 71, *168*
Lee, Francis, xxv, 47, 64, 66, 71, *168*, 205
Lehmann, Hartmut, *xvii*, xix, xxvi
Lehmann, Arno, *xxiv*
Leutbecker, Caspar, 263
Lewis, George, 115, 119, 139–40, 226–27, 231–32, 235
Lindberg, Carter, xxiii
Lothrop, Samuel Kirkland, *72*
Louis XIV, King of France, 166, 213–14
Lovelace, John, Fourth Baron Lovelace, 35
Lubomirsky, I. A., 23–25
Ludolf, Heinrich, 49, *50*, 95, 99, 102, 125, 131–34, 140, 146, 157–59, 195, 239–40, 257
Ludolf, Georg Melchior, 131
Ludolf, Hiob, 49, *61*
Lund, Eric, xxii
Luther, Martin, xxii–xxiv, 174–79, 185, 228
Lütkens, Franz Julius, 141
Lysius, Heinrich, 132, 134

Macarius, of Egypt, *236*, 237
Mackenzie, Sir George, 203
Macray, William Dunn, *181*
Maleiappan, Peter, *142*
Malena, Adelisa, xxv, *134*

Mapletoft, John, *272*
Marion, Élie, 191, *207*
Martin, Lucinda, *69*
Martini, Johann Christoph, *132*
Mary of Modena, Queen of England, *266*
Mather, Cotton, xi, xix, xxiv, 125, 144–45, 233, 243, 264–65
Mathisin, Maria Elisabeth, 208, 211
Matthias, Markus A., *143*
McKenzie, Edgar C., *xxiv*
Michaelis, Johann Heinrich, 61
More, Henry, *93*, 236
Moritzen, Niels-Peter, *141*
Mothe, Claude Grostête de La, 170
Muhlenberg, Henry, 263, *298*

Neander, Joachim, 38
Negri, Solomon, 99, 239–41, 244
Nelson, Robert, 236
Ners, Peter Anthony Delon Seigneur de, xxvi, xxix, 97, 102, 106, 121, 127, 235, 267–68, 270
Neubauer, George Heinrich, 144, 183, 217, 264
Newman, Henry, 30, 180, 184, 186, 188, 196, 244, 272, 284
Newton, Sir Isaac, *191*, *238*, *241*
Niclaes, Hendrik, *107*
Nishikawa, Sugiko, *184*
Noll, Mark A., *xvii*, xxi–xxii
Nurigian, Luke, 181
Nuttall, Geoffrey, xxi

O'Connor, Daniel, *xxiv*
Olson, Roger, xx, *xxi*, xxii, *xxiii*
Olson, Alison G., *xxiii*
Ostervald, Jean-Frédéric, 252, 259
Otterness, Philip, *xxiii*
Oynhausen, Anna Catharina, 271

Palatine Emigration, xi, xxiii, *16*, 33–40, 42–43, 48, 52, 54–56, 72, 78, 97, 100, 102, 104, 108–9, 121–22, 127–28, 185, 269–70
Pannenberg, Wolfhart, xxii
Pardoe, Elizabeth Lewis, *58*

INDEX

Pastorius, Francs Daniel, 70
Pattie, Mark III, *xxi*
Peirce, James, 187
Penn, William, 70, 74, 237
Pertack, 24
Petersen, Johann Wilhelm, xxv, 69
Petersen, Johanna Eleonora, 69
Philadelphia Society, 65, *66*, 71, 168, 186
Philipps, Mary, 147–48
Philipps, Sir John, *148*
Phillips, Charlie, *xxi*
Plütschau, Heinrich, 96, 103, 105, 112, 137–38, 140, *142*, 148, 203
Poiret, Pierre, *192*
Poole, Matthew, 180
Pordage, John, xxv, *48*, 66, *71*, 201
Portalès, Charles, *207*
Porterfield, Amanda, xxi
Pritius, Johann Georg, 223, 236
Pufendorf, Samuel Freiherr von, 220, 224

Quesnel, Pasquier, 188, 213

Rambach, Johann Jakob, xxviii
Ramsey, William L., 252
Reed, Benjamin, 187, 212
Rivet, André, 268
Roach, Richard, xxv, 168, 186, *195*
Robinson, John, 204
Roche, Michel de La, 157, 187
Rochegude, Le Marquis Jacques de, 166
Rodokonakis, 158–59
Roeber, A. Gregg, *xviii*
Rosenroth, Christian Knorr von, xxv, 56
Rous, Francis, 156
Ruperti, Georg Andreas, 36, *44*, 108, 127, 169

Sacheverell, Henry, 49, 64, 222
Sachse, Julius F., *59*
Sames, Arno, *xvii–xviii, xxviii*, 12, *192*
Schade, Johann Kaspar, 28

Scheffler, Johann (see Silesius, Johann Angelus)
Scherer, Ulrich, *36*
Schulenburg, Ehrengard Melusine von der, Duchess of Kendal, Duchess of Munster, 270
Schunka, Alexander, *xvii*,
Schwartz, Hillel, *207*
Seaman, William, 239, *240*, 241
Seelig, Johann Gottfried, xxv, *59*, 206
Seneca, Lucius Annaeus, 285
Seraphim, Greek Archbishop, 258
Servetus, Michael, 157
Sharp, Dr., 250
Sharp, John, 125
Shute, Henry, 71
Silesius, Johann Angelus, 38–39
Simmons, George C., *250*
Slare, Frederick, xxvi, 16, 18, *21*, 71
Slare, Jane, xxvi, 21–22, 26, 31, 128–29, 145–47, 158, 251, 259, 273–74
Smith, Anthony, *148*
Societies, Voluntary
  Charity Schools, 16, *24*, 97, 204
  Religious Societies, xx, 108, 113, 261
  Societies for the Reformation of Manners, xx, 94, 113
  Society for Promoting Christian Knowledge, xv, xvii, xxiv, xxvii, *16*, *24*, 30, *44*, *71*, *93*, 96–97, 101, 103–6, 111–16, *119*, *125*, 134–35, 137, 142, *148*, 149, 157, 170, 173–76, 179–81, 184, 186, 188, 196–200, 204, 226–27, 231–32, 235, *244*, 252, 259–60, 266, 272, 285
  Society for the Propagation of the Gospel in Foreign Parts, xv, xxvii–xxviii, *16*, 24, *93*, 96, 106, 114–15, 245, 250
  Society of the Woman in the Wilderness, 70
Söderblom, Nathan, *xxiii*

Somerset, Henry, 2nd Duke of
  Beaufort, 78
Sophia Hedwig, Princess of
  Denmark and Norway, 197
Sophie Henriette, Countess of
  Waldeck, 12–13
Spademan, John, 72
Spanheim, Ezekiel, Freiherr von, 185
Spener, Philip Jakob, xviii, xix, 28, 69, 178–79, 225, 258, 299
Splitter, Wolfgang, 145
Steele, Sir Richard, 185
Stein, Stephen J., xviii
Stewart, Kenneth, xxi
Stiffer, Dr., 210
Stoeffler, F. Ernest, xviii–xx, xxii
Strandiger, Otto Lorentzen, 63
Sträter, Udo, 126
Stratton, Richard, 72
Strom, Jonathan, xii, xviii
Stuart, James Francis Edward,
  Prince of Wales, the
  "Pretender", 215, 251, 266
Superville, Daniel de, 267
Sylvester, Matthew, 136

Tauler, Johann, xxv, 22, 28, 67, 83
Taylor, Christopher, 72
Tenison, Thomas, xxiv, 40, 111, 172–73, 266
Timothy, 142, 149
Townshend, Charles, Viscount
  Townshend, 221
Tribbeko, John, 36, 92, 109

Undereyck, Theodor, xviii
Urlsperger, Samuel, xxv, 44, 49, 64, 127, 132, 167, 220

Vanandets'i, Thomas, 181
Virgil (Vergilius), Publius Maro, 277

Wake, William, 266
Wallmann, Johannes, xviii
Walsh, John D., v, xxii
Walton, Brian, 72
Ward, Richard, 236
Ward, W.R., xvii, xix, xxi
Watson, George, 115
Watts, Isaac, 295–96
Watts, Robert, 221, 225
Wendt, Christopher, xxvii, 198, 231, 244
Wesley, John, xxi, 237
Whiston, William, 238
White, Jeremiah, xxiv, 195
Whitefield, George, xxi
Whitrow, Abraham, 194
William III, King of England, 70, 215, 237
Williams, Mr., 283, 290–92, 294
Williams, Kim-Eric, 58, 298
Woodward, Josiah, 113, 144, 195, 233
Wornley, Conradus, 36
Worthington, John, 106–7

Yamasee Raids, xxvii, 251–52
Yoder, Peter James, xix

Zaunstöck, Holger, xvii
Ziegenbalg, Bartholomäus, 103, 104, 105, 112, 116, 137, 139, 142, 143, 171, 175, 225, 244, 252–53, 259–61, 266, 269, 271

www.ingramcontent.com/pod-product-compliance
Lightning Source LLC
Chambersburg PA
CBHW061424300426
44114CB00014B/1531